EXPERIENCING SOCIAL PSYCHOLOGY

EXPERIENCING SOCIAL PSYCHOLOGY
READINGS AND PROJECTS

AYALA PINES
CHRISTINA MASLACH
UNIVERSITY OF CALIFORNIA, BERKELEY

ALFRED A. KNOPF · NEW YORK

FOR OUR CHILDREN: ITAI, SHANA, AND ZARA

THIS IS A BORZOI BOOK PUBLISHED BY ALFRED A. KNOPF, INC.

INTRODUCTION

It was not too many years ago that social psychology was considered a distant and not always welcome relative of general psychology. Whereas social psychology was concerned with groups, the focus of general psychology was supposed to be the individual. Social psychologists studied practical affairs of everyday life: conformity, prejudice, persuasion, violence, and the like. Meanwhile, the mainstream of psychological research remained aloof from such mundane matters. "Soft-headed" social psychologists insisted on understanding the unique content of private human experience and its public expression; "hard-headed" psychologists sought to discover quantifiable laws for the behavior of organisms.

But within the last decade, social psychology has quietly moved into the inner circle of psychology, so that it is now at the core of virtually all psychological disciplines. This quiet revolution was assisted during the late 1960s by students who called for social relevance in their courses and who responded to social psychology's problem-centered approach to the study of the human condition. At about the same time, behavioristic psychology, largely based on animal learning experiments, came to be regarded as too limited to be the foundation for understanding the complexities of human behavior. Similarly, the recent emergence of the cognitive psychology of information processing found social psychologists already oriented toward the study of mental states, expectations, intentions, and inferences.

At present, then, it is safe to say that there are few areas of psychological investigation—social learning, social development, social perception, social cognition, social emotionality, social pathology, and so forth—that have not been influenced by social psychology. Nevertheless, the message of modern social psychology is not that it has moved from the attic of the house of psychology to the main floor, where it might annex other areas of psychology; rather, I believe, its contribution to other branches of psychology lies in its ability to point out that exciting views of human experience do exist on many different levels. The social psychologist is equally interested in the individual and in the group, equally challenged by testing an abstract theoretical derivation and by illuminating a common aspect of daily life, equally stimulated by discovering how the mind works and by helping to improve the quality of human life.

In the pages that follow, all these dimensions of social psychology will be revealed to you. Ayala Pines and Christina Maslach are both gifted, energetic individuals who love to teach as much as they love to conduct research. Consequently, they will be very knowledgeable guides for your journey into the workings of social psychology. This book is, in fact, a labor of love. In it you will find ideas, reports, perspectives, and projects that students have responded to with enthusiasm. Pines and Maslach share with us the challenge, complexity, and concerns that constitute the endeavor to understand how individuals are influenced by others and, in turn, shape their social environment. They lead us—sometimes gently, sometimes gingerly—from classic areas of social psychology to emerging frontiers of research. Their concern is always to involve you, to get you to think about what all this means for your life, to participate actively in the observations and experiments suggested. In some languages, *experiment* translates as *experience*. Here's to a most enjoyable experience in learning about the social animal that is you.

Philip G. Zimbardo

TO THE READER

Experiencing Social Psychology: Readings and Projects is designed to supplement your introductory textbook. To make this handbook as useful and adaptable as possible, we have chosen to organize the chapters around twelve topics that are generally considered to be the central concerns of social psychologists. Each chapter begins with a brief general introduction, placing the topic within the context of contemporary theory and research and relating it to conditions of daily life.

In each chapter we have included at least two readings, each of which is preceded by a short introduction that highlights its significance in relation to the chapter topic. These readings, drawn from many sources, represent a mixture of current topics and classic issues. They are meant to extend the ideas you encounter in your textbook or to indicate recent thinking and controversies in a given area. Throughout the book we have also inserted brief excerpts from works of literature, anecdotes, cartoons, and topical discussions that illustrate important principles in thought-provoking ways.

It is our strong conviction that the best way to learn about social psychology is to do it, to take part in the research adventure from which the information and theoretical positions described and analyzed in your textbook are derived.

The insights you gain from course lectures, your textbook, and the readings and boxed features in this book will almost certainly take on a special immediacy and significance when you put them to the test of empirical investigation.

With this in mind, we have included several research projects in each chapter. Here you can test some of the ideas and concepts developed in your text or by your instructor and see how they apply to yourself and to your friends. Some of the projects cast you in the role of the investigator who collects data from surveys and rating scales or by observing other people. Others require you to be your own subject. In addition, we have included projects that can be done in field settings on campus, in your neighborhood, or at work. Others might be done as part of a class project organized by your instructor. Your active participation in carrying out these projects will help reinforce what you have already learned and will show you—through your own work—the basic forms of research that psychologists engage in.

We hope that our book serves its intended purpose well and helps you learn more about the complex, varied, and fascinating field of social psychology and leads you to a better understanding of your own behavior and the behavior of those around you.

Ayala Pines
Christina Maslach

CONTENTS

---

⑥

AGGRESSION 117

---

⑦

ALTRUISM 149

---

⑧

PERSON PERCEPTION 171

⑨

GROUP PROCESSES 195

⑩

THE HUMAN ENVIRONMENT 219

⑪

SOCIAL PATHOLOGY 245

⑫

ETHICS 273

EXPERIENCING SOCIAL PSYCHOLOGY

1
RESEARCH

Virtually everyone has a set of ideas to explain why people behave the way they do. These ideas, or beliefs, which usually strike us as being right, may be based on personal experience or on common sense. If knowledge about human behavior is so easy to acquire, then what do social psychologists have to offer us? Essentially, they offer us the *scientific method.* Social psychologists also use personal experience and common sense as a source of ideas, but, unlike the layperson, they then test the validity of these ideas, using objective research procedures. Because there are so many different beliefs about human behavior, it is the task as well as the goal of the social psychologist to determine which assumptions are scientifically valid.

The research approach that social psychologists use most frequently is the laboratory experiment. In a laboratory setting, the researcher can create and control various social stimuli and then carefully record the behavior of the participants. The primary advantage of laboratory research is that the experimental findings can be understood in causal terms.

Because the laboratory researcher intervenes by determining what will occur, he or she is in a better position to infer why the subjects behaved as they did. In contrast, the researcher who studies social interaction in real-life settings by means of passive observation often cannot control what is going on and usually can point only to correlations rather than to causes. That is, the field researcher can identify different behaviors that seem to be related, but is less able to specify their causes. Although field studies have the advantage of focusing on naturally occurring behavior (as opposed to the more contrived behavior that is so often characteristic of the laboratory experiment), they are often enormously complex, time consuming, expensive, and difficult to carry out. For all these reasons, field research has *not* been the primary mode of scholarly endeavor among social psychologists, although a great deal of lip service is paid to the ideal of doing more work in the field. Reports on the results of controlled laboratory experiments continue to dominate the journals and textbooks.

SOME REFLECTIONS UPON LOSING OUR SOCIAL PSYCHOLOGICAL PURITY

JEROME E. SINGER and DAVID C. GLASS

Social psychology has been called upon more extensively than most other branches of psychology to apply its knowledge to solving social problems. Many within as well as outside the profession have maintained that social psychologists should actually do something about a problem rather than study it for its own sake. In fact, social psychology began largely as an applied discipline. During the 1930s and 1940s, when social psychology emerged

1

as a distinct field of study, research was either inspired by current social issues (e.g., reducing prejudice or understanding the dynamics of fascist leadership) or designed for direct use during World War II (e.g., studies of persuasion and propaganda techniques). After the war, social psychologists attempted to enhance the reputation of their discipline by turning away from applied research and concentrating on pure research. Today, however, the pendulum seems to be swinging back toward applied research. Although not as yet a mass movement, there is a tendency among more and more social psychologists to consider the pros and cons of doing applied research.

That tendency is strikingly illustrated in the article "Some Reflections upon Losing Our Social Psychological Purity." Singer and Glass describe how they studied the social problem of urban stress, including their initial involvement with the problem, their choice of method for the study, and their theoretical explanations of stress as social phenomenon. Rather than presenting the results of their studies (which are contained in their book Urban Stress*), they give the reader a look at how applied research is done and how it differs from pure research.*

The eminent British mathematician, G. H. Hardy, was widely quoted outside of mathematical circles for his famous comment, "I have never done anything useful." And if his pre–World War II remark was interesting at the time it was uttered, it is even more curious now, for it turns out that Hardy was triply wrong. He was wrong in the most literal sense in that time and technology combined in his undoing; his work in number theory provided the basis for the solution of several problems in circuitry and switching theory. He was also wrong in a general historical sense. He was engaged in creating products of the intellect and his mathematics, like other artistic creations, have always, at least in Western society, been found useful enough to command both respect and support from the larger society. It would be a strange culture or age that did not cherish some purely aesthetic endeavors. This may seem to be somewhat of a quibble, but since we are only one or two years away from seeing many of the best products of our universities discarded for having failed to meet some vague criterion of relevance, it is worth restating the point that there is a satisfaction, elegance, and utility to "pure" work. Finally, at the heart of the matter, Hardy was most seriously and perniciously wrong in all that his statement implied; that is, there was something a little suspect, déclassé, or even tawdry about research or scholarship which had a direct application. It is impossible and even irrelevant to determine whether Hardy was merely an echo of his times or a formulator of opinions; he was probably a little of both. What is important to note is that his succinct statement of the mathematician's scorn of the engineer as a mere technician somehow found its way into the graduate training of the social psychologists of our generation.

Our rallying cry was not Hardy's mot, but Lewin's ("There is nothing so practical as a good theory!"), which we shrewdly managed to distort into an equivalent meaning. Our interpretation was simple: if theory was good, it was certainly better to stay in its rarefied domain than to deal with less useful, nongeneral, applied problems. And the very structure of the world around us, from the prize fellowships to the honors given to our faculty advisors, echoed the same theme: to be a major contribution a study must deal with basic, not applied, problems.

There was, of course, some backsliding and some ambivalence to these dictums. After all, didn't many respectable social psychologists work on applied problems during the second world war? Yet their success only reinforced our attitudes: we could do significant applied work if we wished to, but without the pressure of a national emergency we did not wish to. But we did go into the field occasionally. It was nice to be able to show that dissonance theory works in discount houses or in automobile salesrooms, but once again the focus was on the theory, not the sales.

. . .

The point of our introduction is not that we were misguided, saw the light, and then reformed,

Reprinted, with minor deletions, from M. Deutsch and H. A. Hornstein (eds.), *Applying Social Psychology*. Hillsdale, New Jersey: Lawrence Erlbaum Associates, 1975, by permission of the Social Science Research Council and the authors.

but rather that a set of inappropriate values guided our training and early research styles. Paradoxically, we now believe that our training and experiences devoted to the pursuit of the pristine have been precisely the best set of tools for the study of applied social problems. The future training goal, of course, is to impart these skills with a more humane set of values.

. . .

THE APPLIED ORIENTATION

The theme of this presentation is unusual because it concerns the natural history of the conduct of the research rather than a description of the research per se. . . .

The Rotten City and Why Do People Love to Live There?

About a half dozen years ago, we were engaged in a series of conversations filled with the usual sort of small talk that passes for conversation among social psychologists when we discovered that we shared a curiosity about an inconsistency of life in New York City. Just at the time when many newspapers and magazines were printing a spate of articles bemoaning the worsening plight of the cities and highlighting every conceivable peril, we were struck by the fact that several of our friends were striking Faustian bargains, selling their souls, as it were, to remain in the city. We were, of course, aware of the advantages of city life, with its conveniences and opportunities, as well as of its disadvantages. The question that intrigued us was how people managed to cope with urban stress. We could understand how people could value a city's attractions enough for them to outweigh its repugnancies, but how were people able to manage with the problems, such as crowding, noise, bureaucracy, garbage, traffic, crime, etc., which even the most ardent urbanophile could hardly deny. Our first statement of the problem was simple: "How do people cope with urban stress?"

What Precisely Was Our Problem?

One way of attacking our problem was to begin by consulting those studies dealing with stress. At this stage of our work, they were of little help as most stress research dealt with specific and identifiable stressors and we were considering amorphous and all-enveloping living conditions. So we made our first decision to delimit our study to specific stressors. Hopefully, we would conduct

investigations on a wide variety of stressors moving sequentially on to new ones as we solved the problems of the old. But, for a start, we decided to investigate the effects of noise and of bureaucracy on people and spent most of our efforts investigating noise.

Without much discussion, we settled early on the laboratory as the place to start, not because we thought that lab work was superior to field studies, but because of two practical reasons. First, most of our training and experience was in conducting lab studies, and, in an area where we had so little previous work to guide us, we thought that it would be better to avoid, at the start, those techniques in which we were relative neophytes. Second, our immediate resources and our assistants were already at work in the laboratories and the couching of the problems in laboratory frameworks seemed a way to save us from that almost interminable tooling-up process that seems to plague most of our new research endeavors. In retrospect, it may be that we made the right decision for the wrong reasons. We had no need to worry about our field study capabilities. Most veteran investigators have learned the general strategy of doing research, and a questionnaire in the home is not all that different from one in the laboratory. Similarly, it is not that hard to start a field study and, conversely, one can spend as much time fiddling with polygraphs as with any field instrument.

The best reason for our having started in the laboratory was our comparative ignorance of the field. It was our belief that a laboratory study, with its relatively well-defined variables, would soon reveal whether or not there are any results. An initial field study, packed with every variable which we at first believed would have any impact, would have swamped us with data. In short, we felt that not all the possible internal analyses attempted in the name of "salvage" could really convince us that our failed study actually did succeed, while an ill-defined survey, for example, could generate enough data to keep us and our staff of programmers happy for months blithefully unaware of the study's outcome. When we finally did engage in field research, the studies were focused, small in scope, and well addressed to specific problems isolated by our preliminary laboratory work. Just as confirmation in the field adds generalization to the more restricted lab results, those very same lab studies impart a certain elegance to the field studies. In any event, having decided almost by default to start in the lab, exactly what did we want to study?

Enjoy Now, Stress Later

We started our design of the noise studies with an attack on the related literature. This turned out to be a Herculean task and if we had resolved to exhaust the literature before starting, we would still be reading. Even now, a good seven years after we have begun our projects, we still find and are directed to studies we have overlooked or to journals of whose existence we were unaware. But in the material we did read, two seemingly unrelated facts caught our attention. Almost all the studies reviewing the effects of noise upon humans showed that there were very few times and very rare conjunctions of circumstances in which noise produced any direct behavioral deficits. This conclusion, soundly documented, was at odds not only with our own experience and intuition, but also with that of the public at large who was busily forming antinoise committees, with environmentalists who were waging suit against airport expansions, and with almost all social critics from the futurists to the Cassandras. Our initial resolution of this dilemma was to take a biological model of stress and adaptation proposed by Selye* and metaphorically adapt it to our problem. Selye pointed out that for many physical stressors, organisms are able to adapt, but that they pay a cost of adaptation such that the stressor's effects are revealed in later activities. We reasoned that noise could function in much the same way. People in a noisy environment learn to cope with it, but . . . they pay a psychic price for this adaptation which only surfaces in their later activities. Thus, a worker in a noisy office learns to work in a fashion such that his production is equal to that of a colleague in a quieter setting, but . . . he, unlike his sheltered counterpart, is more apt to yell at his family and kick the dog when he returns home from work in the evening.

This cost of adaption hypothesis, although ultimately much revised by our cumulative findings, was the thread upon which we hung the conception of our studies. . . . Our start then, came not from social psychology, but from an odd mixture of human performance studies, evolutionary biology, and urban journalism.

Adding Social Psychology

We ran an initial study and we were fortunate enough to obtain the results that we had hypothe-

*Hans Selye, *The stress of life*, New York: McGraw-Hill, 1956.

sized and intuited; that is, our subjects did adapt to the stressor of noise; after a short period of time, their performance under intense noise stress was no different from that of control subjects performing identical tasks in the absence of noise. Yet at the same time we were able to show that those people who had worked under noise stress manifested aftereffect deficits. They did not perform as well on tasks administered in quiet, after the noise session was over, as did the controls. Encouraging as this finding was, there were three corollary results that added to our interest. One was the fact that physical intensity of the noise was not as powerful a factor as originally supposed. . . . The second interesting result was that the . . . context and interpretation of the situation in which the noise was presented had a greater impact upon the subject than the characteristics of the noise itself. The third related finding of interest was that there was a lack of coordination between the subjects' ratings of the noise and its effects upon their behavior; . . . in fact, there were no direct performance differences between differing loudnesses. And the magnitude of the aftereffects was a function of social-cognitive factors and not of perceived irritation.

Taken together these factors greatly heartened us, for they enabled us to define the problem of noise stress (and by both analogy and subsequent study, urban stress, in general) in terms relating to social psychology, not audition and psychoacoustics. We were able to redefine and narrow our major goal into the study of what social and cognitive factors meliorate or exacerbate the aversive aftereffects of a noise stress.

How to Put Context in Its Place

The nonphysical factor which we had included in our first study concerned predictability, whether or not the noise bursts the subjects heard were possible to anticipate. For half of our subjects, the bursts came at fixed intervals, that is, at regular times and of regular duration. For the other half of the subjects, the bursts were of unequal length and occurred at random intervals during the experimental session. . . . This cognitive variable overrode the effects of intensity. But it immediately presented us with three problems, any one of which could provide the basis for a series of coordinated studies. Our interest in all three of these facets and our appreciation of the large number of questions raised by the results of the first study made us unwilling to concentrate on any one aspect, so we engaged in a four-pronged research effort starting with a continuation of our original problem.

1. Since any experiment is unlikely to be definitive in the sense that it discounts all possible alternatives to the proposed explanation of the data, it was necessary for us to explore what kinds of predictability and circumstances influenced the effects of noise. These studies did not extend our findings to more general conclusions, but they enabled us to demonstrate the robustness of our results, to sharpen our theoretical explanations, and to eliminate possible methodological flaws.

2. Having opened the phenomenon of noise-produced behavioral deficits to the possibility of cognitive modification, if not cognitive control, we proceeded to explore other cognitive factors that would also modify the social environment sufficiently to show moderating effects upon the noise stress. Ultimately, we studied five such variables in some depth. These were predictability, controllability, relative deprivation, necessity, and expectation. . . .

3. As we began to examine the cumulative results of our experiments, not unexpectedly we found it necessary to modify our initial theoretical position. Our initial Selyean position required that subjects adapt to a stressor in order to study aftereffects. We had some reason to question whether or not adaptation was a necessary phase for the production of deleterious aftereffects. Consequently, we conducted several experiments to explore the implications of our preliminary theorizing. These studies, which were an important link in our reasoned explanations of the noise phenomena, would have never been conceived of at the start of our project.

4. We had originally begun our speculations about the general effects of urban stress, but partly out of convenience much of our early work consisted of laboratory studies of noise. As that part of our program developed, we broadened our investigations to keep pace with our speculations by engaging in laboratory studies of bureaucracy, economic discrimination, field studies of noise, and aspects of the stresses in automobile traffic, street litter, and garbage.

FITTING THE THEORY TO THE DATA

As our research progressed, we found ourselves engaged in a reversal of our usual processes of explanation. In most previous circumstances, we had undertaken studies to test a hypothesis or to decide between two or more counterposed ones. When the data had been collected, our analytical task was to ascertain how well it fit each postulated theory. Granted that there was still plenty of room for internal analyses, fiddling with the data, and stretching of our points, our fundamental strategy was still to look for an answer to a question of the sort, "Were we right in expecting events to occur for the reasons we originally proposed?" When we switched to applied problems, our questions, and hence, our way of thinking underwent a change. We asked, "Now that we have created an effect, what caused it?"

The reason for this inversion is not difficult to understand. In most laboratory studies, the experimental situation has been specifically created to be a credible realization of the theory's preconditions. It does not matter that the situation has no exact real world counterpart. . . . But in dealing with a laboratory recreation of an actual world event, a high degree of abstraction is impossible. Unless the problem is well defined and demarcated—and the interesting ones never are—you never know whether the features neglected in your abstract are the most important. The experimenter's ingenuity is put to the test to create a workable replica of the social problem in the lab. It is no great surprise, then, that when his experimental design satisfies the requirement of matching an actual situation, it no longer can neatly be described by any single existing theory. Our own procedure was to speculate, with a mixture of reason, intuition, and common sense, about what could cause the phenomena we hoped to create. When we produced an effect, we then respeculated; modifying, adding, and discarding theory when necessary.

THE WORLD IS A THEORETICAL BAZAAR

We got our theory from wherever we could find it. Because our problems were so complex, usually we were as likely to find explanatory help outside the domain of social psychology as within it. Most of our efforts were attempts at a synthesis of rags and snatches of ideas and concepts from a variety of sources. As a result our receptivity to the ideas and reactions of our colleagues was much greater than when we were engaged in the relatively single-minded pursuit of an hypothesis test. For example, we learned more from the reactions to our own colloquia during this research than before; not that the proportion of dunderheads and self-propagandists in our audiences had changed, but rather, since we were no longer talking about a somewhat narrow social psychological problem, but a much broader social one, people in our audiences from a wider variety of backgrounds and interests could contribute with possible explanations, disconfirmations, and related studies.

A need for more techniques and a wider command of the psychological literature also developed because it was the problems instead of the experimental designs which placed the limits on what we had to study. It is possible for an investigator to go through a career in social psychology without once being concerned with personality measurement; that is, the ability to randomize subjects across conditions will usually allow him to ignore any potential influence from a personality factor. However, when looking at an actual problem in the real world, rarely have people been assigned different lots in life by a random process. To study some of these nonrandom conditions one must either be able to create a manipulated analogue of the factor involved or somehow to measure and adjust for it. And in field studies, the situation is even more acute. As a result, the references in our work are rather diverse with respect to theory, methods, and content. . . . It is our . . . feeling that it is as creative to weave a tapestry out of old and varied theoretical strands as to produce a new theory out of whole cloth. And we have some historical justification in the belief that any newly proffered idea was probably proposed earlier by someone else. There are professional genealogists in psychology who, on request, can trace any idea back to Aristotle, the Talmud, or the Ming Dynasty as the occasion demands. And as Aristotle was expounding on the nature of the dramatic event, some fellow Athenian was probably remarking that Ab of the Urs thought of it first. Be that as it may, whatever the aesthetic or intellectual value of our procedures, they were the only ones which we were able to use.

APPLIED SOCIAL PSYCHOLOGY IS LIKE EATING SALTED PEANUTS

Our original conception of our research program was broadly conceived and the choice of starting with the study of noise was, we believed, just the first step in the study of a wide range of urban stressors. But if starting was difficult, stopping was even harder. Our book, *Urban stress*, contains about two dozen experiments; all but three of them deal with some aspect of noise as a stressor. Yet when we review what we know and don't know about noise, either by ourselves or with colleagues, it becomes painfully obvious that even within our limited framework we have only scratched the surface. . . .

There is no necessary reason why the problem of stopping should be confined to applied work; surely basic researchers may spend their lives on a single problem. But the situation is more troublesome for the applied social psychologist. The basic researcher essentially is trying to document a theory. He can stop his studies when the facts give him sufficient confidence in the veracity of his conjectures. If others deem him intellectually irresponsible for not fully proving his speculations, it is between [him] and his ego ideal to settle. For an applied problem, the criterion of when the solution is complete is a more difficult one for two reasons. More social consensus is involved in determining whether the proposed solution is satisfactory and the issue of social responsibility is involved; that is, a researcher who chooses to investigate some applied area, particularly one of a general social nature, has made a self-declaration of social involvement and concern. This declaration is inconsistent, dissonant, if you will, with the act of abandoning the research before the completion of the problem. . . .

WHAT WE DID: A REPRISE

We have been somewhat discursive in discussing our studies of a problem in applied social psychology, and somehow that is only fitting, for we are merely recapitulating our discursive experiences with the problem. In retrospect, however, there may be more order than we realized in our procedures because now that we are studying stressors other than noise, we can see the same steps being repeated. In brief, the following order represents the chronology of our method of attacking a problem:

1. Find a problem that interests us. Discuss it at length informally in its various aspects until we can agree on the facet of major interest.

2. Speculate, if possible in an informed manner, on the reasons for the occurrence of the phenomena. Read the most salient of the relevant literature. Since a theory is usually not possible at this point, arrive at a working speculation.

3. Try to create a laboratory simulation for the conditions of the problem. The theory at this point is flexible enough to defer to the requirements of making the simulation faithful to the original problem.

4. Run some studies to see if your original hunch has any validity. You may find it necessary

to engage in more replication than formerly because parameters as well as relationships are under investigation.

5. Review your theory and cast a critical eye at your findings. Scavenge around wherever you can for usable explanations. Examine your work for different kinds of loose ends.

6. Expand the scope of your work by generalizing to other similar studies on related problems, and try to find field tests of your current theoretical beliefs. Contrast the results of these different procedures.

7. Don't make your current explanations too irrevocable. Continue to be sensitive to new possibilities of both explanations and unexplored aspects of the basic problem.

8. Try to arrive at a socially responsible balance between the intractability of the problem and the requirements of your own nervous system for variety when deciding to leave the problem for other pursuits.

Let us repeat that this procedural résumé is what we actually did, and as such reflects our biases, predilections, and strengths and weaknesses as researchers. We think that our experience has some didactic value as a loose informal guide to the application of social psychology but that preferences for starting work in the laboratory, the field, or elsewhere should of necessity be determined by the nature of the problems and the particular research preferences of the investigators.

SOME SERENDIPITOUS COCKTAIL PARTY BENEFITS

One disadvantage of being a pure social psychologist is that you can never do anybody any good. When schmoozing with friends about the real world, the best you can do as a professional is to make extrapolations which may or may not be plausible. You may be ingenious enough to think of a possible way . . . to predict the winner of a chessmatch through an analysis of ordinal position of birth, but it's pretty hard to take yourself seriously. One of the advantages of dealing with applied social psychology is that the problems are real ones and lend themselves to immediate application. So when the neighborhood coffee klatch starts talking about how dismal life in the cities has become and the horrors of the impending new jetport, you find that you actually know something. G. H. Hardy notwithstanding, that is a very satisfying feeling.

UNOBTRUSIVE HOLMES

I had called upon my friend Mr. Sherlock Holmes, one day in the autumn of last year, and found him in deep conversation with a very stout, florid-faced, elderly gentleman, with fiery red hair. With an apology for my intrusion, I was about to withdraw, when Holmes pulled me abruptly into the room, and closed the door behind me.

"You could not possibly have come at a better time, my dear Watson," he said cordially.

"I was afraid that you were engaged."

"So I am. Very much so."

"Then I can wait in the next room."

"Not at all. This gentleman, Mr. Wilson, has been my partner and helper in many of my most successful cases, and I have no doubt that he will be of the utmost use to me in yours also."

. . .

The portly client puffed out his chest with an appearance of some little pride, and pulled a dirty and wrinkled newspaper from the inside pocket of his greatcoat. As he glanced down the advertisement column, with his head thrust forward, and the paper flattened out upon his knee, I took a good look at the man, and endeavoured after the fashion of my companion to read the indications which might be presented by his dress or appearance.

I did not gain very much, however, by my inspection. Our visitor bore every mark of being an average commonplace British tradesman, obese, pompous, and slow. He wore rather baggy grey shepherds' check trousers, a not over-clean black frock-coat, unbuttoned in the front, and a drab waistcoat with a heavy brassy Albert chain, and a square pierced bit of metal dangling down as an ornament. A frayed top-hat, and a faded brown overcoat with a wrinkled velvet collar lay upon a chair beside him. Altogether, look as I would, there was nothing remarkable about the man save his blazing red head, and the expression of extreme chagrin and discontent upon his features.

Sherlock Holmes's quick eye took in my occupation and he shook his head with a smile as he noticed my questioning glances. "Beyond the obvious facts that he has at some time done manual labour, that he takes snuff, that he is a Freemason, that he has been in China, and that he has done a considerable amount of writing lately, I can deduce nothing else."

Mr. Jabez Wilson started up in his

From *The Adventures of Sherlock Holmes* by Sir Arthur Conan Doyle.

chair, with his forefinger upon the paper, but his eyes upon my companion.

"How, in the name of good fortune, did you know all that, Mr. Holmes?" he asked. "How did you know, for example, that I did manual labour? It's as true as gospel, and I began as a ship's carpenter."

"Your hands, my dear sir. Your right hand is quite a size larger than your left. You have worked with it, and the muscles are more developed."

"Well, the snuff, then, and the Freemasonry?"

"I won't insult your intelligence by telling you how I read that, especially as, rather against the strict rules of your order, you use an arc-and-compass breastpin."

"Oh, of course, I forgot that. But the writing?"

"What else can be indicated by that right cuff so very shiny for five inches, and the left one with the smooth patch near the elbow where you rest it upon the desk."

"Well, but China?"

"The fish which you have tattooed immediately above your right wrist could only have been done in China. I have made a small study of tattoo marks, and have even contributed to the literature of the subject. That trick of staining the fishes' scales of a delicate pink is quite peculiar to China. When, in addition, I see a Chinese coin hanging from your watch-chain, the matter becomes even more simple."

Mr. Jabez Wilson laughed heavily. "Well, I never!" said he. "I thought at first you had something clever, but I see that there was nothing in it after all."

UNOBTRUSIVE MEASURES: NONREACTIVE RESEARCH IN THE SOCIAL SCIENCES

EUGENE J. WEBB, DONALD T. CAMPBELL,
RICHARD D. SCHWARTZ, and LEE SECHREST

Although laboratory studies are undeniably and uniquely valuable, there are other viable means of doing psychological research. But with many research techniques, the researcher runs the risk of influencing and perhaps distorting the phenomenon under study. This problem is illustrated by the following science fiction story:

Two scientists wish to discover the origins of an ancient god. According to legend, this winged god visited Earth and then vanished. Using a special time machine, the scientists go back in time and experience many thrilling adventures. At the end, they are pursued by a group of angry warriors and barely make it back to the time machine to escape to their modern life. Once safely home again, the scientists recount their adventures, noting that they have failed to find the origin of the winged god. Suddenly, they realize that they themselves, visiting the ancient people and later disappearing in their time machine amid clouds of smoke and fire, must have been the origin of that legend.

Just as these fictional scientists unwittingly created the phenomenon they wanted to study, social psychologists can directly or indirectly create or bias the behaviors they are investigating. For example, through direct questions and measures, the researcher makes people aware that they are objects of study, and this knowledge can itself cause them to react differently than they would in everyday situations. Experimental subjects may hide their true feelings and give answers that they think are more socially appropriate, or they may try to second-guess the experimenter by giving the answers they think he or she is looking for. In either case, their responses are not true reflections of the behavior being studied.

How does the social psychologist deal with this pitfall of research? One answer is provided in the article "Unobtrusive Measures," which is composed of excerpts from the classic book of the same title. The authors describe techniques that the researcher can use to gain valuable behavioral data without intruding directly upon the subject's life and awareness.

This survey directs attention to social science research data *not* obtained by interview or questionnaire. Some may think this exclusion does not leave much. It does. Many innovations in research methods are to be found scattered throughout the social science literature. Their use, however, is unsystematic, their importance understated. Our review of this material is intended to broaden the social scientist's currently narrow range of utilized methodologies and to encourage creative and opportunistic exploitation of unique measurement possibilities.

Today, the dominant mass of social science research is based upon interviews and questionnaires. We lament this overdependence upon a single, fallible method. Interviews and questionnaires intrude as a foreign element into the social setting they would describe, they create as well as measure attitudes, they elicit atypical roles and responses, they are limited to those who are accessible and will cooperate, and the responses obtained are produced in part by dimensions of individual differences irrelevant to the topic at hand.

But the principal objection is that they are used alone. No research method is without bias. Interviews and questionnaires must be supplemented by methods testing the same social science variables but having *different* methodological weaknesses.

In sampling the range of alternative approaches, we examine their weaknesses, too. The flaws are serious and give insight into why we do depend so much upon the interview. But the issue is not choosing among individual methods. Rather it is the necessity for a multiple operationism, a collection of methods combined to avoid sharing the same weaknesses. The goal of this [article] is not to replace the interview but to supplement and cross-validate it with measures that do not require the cooperation of a respondent and that do not themselves contaminate the response.

Here are some samples of the kinds of methods we will be surveying:

From Eugene J. Webb, Donald T. Campbell, Richard D. Schwartz, and Lee Sechrest, *Unobtrusive Measures: Nonreactive Research in the Social Sciences,* © 1966 by Rand McNally College Publishing Company, Chicago, pp. 1, 2, 35–41, 53, 57, 58, 75–77, 112, 115–117, 119, 121–125, 171–174.

The floor tiles around the hatching-chick exhibit at Chicago's Museum of Science and Industry must be replaced every six weeks. Tiles in other parts of the museum need not be replaced for years. The selective erosion of tiles, indexed by the replacement rate, is a measure of the relative popularity of exhibits.

The accretion rate is another measure. One investigator wanted to learn the level of whisky consumption in a town which was officially "dry." He did so by counting empty bottles in ashcans.

The degree of fear induced by a ghost-story-telling session can be measured by noting the shrinking diameter of a circle of seated children.

Chinese jade dealers have used the pupil dilation of their customers as a measure of the client's interest in particular stones, and Darwin in 1872 noted this same variable as an index of fear.

Library withdrawals were used to demonstrate the effect of the introduction of television into a community. Fiction titles dropped, nonfiction titles were unaffected.

The role of rate of interaction in managerial recruitment is shown by the overrepresentation of baseball managers who were infielders or catchers (high-interaction positions) during their playing days.

Sir Francis Galton employed surveying hardware to estimate the bodily dimensions of African women whose language he did not speak.

The child's interest in Christmas was demonstrated by distortions in the size of Santa Claus drawings.

Racial attitudes in two colleges were compared by noting the degree of clustering of Negroes and whites in lecture halls.

PHYSICAL TRACES: EROSION AND ACCRETION

. . . In this [section] we look at research methods geared to the study of physical traces surviving from past behavior. Physical evidence is probably the social scientist's least-used source of data, yet because of its ubiquity, it holds flexible and broad-gauged potential.

It is reasonable to start a discussion of physical evidence by talking of Sherlock Holmes. He and his paperbacked colleagues could teach us much. Consider that the detective, like the social scientist, faces the task of inferring the nature of past behavior (Who did the Lord of the Manor in?) by the careful generation and evaluation of current evidence. Some evidence he engineers (by questioning), some he observes (Does the witness develop a tic?), some he develops from extant physical evidence (Did the murderer leave his eyeglasses behind?). From the weighing of several different types of hopefully converging evidence, he makes a decision on the plausibility of several rival hypotheses. For example:

H_1: The butler did it.

H_2: It was the blacksheep brother.

H_3: He really committed suicide.

This [section] discusses only the physical evidence, those pieces of data not specifically produced for the purpose of comparison and inference, but available to be exploited opportunistically by the alert investigator. It should be emphasized that physical evidence has greatest utility in consort with other methodological approaches. Because there are easily visible population and content restrictions associated with physical evidence, such data have largely been ignored. It is difficult even to consider a patently weak source of data when research strategy is based on single measures and definitional operationism. The visibly stronger questionnaire or interview looks to be more valid, and it may be if only one measure is taken. In a multimethod strategy, however, one does not have to exclude data of any class or degree solely because it is weak. If the weaknesses are known and considered, the data are usable.

It may be helpful to discriminate between two broad classes of physical evidence, a discrimination similar to that between the intaglio and the cameo. On one hand, there are the *erosion measures*, where the degree of selective wear on some material yields the measure. . . . On the other hand, there are *accretion measures*, where the research evidence is some deposit of materials.

Natural Erosion Measures

Let us look first at some erosion measures. A committee was formed to set up a psychological exhibit at Chicago's Museum of Science and Industry. The committee learned that the vinyl tiles around the exhibit containing live, hatching chicks had to be replaced every six weeks or so; tiles in other areas of the museum went for years without replacement (Duncan, 1963). A compara-

tive study of the rate of tile replacement around the various museum exhibits could give a rough ordering of the popularity of the exhibits. Note that although erosion is the measure, the knowledge of the erosion rate comes from a check of the records of the museum's maintenance department.

In addition to this erosion measure, unobtrusive observation studies showed that people stand before the chick display longer than they stand before any of the other exhibits. With this additional piece of evidence, the question becomes whether or not the erosion is a simple result of people standing in one location and shuffling their feet, or whether it really does indicate a greater frequency of different people viewing the exhibit. Clearly an empirical question. The observation and the tile erosion are two partially overlapping measures, each of which can serve as a check on the other. The observation material is more textured for studies of current behavior, because it can provide information on both the number of viewers and how long each views the display. The erosion data cannot index the duration of individual viewing, but they permit an analysis of popularity over time, and do so with economy and efficiency.

The wear on library books, particularly on the corners where the page is turned, offers an example of a possible approach that illustrates a useful overlap measure. One of the most direct and obvious ways to learn the popularity of books is to check how many times each of a series of titles has been removed from a library. This is an excellent measure and uses the records already maintained for other purposes. But it is only an indirect measure for the investigator who wants to know the relative amount of reading a series of books get. They may be removed from the library, but not read. It is easy to establish whether or not there is a close relationship between degree of wear and degree of checkouts from the library. If this relationship is positive and high, the hypothesis that books are taken out but selectively not read is accounted for. Note that the erosion measure also allows one to study the relative use of titles which are outside the span of the library-withdrawal measure. Titles placed on reserve, for example, are typically not noted for individual use by library bookkeeping. An alternative accretion measure is to note the amount of dust that has accumulated on the books studied.

Mosteller (1955) conducted a shrewd and creative study on the degree to which different sections of the *International Encyclopedia of the Social*

Sciences were read. He measured the wear and tear on separate sections by noting dirty edges of pages as markers, and observed the frequency of dirt smudges, finger markings, and underlining on pages. In some cases of very heavy use, ". . . dirt had noticeably changed the color of the page so that [some articles] are immediately distinguishable from the rest of the volume" (p. 171). Mosteller studied volumes at both Harvard and the University of Chicago, and went to three libraries at each institution. He even used the *Encyclopaedia Britannica* as a control.

Natural Accretion Measures

There are large numbers of useful natural remnants of past behavior that can be exploited. We can examine now a few examples of behavior traces which were laid down "naturally," without the intervention of the social scientist.

The detective-story literature . . . is instructive. In a favorite example (Barzun, 1961), a case hinged on determining where a car came from. It was solved (naturally) by studying the frequencies to which the car's radio buttons were tuned. By triangulation of the frequencies, from a known population of commercial-station frequencies, the geographic source of the car was learned. Here was a remnant of past behavior (someone setting the buttons originally) that included several component elements collectively considered to reach a solution. Unimaginatively, most detective fiction considers much simpler and less elegant solutions—such as determining how fast a car was going by noting the degree to which insects are splattered on the windshield.

Modern police techniques include many trace methods, for example, making complex analyses of soil from shoes and clothing to establish a suspect's probable presence at the scene of a crime. One scientist (Forshufvud, 1961) uncovered the historic murder of Napoleon in 1821 on the basis of arsenic traces in remains of his hair.

Radio-dial settings are being used in a continuing audience-measurement study, with mechanics in an automotive service department the data-gatherers (Anonymous, 1962). A Chicago automobile dealer, Z. Frank, estimates the popularity of different radio stations by having mechanics record the position of the dial in all cars brought in for service. More than 50,000 dials a year are checked, with less than 20 per cent duplication of dials. These data are then used to select radio stations to carry the dealer's advertising. The generalization of these findings is sound if (1)

the goal of the radio propaganda is to reach the same type of audience which now comes to the dealership, and (2) a significant number of cars have radios. If many of the cars are without radios, then a partial and possibly biased estimate of the universe is obtained. It is reported, "We find a high degree of correlation between what the rating people report and our own dial setting research" (p. 83).

. . .

DuBois (1963) reports on a 1934 study which estimated an advertisement's readership level by analyzing the number of different fingerprints on the page. The set of prints was a valid remnant, and the analysis revealed a resourceful researcher. Compare this with the anthropologist's device of estimating the prior population of an archeological site by noting the size of floor areas (Naroll, 1962). Among the consistently detectable elements in a site are good indicators of the floor areas of residences. When these can be keyed to knowledge of the residential and familial patterns of the group, these partial data, these remnants, serve as excellent population predictors.

Other remnants can provide evidence on the physical characteristics of populations no longer available for study. Suits of armor, for example, are indicators of the height of medieval knights.

The estimable study of McClelland (1961), *The Achieving Society*, displays a fertile use of historical evidence. Most of the data come from documentary materials such as records of births and deaths, coal imports, shipping levels, electric-power consumption, and remaining examples of literature, folk tales, and children's stories. We consider such materials in our discussion of archival records, but they are, in one sense, a special case of trace analysis. McClelland further reports on achievement-level estimates derived from ceramic designs on urns, and he indexes the geographic boundaries of Greek trade by archeological finds of vases. Sensitive to the potential error in such estimates, McClelland writes,

> So, rough though it is, the measure of the economic rise and fall of classical Greece was taken to be the area with which she traded, in millions of square miles, as determined by the location of vases unearthed in which her chief export commodities were transported [p. 117].

This measure was related to the need-for-achievement level of classical Greece, estimated from a content analysis of Greek writings.

. . .

THE RUNNING RECORD

> Possibly a wife was more likely to get an inscribed tablet if she died before her husband than if she outlived him.

The tablet cited here is a tombstone, and the quotation is from Durand's (1960) study of life expectancy in ancient Rome and its provinces. Tombstones are but one of a plethora of archives available for the adventurous researcher, and all social scientists should now and then give thanks to those literate, record-keeping societies which systematically provide so much material appropriate to novel analysis.

The purpose of this section is to examine and evaluate some uses of data periodically produced for other than scholarly purposes, but which can be exploited by social scientists. These are the ongoing, continuing records of a society, and the potential source of varied scientific data, particularly useful for longitudinal studies.

. . . Here the data are the actuarial records, the votes, the city budgets, and the communications media which are periodically produced, and paid for, by someone other than the researcher.

Actuarial Records

Birth, marriage, death. For each of these, societies maintain continuing records as normal procedure. Governments at various levels provide massive amounts of statistical data, ranging from the federal census to the simple entry of a wedding in a town-hall ledger. Such formal records have frequently been used in descriptive studies, but they offer promise for hypothesis-testing research as well.

Take Winston's (1932) research. He wanted to examine the preference for male offspring in upper-class families. He could have interviewed prospective mothers in affluent homes, or fathers in waiting rooms. Indeed, one could pay obstetricians to ask, "What would you like me to order?" Other measures, nonreactive ones, might be studies of adoption records, the sales of different layette colors (cutting the data by the class level of the store), or the incidence of "other sex" names—such as Marion, Shirley, Jean, Jerry, Jo.

But Winston went to the enormous data bank of birth records and manipulated them adroitly. He simply noted the sex of each child in each birth order. A preference for males was indicated, he hypothesized, if the male-female ratio of the last child born in families estimated to be complete was greater than that ratio for all children in the same families. With the detail present in birth records, he was able to segregate his upper-class sample of parents by the peripheral data of occupation, and so forth. The same auxiliary data can be employed in any study to serve as a check on evident population restrictions—a decided plus for detailed archives.

This study also illustrates the time-sampling problem. For the period studied, and because of the limitation to upper-class families, Winston's measure is probably not contaminated by economic limitations on the absolute number of children, a variable that may operate independently of any family sex preference. Had his study covered only the 1930's, or were he making a time-series comparison of economically marginal families, the time factor could offer a substantial obstacle to valid comparison. The argument for the existence of such an economic variable would be supported if a study of the 1930's showed no sex difference among terminal children, but did show significant differences for children born in the 1940's.

The Mass Media

Among the most easily available and massive sources of continuing secondary data are the mass media. The variety, texture, and scope of this enormous data pool have been neglected for too long. In this section, we present a selected series of studies which show intelligent manipulation of the mass media. We have necessarily excluded most content analyses and focused on a few which illustrate particular points.

It is proper to start this section by citing Zipf, who sought order in diverse social phenomena by his inventive use of data that few others would perceive as germane to scientific inquiry. In a model study, Zipf (1946) looked at the determinants of the circulation of information. His hypothesis was that the probability of message transfer between one person and another is inversely proportional to the distance between them. (See also Miller, 1947; Stewart, 1947; Zipf, 1949.) Without prejudice for content, he made use of the content of the mass media, as well as sales performance. How many and how long were out-of-town obituaries in the *New York Times?* How many out-of-town items appeared in the *Chicago Tribune?* Where did they originate? What was the sales level in cities besides New York and Chicago of the *Times* and *Tribune?* To this information from and about the mass media, Zipf added other archival sources. He asked the number of tons of goods moved by Railway Express between various points, and checked on the number of bus, railroad, and air passengers between pairs of cities. All of these were appropriate outcroppings for the test of his hypothesis on inverse proportionality, and in all cases the data conform, more or less closely, to his prediction.

Other investigators have used the continuing record of the newspaper for their data. Grusky (1963b) wanted to investigate the relationship between administrative succession and subsequent change in group performance. One could manipulate leaders in a small-group laboratory, but, in addition, one can go, as Grusky did, to the newspapers for more "natural" and less reactive intelligence. From the sports pages and associated records, Grusky learned the performance of various professional football and baseball teams, as well as the timing of changes in coaches and managers. Does changing a manager make a difference, or is it the meaningless machination of a front office looking for a scapegoat? It does make a difference, and this old sports-writer's question is a group-dynamics problem, phrased through the stating of two plausible rival hypotheses. In another study, Grusky (1963a) used baseball record books to study "The Effects of Formal Structures on Managerial Recruitment." He learned that former infielders and catchers (high-interaction personnel) were overrepresented among managers, while former pitchers and outfielders (low-interaction personnel) were underrepresented.

This public-record characteristic of the newspaper also allows linguistic analysis. If verbal behavior really is expressive, then one should be able to study a President's position on issues by studying the transcripts of his press conferences. Those answers on which a President stumbles in syntax, or which are prefaced by a string of evasive dependent clauses, may be symptomatic of trouble areas. Similarly, those questions which receive unusually long or short replies may reflect significant content areas.

Analysis of transcripts such as these can be very difficult, and often not enough substantive knowledge is available to rule out alternative hypotheses. A President is briefed on what are likely to be the topics of reporters' questions, and he has an opportunity to rehearse replies. The setting is not a nonreactive one, and the awareness of his visibility and the import of his answers may influence their content and form. One must also make each President his own control. The verbal styles of Eisenhower, Kennedy, and Johnson varied so greatly that any verbal index of syntax, glibness, or folksiness must be adjusted for the response tendencies of the individual President.

. . .

SIMPLE OBSERVATION

Who could he be? He was evidently reserved, and melancholy. Was he a clergyman?—He danced too well. A barrister?—He was not called. He used very fine words, and said a great deal. Could he be a distinguished foreigner come to England for the purpose of describing the country, its manners and customs; and frequenting city balls and public dinners with the view of becoming acquainted with high life, polished etiquette, and English refinement?—No, he had not a foreign accent. Was he a surgeon, a contributor to the magazines, a writer of fashionable novels or an artist?—No: to each and all of these surmises there existed some valid objection.—"Then," said everybody, "he must be somebody."—"I should think he must be," reasoned Mr. Malderton, with himself, "because he perceives our superiority, and pays us much attention."

(Sketches from Boz)

Charles Dickens displayed a ready touch for observationally scouring the behavior of this mysterious gentleman for evidence with which to classify him—even going so far as to put out the hypothesis that the man was a participant observer. In this [section] . . . our interest is focused on situations in which the observer has no control over the behavior or sign in question, and plays an unobserved, passive, and nonintrusive role in the research situation.

. . .

Exterior Physical Signs

Most of the exterior physical signs discussed are durable ones that have been inferred to be expressive of current or past behavior. A smaller number are portable and shorter-lived. The bullfighter's beard is a case in point. Conrad (1958) reports that the bullfighter's beard is longer on the day of the fight than on any other day. There are supporting comments among matadors about this phenomenon, yet can one measure the torero's anxiety by noting the length of his beard? The physical task is rather difficult, but not impossible in this day of sophisticated instrumentation. As in all these uncontrolled measures, one must draw inferences about the criterion behavior. Maybe it wasn't the anxiety at all. Perhaps the bullfighter stands farther away from the razor on the morning of the fight, or he may not have shaved that morning at all (like baseball pitchers and boxers). And then there is the possible intersubject contaminant that the more affluent matadors are likely to be shaved, while the less prosperous shave themselves.

In a report whose authors choose to remain anonymous (Anonymoi, 1953–1960), it was discovered that there is a strong association between the methodological disposition of psychologists and the length of their hair. The authors observed the hair length of psychologists attending professional meetings and coded the meetings by the probable appeal to those of different methodological inclinations. Thus, in one example, the length of hair was compared between those who attended an experimental set of papers and those who attended a series on ego-identity formation. The results are clear cut. The "tough-minded" psychologists have shorter-cut hair than the long-haired psychologists. Symptomatic interpretations, psychoanalytic inquiries as to what is cut about the clean-cut young man, are not the only possibilities. The causal ambiguity of the correlation was clarified when the "dehydration hypothesis" (i.e., that lack of insulation caused the hard-headedness) was rejected by the "bald-head control," i.e., examining the distribution of baldheaded persons (who by the dehydration hypothesis should be most hard-headed of all).

. . .

Expressive Movement

The more plastic variables of body movement historically have interested many observers. Charles Darwin's (1872) work on the expression of emotions continues to be the landmark commentary. His exposition of the measurement of frowning, the uncovering of teeth, erection of the hair, and the like remains provocative reading.

A journalistic account of the expressive behavior of hands has been given by Gould (1951). Here is his description of Frank Costello's appearance before the Kefauver crime hearings:

As he [Costello] sparred with Rudolph Halley, the committee's counsel, the movement of his fingers told their own emotional story. When the questions got rough, Costello crumpled a handkerchief in his hands. Or he rubbed his palms together. Or he interlaced his fingers. Or he grasped a half-filled glass of water. Or he beat a silent tattoo on the table top. Or he rolled a little ball of paper between his thumb and index finger. Or he stroked the side

piece of his glasses lying on the table. His was video's first ballet of the hands [p. 1].

It is of interest that conversations of male students with females have been found to be more frequently punctuated by quick, jerky, "nervous" gestures than are conversations between two males (Sechrest, 1965).

Schubert (1959) has suggested that overt personal behavior could be used in the study of judicial behavior. In presenting a psychometric model of the Supreme Court, he suggests that the speech, grimaces, and gestures of the judges when hearing oral arguments and when opinions are being delivered are rich sources of data for students of the Court.

On the other side of the legal fence, witnesses in Hindu courts are reported to give indications of the truth of their statements by the movement of their toes (Krout, 1951). The eminent American legal scholar J. H. Wigmore, in works on judicial proof and evidence (1935; 1937), speaks of the importance of peripheral expressive movements as clues to the validity of testimony.

The superstitious behavior of baseball players is a possible area of study. Knocking dust off cleats, amount of preliminary bat swinging, tossing dust into the air, going to the resin bag, and wiping hands on shirts may be interpreted as expressive actions. One hypothesis is that the extent of such superstitious behavior is related to whether or not the player is in a slump or in the middle of a good streak. This study could be extended to other sports in which the central characters are relatively isolated and visible. It should be easier for golfers and basketball players, but more difficult for football players.

From a practical point of view, of course, coaches and scouts have long studied the overt behavior of opponents for clues to forthcoming actions. (It is known, for example, that most football teams are "right sided" and run a disproportionate number of plays to the right [Griffin, 1964].) Does the fullback indicate the direction of the play by which hand he puts on the ground? Does the linebacker rest on his heels if he is going to fall back on pass defense? Does the quarterback always look in the direction in which he is going to pass, or does he sometimes look the other way, knowing that the defense is focusing on his eyes?

. . .

Physical Location

. . . There are the familiar newspaper accounts of who stood next to whom in Red Square reviewing the May Day parade. The proximity of a politician to the leader is a direct clue of his status in the power hierarchy. His physical position is interpreted as symptomatic of other behavior which gave him the status position befitting someone four men away from the Premier, and descriptive of that current status position. In this more casual journalistic report of observations, one often finds time-series analysis: Mr. B. has been demoted to the end of the dais, and Mr. L. has moved up close to the middle.

The clustering of Negroes and whites was used by Campbell, Kruskal, and Wallace (1965) in their study of seating aggregation as an index of attitude. Where seating in a classroom is voluntary, the degree to which the Negroes and whites present sit by themselves versus mixing randomly may be taken as a presumptive index of the degree to which acquaintance, friendship, and preference are strongly colored by race, as opposed to being distributed without regard to racial considerations. Classes in four schools were studied, and significant aggregation by race was found, varying in degree between schools. Aggregation by age, sex, and race has also been reported for elevated trains and lunch counters (Sechrest, 1965).

Feshbach and Feshbach (1963) report on another type of clustering. At a Halloween party, they induced fear in a group of boys, aged nine to twelve, by telling them ghost stories. The boys were then called out of the room and were administered questionnaires. The induction of the fear state was natural, but their dependent-variable measures were potentially reactive. What is of interest to us is a parenthetical statement made by the authors. After describing the ghost-story-telling situation, the Feshbachs offer evidence for the successful induction of fear: "Although the diameter of the circle was about eleven feet at the beginning of the story telling, by the time the last ghost story was completed, it had been spontaneously reduced to approximately three feet" (p. 499).

Sommer (1961) employed the position of chairs in a descriptive way, looking at "the distance for comfortable conversation." Normal subjects were used, but observations were made after the subjects had been on a tour of a large mental hospital. Distances among chairs in a lounge were systematically varied, and the people were brought into the lounge after the tour. They entered by pairs, and each pair was asked to go to a designated area and sit down. A simple record was made of the chairs selected.

The issue here is what one generalizes to. Just as the Feshbachs' subjects drew together during the narration of ghost stories, it would not be

unrealistic to expect that normal adults coming from a tour of a mental hospital might also draw closer together than would be the case if they had not been on the tour. Their seating distance before the tour would be an interesting control. Do they huddle more, anticipating worse than will be seen, or less?

Sommer (1959; 1960; 1962) has conducted other studies of social distance and positioning, and in the 1959 study mentions a "waltz technique" to measure psychological distance. He learned that as he approached people, they would back away; when he moved backward during a conversation, the other person moved forward. The physical distance between two conversationalists also varies systematically by the nationality of the talkers, and there are substantial differences in distance between two Englishmen talking together and two Frenchmen in conversation. In a cross-cultural study, this would be a response-set characteristic to be accounted for.

. . .

A FINAL NOTE

In the dialectic between impulsivity and restraint, the scientific superego became too harsh—a development that was particularly effective in intimidating adventurous research, because the young were learning more about methodological pitfalls than had their elders. . . .

(Riesman, 1959, p. 11)

David Riesman's remarks on the evolution of communications research apply equally well to the broader panoply of the study of social behavior. As social scientists, we have learned much of the labyrinth that is research on human behavior, and in so doing discovered an abundance of cul-de-sacs. Learning the complexities of the maze shortened our stride through it, and often led to a pattern of timid steps, frequently retraced. No more can the knowledgeable person enjoy the casual bravura that marked the sweeping and easy generalizations of an earlier day.

The facile promulgation of "truth," backed by a few observations massaged by introspection, properly met its end—flattened by a more questioning and sophisticated rigor. The blackballing of verification by introspection was a positive advance, but an advance by subtraction. Partly as a reaction to the grandiosities of the past, partly as a result of a growing sophistication about the opportunities for error, the scope of individual research studies shrank, both in the range of content considered and in the diversity of procedures.

The shrinkage was understandable and desirable, for certainly no science can develop until a base is reached from which reliable and consistent empirical findings can be produced. But if reliability is the initial step of a science, validity is its necessary stride. The primary effect of improved methodological practices has been to further what we earlier called the internal validity of a comparison—the confidence that a true difference is being observed. Unfortunately, practices have not advanced so far in improving external validity—the confidence with which the findings can be generalized to populations and measures beyond those immediately studied.

Slowing this advance in ability to generalize was the laissez-faire intellectualism of the operational definition. Operational definitionalism (to use a ponderously cumbersome term) provided a methodological justification for the scientist not to stray beyond a highly narrow, if reliable, base. One could follow a single method in developing data and be "pure," even if this purity were more associated with sterility than virtue.

The corkscrew convolutions of the maze of behavior were ironed, by definitional fiat, into a two-dimensional *T* maze. To define a social attitude, for example, solely by the character of responses to a list of questionnaire items is eminently legitimate—so much so that almost everything we know about attitudes comes from such research. Almost everything we know about attitudes is also suspect because the findings are saturated with the inherent risks of self-report information. One swallow does not make a summer; nor do two "strongly agrees," one "disagree," and an "I don't know" make an attitude or social value.

Questionnaires and interviews are probably the most flexible and generally useful devices we have for gathering information. Our criticism is not against them, but against the tradition which allowed them to become the methodological sanctuary to which the myopia of operational definitionalism permitted a retreat. If one were going to be limited to a single method, then certainly the verbal report from a respondent would be the choice. With no other device can an investigator swing his attention into so many different areas of substantive content, often simultaneously, and also gather intelligence on the extent to which his findings are hampered by population restrictions.

The power of the questionnaire and interview has been enormously enhanced, as have all methods, by the development of sensitive sampling procedures. With the early impetus provided by the Census Bureau to locational sampling, particularly to the theory and practice of stratification, concern about the population restrictions of a research sample has been radically diminished. Less well developed is the random sampling of time units—either over long periods such as months, or within a shorter period such as a day. There is no theoretical reason why time sampling is scarce, for it is a simple question of substituting time for location in a sampling design. Time sampling is of interest not only for its control over population fluctuations which might confound comparisons, but also because it permits control over the possibility of variable content at different times of the day or different months of the year.

The cost is high. And for that reason, government and commercial research organizations have led in the area, while academic research continues to limp along with conscripted sophomores. The controlled laboratory setting makes for excellent internal validity, as one has tight control over the conditions of administration and the internal structure of the questionnaire, but the specter of low generalizability is ever present.

That same specter is present, however, even if one has a national probability sample and the most carefully prepared questionnaire form or interview schedule. So long as one has only a single class of data collection, and that class is the questionnaire or interview, one has inadequate knowledge of the rival hypotheses grouped under the term "reactive measurement effects." These potential sources of error, some stemming from an individual's awareness of being tested, others from the nature of the investigator, must be accounted for by some other class of measurement than the verbal self-report.

It is too much to ask of any single class that it eliminate all the rival hypotheses subsumed under the population-, content-, and reactive-effects groupings. As long as the research strategy is based on a single measurement class, some flanks will be exposed, and even if fewer are exposed with the choice of the questionnaire method, there is still insufficient justification for its use as the only approach.

If no single measurement class is perfect, neither is any scientifically useless. Many studies and many novel sources of data have been mentioned in these pages. The reader may indeed have wondered which turn of the page would provide a commentary on some Ouija-board investigation. It would have been there had we known of one, and had it met some reasonable criteria of scientific worth. These "oddball" studies have been discussed because they demonstrate ways in which the investigator may shore up reactive infirmities of the interview and questionnaire. As a group, these classes of measurement are themselves infirm, and individually contain more risk (more rival plausible hypotheses) than does a well-constructed interview.

This does not trouble us, nor does it argue against their use, for the most fertile search for validity comes from a combined series of different measures, each with its idiosyncratic weaknesses, each pointed to a single hypothesis. When a hypothesis can survive the confrontation of a series of complementary methods of testing, it contains a degree of validity unattainable by one tested within the more constricted framework of a single method (Campbell & Fiske, 1959). Findings from this latter approach must always be subject to the suspicion that they are method-bound: Will the comparison totter when exposed to an equally prudent but different testing method? There must be a multiple operationalism. E. G. Boring (1953) put it this way:

. . . as long as a new construct has only the single operational definition that it received at birth, it is just a construct. When it gets two alternative operational definitions, it is beginning to be validated. When the defining operations, because of proven correlations, are many, then it becomes reified [p. 222].

This means, obviously, that the notion of a single "critical experiment" is erroneous. *There must be a series of linked critical experiments, each testing a different outcropping of the hypothesis.* It is through triangulation of data procured from different measurement classes that the investigator can most effectively strip of plausibility rival explanations for his comparison. . . .

REFERENCES

Anonymoi. Hair style as a function of hard-headedness vs. long-hairedness in psychological research, a study in the personology of science. Unprepared manuscript. Northwestern Univer. & Univer. of Chicago, 1953–1960.

Anonymous. Z-Frank stresses radio to build big Chevy dealership. *Advertising Age*, 1962, *33*, 83.

Barzun, J. *The delights of detection.* New York: Criterion Books, 1961.

Boring, E. G. The role of theory in experimental psychology. *American Journal of Psychology*, 1953, *66*, 169–184. (Reprinted in E. G. Boring, *History, psychology, and science.* Ed. R. I. Watson & D. T. Campbell, New York: Wiley, 1963. Pp. 210–225.)

Campbell, D. T., & Fiske, D. W. Convergent and discriminant validation by the multitrait-multimethod matrix. *Psychological Bulletin*, 1959, *56*, 81–105.

Campbell, D. T., Kruskal, W. H., & Wallace, W. P. Seating aggregation as an index of attitude. *Sociometry*, 1966, *29*, 1–15.

Conrad, B. *The death of Manolete.* Cambridge: Houghton Mifflin, 1958.

Darwin, C. *The expression of the emotions in man and animals.* London: Murray, 1872.

DuBois, C. N. Time Magazine's fingerprints' study. *Proceedings: 9th Conference, Advertising Research Foundation.* New York: Advertising Research Foundation, 1963.

Duncan, C. P. Personal communication, 1963.

Durand, J. Mortality estimates from Roman tombstone inscriptions. *American Journal of Sociology*, 1960, *65*, 365–373.

Feshbach, S., & Feshbach, N. Influence of the stimulus object upon the complementary and supplementary projection of fear. *Journal of Abnormal and Social Psychology*, 1963, *66*, 498–502.

Forshufvud, S. *Vem mordade Napoleon?* Stockholm: A. Bonnier, 1961.

Gould, J. Costello TV's first headless star; only his hands entertain audience, *New York Times*, March 4, 1951, *100* (34), 1. Cited in I. Doig, Kefauver and crime; the rise of television news and a senator. Unpublished master's thesis. Northwestern Univer., 1962.

Griffin, J. R. Coia "catch," kicking draw much criticism. *Chicago Sun Times*, October 27, 1964, *17*, 76.

Krout, M. H. Gestures and attitudes: an experimental study of the verbal equivalents and other characteristics of a selected group of manual autistic gestures. Unpublished doctoral dissertation, Univer. of Chicago, 1951.

McClelland, D. C. *The achieving society.* Princeton: Van Nostrand, 1961.

Miller, G. A. Population, distance and the circulation of information. *American Journal of Psychology*, 1947, *60*, 276–284.

Mosteller, F. Use as evidenced by an examination of wear and tear on selected sets of ESS. In K. Davis *et al.*, A study of the need for a new encyclopedic treatment

---

Page 18 — EXPERIENCING SOCIAL PSYCHOLOGY

of the social sciences. Unpublished manuscript, 1955. Pp. 167–174.

Naroll, R. *Data quality control.* Glencoe, Ill.: Free Press, 1962.

Riesman, D. Comment on "The State of Communication Research." *Public Opinion Quarterly,* 1959, *23,* 10–13.

Schubert, G. *Quantitative analysis of judicial behavior.* Glencoe, Ill.: Free Press, 1959.

Sechrest, L. Situational sampling and contrived situations in the assessment of behavior. Unpublished manuscript, Northwestern Univer., 1965. (Mimeographed.)

Sommer, R. Studies in personal space. *Sociometry,* 1959, *22,* 247–260.

Sommer, R. Personal space. *Canadian Architect,* 1960, pp. 76–80.

Sommer, R. Leadership and group geography. *Sociometry,* 1961, *24,* 99–110.

Sommer, R. The distance for comfortable conversations: further study. *Sociometry,* 1962, *25,* 111–116.

Stewart, J. Q. Empirical mathematical rules concerning the distinction and equilibrium of population. *Geographical Review,* 1947, *37,* 461–485.

Wigmore, J. H. *A student's textbook of the law of evidence.* Brooklyn: Foundation Press, 1935.

Wigmore, J. H. *The science of judicial proof as given by logic, psychology, and general experience and illustrated in judicial trials.* (3rd ed.) Boston: Little, Brown, 1937.

Zipf, G. K. Some determinants of the circulation of information. *American Journal of Psychology,* 1946, *59,* 401–421.

Zipf, G. K. *Human behavior and the principle of least effort.* Cambridge: Addison-Wesley, 1949.

IT STANDS TO REASON

The following story is attributed to Sigmund Freud, who told it as an example of scientific deduction in psychology:

An old Jew went on a train ride from Budapest back to his little village. Sitting in front of him was a distinguished-looking young man reading a book. The ride was long, and as the train was pulling out of the next-to-last station, the old man noticed that the young man was still on the train. That seemed rather surprising because the village at the last station was very poor and primitive. "Since he is reading a book, he must be a Jew," thought the old man, "and since he is so well dressed he must be prosperous. But what could a young, prosperous Jew possibly want in my little village? I guess he must have relatives there . . . in that case, it is probably Cohen's son who went to study medicine in Budapest. But if it's indeed Cohen's son, he couldn't be possibly coming for a visit because both Cohen and his wife are dead. What other reason could he have for coming to the village? It must be to get married. But to whom? Schull has two daughters; his oldest one is already married, so it must be the younger one. And Schull always wanted a prosperous doctor for a son-in-law. But a doctor could not be prosperous in Budapest with a name like Cohen, so he probably changed it to the Hungarian equivalent, Covax."

As the train was pulling into its final destination, the old Jew stood up and said, "Dr. Covax, if Mr. Schull is not in the station, I'll be happy to give you a ride to his house."

Flabbergasted, the young man looked at him and said, "How did you know my name, and that I'm to meet Mr. Schull?"

"It stands to reason," came the reply.

A GUIDE TO READING RESEARCH ARTICLES

The best way to assess the evidence supporting a particular theory, proposition, conclusion, or fact is to read the original research report. That will enable you to evaluate the logic of the researcher's theory, the adequacy of the research design, and the interpretation of the results. However, many students are reluctant to read original research because they believe that it is too complicated to understand. Actually the task is not so difficult as it may at first appear to be. Research articles generally follow a standard format and are divided into distinct sections and subsections that discuss different aspects of the study. We have added explanatory comments to excerpts from an actual research article in order to illustrate this format and guide your reading and understanding of research material.

Social and Personal Bases of Individuation

CHRISTINA MASLACH

Male and female subjects participated in a group experiment which provided them with opportunities (both verbal and nonverbal) to either individuate or deindividuate themselves. When the subjects anticipated the possibility of positive rewards, they made many more attempts to individuate themselves than when they expected that negative consequences were forthcoming. The pattern of individuating behavior was also affected by the subject's sex and prior level of experienced uniqueness. These findings have important implications for theoretical models of individuation and also provide a conceptual link between the phenomena of conformity, deviancy, and personal identity.

◄ Articles usually begin with an abstract that summarizes the purpose, method, and findings of the study. This gives the reader a quick overview of the entire study. In some journals, the summary appears as a concluding statement.

A woman living in a housing project reports ◄ that she feels safer because all the apartments look alike from the outside; there is nothing special to attract a burglar to her particular apartment. Men in basic military training quickly learn not to make themselves stand out from the rest of the platoon because if they do, they are more likely to be chosen for the most menial jobs. When a volunteer for an unpopular task is asked for from a group of school children, they often slump down in their chairs, look away, or put their hands in front of their faces in an effort to melt into the crowd and not look different from the others. However, when one of them is going to be chosen for a special reward, they yell, wave their arms, and jump up and down in order to draw attention to themselves. Similarly, contestants on such television shows as "The Dating Game" try very hard to make themselves appear unusual and unique, so that they have a better chance of being chosen for a glamorous date. Many people use clothes to make themselves stand out from others and

The first section of the research article, the Introduction, begins with a statement of the general problem under investigation.

Maslach, C. Social and personal bases of individuation. *Journal of Personality and Social Psychology*, 1974, *29*(3), 411–425. Copyright 1974 by the American Psychological Association. Reprinted by permission.

are sometimes upset if they find someone else wearing an outfit identical to theirs. On the other hand, such individuality in clothing usually occurs within the limits of the latest fashion trend, so that people wear what is "in" and not what is "out."

These and many other examples drawn from real life point up an intriguing behavioral paradox: People try to make themselves different and to stand out from others, but they also try to minimize their differences and to be just like everyone else. What are the reasons for engaging in such seemingly contradictory behaviors? When is one more likely to occur than the other? Although little work has focused directly on the dual question of why people want to be different from others but also similar to them, there are several areas of theory and research that are concerned with either one or the other aspect of the problem.

. . .

CONFORMITY

If being different from others is a negative characteristic, then we would expect people to try to be more like others by concealing or minimizing their dissimilarity. This idea is clearly supported by the work of social psychologists on conformity. Both Festinger (1950) and Kelley (1952) have discussed the various pressures toward uniformity in groups which cause an individual member to conform to the group norms. The classic experiments of Asch (1951, 1956) have demonstrated that subjects often agree with a unanimous (but clearly incorrect) majority rather than be the only one in the group who disagrees. However, when the subject is joined by someone who agrees with him, the amount of conformity drops sharply. In fact, a consistent minority can sometimes influence the majority (Moscovici, Lage, & Naffrechoux, 1969) probably because the minority opinion cannot then be regarded as an idiosyncrasy on the part of a single individual. Conformity is also greater when the subject's responses are public than when they are private or made anonymously (Deutsch & Gerard, 1955; Mouton, Blake & Olmstead, 1956).

. . .

The major hypothesis of this study, which was derived from these formulations, states that people work to individuate themselves when a positive event is forthcoming in the environment, but work to deindividuate themselves in the face of an impending negative event. In other words, people try to make themselves different and stand out

◄ Next, there is a literature review that discusses previous theorizing and research relevant to the current problem. Each reference is indicated by the author's last name and the date of publication; the complete reference is found in the References section at the end of the article (e.g., in case you want to go to the library and read Festinger's 1950 paper on social communication).

◄ The final part of the Introduction is the researcher's own hypotheses, which are the specific ideas that were tested in the experiment.

from the crowd in order to enhance their chances of receiving available positive rewards. However, they try to melt into the crowd, becoming relatively anonymous, as the likelihood of punishment or other negative consequences increases. A second hypothesis, in which individuation is both the independent and dependent variable, involves a person's prior level of experienced individuation. People who are already in a deindividuated state should have to work harder to make themselves stand out than people who already feel individuated, but should have to work less hard to make themselves anonymous. In contrast, people who are in an individuated state should show the reverse pattern. Finally, there was no reason to predict that these general principles about individuation would not hold true for both males and females. However, the study explored the hypothesis that the two sexes would use different techniques to call attention to themselves, as a result of previously learned sex roles.

METHOD

Overview of Design

Male and female subjects were run in groups of 4 in an experiment which was presumably concerned with group dynamics. After completing several preliminary activities, one of the subjects was to be chosen to be the designer in a city planning game. Half of the groups were told that the designer would win extra money (positive environment), while the others were told that the designer would receive electric shocks (negative environment). Within each group, two of the subjects were called by name, had personal comments made to them, had greater eye contact with the experimenter, and were in closer physical proximity to him (individuation condition). The other two subjects were addressed more impersonally and were not in such close contact with the experimenter (deindividuation condition). The subjects took several tests and participated in a group discussion, all of which were designed to allow them to make either unique or normative responses and thus either individuate or deindividuate themselves. With two levels of each of three independent variables (environment, individuation, and sex of subject), the basic design of

this study was a $2 \times 2 \times 2$ factorial. Ten subjects were run in each of the eight cells of the design for a total of 80 subjects.

◀ The Method section is the second section of the research article. It provides a detailed description of how the study was carried out. In some cases, when the study is rather complex, the Method section will begin with a summary of the design in order to give the reader a broad view of what went on.

◀ An independent variable (IV) is one that is deliberately manipulated by the experimenter in order to determine its effects on other behaviors, dependent variables (DVs).

◀ A factorial design is one in which there are two or more IVs; each level of each IV is completely crossed with the others. Each subject is assigned to only one cell (*a* to *h*) by random assignment (in this case, within each sex). The factorial design described here has three IVs and can be diagramed as follows:

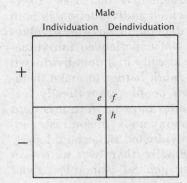

Subjects

Forty male and 40 female undergraduates at Stanford University participated in the experiment, which was described as a study on group processes. Most of them were paid for their participation, while a few completed the experiment in order to satisfy a course requirement in introductory psychology. All of the subjects were contacted by telephone, and precautions were taken to assign them to a group where they were unacquainted with the other subjects.

◄ A subsection describes characteristics of the people who made up the subject population of the study, including their number, age, sex, the population from which they were drawn, and how they were recruited.

Procedure

A group of four subjects was run in each session, with the sex of the group (either all males or all females) being randomly determined. After arriving at the experimental room, the subjects were greeted by Experimenter 1 and told that the study was concerned with different aspects of group behavior. In the first part of the study, group norms were to be obtained on personal associations and reactions, while in the second part, the subjects were going to engage in a group discussion.

◄ A subsection presents the details of the experimental procedure, including what subjects were told, what experimental treatments they experienced, and what they were asked to do.

. . .

Environment manipulation. In the third and last part of the study, the subjects were supposed to play a game of city planning, in which one person was to be the "designer," while the other three were to be "consultants." The designer was supposed to build a model city based on the informational cues provided by the consultants. Half of the groups (randomly assigned) were told that the designer would receive money for each trial where he or she correctly integrated the information provided (positive environment

◄ *Random assignment* of subjects to experimental treatment means that there is no systematic variable other than the treatment that is likely to cause the observed effects.

condition). The other groups were told that the designer would receive an electric shock each time he or she made a mistake in using the consultants' information (negative environment condition). After the procedure was described, each group saw one of four stimulus videotapes (with appropriate environment condition and sex) of "previous subjects" engaging in the city planning game. In addition to clearly showing the roles of the designer and the consultants in the game, the tape emphasized the rewarding aspects of the positive environment condition (the designer smiled and joked about all of the money he or she was winning) or the unpleasant ones of the negative environment condition (the designer was fairly grim-faced and visibly reacted to the shocks).

Experimenter 1 then explained to the subjects that one of them would be chosen to be the designer by Experimenter 2, who would be running the rest of the study. His decision would be based on the subject's performance on the association tests and in the group discussion.

In terms of experimental control, the use of two experimenters instead of one meant that each of them was blind to one of the experimental ◀ variables. Experimenter 2 was blind to the environment condition, while Experimenter 1 was unaware that the interviews were part of an experimental manipulation and thus was blind to the individuation variable.

An experimenter is *blind* to an independent variable when he or she is prevented from knowing which treatment the subject is in. As a result, this procedural control prevents the experimenter from systematically biasing the subject's responses, either consciously or unconsciously.

. . .

The ostensible purpose of these presentations ◀ was to provide the group members with information on which they could base a discussion. Experimenter 2 then asked the subjects to engage in a discussion for about 10 minutes while he made observations. Both the presentations and the discussion of each group were recorded on videotape for subsequent analysis. In addition, there were two observers behind a one-way glass who rated the subjects' verbal and nonverbal behavior on standardized check lists.

The way in which the dependent variables were recorded and coded is presented either with the procedure (as it is here) or in a separate subsection on dependent measures.

RESULTS

. . . It was critical to the design of the present ◀ study that the subjects clearly perceive a connection between their test and discussion behavior and the selection of one of them as the designer. At the end of the study, the subjects were asked to state what they thought were the reasons for the selection that was made. Virtually all of the subjects indicated that their test answers and

The third section of the research article describes the results of the study and presents the statistical analyses. This is the crux of the article: what was found.

In many cases, the Results section of a social psychology experiment involving a manipulation of the subject's motives or perception begins with an assessment of whether subjects actually perceived the instructions and experimental treatments accurately (i.e., as the researcher intended).

discussion participation were the basis for the experimenter's decision.

... The major hypothesis, that positive environment subjects would try to individuate themselves more than negative environment subjects, received a good deal of empirical support. ... Positive environment subjects gave more unusual self-descriptions ($F = 4.72$, $df = 1/72$, $p < .05$), which were accompanied by more expressive arm gestures ($F = 5.46$, $df = 1/66$, $p < .025$), than did negative environment subjects.

Following this check of experimental manipulations, the Results section presents data that are relevant to evaluating the hypotheses.

The numbers in parentheses refer to a particular statistical analysis. An F-value is the result of an analysis of variance. It is performed when there are more than two groups being compared and tells how much of the variability in the dependent variable is caused by the independent variable and how much by other (chance) factors. The df term refers to the degrees of freedom used in the analysis, which are a function of number of subjects and number of variables. The p-value is the level of significance and indicates the probability that the observed finding could have occurred by chance alone (rather than by experimental manipulation). In the first example here, $p < .05$ means that the probability of this finding occurring by chance is less than 5 times in 100 and that the finding is considered significantly different from chance. In other words, 95 times in 100 this result would probably be caused by the experimental treatment. After the F-value and df are computed, prepared tables in statistics books are consulted to determine what p-values are associated with those particular figures.

... When the test items included norms, individuated subjects gave much less unusual public answers than when no norms were involved ($t = 4.15$, $df = 38$, $p < .001$). In contrast, deindividuated subjects showed no such differences ($t = .83$, ns).

The t-values refer to the results of a statistical analysis called a t-test (comparing mean differences in two groups). In the first example, $p < .001$ means that the probability of this finding occurring by chance is less than 1 in 1,000. Therefore, the probability is very strong indeed. In the second example, ns means that the finding is not significantly different from what would occur by chance alone. By convention, $p < .05$ is the smallest probability value at which a result is judged significant.

... Females who spent a lot of time in describing themselves were less likely to smile ($r = -.52$, $p < .001$) or to joke ($r = .34$, $p < .04$) during the discussion.

The r-value refers to the degree of correlation between two variables. It describes the strength of the association between them.

[Subjects who had high social desirability scores were distributed equally throughout the experimental conditions ($\chi = 1.60$, $df = 3$, ns).]

The χ-value refers to the result of a chi-square test, which is used to compare whether different *frequencies* observed could be expected to occur by chance alone.

DISCUSSION

On reviewing this complex set of data, several clear behavioral patterns emerge. Some subjects made attempts to individuate themselves, while others did not. Those who did were primarily

The fourth and final section of a research article is the Discussion. Here the researcher evaluates and interprets the results of the study. The Discussion usually begins with a review of the findings in terms of the original hypotheses. The in the positive environment and deindividuated conditions, as predicted. Individuating behavior was both verbal (more unusual and longer self-descriptions, more unusual test answers) and nonverbal (more expressive arm gestures, more looking at the experimenter). Because of the nature of the experiment, the subjects who wanted to deindividuate themselves could not do so in very extreme ways (such as disguising themselves or getting lost in a large crowd). However, these subjects did take the deindividuating options that were available to them by conforming more often, exhibiting a different type of conversational behavior (many short, unrevealing comments), and often looking away from the other people. In addition to these individuation differences, subjects showed different emotional responses which generally corresponded with the environment manipulation. Positive environment subjects were relaxed and enjoying the study, while negative environment subjects (particularly those in the negative individuated condition) felt more uncomfortable and behaved in a rather boisterous and agitated way. Overall, the above pattern of results was more striking for female subjects than for males.

One of the major outcomes of the present ◄ study is that is has underscored the complexity of the individuation process. A particularly critical problem is the way in which the process is put into operation. . . . Since being different obviously necessitates the use of a reference group, the first step is to evaluate the other people in the particular situation and determine the dimensions on which one could differ from them. For example, a person could disagree with a position taken by the others, could dress differently from them, could disrupt some ongoing activity, could react with more extreme emotion. . . .

Throughout the present study, the concern has ◄ been with how and why the single individual tries to be different from others. However, there are also collective attempts at individuation, in which people become members of a group that behaves very differently from the rest of society. . . . In collective individuation, the individual group member must first become very similar to some people in order to become very different from others, while such sameness is not a necessary prerequisite for singularity. Interesting questions raised by the collective phenomenon are how much group members want to be individuated within the group, and the extent to which such individuation could occur before the person

reader should be sure to evaluate whether the conclusions drawn are appropriate to the actual results and to note conclusions that take too much liberty with the data.

The Discussion also develops important theoretical points arising from the study,

raises new issues for consideration,

risked the loss of the collective identity.

In this experiment, . . . the hypothesis was operationalized by varying an outcome that was external to the subject (i.e., money or electric shocks). However, it would be misleading to assume that this hypothesis only applied to human behavior that is controlled by external consequences. People often change their behavior as a function of chronic, internal, self-evaluative processes, such as pride or shame, and one would expect that the general hypothesis would also apply in such instances. For example, a person who anticipates feeling embarrassed or ashamed should try to deindividuate himself in order to minimize the chance of this occurring.

◄ and proposes new hypotheses for the researcher to follow up in his or her next study or for other investigators to test.

REFERENCES

◄ The References section gives you an alphabetically arranged listing of the sources cited in the article. Each of those sources has its own reference list. Thus, the reader can readily become well informed in the general area under investigation by reading the references (and their references) as well.

Asch, S. E. Effects of group pressure on the modification and distortion of judgments. In H. Geutzkow (ed.), *Groups, leadership, and men*. Pittsburgh: Carnegie Press, 1951.

Asch, S. E. Studies of independence and conformity: I. A minority of one against a unanimous majority. *Psychological Monographs*, 1956, **70**(9, Whole No. 416).

Deutsch, M., & Gerard, H. B. A study of normative and informational social influences upon individual judgment. *Journal of Abnormal and Social Psychology*, 1955, **51**, 629–636.

Festinger, L. Informal social communication. *Psychological Review*, 1950, **57**, 271–282.

Kelley, H. H. The two functions of reference groups. In G. E. Swanson, T. M. Newcomb, & E. L. Hartley (eds.), *Readings in social psychology*. (2nd ed.) New York: Holt, 1952.

Moscovici, S., Lage, E., & Naffrechoux, M. Influence of a consistent minority on the responses of a majority in a color perception task. *Sociometry*, 1969, **32**, 365–380.

Mouton, J. S., Blake, R. R., & Olmstead, J. A. The relationship between frequency of yielding and the disclosure of personal identity. *Journal of Personality*, 1956, **24**, 339–347.

ON EXPERIMENTAL DESIGN

[Mark Twain]

I constructed four miniature houses of worship—a Mohammedan mosque, a Hindu temple, a Jewish synagogue, a Christian cathedral—and placed them in a row. I then marked 15 ants with red paint and turned them loose. They made several trips to and fro, glancing in at the places of worship, but not entering.

I then turned loose 15 more painted blue; they acted just as the red ones had done. I now gilded 15 and turned them loose. No change in the result; the 45 traveled back and forth in a hurry persistently and continuously visiting each fane, but never entering. This satisfied me that these ants were without religious prejudices—just what I wished; for under no other conditions would my next and greater experiment be valuable. I now placed a small square of white paper within the door of each fane; and upon the mosque paper I put a pinch of putty, upon the temple paper a dab of tar, upon the synagogue paper a trifle of turpentine, and upon the cathedral paper a small cube of sugar.

First I liberated the red ants. They examined and rejected the putty, the tar and the turpentine, and then took to the sugar with zeal and apparent sincere conviction. I next liberated the blue ants, and they did exactly as the red ones had done. The gilded ants followed. The preceding results were precisely repeated. This seemed to prove that ants destitute of religious prejudice will always prefer Christianity to any other creed.

However, to make sure, I removed the ants and put putty in the cathedral and sugar in the mosque. I now liberated the ants in a body, and they rushed tumultuously to the cathedral. I was very much touched and gratified, and went back in the room to write down the event; but when I came back the ants had all apostatized and had gone over to the Mohammedan communion.

I saw that I had been too hasty in my conclusions, and naturally felt rebuked and humbled. With diminished confidence I went on with the test to the finish. I placed the sugar first in one house of worship, then in another, till I had tried them all.

With this result: whatever Church I put the sugar in, that was the one the ants straightway joined. This was true beyond a shadow of doubt, that in religious matters the ant is the opposite of man, for man cares for but one thing; to find the only true Church; whereas the ant hunts for the one with the sugar in it.

A KEY TO SCIENTIFIC RESEARCH LITERATURE

What was said	What was meant	What was said	What was meant
It has long been known that . . .	I haven't bothered to look up the original reference but . . .	satisfactory	doubtful
		fair	imaginary
Of great theoretical and practical importance . . .	Interesting to me.		
While it has not been possible to provide definite answers to these questions . . .	The experiment didn't work out, but I figured I could at least get a publication out of it.	It is suggested that . . . It is believed that . . . It may be that . . .	I think.
The operant conditioning technique was chosen to study the problem . . .	The fellow in the next lab already had the equipment set up.	It is generally believed that . . .	A couple of other guys think so too.
Three of the Ss were chosen for detailed study . . .	The results on the others didn't make sense.	It is clear that much additional work will be required before a complete understanding . . .	I don't understand it.
Typical results are shown . . .	The best results are shown . . .		
Agreement with the predicted curve is:		Unfortunately, a quantitative theory to account for these results has not been formulated.	I can't think of one and neither has anyone else.
excellent	fair		
good	poor	Correct within an order of magnitude . . .	Wrong.

Hodge, M. H. Table 1. A key to scientific research literature. *The American Psychologist*, March 1962, p. 154. Copyright © 1962 by the American Psychological Association. Reprinted by permission.

Thanks are due to Joe Glotz for assistance with the experiments and to John Doe for valuable discussion.	Glotz did the work and Doe explained what it meant.

PROJECTS

Name _____

Date _____

1.1: UNOBTRUSIVE MEASURES

The goal of this project is to give you some firsthand experience in designing research that uses unobtrusive measures. Imagine you are a social psychologist who is interested in studying altruism. In particular, you wish to discover what factors influence people's decisions to give help to a needy person. Rather than rely on a questionnaire about altruism, you decide to use some unobtrusive measures of helping. What might these measures be? How would you collect the data? What are the limitations of these measures?

1. Describe one or more unobtrusive measures of helping behavior.

2. What specific procedures would you use to collect data with these measures?

3. List the advantages and disadvantages (e.g., cost, time, access, accuracy) of using each measure.

4. Present a hypothesis about the effect of a variable—such as age or sex of the helper and recipient, presence of bystanders, etc.—on helping behavior, and describe how you would test this hypothesis, using at least one unobtrusive measure of helping.

Name _____

Date _____

1.2: RESEARCH CRITIQUE

An enterprising student decided to do an original experiment on racism that would be a distinct improvement over previous studies. However, the student's description of the experiment is clear evidence that good intentions do not ensure good research skills. On the worksheet below, first list all the errors in the study, and then indicate a way in which each could be corrected or improved.

RACISM AND GROUP INFLUENCE

Even though a lot of studies have been done on the subject of racist attitudes, I felt that they were all bad, and so I carried out a study of my own. I contacted fifteen schools, but only one was willing to let me use some of its pupils as subjects—on the condition that the teachers would select them. Over sixty names were given to me, and from them I selected, by using a pretest racism questionnaire, those subjects who expressed some racist attitudes ($n = 25$). Because some of the subjects were young, I thought it necessary to use simple statements that were all worded in one direction (i.e., agreement with each item always indicated racism). This pretest was done a few days before the experimental group discussion. The second measure (using the very same questionnaire) was done a few days after the group discussion. In the group situation, items from the racism scale were presented for group discussion. Confederates planted in the group responded in a systematic, nonracist way. From the total of 25 subjects, I took only the top 10 subjects (those who scored highest on the pretest) for the analysis to be reported here. The analysis I used was analysis of variance. The mean score for the pretest was 87.4, SD = 20.85. After the experimental induction of the group discussion, the mean score was 83.13, SD = 15.62. Because the score on the racism questionnaire was lower after the discussion session, this study clearly shows that racism can be reduced through group discussion.

Errors

Corrections or Improvements

2
THE SELF

When you think about your "self"—the part of you that is your essence, your core, your very own—what do you see? Do you, like some psychoanalysts, see the self as being somewhat similar to an iceberg, with the greater part of its mass hidden beneath the surface of everyday consciousness and your behavior motivated mainly by deep impulses linked to childhood? Or do you perhaps share the view of B. F. Skinner that the self is a vacuum, a black box, an unknowable organism that is motivated mainly by external environmental forces. You may also see the self as Jung saw it: an island rising above water, joined to others by a collective unconscious. Or do you see the self as a mirror reflecting the world and other people around you, or as a series of roles, rather like the layers of an onion—a ball of persons with no real substance at the core? You may share the view of Erikson and the existential philosophers, that the self is an active selector which reflects its own free will through the essential human ability to choose. If you do not see yourself as any of these things, the conceptualizations proposed by other psychologists, who

have characterized the self as, among other things, a "digital computer," a "child of God," a "pilgrim," and a "godhead," may strike you as more to the point. And if none of these metaphors fits your own self-concept, then maybe, as suggested by some, you are just an "illusion" or a "ghost in the machine." Maybe in reality there is no "you" at all!

Clearly, there are many definitions of the self in everyday language and many more in the psychological literature. In addition to their dramatic-pictorial effect, these metaphors and definitions share the notion of the self as that part of human experience that we regard as essentially us—unique, stable, coherent, organized, consistent, and integrated. Nevertheless, most of us behave, think, and feel very differently with different people at different times. Quite appropriately, we experience and express rather different selves with our parents, friends, supervisors, and lovers. Furthermore, things such as weather, music, drugs, meditation, and even clothing can affect our self-perception.

A good example of the effects of social atmo-

ADVICE FROM A CATERPILLAR

The Caterpillar and Alice looked at each other for some time in silence: at last the Caterpillar took the hookah out of his mouth, and addressed her in a languid, sleepy voice.

"Who are *you?*" said the Caterpillar.

This was not an encouraging opening for a conversation. Alice replied, rather shyly, "I—I hardly know, Sir, just at present—at least I know who I *was* when I got up this morning,

but I think I must have changed several times since then."

"What do you mean by that?" said the Caterpillar, sternly. "Explain yourself!"

"I ca'n't explain *myself,* I'm afraid, Sir," said Alice, "because I'm not myself, you see."

"I don't see," said the Caterpillar.

"I'm afraid I ca'n't put it more clearly," Alice replied, very politely, "for I ca'n't understand it myself, to begin with; and being so many different sizes in a day is very confusing."

"It isn't," said the Caterpillar.

"Well, perhaps you haven't found it so yet," said Alice: "but when you have to turn into a chrysalis—you will some day, you know—and then after that into a butterfly, I should think you'll feel it a little queer, won't you?"

"Not a bit," said the Caterpillar.

"Well, perhaps *your* feelings may be different," said Alice: "all I know is, it would feel very queer to *me.*"

"You!" said the Caterpillar contemptuously. "Who are *you?*"

From Lewis Carroll, *Alice's Adventures in Wonderland* (New York: Random House).

sphere on the different roles that the self must assume can be observed among people who are called to serve in the military reserves. When they arrive, they are quiet and are dressed conservatively. They may be clerks, executives, bus drivers, teachers. They may be a little overweight and perhaps have balding heads. They are likely to be preoccupied with the cares of the business or job that was left unfinished when the call for service came. Yet, within a short period of time, as they put on the old uniforms and start to carry a gun,

they are transformed. Other selves emerge. The old glitter comes back to the eyes and with it the youthful expression, the old gestures, the special army vocabulary. The atmosphere is radically changed. They are loud and noisy, united—a group. They in fact begin to behave in a way that they themselves would have found rather unacceptable just a few hours earlier. Yet, they clearly have no great difficulty assuming the proper role once they have the proper uniform.

THE CONSCIOUSNESS OF SELF

WILLIAM JAMES

"The Consciousness of Self," by William James, begins with some classic theorizing about the nature of the self. James proposes that the individual has many selves rather than a single one and that some of these selves develop as a function of the different people with whom the individual interacts. He explores the conflicts that can exist among these different selves and the ways in which alterations in the selves can take place. Although James's style and language may seem somewhat archaic, his ideas are very modern. In fact, they provide the theoretical underpinnings for much current work on self and identity.

Let us begin with the Self in its widest acceptation, and follow it up to its most delicate and subtle form. . . .

THE EMPIRICAL SELF OR ME

The Empirical Self of each of us is all that he is tempted to call by the name of *me.* But it is clear that between what a man calls *me* and what he simply calls *mine* the line is difficult to draw. We feel and act about certain things that are ours very much as we feel and act about ourselves. Our fame, our children, the work of our hands, may be as dear to us as our bodies are, and arouse the same feelings and the same acts of reprisal if attacked. And our bodies themselves, are they simply ours, or are they *us?* Certainly men have been ready to disown their very bodies and to regard them as mere vestures, or even as prisons of clay from which they should some day be glad to escape.

We see then that we are dealing with a fluctuating material. The same object being sometimes treated as a part of me, at other times as simply mine, and then again as if I had nothing to do with it at all. *In its widest possible sense,* however, *a man's Self is the sum total of all that he* CAN *call his,* not only his body and his psychic powers, but his clothes and his house, his wife and children, his ancestors and friends, his reputation and works, his lands and horses, and yacht and bank-account. All these things give him the same emotions. If they wax and prosper, he feels triumphant; if they dwindle and die away, he feels cast down,—not necessarily in the same degree for each thing, but in much the same way for all. . . .

1. *The constituents of the Self* may be divided into . . .

(*a*) The material Self;

(*b*) The social Self; and

(*c*) The spiritual Self. . . .

(*a*) The body is the innermost part of *the material Self* in each of us; and certain parts of

---

From William James, *The Principles of Psychology* (New York: Dover).

the body seem more intimately ours than the rest. The clothes come next. The old saying that the human person is composed of three parts—soul, body and clothes—is more than a joke. . . . Next, our immediate family is a part of ourselves. Our father and mother, our wife and babes, are bone of our bone and flesh of our flesh. When they die, a part of our very selves is gone. If they do anything wrong, it is our shame. If they are insulted, our anger flashes forth as readily as if we stood in their place. Our home comes next. Its scenes are part of our life; its aspects awaken the tenderest feelings of affection; and we do not easily forgive the stranger who, in visiting it, finds fault with its arrangements or treats it with contempt. All these different things are the objects of instinctive preferences coupled with the most important practical interests of life. We all have a blind impulse to watch over our body, to deck it with clothing of an ornamental sort, to cherish parents, wife and babes, and to find for ourselves a home of our own which we may live in and "improve."

An equally instinctive impulse drives us to collect property; and the collections thus made become, with different degrees of intimacy, parts of our empirical selves. The parts of our wealth most intimately ours are those which are saturated with our labor. There are few men who would not feel personally annihilated if a life-long construction of their hands or brains—say an entomological collection or an extensive work in manuscript—were suddenly swept away. The miser feels similarly towards his gold, and although it is true that a part of our depression at the loss of possessions is due to our feeling that we must now go without certain goods that we expected the possessions to bring in their train, yet in every case there remains, over and above this, a sense of the shrinkage of our personality, a partial conversion of ourselves to nothingness, which is a psychological phenomenon by itself. . . .

(b) *A man's Social Self* is the recognition which he gets from his mates. We are not only gregarious animals, liking to be in sight of our fellows, but we have an innate propensity to get ourselves noticed, and noticed favorably, by our kind. No more fiendish punishment could be devised, were such a thing physically possible, than that one should be turned loose in society and remain absolutely unnoticed by all the members thereof. If no one turned round when we entered, answered when we spoke, or minded what we did, but if every person we met "cut us dead," and acted as if we were non-existing things, a kind of rage

and impotent despair would ere long well up in us, from which the cruellest bodily tortures would be a relief. . . .

Properly speaking, *a man has as many social selves as there are individuals who recognize him* and carry an image of him in their mind. To wound any one of these his images is to wound him. But as the individuals who carry the images fall naturally into classes, we may practically say that he has as many different social selves as there are distinct *groups* of persons about whose opinion he cares. He generally shows a different side of himself to each of these different groups. Many a youth who is demure enough before his parents and teachers, swears and swaggers like a pirate among his "tough" young friends. We do not show ourselves to our children as to our club-companions, to our customers as to the laborers we employ, to our own masters and employers as to our intimate friends. From this there results what practically is a division of the man into several selves; and this may be a discordant splitting, as where one is afraid to let one set of his acquaintances know him as he is elsewhere; or it may be a perfectly harmonious division of labor, as where one tender to his children is stern to the soldiers or prisoners under his command.

. . .

(c) By the Spiritual Self, so far as it belongs to the Empirical Me, I mean a man's inner or subjective being, his psychic faculties or dispositions, taken concretely. . . . These psychic dispositions are the most enduring and intimate part of the self, that which we most verily seem to be. We take a purer self-satisfaction when we think of our ability to argue and discriminate, of our moral sensibility and conscience, of our indomitable will, than when we survey any of our other possessions. Only when these are altered is a man said to be *alienatus a se.*

. . .

RIVALRY AND CONFLICT OF THE DIFFERENT SELVES

With most objects of desire, physical nature restricts our choice to but one of many represented goods, and even so it is here. I am often confronted by the necessity of standing by one of my empirical selves and relinquishing the rest. Not that I would not, if I could, be both handsome and fat and well dressed, and a great athlete, and make a million a year, be a wit, a *bon-vivant,* and a lady-killer, as well as a philosopher; a philanthropist, statesman, warrior, and African explorer, as well as a "tone-poet" and saint. But the thing is simply impossible. The millionaire's work would run counter to the saint's; the *bon-vivant* and the philanthropist would trip each other up; the philosopher and the lady-killer could not well keep house in the same tenement of clay. Such different characters may conceivably at the outset of life be alike *possible* to a man. But to make any one of them actual, the rest must more or less be suppressed. So the seeker of his truest, strongest, deepest self must review the list carefully, and pick out the one on which to stake his salvation. All other selves thereupon become unreal, but the fortunes of this self are real. Its failures are real failures, its triumphs real triumphs, carrying shame and gladness with them.

. . .

I, who for the time have staked my all on being a psychologist, am mortified if others know much more psychology than I. But I am contented to wallow in the grossest ignorance of Greek. My deficiencies there give me no sense of personal humiliation at all. Had I "pretensions" to be a linguist, it would have been just the reverse. So we have the paradox of a man shamed to death because he is only the second pugilist or the second oarsman in the world. That he is able to beat the whole population of the globe minus one is nothing; he has "pitted" himself to beat that one; and as long as he doesn't do that nothing else counts. He is to his own regard as if he were not, indeed he *is* not.

Yonder puny fellow, however, whom every one can beat, suffers no chagrin about it, for he has long ago abandoned the attempt to "carry that line," as the merchants say, of self at all. With no attempt there can be no failure; with no failure no humiliation. So our self-feeling in this world depends entirely on what we *back* ourselves to be and do. It is determined by the ratio of our actualities to our supposed potentialities; a fraction of which our pretensions are the denominator and the numerator our success: thus,

$$\text{Self-esteem} = \frac{\text{Success}}{\text{Pretensions}} \ . \ . \ . \ .$$

To give up pretensions is as blessed a relief as to get them gratified; and where disappointment is incessant and the struggle unending, this is what men will always do. . . .

THE MUTATIONS OF THE SELF

may be divided into two main classes:

1. Alterations of memory; and
2. Alterations in the present bodily and spiritual selves.

1. *Alterations of memory* are either *losses* or false recollections. In either case the *me* is changed. Should a man be punished for what he did in his childhood and no longer remembers? Should he be punished for crimes enacted in post-epileptic unconsciousness, somnambulism, or in any involuntarily induced state of which no recollection is retained? Law, in accord with common-sense, says: "No; he is not the same person forensically now which he was then." These losses of memory are a normal incident of extreme old age, and the person's *me* shrinks in the ratio of the facts that have disappeared.

In dreams we forget our waking experiences; they are as if they were not. And the converse is also true. As a rule, no memory is retained during the waking state of what has happened during mesmeric trance, although when again entranced the person may remember it distinctly, and may then forget facts belonging to the waking state. We thus have, within the bounds of healthy mental life, an approach to an alternation of *me's*.

False memories are by no means rare occurrences in most of us, and, whenever they occur, they distort the consciousness of the me. Most people, probably, are in doubt about certain matters ascribed to their past. They may have seen them, may have said them, done them, or they may only have dreamed or imagined they did so. The content of a dream will oftentimes insert itself into the stream of real life in a most perplexing way. The most frequent source of false memory is the accounts we give to others of our experiences. Such accounts we almost always make both more simple and more interesting than the truth. We quote what we should have said or done, rather than what we really said or did; and in the first telling we may be fully aware of the distinction. But ere long the fiction expels the reality from memory and reigns in its stead alone. This is one great source of the fallibility of testimony meant to be quite honest.

. . .

2. When we pass beyond alterations of memory to abnormal *alterations in the present self* we have

still graver disturbances. These alterations are of three main types, from the descriptive point of view. But certain cases unite features of two or more types; and our knowledge of the elements and causes of these changes of personality is so slight that the division into types must not be regarded as having any profound significance. The types are:

(1) Insane delusions;

(2) Alternating selves;

(3) Mediumships or possessions.

1) In insanity we often have delusions projected into the past. . . . But the worst alterations of the self come from present perversions of sensibility and impulse which leave the past undisturbed, but induce the patient to think that the present *me* is an altogether new personage. Something of this sort happens normally in the rapid expansion of the whole character, intellectual as well as volitional, which takes place after the time of puberty. . . .

. . .

With the beginnings of cerebral disease there often happens something quite comparable to this:

Masses of new sensation, hitherto foreign to the individual, impulses and ideas of the same inexperienced kind, for example terrors, representations of enacted crime, of enemies pursuing one, etc. At the outset, these stand in contrast with the old familiar *me*, as a strange, often astonishing and abhorrent *thou*. Often their invasion into the former circle of feelings is felt as if the old self were being taken possession of by a dark overpowering might, and the fact of such "possession" is described in fantastic images. Always this doubleness, this struggle of the old self against the new discordant forms of experience, is accompanied with painful mental conflict, with a passion, with violent emotional excitement. . . .

. . .

What the particular perversions of the bodily sensibility may be, which give rise to these contradictions, *is for the most part impossible* . . . to conceive. One patient has another self that repeats all his thoughts for him. Others, among whom are some of the first characters in history, have familiar demons who speak with them, and are replied to. In another someone "makes" his thoughts for him. Another has two bodies, lying in different beds. Some patients feel as if they had lost parts of their bodies, teeth, brain, stomach, etc. In some it is made of wood, glass, butter, etc. In some it does not exist any longer, or is dead, or is a foreign object quite separate from the speaker's self. Occasionally, parts of the body lose their connection for consciousness with the rest, and are treated as belonging to another person and moved by a hostile will. Thus the right hand may fight with the left as with an enemy. Or the cries of the patient himself are assigned to another person with whom the patient expresses sympathy. . . .

. . .

A case with which I am acquainted through Dr. C. J. Fisher of Tewksbury has possibly its origin in this way. The woman, Bridget F.,

has been many years insane, and always speaks of her supposed self as "the rat," asking me to "bury the little rat," etc. Her real self she speaks of in the third person as "the good woman," saying, "The good woman knew Dr. F. and used to work for him," etc. Sometimes she sadly asks: "Do you think the good woman will ever come back?" She works at needlework, knitting, laundry, etc., and shows her work, saying, "Isn't that good for only a rat?" She has, during periods of depression, hid herself under buildings, and crawled into holes and under boxes. "She was only a rat, and wants to die," she would say when we found her.

2. The phenomenon of *alternating personality* in its simplest phases seems based on lapses of memory. Any man becomes, as we say, *inconsistent* with himself if he forgets his engagements, pledges, knowledges, and habits; and it is merely a question of degree at what point we shall say that his personality is changed. In the pathological cases known as those of double or alternate personality the lapse of memory is abrupt, and is usually preceded by a period of unconsciousness or syncope lasting a variable length of time. In the hypnotic trance we can easily produce an alteration of the personality, either by telling the subject to forget all that has happened to him since such or such a date, in which case he becomes (it may be) a child again, or by telling him he is another altogether imaginary personage, in which case all facts about himself seem for the time being to lapse from out his mind, and he throws himself into the new character with a vivacity proportionate to the amount of histrionic imagination which he possesses. But in the pathological cases the transformation is spontaneous.

The most famous case, perhaps, on record is that of Félida X., reported by Dr. Azam of Bordeaux. At the age of fourteen this woman began to pass into a "secondary" state characterized by a change in her general disposition and character, as if certain "inhibitions," previously existing, were suddenly removed. During the secondary state she remembered the first state, but on emerging from it into the first state she remembered nothing of the second. At the age of forty-four the duration of the secondary state (which was on the whole superior in quality to the original state) had gained upon the latter so much as to occupy most of her time. During it she remembers the events belonging to the original state, but her complete oblivion of the secondary state when the original state recurs is often very distressing to her, as, for example, when the transition takes place in a carriage on her way to a funeral, and she hasn't the least idea which one of her friends may be dead. She actually became pregnant during one of her early secondary states, and during her first state had no knowledge of how it had come to pass. Her distress at these blanks of memory is sometimes intense and once drove her to attempt suicide.

To take another example, Dr. Rieger gives an account of an epileptic man who for seventeen years had passed his life alternately free, in prisons, or in asylums, his character being orderly enough in the normal state, but alternating with periods, during which he would leave his home for several weeks, leading the life of a thief and vagabond, being sent to jail, having epileptic fits and excitement, being accused of malingering, etc., etc., and with never a memory of the abnormal conditions which were to blame for all his wretchedness.

"I have never got from anyone," says Dr. Rieger, "so singular an impression as from this man, of whom it could not be said that he had any properly conscious past at all. . . . It is really impossible to think one's self into such a state of mind. His last larceny had been performed in Nürnberg, he knew nothing of it, and saw himself before the court and then in the hospital, but without in the least understanding the reason why. That he had epileptic attacks, he knew. But it was impossible to convince him that for hours together he raved and acted in an abnormal way."

. . .

3. In *"mediumships"* or *"possessions"* the invasion and the passing away of the secondary state are both relatively abrupt, and the duration

of the state is usually short—i.e., from a few minutes to a few hours. Whenever the secondary state is well developed no memory for aught that happened during it remains after the primary consciousness comes back. The subject during the secondary consciousness speaks, writes, or acts as if animated by a foreign person, and often names this foreign person and gives his history. In old times the foreign "control" was usually a demon, and is so now in communities which favor that belief. . . . Usually he purports to be the spirit of a dead person known or unknown to those present, and the subject is then what we call a "medium." Mediumistic possession in all its grades seems to form a perfectly natural special type of alternate personality, and the susceptibility to it in some form is by no means an uncommon gift, in persons who have no other obvious nervous anomaly. The phenomena are very intricate, and are only just beginning to be studied in a proper scientific way. The lowest phase of mediumship is automatic writing, and the lowest grade of that is where the Subject knows what words are coming, but feels impelled to write them as if from without. Then comes writing unconsciously, even whilst engaged in reading or talk. Inspirational speaking, playing on musical instruments, etc., also belong to the relatively lower phases of possession, in which the normal self is not excluded from conscious participation in the performance, though their initiative seems to come from elsewhere. In the highest phase the trance is complete, the voice, language, and everything are changed, and there is no after-memory whatever until the next trance comes. . . .

. . .

I am myself persuaded by abundant acquaintance with the trances of one medium that the "control" may be altogether different from any *possible* waking self of the person. In the case I have in mind, it professes to be a certain departed French doctor; and is, I am convinced, acquainted with facts about the circumstances, and the living and dead relatives and acquaintances, of numberless sitters whom the medium never met before, and of whom she has never heard the names. I record my bare opinion here unsupported by the evidence, not, of course, in order to convert anyone to my view, but because I am persuaded that a serious study of these trance-phenomena is one of the greatest needs of psychology, and think that my personal confession may possibly draw a reader or two into a field which the *soi-disant* "scientist" usually refuses to explore.

MULTIPLE IDENTITY: THE HEALTHY, HAPPY HUMAN BEING WEARS MANY MASKS

KENNETH J. GERGEN

In "Multiple Identity: The Healthy, Happy Human Being Wears Many Masks," Gergen raises doubts about the belief, held by many clinical and personality psychologists, that there is such a thing as a single stable, consistent, and integrated self that fits one personality profile. Like James, Gergen argues for the notion of multiple selves. He maintains that several healthy characters coexist in every individual. Each person is a social being and therefore may display very different facets of his or her personality under different circumstances and with different people. How we see ourselves and others depends on the role we are playing at any given time.

To thine own self be true, and it must follow, as the night the day, Thou canst not then be false to any man.

—Polonius to Laertes
Hamlet, Scene I, Act III

Polonius undoubtedly had good intentions; his counsel to his son seems immanently reasonable. It has a ring of validity and it fits our religious and moral values. But it is poor psychology. I think we are not apt to find a single, basic self to which we can be true.

I came to this belief after writing letters to close friends one evening. When I read over what I had written, I was first surprised, then alarmed. I came across as a completely different person in each letter: in one, I was morose, pouring out a philosophy of existential sorrow; in another I was a lusty realist; in a third I was a lighthearted jokester; and so on.

I had felt completely honest and authentic as I wrote each letter; at no time was I aware of putting on a particular style to please or impress a particular friend. And yet, a stranger reading those letters all together would have no idea who I am. This realization staggered me. Which letter, if any, portrayed the true me? Was there such an entity—or was I simply a chameleon, reflecting others' views of me?

PARCELS

Such questions I find are widespread in our culture. One young woman described the problem to her encounter group thus: "I feel like I'm contradictory . . . and people keep hitting me with the *you're-not-what-you-seem* issue, and it's really wearing me down . . . it's like I feel I can only give part here to one person and part there to another, but then I become a bunch of parcels. If I could just get all my reactions together . . ."

Her difficulties evoke Erik Erikson's classical description of identity diffusion: a state of bewilderment, typical of the young, at the lack of a firm sense of self. Other psychiatrists speak of self-alienation, a depressed feeling of estrangement from the masks of identity that society forces on the individual. Contemporary critics argue that rapid social and technological upheaval has created a crisis of identity: an individual no longer can develop and maintain a strong, integrated sense of personal identity. Writers from Alexander Pope to sociologist Erving Goffman have been alternately impressed and irritated at the use of masks in social life.

BASES

Such critics and psychologists have been working on two assumptions:

1) that it is normal for a person to develop a firm and coherent sense of identity, and

2) that it is good and healthy for him to do so, and pathological not to.

The first assumption underlies virtually all psychological research on the development of the self. Psychologists maintain that the child learns to identify himself positively (high self-esteem) or negatively (the inferiority complex); they have sought the origins of such feelings in different kinds of home environments and socialization styles. They believe that once the sense of self is fixed, it remains a stable feature of personality. Moreover, knowing a person's fixed level of self-esteem allows us to predict his actions: his neurotic or healthy behavior, his assertiveness in social relations, his academic performance, his generosity, and more.

The second assumption—that a unified sense of self is good and that inconsistency is bad—is so pervasive in our cultural traditions that it is virtually unquestioned. At the turn of the century William James said that the person with a divided sense of self had a "sick soul": he was to be pitied and redeemed. The psychologist Prescott Lecky argued that inconsistency of self was the very basis of neurotic behavior. And of course we are all apt to applaud the person of firm character who has self-integrity; we think of the inconsistent person as wishy-washy, undependable, a fake.

DOUBT

My research over the past few years has led me to question both of these assumptions very seriously. I doubt that a person normally develops a coherent sense of identity, and to the extent that he does, he may experience severe emotional distress. The long-term intimate relationship, so cherished in our society, is an unsuspected cause of this distress because it freezes and constricts identity.

My colleagues and I designed a series of studies to explore the shifting masks of identity, hoping to document the shifts in an empirically reliable way. We wanted to find the factors that influence the individual's choice of masks; we were interested in both outward appearances and inward feelings of personal identity. To what extent are we changeable, and in what conditions are we most likely to change? Do alterations in public identity create a nagging sense of self-alienation? How do we reconcile social-role-playing with a unified personality?

Our studies dealt with the influence of the other person, the situation, or the individual's motives. In each experiment, we would vary one of these three factors, holding the other factors constant. We would thus assess their impact on the subject's presentation of himself; and when the whole procedure was over, we explored the participant's feelings of self-alienation and sincerity.

SELVES

William James believed that one's close friends mold his public identity: "a man has as many different social selves as there are distinct groups of persons about whose opinion he cares." Our research supports this Jamesian hypothesis, and goes further. One's identity will change markedly even in the presence of strangers.

For instance, in one experiment a woman co-worker whom we identified as a clinical trainee interviewed 18 women college students. She asked each student a variety of questions about her background, then 60 questions about how she saw herself. Every time that the student gave a self-evaluation that was more positive than the norm, the interviewer showed subtle signs of approval: she nodded her head, smiled, occasionally spoke agreement. Conversely, she would disapprove of the student's negative self-evaluations: she would shake her head, frown, or speak disagreement. It became clear to the student that the trainee took a very positive view of her.

As a result of this procedure, the students' self-evaluation became progressively more positive. This increase was significantly greater than the minimal change that occurred in the control condition, where students received no feedback from the trainee.

This finding demonstrates that it is easy to modify the mask of identity, but it says little about underlying feelings. Did the young women think they were misleading the interviewer—telling her one thing while they secretly believed something else? To check on their private evaluations of themselves, after the interview we asked the students to undertake honest self-ratings that were not be be seen by the interviewer. We found significant increases in the self-esteem of students who had received the positive feedback; we found no such increases in the control condition. (We compared these self-ratings with those taken in other circumstances a month earlier.) One student in the experimental group told me later: "You know, it's very strange; I spent the rest of the day whistling and singing. Something about that interview really made me happy."

Our next experiment found that even this minimal amount of supportive reinforcement is not necessary to raise one's self-esteem. Sometimes another's outward characteristics are sufficient by themselves to change our self-concepts. Consider our response to the braggart, who spins glorious tales of success, and the whiner, who snivels and frets about his failures. My research with Barbara Wishnov suggests that these two types create entirely different identities in those around them.

Wishnov asked 54 pairs of young women college students to write descriptions of themselves. She explained that she would give the descriptions from one member to the other in each pair. Actually, instead, what she passed along to each was an evaluation that we had prepared in advance.

Each member of one group of students found herself reading the words of a braggart—a peer of impeccable character who described herself as being cheerful, intelligent and beautiful. She loved school, had had a marvelous childhood, and was optimistic about the future.

In contrast, each member of a second group read a description of a fellow student who might have been a dropout from psychotherapy: she was a whiner, unhappy, ugly, and intellectually dull; her childhood had been miserable; she hated school; and she was intensely fearful of the future.

The experimenter then asked each student to respond to this supposed partner by describing herself as honestly as possible in direct response to her.

Self-evaluations soared among the students who read positive evaluations of their peers; they found positive qualities in themselves that were nowhere in evidence in the self-appraisals they had made a month before; they hid negative characteristics. The braggart may produce a power imbalance that persons try to equalize by affirming their own virtues. It is as if they are saying: *You think you're so great; well, I'm pretty terrific too.*

The whiner produced strikingly different results in the students who read the negative evaluations. These young women responded by admitting to an entire array of shortcomings that they had not previously acknowledged. They adopted a mask that seemed to say: *I know what you mean; I've got problems too.* Even so, they resisted admitting that they were just as unfortunate as the whiner: perhaps they sought to avoid budding friendships based on misery. Thus they did not conceal the virtues they had claimed for themselves a month earlier.

UNDER

Again we tried to explore beneath these masks. We asked the students a variety of questions after the interchange: *is it possible that anything the other* [*young woman*] *said about herself may have influenced you in any way? How honest did you feel you could be with her? Do you feel that your self-evaluations were completely accurate?*

About 60 percent of the subjects said that they felt completely comfortable with the selves they had presented to the partner. The partner had had no effect, they replied, and their own self-evaluations were completely honest and accurate. Moreover, they did not differ at all from the 40 percent who had felt alienated from their self-presentations. The young women shifted their masks with little conscious awareness that they were doing so.

LOOKS

A third experiment showed that we can induce changes in the way one presents oneself simply by varying the physical appearance of the other person.

In an experiment at the University of Michigan, Stanley J. Morse and I sought male applicants for an interesting summer job that paid well. As each volunteer reported in, we seated him alone in a room with a long table, and gave him a battery of tests to fill out. Among them, of course, was a self-evaluation questionnaire. We explained that his responses on this questionnaire would have nothing to do with his chances for being hired, but that we needed his honest answers to construct a good test. As the applicant sat there working, we sent in a stooge—supposedly another applicant for the job.

STOOGES

In half of the cases, the stooge was our Mr. Clean. He was a striking figure: well-tailored business suit, gleaming shoes, and a smart attaché case, from which he took a dozen sharpened pencils and a book of Plato. The other half of the job applicants met our Mr. Dirty, who arrived with a torn sweat shirt, pants torn off at the knees, and a day's growth of beard. He had no pencils, only a battered copy of Harold Robbins' *The Carpetbaggers.* Neither stooge spoke to the real applicants as they worked on self-ratings.

We then compared the evaluations before and after the arrival of the stooge. Mr. Clean produced a sharp drop in self-esteem. Applicants suddenly felt sloppy, stupid and inferior by comparison; indeed, Mr. Clean was an intimidating character. But Mr. Dirty gave everyone a psychological lift. After his arrival, applicants felt more handsome, confident and optimistic. We might conclude that the slobs of the world do a great favor for those around them: they raise self-esteem.

SIGNALS

The behavior and appearance of others inspire self-change, but the setting in which we encounter other persons also exerts an influence. For example, work situations consistently reward serious, steadfast, Calvinistic behavior. But for a person to act this way in all situations would be unfortunate, especially when the situation demands spontaneity and play. No one wants to live with the Protestant Ethic 24 hours a day; in this sense, the office door and the door to one's home serve as signals for self-transformation.

Margaret Gibbs Taylor and I showed how this transformation-by-setting occurs, in a study of 50 Naval-officer trainees. We told the trainees that they would be working in two-man teams on a task (their partners would be in an adjoining room). We put half of the trainees in the work condition, where they expected to have to solve a problem in fleet maneuvers. We showed them a large board on which we placed a variety of model ships. Their task, we said, would be to maneuver a model submarine out of danger in conditions of great stress. To succeed, the team would have to work with great precision in processing an array of complex information.

By contrast, we told the other half of the trainees that while they would be discussing fleet maneuvers with their partners, their primary aim should be to get along with each other as well as possible. We told them to pay special attention to each other's opinions and feelings, and to accommodate themselves to each other. We then asked all trainees to describe themselves to their partners in writing and, as accurately as possible, what they were really like as persons—in preparation for the actual interchange. We then compared these descriptions with those they had written about a month earlier.

FACES

The trainees in the hard-work condition described themselves in a way that would have made Calvin

proud: they came across as significantly more logical, well-organized, and efficient than they had a month before. The trainees in the social-solidarity condition put on opposite masks: they described themselves as far more free and easy in disposition, more friendly and illogical, than they had earlier. Each group, in short, adopted the proper face for the occasion.

When the experiment was over, we asked the trainees how they had felt about their self-descriptions. More than three quarters felt that they had been completely accurate and honest; and their self-evaluations did not differ from those of the 25 percent who had felt alienated from their self-presentations.

LESSON

Freudian theory awakened us to the motives that underlie behavior; for instance, we have become aware of the self-gratifying aspects of even the most altruistic behavior. I think that we can apply this lesson to the study of public identity. If someone appears open, warm and accepting, we may ask why that person adopts such a mask. We may inquire what the cold and aloof individual hopes to attain with that appearance. We should not, however, conclude that the mask is a sure sign of the person's deep-seated character. When motives change, conviviality may turn to coolness, the open man may become guarded.

We studied the relationship between masks and motives in several experiments, most of them based on approval-seeking. Carl Rogers pointed out that the warm regard of others is vital to feelings of self-regard and hence to feelings of personal worth. So we asked: *how do individuals present themselves when they want to gain the approval of others?*

In experiments designed to answer this question, we varied the characteristics of the other in systematic ways. He might be senior to our subject in authority, or junior; open and revealing, or closed and remote; a stern taskmaster or an easy-going boss. When an individual seeks approval from this diverse range of personalities, he adopts wholly different masks or public identities. When he is not seeking approval, self-presentation is much different in character.

GLOW

I will use one of our experiments on authority figures as an illustration. A woman who was senior in age and status interviewed 18 undergraduate women. Before the session began, we took each student aside and asked if she would help us by trying as best as she could to gain the liking of the interviewer. We told her that she could do or say anything she wished to achieve this goal.

We observed the students' behavior in the interviews; all identified themselves to the interviewer in glowing terms. They indicated they were highly accepting of others, socially popular, perceptive, and industrious in their work. Students in the control condition, who had not been instructed to seek approval, showed no such change of masks.

So far, no surprise. What startled us was that this conscious role-playing had marked effects on the students' feelings about themselves. After the interview each student made a private self-appraisal, and we compared her rating to tests she had taken a month earlier. Apparently, in trying to convince the interviewer of their sterling assets, the students succeeded in convincing themselves. There was no such change in self-esteem in the control group.

In subsequent research we found that persons can improve their feelings about themselves simply by thinking about their positive qualities. It is not necessary to act the role; fantasizing about how they would act is sufficient.

PLASTIC

Taken together, our experiments document the remarkable flexibility of the self. We are made of soft plastic, and molded by social circumstances. But we should not conclude that all of our relationships are fake: subjects in our studies generally believed in the masks they wore. Once donned, mask becomes reality.

I do not want to imply that there are no central tendencies in one's concept of self. There are some lessons that we learn over and over, that remain consistent through life—sex-typing, for example. Men learn to view themselves as "masculine," women as "feminine." Some of us have been so rigorously trained to see ourselves as "inferior" or "superior" that we become trapped in these definitions. Often we cannot escape even when the self-concepts become inappropriate or unwanted.

But we have paid too much attention to such central tendencies, and have ignored the range and complexity of being. The individual has many potential selves. He carries with him the capacity to define himself, as warm or cold, dominant or submissive, sexy or plain. The social conditions around him help determine which of these options are evoked.

I believe we must abandon the assumption that normal development equips the individual with a coherent sense of identity. In the richness of human relations, a person receives varied messages about who he is. Parents, friends, lovers, teachers, kin, counselors, acquaintances all behave differently toward us; in each relationship we learn something new about ourselves and, as the relations change, so do the messages. The lessons are seldom connected and they are often inconsistent.

WORRY

In this light, the value that society places on a coherent identity is unwarranted and possibly detrimental. It means that the heterosexual must worry over homosexual leanings, the husband or wife over fantasies of infidelity, the businessman over his drunken sprees, the commune dweller over his materialism. All of us are burdened by the code of coherence, which demands that we ask: *How can I be X if I am really Y, its opposite?* We should ask instead: *What is causing me to be X at this time?* We may be justifiably concerned with tendencies that disrupt our preferred modes of living and loving; but we should not be anxious, depressed, or disgusted when we find a multitude of interests, potentials and selves.

Indeed, perhaps our true concern should be aroused when we become too comfortable with ourselves, too fixed in a specific identity. It may mean that our environment has become redundant—we are relating to the same others, we encounter the same situations over and over. Identity may become coherent in this fashion, but it may also become rigid and maladaptive. If a man can see himself only as powerful, he will feel pain when he recognizes moments of weakness. If a woman thinks of herself as active and lively, moments of quiet will be unbearable; if we define ourselves as weak and compliant we will cringe ineptly when we are challenged to lead.

The social structure encourages such one-dimensionality. We face career alternatives, and each decision constricts the possibilities. Our social relationships stabilize as do our professional commitments; eventually we find ourselves in routines that vary little from day to day.

INTIMACY

Many of us seek refuge from the confining borders and pressures of careers in long-term intimate relationships. Here, we feel, we can be liberated: we can reveal our true selves, give and take spontaneously, be fully honest.

Unfortunately, salvation through intimacy usually is a false hope, based on Western romantic myth. Marriage, we are taught, soothes the soul, cures loneliness, and frees the spirit. It is true that at the outset, love and intimacy provide an experience in personal growth. The loved one comes to see himself as passionate, poetic, vital, attractive, profound, intelligent, and utterly lovable. In the eyes of his beloved, the individual becomes all that he would like to be: he tries on new masks, acts out old fantasies. With the security of love, identity may flower anew.

RIGIDITY

I have had a broad range of experience with young married couples, and I observe that for most of them the myth of marriage dies quickly. In a matter of months they feel the pain of identity constriction; the role of mate becomes stabilized and rigid. I think that such stabilization occurs for at least three reasons:

1) *The reliance of each spouse on the other for fulfillment of essential needs.* To the extent that each partner needs the other for financial support, food-preparation, care of children, housekeeping, and so on, stable patterns of behavior must develop. Each begins to hold the other responsible for certain things, and if these expectations are not met the violator is punished. *But you can't just quit your job,* one asserts; *You call this dinner?* the other complains; and *How many times do I have to tell you not to make plans on Sunday when I'm watching the game?* Interdependency fosters standardized behavior. And along with standardized behavior comes a limited identity.

2) *Our general inability to tolerate inconsistencies in others.* From infancy we learn that, to survive, we must locate the consistencies in our environment and maintain them. If we could not predict from moment to moment whether a friend would respond to us with laughter, sadness, boredom or rejection, we would rapidly become incapable of action. Thus we reward consistent identity in others and punish variations. This process eases interaction, makes it predictable,

and greases the wheels of social discourse. In an intimate relationship, it also constricts identity.

3) *Our inability to tolerate extreme emotional states for long periods of time.* The new identities that emerge in the early stage of a relationship depend in part on the emotional intensity of this period—an intensity fired by the discovery of another's love, the risk in trying new masks, the prospect of a major commitment, and sexual arousal. But it is seldom that we can sustain such grand passion, or tolerate the anger and depression that are its inevitable counterparts. We weary of the emotional roller coaster, and replace passion with peace. It is difficult to restore intense feelings once we have quelled them, though some events may ignite them again temporarily.

AROUND

This picture is depressing, I realize. Probably most of us have friends who now settle for contentment in place of joy, and we know others who ceaselessly search for ecstasy in new relationships—only to see it vanish at the moment of capture. Solutions are elusive, because the tightening of identity moves so slowly that only cumulative effects are visible.

But if we are aware of the process that limits identity, we can subvert it. We can broaden our experiences with others: the more unlike us they are, the more likely we are to be shaken from a rigid sense of identity. Lovers can pursue new experiences: confront a foreign culture, meet at odd times or places, drastically alter the schedule of who-does-what-and-when, develop individual interests. If each partner presents new demands, the stage is set for trying on new masks—and this in turn awakens new feelings about the self. Honest communication—*this is how I think you are now*—is essential. Once in the open, such images usually prove quite false; and as impressions are broken, expectations become more pliable and demands for consistency lose urgency. Finally, if playing a role does in fact lead to real changes in one's self-concept, we should learn to play more roles, to adopt any role that seems enjoyable—a baron, a princess, a secret agent, an Italian merchant—and, if the other is willing to play, a storehouse of novel self-images emerges.

The mask may be not the symbol of superficiality that we have thought it was, but the means of realizing our potential. Walt Whitman wrote: "Do I contradict myself? Very well then, I contradict myself. (I am large. I contain multitudes)."

BIBLIOGRAPHY

Erik Erikson, "The Problem of Ego Identity," *Journal of the American Psychoanalytic Association*, Vol. 4, pp. 56–121, 1956.

Kenneth J. Gergen, "The Effects of Interaction Goals and Personalistic Feedback on the Presentation of Self," *Journal of Personality and Social Psychology*, Vol. 1, pp. 413–424, 1965.

Kenneth J. Gergen, *The Concept of Self*, New York: Holt, Rinehart and Winston, 1971.

Kenneth J. Gergen and Stanley J. Morse, "Social Comparison, Self-Consistency, and the Concept of Self," *Journal of Personality and Social Psychology*, Vol. 16, pp. 148–156, 1970.

Kenneth J. Gergen and M. G. Taylor, "Social Expectancy and Self-Presentation in a Status Hierarchy," *Journal of Experimental Social Psychology*, Vol. 5, pp. 79–92, 1969.

Kenneth J. Gergen and Barbara Wishnov, "Others' Self-Evaluations and Interaction Anticipation as Determinants of Self Presentation," *Journal of Personality and Social Psychology*, Vol. 2, pp. 348–358, 1965.

Erving Goffman, *The Presentation of Self in Everyday Life*, Garden City, N.Y.: Doubleday, 1959.

Chad Gordon and Kenneth J. Gergen, eds., *The Self in Social Interaction*, Vol. I, New York: Wiley, 1968.

Sidney M. Jourard, *Transparent Self* (2nd ed.), New York: Van Nostrand, 1971.

Ruth C. Wylie, *The Self Concept*, Lincoln: University of Nebraska Press, 1961.

PROJECTS

Name _____

Date _____

2.1: WHO AM I?

Each of us is a unique individual, quite distinct from other people. Yet, we all have much in common. You probably have your own theory about what makes you such a special person, what characteristics, behaviors, goals, accomplishments, and so on that add up to "you." But do others see the same person that you see? Would they characterize you in the same way? If they see you differently, what is the basis for their divergent perceptions? The following exercise is designed to stimulate your thinking about the multiple identities or masks that you may possess.

A. Give 10 answers to the question: Who am I? Do this quickly, writing down your answers exactly as they come to mind.

1. _____

2. _____

3. _____

4. _____

5. _____

6. _____

7. _____

8. _____

9. _____

10. _____

B. Answer the same question the way you think your father or mother (choose one) would have answered it *about you.*

1. _____

2. _____

3. _____

4. _____

5. _____

6. _____

7. _____

8. _____

9. _____

10. _____

C. Answer the same question the way you think your best friend would have answered it *about you*.

1. _____

2. _____

3. _____

4. _____

5. _____

6. _____

7. _____

8. _____

9. _____

10. _____

D. Compare your three sets of answers and indicate the following:

1. What are the similarities? _____

_____

_____

_____

_____

_____

2. What are the differences? _____

_____

_____

_____

_____

_____

3. If there are differences, in what ways are they attributable to *you?* That is, to what extent do you act differently and adopt varying roles with others?

_____

_____

_____

_____

_____

4. In what ways are the differences attributable to *others?* That is, how do *their* personalities and expectations shape the "you" that they see?

_____

_____

_____

_____

_____

5. In evaluating your self-description (exercise A), indicate which of the 10 answers referred to

a. physical characteristics _____

_____

b. psychological characteristics _____

_____

c. social roles _____

_____

6. Now indicate the *priority* you gave to these different types of characteristics. That is, which did you list first, second, and so on? Which type of characteristics did you use to describe yourself, and what implications might this have for your conception of self?

_____

_____

_____

_____

_____

Name _____

Date _____

2.2: THE SELF AS A PERCEIVER

When we interact with people, we usually find that we like or dislike them. We also develop certain perceptions about them. We tend to assume that these perceptions are a result of people's inherent characteristics, that those characteristics compel us to feel the way we do. This exercise is designed to demonstrate the existence of variables that are outside of the stimulus person and inside ourselves that may affect our feelings toward that person. This can be seen in relation to people you know very well and toward whom you have very different feelings.

A. Think of two people you love very much. (Use their initials to identify them.) Indicate what characteristics you love in them.

Name 1. _____   Name 2. _____

Characteristics

1. _____   1. _____
2. _____   2. _____
3. _____   3. _____
4. _____   4. _____
5. _____   5. _____

B. Think of two people you dislike very much. (Use their initials to identify them.) Indicate what characteristics you dislike in them.

Name 1. _____   Name 2. _____

Characteristics

1. _____   1. _____
2. _____   2. _____
3. _____   3. _____
4. _____   4. _____
5. _____   5. _____

C. After indicating all these characteristics, you will be able to see the ways in which the two people you love are similar. For instance, do both lists include the adjectives *warm* and *generous?* You can make the same comparison for the next two lists and see the ways in which the two people you dislike are similar. For instance, are both *cold, rigid, belittling?* Now compare all four lists, and identify what dimensions in these people make *you* love them, what things are important to *you,* what *you* look for in the people you love and resent in those you dislike (e.g., the warm-cold dimension). Write down your conclusions on the following blank page.

Name _____

Date _____

2.3: WHAT DO I DO THAT I WOULD RATHER NOT DO, AND WHAT DO I NOT DO THAT I WOULD LIKE TO DO?

We all get overly involved in doing things we do not like, things that keep us from doing what we do like. Culture and society emphasize and reward certain activities and therefore are partly to blame. The self can be seen as having two parts: One is verbal, communicative, future-oriented; the other is nonverbal, physical, present-oriented. Modern Western society, with its emphasis on competition, work, and achievement, thus encourages one aspect of the self at the expense of the other. The goal of this exercise is to explore the effect of that emphasis on your choice of activities and on the way you feel about your choices.

A. Indicate three things that you would like to do more often in your life.

1. _____

2. _____

3. _____

B. Indicate three things that you would like to stop doing as much as you do and perhaps even hate doing.

1. _____

2. _____

3. _____

C. Explain briefly why you do not do enough of A and do too much of B.

_____

_____

_____

3
ATTITUDE AND BEHAVIOR CHANGE

Throughout our lives, we influence other people and are influenced by them. Sometimes, we attempt to change a person's attitude. For example, we may try to change someone's opinion about the trustworthiness of a particular politician, the value of a proposed law, or the usefulness of a new product. At other times, we may seek to influence a person's behavior. For example, we may try to persuade someone to vote for one candidate rather than another, to buy a certain gift, or to join us for a cup of coffee. However, whether we focus our efforts on changing attitudes or behavior, we usually assume that the two go together. Thus, if we succeed in changing someone's attitude toward a political candidate, we expect corresponding changes in his or her behavior toward that candidate (votes, campaign contributions, endorsements, and so on). The link between attitudes and behavior is presumed to be a causal one. Furthermore, in most

cases, it is believed that internal attitudes cause and direct external behavior.

Social psychologists have done a vast amount of research into the nature of attitudes, their development, and the ways in which they change. Various definitions of *attitude* have been proposed, all of which assume a consistency between attitudes and behavior. Indeed, some definitions include behavior as one of the components of attitude. Several models of attitude formation and change have been developed, some of which also support the common-sense view that changes in attitudes cause corresponding changes in behavior. However, other theories (most notably, cognitive dissonance and self-perception) argue the reverse: that changes in behavior cause corresponding changes in attitudes. The practical implications of these theories are obviously quite different because they suggest opposite approaches to bringing about change in others.

FOCUSING ON PRACTICAL APPLICATIONS OF PRINCIPLES OF ATTITUDE AND BEHAVIOR CHANGE

PHILIP G. ZIMBARDO, EBBE B. EBBESEN, and CHRISTINA MASLACH

Much of the research on attitude and behavior change has been carried out in controlled laboratory settings. The laboratory approach has numerous advantages for the development of theory because it allows the researcher to specify critical variables in order to study the pattern of causal relationships. But what happens when we move from the laboratory to events in the real world? How well do the research models predict and explain the effects of the many influences to which we are all subjected all the time? According to Zimbardo, Ebbesen, and Maslach, there is still a large gap between the questions posed by practical problems and the answers provided by theory and research. However, they demonstrate that an analysis of actual attempts to influence attitudes and behavior can also provide some answers to these questions by showing us what does and does not work in various situations.

We ask you to consider with us the following range of problems, from which will be drawn practical, concrete illustrations of attitude and behavior change programs in action. Is "creating an image" a *new* Madison Avenue approach? In what sense is our educational system a propaganda mill? . . . How can the prejudiced attitudes of a given woman toward a minority group be changed? . . . How can a person's need for freedom and self-assertion be incorporated into a persuasion program? . . .

CREATING AN IMAGE, OR "PACKAGING" THE COMMUNICATOR

Television has made us aware of the extensive use of public relations firms to promote the campaigns of political candidates. Hair style, clothes style, and speech style are modified to fit an image fashioned by opinion polls, advisers, and media experts. Thus former President Ford was trained to use hand gestures, albeit woodenly, when making key points during TV speeches. This image management strategy was first used many years ago. An enterprising public relations man (whose pseudonym was Ivy Lee) was hired to change the prevailing stereotype of John D. Rockefeller. Mr. Rockefeller was generally considered a self-aggrandizing robber baron. A complete image reversal was called for, one in which the public would view him as a philanthropic, kindly gentleman. The strategy was deceptively simple: one of the most effective techniques was to publicize pictures and stories of Rockefeller giving shiny new dimes to every child he met in the streets. It is tougher on the tummy these days with urban politicians having to appeal to diverse ethnic constituencies. The TV image comes to mind of suave John Lindsay, New York's former Mayor, making the rounds eating knishes, pizza, Polish sausage, ribs, fried bananas, and egg rolls, topped off with an all-American hot dog from Nathan's delicatessen.

Reprinted by special permission from Zimbardo, Ebbesen, Maslach, *Influencing Attitudes and Changing Behavior,* 2nd Edition, 1977, Addison-Wesley, Reading, Mass.

EDUCATION: HIDDEN PROPAGANDA FOR THE ESTABLISHMENT

Traditionally, *propaganda* is defined as an attempt to influence public opinion and public behavior through specialized techniques. It is contrasted with *education,* in which there is also an attempt to change attitudes and behavior, but through information, evidence, facts, and logical reasoning. In an ideal sense, educators teach students not *what* to think, but only *how* to think. In this way, propagandists differ from educators because they intentionally try to bias what people see, think, and feel in the hope that they will adopt their viewpoint.

But are there concealed, subtle forms of indoctrination in education that cloud these neat distinctions? Think back to the examples used in your textbooks to teach you the purely objective, academic discipline of mathematics. Most of the work problems dealt with buying, selling, renting, working for wages, and computing interest. These examples not only reflect the system of economic capitalism in which the education takes place, but are also an endorsement or subconscious legitimization of it. To illustrate, take an example that might be used to make concrete the arithmetic operations involved in dividing 90 by 60. "John wants to borrow $90, but Joe can only lend him $60. What percentage of the amount he wanted does John obtain?" The same conceptual operations could be equally well learned with a different illustration, perhaps less likely in our country: "John earns $60 a week for his labor from Company *X.* Medical and health authorities are agreed that the weekly cost of living for a family of four is $90. What percentage of a decent, acceptable minimal wage does Company *X* pay John?"

While such an example may seem farfetched, consider the complaints of the black community that textbooks in all areas omit reference in word or picture to the reality of black history, black culture, or even black existence—except as related to slavery and primitive native customs. Such an omission fosters the majority attitude among black and other minority children that their race (and they as members of it) is insignificant. If this is not an intentional goal of our educational process, then its impact should be assessed, and correctives considered.

. . .

WHO'S PREJUDICED? YOUR MOTHER!

Racial, ethnic, and religious prejudice may be viewed as a negative evaluation, and as a rejection of an individual solely because of his or her membership in a particular group. If those discriminated against (as well as those who are prejudiced) suffer because of this prejudice, then why do we not eliminate it? Dedicated social scientists and humanitarians have been concerned with this problem for a number of years. The United Nations and the United States have spent millions of dollars on *information* campaigns to correct stereotypes about minority groups, to present the facts, and to help people to get to know one another. They assumed that prejudice was based on ignorance and that every person's desire to know the truth would dispel false beliefs. From every indication we have, these campaigns have been very limited in their effectiveness.

A second approach used to combat prejudiced attitudes has assumed that *contact,* or physical proximity between members of the group in question, would make attitudes more favorable. For example, you take a class of white students on a tour of Harlem, or you mix races in a public housing project, a summer camp, an infantry outfit, or the classroom.

There is some equivocal evidence that as long as the contact continues, the prejudiced attitudes may weaken. However, once the person returns to a situation where the norms do not support tolerant attitudes, the newfound tolerance slips back into old prejudiced habits of thought, speech, and action. This raises the key issue not only of whether the techniques used produce a big immediate change, but also of whether the change generalizes to the social environment or group that supports the old behavior. Criminal recidivism and the return to drugs by "cured" drug addicts may be traced to "changed" individuals being sent back to an unchanged social setting in which their new attitudes and behavior are not socially supported. A newly emerging philosophy of change in therapeutic communities such as Synanon and San Francisco's Delancey Street Foundation (for former prisoners, prostitutes, and drug addicts) is to *not* send the members back if they want to stay on. You cannot go home to old stimuli and expect old responses not to be evoked. You cannot put cucumbers in a vinegar barrel and expect them not to emerge as pickles.

Judge for yourself whether information and contact alone are sufficient conditions for changing prejudice. Here is a case study of a college freshman trying to persuade a middle-aged housewife that she holds untenable attitudes toward Puerto Ricans who were then (1954) just beginning to move into "her" Southeast Bronx neighborhood. The woman has already had a great deal of contact with Puerto Ricans who live in her building, shop at the same stores, own some of these stores, and are friends of her daughters. The boy provides sensible, rational arguments in favor of a general attitude of tolerance and understanding of the problems of this new group of migrants to the American melting pot. In reading this account of the transcript,[1] note not only the student's efforts to change the woman's attitude, but also the techniques the woman uses to bolster her position. Also, try to see beyond her rational manifest concern to the nature and the variety of topics she raises, especially those that emerge when the student has trapped her in an inconsistency. There seems to be something lurking below the surface of her conscious rationality.

INTERVIEWER (P. ZIMBARDO): You've been living in this neighborhood quite a number of years. Do you think there's been any change in the composition of the neighborhood?

WOMAN: There certainly has. I've been living in this house now for twenty-one years, and I daresay I'm ashamed to tell people that I live in the neighborhood I do.

STUDENT: Why is that?

WOMAN: Because of what the Puerto Ricans have done to it.

STUDENT: What do you mean, specifically?

WOMAN: Well, to start with, their filth. Second, the language they use, and third, because the teachers waste eight hours a day with them in school and find that they get nowhere the minute the children are released.

STUDENT: You mean you never heard that language from anyone else but a Puerto Rican?

WOMAN: I certainly have, but not as much as I hear it from them.

STUDENT: Maybe you listen to it from them more often than you listen to it from others.

---

[1] A transcript of a tape recording made by Zimbardo in a community center in New York City. The participants agreed to talk about conditions in their neighborhood and were aware they were being recorded. Comments by other participants were deleted from this presentation for purposes of space.

WOMAN: I can't help it, because the streets are over-crowded with them.

STUDENT: Well, why are they overcrowded with them?

WOMAN: It doesn't have to be overcrowded, they can live somewhere else, or gather somewhere else. But I find that this is the biggest dope center, because there's nothing done about it. We pay police the salaries that we do, we pay taxes, and yet what has been done?

STUDENT: What do you know about dope centers? You say this is the *biggest* dope center. Do you know of other dope centers . . . ?

WOMAN: I think they're the filthiest race, they're devoid of brains, and it's a disgrace with what goes on.

STUDENT: Why do you say they're the filthiest race?

WOMAN: They are, because I've worked with colored people, and I find that they're 50 percent more immaculate than the Puerto Ricans.

STUDENT: Well why are they dirty? Isn't there a reason why they're dirty?

WOMAN: They don't know any better, unfortunately.

STUDENT: So then how can you condemn them because they don't know better? If you find a person that's ignorant, are you gonna condemn him?

WOMAN: You can condemn people for being poor, but you can't condemn them for being filthy. [She means the opposite, or does she?] Soap and water doesn't cost much. If a person is ignorant, he knows nothing about cleanliness. And if he's devoid of brains, he certainly doesn't know.

STUDENT: All right, look, you say they're filthy and all that. But look at the sanitation problems in Puerto Rico.

WOMAN: I've never been to Puerto Rico, so I can't speak about Puerto Rico. I live in the Bronx and I can only tell you what happens here.

STUDENT (overlaps): In New York here or even in the United States we have the highest standard of living. They don't have that in other places; if a person just comes over from a low standard of living into a high standard of living. . . .

WOMAN (interrupts): Why is it that most of the Puerto Ricans own the most beautiful cars, and yet 90 percent of them are on relief [social welfare]?

STUDENT: A lot of people own cars and don't have a lot of money.

WOMAN: Not a lot. Puerto Ricans more than any other race.

STUDENT: Why Puerto Ricans more than any other race?

WOMAN: 'Cause I happen to know someone that works on the Home Relief Bureau [Welfare Service]; and more Puerto Ricans than any other race. . . . But they know how to make babies every nine months.

STUDENT: So are you going to condemn them for having *kids?*

WOMAN: Why do they have so many of them? *You could condemn them for having kids.* They should go out and look for jobs! The hospitals are flooded with them today. Do they know about going to pediatricians? No! Do they know how to raise children? No! What do they bring them up on? When the child's seven months old, it learns to drink beer from a can!

STUDENT (interrupts): My God, the people . . . the people just came over here, how long have they been in the United States? What chance have they had?

WOMAN: They've been here much too long to suit me. [Discussion of Puerto Rican girls going behind the school yard at night with boys.]

STUDENT: So you blame them for being *obvious* instead of hiding it . . . right? Instead of being sneaks about it?

WOMAN: Yes, because their parents don't know enough to take care of them.

STUDENT: How do you know their parents don't know?

WOMAN: Because if you go to dance halls, who do you find there? More Puerto Ricans.

STUDENT: You find anybody at dance halls. You mean before the Puerto Ricans came there were no dance halls?

WOMAN: Refined, but not like now. I lived in a building that was the most upstanding house on the block. Today it's disgraceful, because it's surrounded with Puerto Ricans.

STUDENT: Surrounded with . . . Why? Do you think just because a person's Puerto Rican, right away he's filthy and he's dirty and he's dumb? You think just because a person's a Puerto Rican or something like that, that you call him dumb and ignorant because he's born Puerto Rican? A few years ago there was prejudice against the Jewish people. They weren't allowed in certain jobs, they're not allowed in colleges, they're not allowed in, uh. . . .

WOMAN (not listening): Then they shouldn't come here. They should stay in Puerto Rico.

STUDENT: Is it so easy to find apartments now that you can go out and get all the apartments you want? So then why are you condemning?

WOMAN: It isn't easy, because I'm a little fussy. I want to stay away from them. I want to go to a neighborhood that *restricts them.*

STUDENT: But you still didn't answer a question I asked before. Just because the . . . they're Puerto Ricans or something like that, they're . . . that they're filthy, they're dirty. How many years ago was it before the Jewish people were, uh, discriminated against?

WOMAN: Not that I know of.

STUDENT: Not that you know of! How . . . the Jewish people . . . A Jewish person couldn't get into law school or anything like that then, you couldn't get into the Bell Telephone Company, you couldn't get into . . . to millions of jobs.

WOMAN: That's only hearsay. But can you prove it?

STUDENT: It isn't, yes, I can prove it. I have relatives that tried out for the Bell Telephone Company and they couldn't get in because they were Jewish. I had a . . . one of my relatives graduated from law school. He was one of the first people who graduated like that.

DAUGHTER: So tell us why has the Bronx come down so much?

STUDENT: Because it's overpopulated?

DAUGHTER: With dirty Spics!

STUDENT: So what reason do you have to call them dirty Spics?

DAUGHTER: What reason!

WOMAN: One, because they don't know how to bring up children. Second, because their morale [morals?] is so low. Third, because they're known to consume more alcohol than any other race in this world. And fourth, they're the biggest marijuana smokers.

STUDENT: Who drinks more beer than Irish people?

WOMAN: Who wanted to shoot the President, if not the Puerto Ricans [reference to assassination attempt on President Truman by Puerto Rican Nationalists]?

STUDENT: What about John Wilkes Booth, who tried to shoot Abraham Lincoln, what was he?

WOMAN: You're going back so many years! You pick up the paper and read about prostitutes. Who's involved? Puerto Ricans.

INTERVIEWER: We seem to be going off on a tangent, so let's wind up the discussion with your views on how the problem could be solved.

WOMAN: It could be solved by dropping a token in the subway and sending them all back where they came from!

The student clearly had good intentions and worked hard to dissuade the woman from her anti-Puerto Rican position. He gave some sound arguments, refuted some of the opposing arguments, gave personal examples of prejudice toward him, and made a sincere appeal to view prejudice as ignorance that can be overcome by simply getting to know your disliked neighbors regardless of their race, religion, or ethnic background. And to what effect? The woman exhibited a "boomerang" effect, reacting with more overt hostility and prejudice than she showed initially.

Good intentions unsupported by sound psychological knowledge may get the student into heaven, but they will never change this woman's attitude. Where he failed was in not assessing the function her attitude serves in her total psychological makeup, and by accepting her rationalizations as rational statements. The major consequence of his puncturing one of her arguments, or directly confronting her with contrary evidence,

was for her to become both emotionally upset (at points, both she and daughter were near hysteria) and more openly hostile over the course of the interview. Her tactical weapon was a non sequitur flank attack. She changed topics and regained her composure, while her adversary was shifting gears in order to make sense of and reply to a non sequitur that she had tossed off. Then she would counter-attack again.

. . .

SELLING FREEDOM: AGREEING TO DISAGREE

The approaches we have outlined so far have been based on experience, trial and error, clinical intuition, psychoanalytic theory, ingenuity, many implicit assumptions, and a smattering of low-level psychological principles. Although some of them have been successful, their success depended more on the particular person who was employing the techniques, or "practicing his or her art," than on a sound social science base. When there is such a base, however, the control of behavior is predicated upon an understanding of the causal relations and, because it is explicitly spelled out, can be implemented by anyone. The approach adopted by Jacobo Varela (1971) tries to achieve this goal through the practical, systematic application of principles derived from psychological theories, and especially from the results of social psychological experiments.

This approach begins by rejecting two of the criticisms often leveled at the possible utility of laboratory-experimental findings: (1) that you cannot extrapolate from the laboratory to the real world when laboratory subjects are a captive audience in a novel environment that is under a high degree of control by the experimenter, and (2) that the time interval used in laboratory studies is rarely more than one hour, while in real life there is no such time constraint.

Instead of insisting on bringing more of real life into the laboratory, this approach says that since laboratory studies are shown to be effective in changing attitudes, then bring the laboratory into real life. If an hour is enough to persuade an intelligent, often critical undergraduate subject, it should be enough to change the behavior of the average businessperson or others—if a planned, concentrated, and powerful manipulation is used and tailored to the target audience.

Varela combines several basic techniques suggested from attitude change research into a systematic persuasion program. This planned program is then brought to bear on particular individuals identified as decision-makers or as holding attitudes or acting in ways that call for change. They might be people who control resources and do not want to buy your product, or who will not give you or certain minorities jobs or improved work/living conditions. They might be people who engage in antisocial behavior that may also be injurious to their health (such as crime, violence, and drug addiction). Or they can be individuals who need help to break phobias (of flying, for example), to control compulsions, or to handle personal family conflicts.

The basic approach is to tailor an individualized program of change to each specific person. This consists of first diagnosing exactly what are the person's relevant attitudes, beliefs, and current behaviors. Then a systematic attempt is made to confront each of these components of the person's overall attitude on the issue.

Attitude Change by Successive Approximations

To change a strongly held set of attitudes and beliefs, Varela proposes a strategy of successive approximations. In this strategy, the most weakly held attitude elements are changed first. Then, one by one, each of the more staunchly endorsed elements [is] subjected to change tactics. To begin with, it is determined how strongly the person feels about various aspects of the issue. This is done by devising a series of statements that range from those that would be accepted by the person to those that would be rejected. These statements may come from one's knowledge of what the person has said previously or from an analysis of possible statements the person would be likely to endorse.

Next, each of these statements is subtly presented to the person during a conversation in order to discover how strongly he or she feels about each one. On the basis of that evaluative information, a scale of statements graded by intensity of affect is constructed. The scale items range from those the person accepts most strongly, to accepts, rejects, and rejects most strongly. Those that are accepted constitute the *latitude of acceptance,* while the rejected statements comprise the *latitude of rejection.* . . .

Armed with this knowledge of where the person stands on the issue and how much feeling and psychological energy are invested in various aspects of the general issue, a person other than the one who collected the initial latitude information proceeds with Part 2 of the change program.

The unique feature of this phase is to create *reactance* in the target person.

According to Jack Brehm's theory of reactance, "the perception that a communication is attempting to influence will tend to be seen as a threat to one's freedom to decide for oneself" (1966, p. 94). This is a reverse use of manipulative intent, and is also the "Marc Antony effect." Reactance can be used in an ingenious way to get the person to disagree with statements that he or she would ordinarily agree with, and to agree with statements that were previously disagreed with. The attitude change agent merely implies that there is some limit on the freedom of the person to decide for himself or herself. Reactance is generated by asserting what the person already agrees with in terms such as, "There is no question but . . . ," "You would have to say that . . . ," "It is always the case that . . . ," and so on. The induced reactance leads the person to mildly disagree with these unqualified assertions, and thus weakens support for his or her original position. Then the change agent proceeds in the same way to strongly disagree with statements in the person's latitude of rejection ("There's no way anyone could support the view that . . ."). The target person continues to disagree with the change agent's persuasive assertion, in order to maintain his or her perceived freedom of opinion, and in so doing agrees with the attitude item that had previously been most strongly rejected.

When this is done, the entire attitude structure has shifted its direction and resistance to change has been substantially weakened. The change agent ultimately reinforces each of the person's disagreements and is seen as "coming around" to agree with him or her. It is almost as if the person being changed perceives the change agent as the one he or she has influenced. Where the goal is to have the target person be more optimistic and positive about the topic (or problem), the latitude of acceptance is expanded. Where the goal is to develop a more negative attitude toward the topic (such as taking drugs), the method used is to expand the latitude of rejection.

Let's look at this approach in actual practice. The salesperson's goal here is to get a retail store owner to stop buying from a competitor and thus to be open to new accounts from—guess who.

The customer has often bought from Company *A,* which is a very reputable firm that has high-quality goods at reasonable prices with excellent payment terms. However, it makes few model changes and does not give exclusive lines. This last point is a source of irritation to many retailers, who do not wish to see the same goods that they are selling available at the lowest-quality stores in lower-class sections of town.

The customer's initial attitudes toward the rival company are systematically manipulated by a combination of the reactance approach and the reinforcement approach. An example of how this technique can be employed follows:

(—3) Company A gives exclusive lines

SALESPERSON: [Saying he liked a style in the customer's store and wonders whether Company A made it] Yes? Well, you are lucky to have that made *exclusively* for you!

RETAILER: No, they don't give exclusives.

(—2) Company A makes frequent style changes

SALESPERSON: [In an apparent defense of Company A] You're right, that's too bad, but at least they make frequent style changes.

RETAILER: Sorry, I must disagree, they rarely do.

(—1) Company A is very regular in deliveries

SALESPERSON: Even if it is true that they don't (and I do believe you), you must admit that they make up for it by being regular and prompt in their deliveries.

RETAILER: Here you're just wrong, they aren't so prompt, and their deliveries are often irregular.

(+1) Company A offers good promotional assistance

SALESPERSON: That's surprising to hear, but judging from what I know of other companies, Company A is certainly good in things like promotional assistance.

RETAILER: [Now disagreeing mildly with a statement he previously would have agreed with] Well, sometimes they do, but you're not right if you mean they always do.

(+2) Company A offers very favorable terms

SALESPERSON: Of course, *you* know better than I do about that, but I've heard that there's *no question* about the very favorable terms Company A offers.

RETAILER: I don't know where you get your information but there *is* some question about that issue; their terms are favorable to them, but not necessarily for the small shopowner.

(+3) Company A is a very responsible firm

[This is the "most accepted" statement that is to be modified.]

SALESPERSON: You may be right, I never thought of it like that, but I am sure that you would *have to say* that Company A is a very responsible firm.

RETAILER: [As actually happened in one case] Not at all! They *used* to be a very responsible firm, but they aren't any longer!

In this way, the customer is not only guided to buy now, and to reject old loyalties to the opposition, but the general approach used is likely to engender a long-term commitment on the part of the client, because he or she has not been forced to buy anything. Rather, the salespeople have been attentive, approving, reinforcing, concerned with his opinions, altruistic in saying nice things about their rivals—and they have allowed most of the work of persuasion to be done by the retailer.

WHAT YOU NEED IS A GOOD LAWYER

Editors' Note: Lawyers are, by definition, practitioners of behavior change. As such, claims Israeli humorist Ephraim Kishon, they know what methods of communication are most effective in producing results.

Tel Aviv—Ten years ago Billitzer borrowed 20 pounds off me for two hours. He promised to return the money within a day. As he didn't, I gave him a call and he asked for a week's grace. After a week I went to see him to demand my money back. He promised he'd fix it by Monday noon. Thursday evening I

consulted a solicitor and he sent Billitzer a notice that "due steps will be taken in default of claim being met within a period of 72 hours after receipt of this communication."

No reply came from Billitzer within a period of two months, following which the solicitor stated that there was nothing more he could do, as Billitzer refused to pay.

I took the case out of his hands

and placed it in those of a better solicitor. We sued Billitzer. The hearing took place after five months, but Billitzer didn't show up because of illness. The hearing was therefore adjourned to a later date next year.

Then it didn't take place either, because Billitzer had meanwhile gone abroad. I waited for a year and a half, but as he didn't come back I applied to another quite well-known lawyer who tried to reopen the proceedings, but the judge refused to conduct the case in the absence of the defendant.

We appealed to a higher court, which rejected the case in accordance with the regulation that a court of that level does not handle civil claims involving less than 50 pounds.

We waited a year or two for Billitzer to come back from abroad, and when he did, I sent him another 30 pounds' loan by notary to raise his debt to a round fifty. Now the higher court did accept our case and ordered the lower court to conduct the hearing in defendant's absentia.

Since, however, defendant wasn't in absentia because Billitzer had meanwhile returned from abroad, as mentioned, the hearing was adjourned pending clarification.

I hired an even better-known lawyer and we petitioned the Supreme Court for an order nisi calling upon the Minister of Justice to show cause why I shouldn't have my money back from Billitzer. The Minister of Justice said I should apply to the courts. Thereupon we renewed the proceedings but they were adjourned because Billitzer asked for an adjournment.

I went to the biggest lawyer in Israel and told him my story. He listened attentively and suggested I go to Billitzer and beat him up.

I went to Billitzer and beat him up. He gave me my 50 pounds in cash right away. It pays to consult a really good lawyer.

WHEN PROPHECY FAILS

LEON FESTINGER, HENRY W. RIECKEN, and STANLEY SCHACHTER

Festinger's theory of cognitive dissonance is one of the most influential theoretical models of attitude and behavior change. When it was first published (1957), it evoked great controversy among social psychologists because it challenged much of the research being done on attitudes. Its motivational basis contrasted with the traditional learning approach then in vogue, and some of its nonobvious predictions were directly opposed to those based on concepts of reinforcement. Furthermore, Festinger argued that discrepancies between attitudes and behavior could be reduced by changing the attitude to fit the behavior. He thus reversed the traditional idea that attitudes are always the cause and therefore the forerunners of behavior.

Although many of the hypotheses derived from cognitive dissonance theory have been tested in elaborately staged experiments, one of the classic studies involved an unusual real-life situation. A woman had announced that a city would be destroyed by flood on a specific date. The basis for this prophecy, she maintained, was a series of messages from beings on another planet. What interested the dissonance researchers about this situation was that the woman and her followers had publicly stated their belief in a forthcoming event that had been pinpointed in time. When, as the researchers assumed, the prophesied event did not occur, what would happen to these people's belief systems? How would they resolve the dissonance between their commitment to the belief and the evidence that that belief was in error? In order to study these issues, the researchers became members of the group of believers. In this way, they were able to take notes on everything that happened both before and after the failure of the predicted flood to occur. This research method is known as participant observation. In their article "When Prophecy Fails," Festinger, Riecken, and Schachter describe the response of the believers to the events that disconfirmed their prophecy and analyze these behavioral changes in terms of cognitive dissonance theory.

A man with a conviction is a hard man to change. Tell him you disagree and he turns away. Show him facts or figures and he questions your sources. Appeal to logic and he fails to see your point.

We are familiar with the variety of ingenious defenses with which people protect their convictions, managing to keep them unscathed through the most devastating attacks.

But man's resourcefulness goes beyond simply protecting a belief. Suppose an individual believes something with his whole heart; suppose further that he has a commitment to this belief and that he has taken irrevocable actions because of it; finally, suppose that he is presented with evidence, unequivocal and undeniable evidence, that his belief is wrong: what will happen? The individual will frequently emerge, not only unshaken, but even more convinced of the truth of his beliefs than ever before. Indeed, he may even show a new fervor for convincing and converting other people to his view.

How and why does such a response to contradictory evidence come about? Let us begin by stating the conditions under which we would expect to observe increased fervor following the disconfirmation of a belief. There are five such conditions.

1. A belief must be held with deep conviction and it must have some relevance to action, that is, to what the believer does or how he behaves.

2. The person holding the belief must have committed himself to it; that is, for the sake of his belief, he must have taken some important action that is difficult to undo. In general, the more important such actions and the more difficult they are to undo, the greater is the individual's commitment to the belief.

3. The belief must be sufficiently specific and sufficiently concerned with the real world so that events may unequivocally refute the belief.

4. Such undeniable disconfirmatory evidence must occur and must be recognized by the individual holding the belief.

The first two of these conditions specify the circumstances that will make the belief resistant to change. The third and fourth conditions, on the other hand, point to factors that would exert powerful pressure on a believer to discard his belief. It is, of course, possible that an individual, even though deeply convinced of a belief, may discard it in the face of unequivo-

cal disconfirmation. We must, therefore, state a fifth condition specifying the circumstances under which it will be maintained with new fervor.

5. The individual believer must have social support. It is unlikely that one isolated believer could withstand the kind of disconfirming evidence we have specified. If, however, the believer is a member of a group of convinced persons who can support one another, we would expect the belief to be maintained and the believers to attempt to proselytize or to persuade nonmembers that the belief is correct.

These five conditions specify the circumstances under which increased proselytizing would be expected to follow disconfirmation. Given this set of hypotheses, our immediate concern is to locate data that will allow a test of the prediction of increased proselytizing. Fortunately, throughout history there have been recurring instances of social movements which satisfy the conditions adequately. These are the millennial or messianic movements, a contemporary instance of which forms the basis for the present study. Let us see just how such movements do satisfy the five conditions we have specified.

Typically, millennial or messianic movements are organized around the prediction of some future events. Our conditions are satisfied, however, only by those movements that specify a date or an interval of time within which the predicted events will occur as well as detailing exactly what is to happen. Sometimes the predicted event is the second coming of Christ and the beginning of Christ's reign on earth; sometimes it is the destruction of the world through a cataclysm (usually with some select group slated for rescue from the disaster); or sometimes the prediction is concerned with particular occurrences that the messiah or a miracle worker will bring about. Whatever the event predicted, the fact that its nature and the time of its happening are specified satisfies the third point on our list of conditions.

The second condition specifies strong behavioral commitment to the belief. This usually follows almost as a consequence of the situation. If one really believes a prediction (the first condition), for example, that on a given date the world will be destroyed by fire, that the sinners will die and the good be saved, he does things about it and makes certain preparations as a matter of course. These actions may range all the way from simple public declarations to the neglect of

worldly things and the disposal of earthly possessions. Through such actions and through the
mocking and scoffing of nonbelievers, the believers usually establish a heavy commitment.
What they do by way of preparation is difficult
to undo, and the jeering of nonbelievers simply
makes it far more difficult for the adherents to
withdraw from the movement and admit that they
were wrong.

Our fourth specification has invariably been
provided. The predicted events have not occurred.
There is usually no mistaking the fact that they
did not occur and the believers know that. In
other words, the unequivocal disconfirmation
does materialize and makes its impact on the
believers.

Finally, our fifth condition is ordinarily satisfied—such movements do attract adherents and
disciples, sometimes only a handful, occasionally
hundreds of thousands. The reasons why people
join such movements are outside the scope of
our present discussion, but the fact remains that
there are usually one or more groups of believers
who can support one another.

History has recorded many such movements.
Ever since the crucifixion of Jesus, many Chris-
tians have hoped for the second coming of Christ
and movements predicting specific dates for this
event have not been rare. However, most of the
very early ones were not recorded in such a fashion
that we can be sure of the reactions of believers
to the disconfirmations they may have experienced. Occasionally historians make passing reference to such reactions as does Hughes in his
description of the Montanists:

Montanus, who appeared in the second half of the
second century, does not appear as an innovator
in matters of belief. His one personal contribution
to the life of the time was the fixed conviction that
the second coming of Our Lord was at hand. The
event was to take place at Pepuza—near the modern
Angora—and thither all true followers of Our Lord
should make their way. His authority for the statement was an alleged private inspiration, and the
new prophet's personality and eloquence won him
a host of disciples, who flocked in such numbers
to the appointed spot that a new town sprang up
to house them. *Nor did the delay of the second
advent put an end to the movement. On the contrary,
it gave new life and form* as a kind of Christianity
of the elite, whom no other authority guided in their

new life but the Holy Spirit working directly upon
them. . . . [Italics ours.]

In this brief statement are all the essential
elements of the typical messianic movement.
There are convinced followers; they commit
themselves by uprooting their lives and going to
a new place where they build a new town; the
Second Advent does not occur. And, we note,
far from halting the movement, this disconfirmation gives it new life.

Why does increased proselytizing follow the
disconfirmation of a prediction? How can we
explain it, and what are the factors that will
determine whether or not it will occur? For our
explanation, we shall introduce the concepts of
consonance and dissonance.

Dissonance and consonance are relations
among cognitions—that is, among opinions, beliefs, knowledge of the environment, and knowledge of one's own actions and feelings. Two
opinions, or beliefs, or items of knowledge are
dissonant with each other if they do not fit
together—that is, if they are inconsistent, or if,
considering only the particular two items, one
does not follow from the other. For example, a
cigarette smoker who believes that smoking is
bad for his health has an opinion that is dissonant
with the knowledge that he is continuing to smoke.

Dissonance produces discomfort and, correspondingly, there will arise attempts to reduce
dissonance. Such attempts may take any or all
of three forms. The person may try to change
one or more of the beliefs, opinions, or behaviors
involved in the dissonance; to acquire new information or beliefs that will increase the existing
consonance and thus cause the total dissonance
to be reduced; or to forget or reduce the importance
of those cognitions that are in a dissonant relationship.

If any of these attempts is to be successful,
it must be met with support from either the
physical or the social environment. In the absence
of such support, the most determined efforts to
reduce dissonance may be unsuccessful.

Theoretically, then, what is the situation of the
individual believer at the predisconfirmation stage
of a messianic movement? He has a strongly held
belief in a prediction—for example, that Christ
will return—a belief that is supported by the other
members of the movement. By way of preparation
for the predicted event, he has engaged in many
activities that are entirely consistent with his
belief. In other words, most of the relations among
relevant cognitions are, at this point, consonant.

P. Hughes, *A Popular History of the Catholic Church* (Garden
City, N.Y.: Doubleday), 1954, p. 10.

Now what is the effect of the disconfirmation, of the unequivocal fact that the prediction was wrong, upon the believer? The disconfirmation introduces an important and painful dissonance. The fact that the predicted events did not occur is dissonant with continuing to believe both the prediction and the remainder of the ideology of which the prediction was the central item. The failure of the prediction is also dissonant with all the actions that the believer took in preparation for its fulfillment. The magnitude of the dissonance will, of course, depend on the importance of the belief to the individual and on the magnitude of his preparatory activity.

In the type of movement we have discussed, the central belief and its accompanying ideology are usually of crucial importance in the believers' lives and hence the dissonance is very strong— and very painful to tolerate. Accordingly, we should expect to observe believers making determined efforts to eliminate the dissonance or, at least, to reduce its magnitude. How may they accomplish this end? The dissonance would be largely eliminated if they discarded the belief that had been disconfirmed, ceased the behavior which had been initiated in preparation for the fulfillment of the prediction, and returned to a more usual existence. Indeed, this pattern sometimes occurs. But frequently the behavioral commitment to the belief system is so strong that almost any other course of action is preferable. It may even be less painful to tolerate the dissonance than to discard the belief and admit one had been wrong. When that is the case, dissonance cannot be eliminated by abandoning the belief.

Alternatively, the dissonance would be reduced or eliminated if the members of a movement effectively blind themselves to the fact that the prediction has not been fulfilled. But most people, including members of such movements, are in touch with reality and simply cannot blot out of their cognition such an unequivocal and undeniable fact. They can try to ignore it, however, and they usually do try. They may convince themselves that the date was wrong but that the prediction will, after all, be shortly confirmed; or they may even set another date. Believers may try to find reasonable explanations, very often ingenious ones, for the failure of their prediction. Rationalization can reduce dissonance somewhat, but for rationalization to be fully effective, support from others is needed to make the explanation or the revision seem correct. Fortunately, the disappointed believer can usually turn to others in the same movement, who have the same dissonance and the same pressures to reduce it. Support for the new explanation is, hence, forthcoming and the members of the movement can recover somewhat from the shock of the disconfirmation.

Whatever the explanation, it is still by itself not sufficient. The dissonance is too important and though they may try to hide it, even from themselves, the believers still know that the prediction was false and all their preparations were in vain. The dissonance cannot be eliminated completely by denying or rationalizing the disconfirmation. There is, however, a way in which the remaining dissonance can be reduced. *If more and more people can be persuaded that the system of belief is correct, then clearly it must, after all, be correct.* It is for this reason that we observe the increase in proselytizing following disconfirmation. If the proselytizing proves successful, then by gathering more adherents and effectively surrounding himself with supporters the believer reduces dissonance to the point where he can live with it.

In the light of this explanation of the phenomenon that proselyting increases as a result of a disconfirmation, we sought a modern instance of disconfirmation, an instance which could be observed closely enough so that our explanation could be put to an empirical test.

One day at the end of September the Lake City *Herald* carried a two-column story, on a back page, headlined: PROPHECY FROM PLANET. CLARION CALL TO CITY: FLEE THAT FLOOD. IT'LL SWAMP US ON DEC. 21, OUTER SPACE TELLS SUBURBANITE. The body of the story expanded somewhat on these bare facts:

Lake City will be destroyed by a flood from Great Lake just before dawn, Dec. 21, according to a suburban housewife. Mrs. Marian Keech, of 847 West School street, says the prophecy is not her own. It is the purport of many messages she has received by automatic writing, she says. . . . The messages, according to Mrs. Keech, are sent to her by superior beings from a planet called "Clarion." These beings have been visiting the earth, she says, in what we call flying saucers. During their visits, she says, they have observed fault lines in the earth's crust that foretoken the deluge. Mrs. Keech reports she was told the flood will spread to form an inland sea stretching from the Arctic Circle to the Gulf of Mexico. At the same time, she says, a cataclysm will submerge the West Coast from Seattle, Wash., to Chile in South America.

Since Mrs. Keech's pronouncement made a specific prediction of a specific event, since she, at least, was publicly committed to belief in it, and since she was apparently interested to some extent in informing a wider public about it, this seemed to be an opportunity to conduct a "field" test of the theoretical ideas to which the reader has been introduced. Therefore, the authors joined Mrs. Keech's group in early October and remained in constant touch with it throughout the events to be narrated here.

About nine months before the newspaper story appeared, Marian Keech had begun to receive messages in "automatic writing" from beings who said they existed in outer space and were instructing her to act as their representative to warn the people of earth of the coming cataclysm. Mrs. Keech told many of her friends and acquaintances of her messages, and by September had attracted a small following of believers. Among them was Dr. Thomas Armstrong, a physician who lived in a college town in a nearby state. Dr. Armstrong spread the word among a group of students ("The Seekers") who met at his home regularly to discuss spiritual problems and cosmology. Dr. Armstrong and his wife also visited Lake City frequently to attend meetings of Mrs. Keech's group there.

Throughout the fall months the groups in Lake City and Collegeville held a series of meetings to discuss the lessons from outer space and to prepare themselves for salvation from cataclysm. As December 21 drew near some members gave up their jobs, others gave away their possessions, and nearly all made public declarations of their conviction. In September, Dr. Armstrong had prepared two "news releases" about the prediction of flood, although Mrs. Keech had not sought any publicity herself and had given only the one interview to the Lake City reporter who called on her after he had seen one of Dr. Armstrong's news releases. Except for that interview, Mrs. Keech had confined her proselyting to friends and acquaintances, and Dr. Armstrong had virtually limited his activities to "The Seekers." During October and November, a policy of increasingly strict secrecy about the beliefs and activities of the believers had been developing in both Collegeville and Lake City.

In December, Dr. Armstrong was dismissed from his hospital post, and the action brought him nation-wide publicity. Had the group been interested in carrying their message to the world and securing new converts, they would have been presented with a priceless opportunity on December 16 when representatives of the nation's major news-reporting services converged on the Keech home, hungry for a story to follow up the news break on Dr. Armstrong's dismissal from the college. But the press received a cold, almost hostile reception, and their most persistent efforts were resisted. In two days of constant vigil, the newspapermen succeeded in winning only one brief broadcast tape and one interview with Dr. Armstrong and Mrs. Keech—and that only after a reporter had virtually threatened to print his own version of their beliefs. A cameraman who surreptitiously violated the believers' prohibition against taking photographs was threatened with a lawsuit. Between December 16 and the early morning of December 21, the Keech home was the object of a barrage of telephone calls and a steady stream of visitors who came seeking enlightenment or even offering themselves for conversion. The telephone calls from reporters were answered by a flat, unqualified "No comment." The visitors, mostly potential converts, were paid the most casual attention and the believers made only sporadic attempts to explain their views to these inquirers.

By the late afternoon of December 20—the eve of the predicted cataclysm—the hullaballoo in the house had died down somewhat, and the believers began making their final preparations for salvation. Late that morning, Mrs. Keech had received a message instructing the group to be ready to receive a visitor who would arrive at midnight and escort them to a parked flying saucer that would whisk them away from the flood to a place of safety, presumably in outer space. Early in the evening, the ten believers from Lake City and Collegeville had begun rehearsing for their departure. First, they went through the ritual to be followed when their escort arrived at midnight. Dr. Armstrong was to act as sentry and, having made sure of the caller's identity, admit him. The group drilled carefully on the ritual responses they would make to the specific challenges of their unearthly visitor, and the passwords they would have to give in boarding the saucer. Next, the believers removed all metal from their persons. The messages from outer space left no doubt in anyone's mind that it would be extremely dangerous to travel in a saucer while wearing or carrying anything metallic, and all of the group complied painstakingly with this order—excepting only the fillings in their teeth.

The last ten minutes before midnight were tense ones for the group assembled in Mrs. Keech's living room. They had nothing to do but sit and wait, their coats in their laps. In the silence two clocks ticked loudly, one about ten minutes faster than the other. When the faster clock pointed to 12:05, someone remarked about the time aloud.

A chorus of people replied that midnight had not yet come. One member affirmed that the slower clock was correct; he had set it himself only that afternoon. It showed only four minutes before midnight.

Those four minutes passed in complete silence except for a single utterance. When the (slower) clock on the mantel showed only one minute remaining before the guide to the saucer was due, Mrs. Keech exclaimed in a strained, high-pitched voice: "And not a plan has gone astray!" The clock chimed twelve, each stroke painfully clear in the expectant hush. The believers sat motionless.

One might have expected some visible reaction, as the minutes passed. Midnight had come and gone, and nothing had happened. The cataclysm itself was less than seven hours away. But there was little to see in the reactions of the people in that room. There was no talking, nor sound of any sort. People sat stock still, their faces seemingly frozen and expressionless.

Gradually, painfully, an atmosphere of despair and confusion settled over the group. They re-examined the prediction and the accompanying messages. Dr. Armstrong and Mrs. Keech reiterated their faith. The believers mulled over their predicament and discarded explanation after explanation as unsatisfactory. At one point, toward 4 A.M., Mrs. Keech broke down and cried bitterly. She knew, she sobbed, that there were some who were beginning to doubt but that the group must beam light to those who needed it most, and that the group must hold together. The rest of the believers were losing their composure, too. They were all visibly shaken and many were close to tears. It was now almost 4:30 A.M. and still no way of handling the disconfirmation had been found. By now, too, most of the group were talking openly about the failure of the escort to come at midnight. The group seemed near dissolution.

But this atmosphere did not continue long. At about 4:45 A.M. Mrs. Keech summoned everyone to attention, announcing that she had just received a message. She then read aloud these momentous words: "For this day it is established that there is but one God of Earth and He is in thy midst, and from his hand thou hast written these words. And mighty is the word of God—and by his word have ye been saved—for from the mouth of death have ye been delivered and at no time has there been such a force loosed upon the Earth. Not since the beginning of time upon this Earth has there been such a force of Good and light as now floods this room and that which has been loosed within

this room now floods the entire Earth. As thy God has spoken through the two who sit within these walls has he manifested that which he has given thee to do."

This message was received with enthusiasm. It was an adequate, even an elegant, explanation of the disconfirmation. The cataclysm had been called off. The little group, sitting all night long, had spread so much light that God had saved the world from destruction.

The atmosphere in the group changed abruptly and so did their behavior. Within minutes after she had read the message explaining the disconfirmation, Mrs. Keech received another message instructing her to publicize the explanation. She reached for the telephone and began dialing the number of a newspaper. While she was waiting to be connected, someone asked: "Marian, is this the first time you have called the newspaper yourself?" Her reply was immediate: "Oh, yes, this is the first time I have ever called them. I have never had anything to tell them before, but now I feel it is urgent." The whole group could have echoed her feelings, for they all felt a sense of urgency. As soon as Marian had finished her call, the other members took turns telephoning newspapers, wire services, radio stations, and national magazines to spread the explanation of the failure of the flood. In their desire to spread the word quickly and resoundingly, the believers now opened for public attention matters that had been thus far utterly secret. Where only hours earlier they had shunned newspaper reporters and felt that the attention they were getting in the press was painful, they now became avid seekers of publicity. During the rest of December 21, the believers thrust themselves willingly before microphones, talked freely to reporters, and enthusiastically proselytized the visitors and inquirers who called at the house. In the ensuing days they made new bids for attention. Mrs. Keech made further predictions of visits by spacemen and invited newspapermen to witness the event. Like the millennial groups of history, this one, too, reacted to disconfirmation by standing firm in their beliefs and doubling their efforts to win converts. The believers in Lake City clearly displayed the reaction to disconfirmation that our theory predicted.

Among the members of the Collegeville group who had not gone to Lake City for the flood, matters took quite a different turn. Most of them were students who had gone to their homes for Christmas vacation. All but two of them spent December 20 and 21 in isolation from each other, surrounded by unbelievers. These isolates reacted to the disconfirmation in a very different fashion from their fellows in Lake City. Instead of recovering from the initial shock of disconfirmation, they either gave up their beliefs completely or found their conviction seriously weakened. There was no upsurge of proselytizing among the stay-at-homes in "The Seekers" even after they had been informed of the message rationalizing the disconfirmation. Indeed, the reverse seems to have occurred in two cases where the individuals attempted to conceal their membership in "The Seekers." Thus, most of the Collegeville group reduced the dissonance created by disconfirmation by giving up all their beliefs, whereas in Lake City the members held fast and tried to create a supportive circle of believers.

The comparison of the two situations—Lake City and Collegeville—permits at least a crude test of the importance of one element of the theory proposed to explain the proselyting reaction to disconfirmation: namely, the element of social support. In Lake City, most of the members were in the constant presence of fellow believers during the period immediately following disconfirmation. They had social support; they were able to accept the rationalization; and they regained confidence in their beliefs. On the other hand, all of the members of the Collegeville group, with the exception of one pair, faced the morning of December 21 and the following days either with people who neither agreed nor disagreed or with people who were openly opposed to the views of "The Seekers." It would seem that the presence of supporting cobelievers is an indispensable requirement for recovery from disconfirmation.

At the beginning of this article, we specified the conditions under which disconfirmation would lead to increased proselytizing and, for most of the members of the Lake City group, these specifications were satisfied. Most of them believed in Mrs. Keech's prediction and were heavily committed to this belief. Disconfirmation was unequivocal, and the attempted rationalization by itself was never completely successful in dispelling dissonance. Finally, the members of the group faced disconfirmation and its aftermath together. The members responded with strong, persistent attempts at proselytizing. Among "The Seekers," all the conditions were the same except that the supportive group of cobelievers was missing. Among these isolates there was no increase in proselyting, no attempt to seek publicity, but rather their characteristic response was to give up their belief and even to conceal their earlier membership.

PROJECTS

Name _____

Date _____

3.1: INFLUENCING ATTITUDES

This project is designed to help you analyze the effects of a group discussion on the formation and change of a particular attitude. Your analysis will be based on the point of view either of someone actively involved in the discussion or of someone who is listening to it. Your instructor will divide the class into two groups, discussants and observers, and will assign a particular topic to be discussed. After the discussion has taken place, answer the following questions.

1. What topic was discussed?

2. Were you a discussant or an observer? _____

3. On the form below, rate the attitudes of the discussants. Begin by listing each discussant by name in the left-hand column. Then indicate what position each argued (circle either "pro" or "anti"). Finally, rate each discussant according to how much you think he or she *actually* believed the position being argued. The rating scale ranges from 1 (did not believe at all) to 7 (believed very strongly). Circle the appropriate rating number.

Discussants	Position Argued		Actual Belief in Position Argued						
			Did Not Believe at All				Believed Very Strongly		
1. _____	pro	anti	1	2	3	4	5	6	7
2. _____	pro	anti	1	2	3	4	5	6	7
3. _____	pro	anti	1	2	3	4	5	6	7
4. _____	pro	anti	1	2	3	4	5	6	7
5. _____	pro	anti	1	2	3	4	5	6	7
6. _____	pro	anti	1	2	3	4	5	6	7
7. _____	pro	anti	1	2	3	4	5	6	7
8. _____	pro	anti	1	2	3	4	5	6	7
9. _____	pro	anti	1	2	3	4	5	6	7
10. _____	pro	anti	1	2	3	4	5	6	7

4. What was the basis for your ratings? That is, what led you to the conclusion that discussants actually did or did not believe what they were arguing?

5. How would you rate *your* attitude on this issue? (Circle the appropriate number.)

1   2   3   4   5   6   7

agree strongly   agree strongly
with "pro" position   with "anti" position

6. Was your own attitude affected by the group discussion?   *Yes*   *No*

7. If you answered yes, describe the way in which your attitude was affected.

8. Do you have any additional comments about the project as a whole or any particular aspect of it?

Name _____

Date _____

3.2: BECOMING AN AGENT OF SOCIAL CHANGE

Imagine that you are a professional specializing in persuasive communications and that you have been hired to bring about change in one of the following areas:

a. Get people to stop discriminating against a particular minority group (e.g., by hiring more people from this group or by changing their attitude toward it)

b. Get people to adopt one or more conservation behaviors (e.g., reducing gasoline consumption or using biodegradable products)

c. Get people to vote for a political candidate who is currently running far behind in the polls

d. [Some other problem devised by you or your instructor]

In answering the following questions, assume that you have access to sufficient money and resources to mount the ideal campaign for change. On the work sheet, list what your *specific* goals would be and then outline the steps that you would take to achieve them. Wherever appropriate, cite the theoretical principles (modeling, reinforcement, dissonance, reactance, and so on) that you are using in developing your change techniques.

1. Which of the problem areas have you chosen to work on?

2. List the *specific* goal(s) that you have set in this change program. In other words, what actual behavior(s) should show a change as a result of your efforts (e.g., more positive scores on an attitude scale, reduced automobile driving)?

3. What techniques would you use to produce the changes you listed in question 2? Give concrete examples: for instance, what the ad would look like, what you would say to people as you conducted your door-to-door campaign, or what incentives or rewards you would give.

4. What are the theoretical principles on which your techniques are based? For example, giving everyone a dime if they buy a new biodegradable product is a technique based on reinforcement principles.

5. How will you know if your behavior change program has been successful? That is, how will you actually assess the amount of change in the behavior(s) that you listed in question 2?

4

PREJUDICE

Suppose you were asked to rate yourself on a scale designed to measure racial prejudice, and the choices ranged from "very racially prejudiced" at one end of the scale to "very racially tolerant" at the other. You would probably place yourself at the tolerant end of the scale. If you were asked to rate yourself on a sexual prejudice scale, your self-evaluation would probably be the same. In fact, few of today's college students would willingly admit to considering racial groups, ethnic minorities, or women inferior. But what about other forms of prejudice? In our youth-oriented society, many people deride old age; "dirty old man" jokes are just one way that our society uses ridicule to censure and ostracize the elderly. Many people, especially those who regard themselves as intellectuals, will openly acknowledge that they cannot tolerate "stupid" people. Somehow, stupidity or lack of education is considered sufficient justification for oth-erwise liberal and humanistic individuals to treat certain human beings in a rude, derogatory manner.

What is it about the way we live that tends to foster prejudicial attitudes? The world around us bombards our senses with an infinite number of stimuli. No one person can perceive and under-stand them all. Therefore, each individual perceives only a selected number of stimuli, organizes them, and encodes their meaning. Social psychologists believe that this process of selective perception of, and response to, our environment may contribute to the formation of prejudice. Such perceptual short-cuts are necessary if the individual is to bring some order to the surrounding chaos, but they inevitably involve a loss of information and consequently pro-duce perceptual distortions. Because these distor-tions may lead to the formation of negative attitudes that can be used to justify discriminatory treatment of others, they are especially dangerous.

DOONESBURY

by Garry Trudeau

Copyright, 1974, G. B. Trudeau / Distributed by Universal Press Syndicate.

A CASE OF PREJUDICE

The ease with which people adopt prejudices and, even worse, the ease with which the subjects of prejudice accept their unjust fate are illustrated by an incident that occurred in Israel in 1967, just before the outbreak of the Six Day War. Egyptian President Gámal Abdel Nasser had closed the Tiran Sea Gates to Africa to Israeli ships, and all diplomatic negotiations had proved futile. Tensions were rising rapidly, and the inevitability of war was becoming increasingly clear to everyone. The only question on people's minds was: When will the war start?

The 5:30 P.M. bus to Hertseliya from Tel Aviv was crowded with rush-hour commuters. All the passengers seemed tired, worried, and sweaty, weary from their long workday and looking forward to getting home and unwinding. Shortly after the bus left Tel Aviv, a confrontation developed in the last two rows of the bus. A young man was listening to his transistor radio. The man sitting behind him told him rather rudely to turn the radio down. The youth's response was predictable: he turned the volume up. With that, the man demanded even more firmly that he turn it down; again, his response was to turn it up even higher.

The incident might have ended with the two arguing it out if the older man had not then abruptly accused the boy of being an Arab spy. He shouted, "Arab! . . . You are an Arab . . . an Arab spy!" Within seconds, everyone on the still-moving bus was involved in the fight. "I am not an Arab spy, I swear. Let me show you my identification card," the youth protested pitifully. No one examined the card. No one listened to him. Suddenly, all the strained, withdrawn faces grew flushed. Eyes shone with excitement at the prospect of capturing an Arab spy.

Although in a great hurry to get home from work, the passengers unanimously decided to make a wide detour and drop the "spy" at the Hertseliya police station. The youth seemed quiet, subdued, totally resigned to his fate as he was taken into the station house by an escort of six enthusiastic volunteers who had been his fellow passengers on the bus.

PREJUDICE AGAINST AN INVISIBLE RACE

NICHOLAS H. PRONKO

When a group of people in a society becomes the target of derogatory stereotypes and discrimination, that group is likely to become segregated from the society. As a result, the group may develop patterns of housing, education, occupation, speech, and so on, that differ from those of the society's controlling group. Thus, the inevitable differences between the isolated group and the rest of the population are often the result of discrimination rather than its cause.

This is true of the Burakumin in Japan, who are described by DeVos and Wagatsuma in Pronko's article "Prejudice Against an Invisible Race." Burakumin are an invisible race because, unlike certain groups in the United States, they are indistinguishable from the rest of the population in any physical sense. Nevertheless, their segregation is justified on racial grounds.

DeVos's and Wagatsuma's study started as an attempt to find a cross-cultural parallel to the ghetto experiences of black American and Mexican-American youth. They found that parallel in the experiences of Buraku youths. DeVos and Wagatsuma came to the conclusion that even if members of America's minority groups looked exactly like the white majority, they would still not become completely equal citizens, because the effects of so many years of inequality in all aspects of life have profoundly affected their life-styles and their perceptions of themselves.

It is a truism that human populations differ in skin color, hair texture, size, and other less noticeable anatomical characteristics. What is the relationship between these attributes and human temperament, skills, and other behavioral potentials?

If we could manipulate humans as we do rats, we could design an experiment to help answer the question. In our experiment, we would want to control *every condition but one* and simply observe the effect of varying that single factor.

We might care to select skin color as the one variable. For example, let two groups of people, one with black skin and the other nonblack, each be equally segregated, equally deprived of educational opportunities, equally hated and mistreated. Other things being equal, the outcome, if different, could be attributed to the skin-color variable. If there were no differences in outcome, we would be justified in concluding that the skin-color variable made no difference.

The thought of designing such a monstrous experiment is revolting. Yet sometimes "nature's experiments" furnish valuable knowledge about humans even though they are not as carefully controlled as laboratory experiments. The following report of an ingenious study is only remotely analogous to the experiment proposed, but it is the best we have and it does shed light on the relationship between race and psychological inquiry.

The fact of white prejudice against the Negro in the United States is an explosive issue today. Its counterpart in Japan concerns a group of two to three million real or imaginary descendants of an untouchable pariah caste known as the Burakumin. In a book that provides the substance of the present article, DeVos and Wagatsuma tell how "racial" prejudice has forced the Burakumin into ghettos of indescribable poverty, wretchedness, and suffering in such representative cities as Osaka, Kobe, Kyoto, and Nara, although they have banded together in rural areas as well.

Officially the Burakumin were emancipated in 1871, at which time they were free to discard the special prescribed garb they had been forced to wear and the occupations that had identified

From *Panorama of Psychology*, by N. H. Pronko. Copyright © 1973 by Wadsworth Publishing Company, Inc. Reprinted by permission of the publisher, Brooks/Cole Publishing Company, Monterey, California.

Editors' Note: Unless otherwise indicated, all quotations in this article are from George DeVos and Hiroshi Wagatsuma, *Japan's Invisible Race* (Berkeley: University of California Press, 1966).

them for over a thousand years. Yet, despite recent radical economic and social changes that have placed Japan among the top four or five countries of the world, the condition of the Burakumin remains unchanged and they suffer the same indignity and lack of opportunity as the Negro in America or the 50 million untouchables in India. Japanese see no inconsistency in their repugnance at any familiarity or contact with a Buraku.

LIFE IN THE OUTCASTE GHETTO

Marriage

The tight, geographical confinement of the Burakumin would obviously limit mate selection. Consequently, intermarriage occurs on a much more "local" basis than in nonoutcaste communities. However, in more recent years inbreeding is very gradually breaking down. For example, according to DeVos and Wagatsuma, although less than 10 percent of Buraku men over 50 years of age married outside their caste, 38 percent of men under 30 have done so. Similarly, of Buraku women over age 30, less than 5 percent married men from the majority population as compared with 30 percent of women under 30 (p. 119).

Occupation

Historically the outcaste group has been connected with the building and guarding of tombs, undertaking, butchering, tanning, leather-working, including shoe- and sandal-making, working in armor, fur, bowstrings, basket making and tea-whisk manufacture. How one's occupation can readily identify one's social position is illustrated effectively in the case of one such outcaste who preferred to live in his ghetto. When asked "If you were to live elsewhere, can you think of any sort of undesirable conditions you might face?" His reply: "Because I am a shoemaker, everyone would know of my Buraku origin [p. 167]."

Food

In a Buddhist setting, meat eating is unthinkable, but the consumption of the internal organs of cows and horses is even more abhorrent. By this conspicuous practice, many Burakumin have succeeded in segregating themselves further from the majority population.

Dress

The Burakumin tend to dress carelessly within the ghetto, but in the larger community they impose greater formality. Weather permitting, children under six are allowed to run around completely naked.

Speech

Vocabulary, such as special or secret words, ruder speech, and identifying accent also tend to set off a person reared in a Buraku ghetto from the majority as well as from the other lower (i.e., non-Buraku) segments of the Japanese population. The Cockney of London offers a parallel example.

Identifying the Burakumin

The people whom Buraku outcastes choose for their mates, their occupations, their food, dress, and speech are all very conspicuous and *visible* "things." And yet DeVos and Wagatsuma refer to the Burakumin as "the *invisible* race." How so? The whole point, one of utmost significance in considering the relationship of biological factors and psychological events, is this. "It is not widely known that Japan has discriminated in the past and continues to discriminate against a pariah caste that is completely indistinguishable *in any physical sense* from the population as a whole, whose segregation nevertheless has long been justified *in racial terms* [p. xx; Pronko's italics]" For a special emphasis of this point, the following statement regarding Japan's pariahs is quoted from Wagatsuma (1967):

> Not racially different in any way from the majority Japanese, they can be identified with certainty only by the registry of place of birth and residence. Nevertheless, many Japanese believe that they are in some way or other visibly identifiable [p. 118].

Most Negroes in America manifest a skin color that permits instant recognition and a resultant expression of any existing prejudice toward them. The black skin triggers the prejudiced response. However, undress a representative outcaste and a representative upperclass citizen of Japan and they are indistinguishable from each other. Ask about the locality where they were born, listen to them talk, eat, note their dress, and once more you can segregate them. "The concept of caste remains a social force because it exists in the emotional structure of individual Japanese [p. xxi]." The point of our discussion is that prejudice can always find food to feed upon. If no distinctive anthropomorphic feature exists between human groups, one can *create* some cultural feature that will serve the same purpose as kinky hair and pigmented skin. A yellow star of David worn on the sleeve will serve equally well. If you herd people into strictly bounded areas, restrict their manner of earning a living or their opportunities for education, if you contrive appropriate historical, economic, and religious factors, and spell out their diet and dress and whom they can marry, you will find that skin color is not indispensable. Skin color is only more obvious.

DeVos and Wagatsuma seem to agree with this thinking:

> Outcaste status and attitudes about untouchability developed within medieval Japanese culture because of a complex set of economic, social, political, and ideological conditions. And once established, outcaste status has had great staying power. The formal rational explanations and protests on the parts of members of the majority society, or by the outcastes themselves, have had little effect on hastening change in outcaste history [p. 13].

Does "Passing" Occur Among Burakumin?

The answer to the above question, as applied to the Negro in North America, is clear cut. Because the vast majority of Negroes cannot erase their distinguishing skin color, they cannot merge into the white population. In Japan, however, since "No scientific fact substantiates the myth that there are hereditary biological factors that separate ordinary Japanese from the former pariahs [p. xxi]," the transition seems easier. Not having a different skin color or other distinguishing anatomical characteristic, the Buraku should be able to blend into the majority population; this is physically possible to them on a much wider scale than for the colorful Negro.

DeVos and Wagatsuma tell us the secrets of "passing." In order to escape completely from the stigma of his past, a Burakumin must make a complete geographical and occupational break with his ghetto and "forge for himself an entirely new identity and in some cases fabricate a past so that he will not be disadvantaged by his lack of ancestry [p. 241]." However, such a step would require extreme challenge and motivation that would be blocked by difficult procedures, steps, risk of discovery, and lack of money, opportunity for employment, and so on.

Buraku individuals who marry across the caste barrier may establish successful and lasting happy marriages *unless* and *until* they are identified by a person out of their past. The result often spells rupture, anguish, guilt, and a break-up or suicide. The consequences of discovery may match the tragedy of *Madame Butterfly*. The following poignant story from DeVos and Wagatsuma makes the point emphatically:

A Buraku woman, named Niwa Mariko, sent her letter to the journal *Buraku*, describing her painful experience.

"I was born in a Buraku, as a youngest daughter. Although my family was relatively well off in the Buraku, I had to work hard as soon as I finished junior high school. I found a job . . . in Kyoto, where I met my future husband. We fell in love with each other, and after talking it over with my brothers and sisters, I married him. . . . A few years after our marriage, my husband was promoted to a position of supervisor in his factory. I was happy.

"Last year, I went to the factory to see my husband, and there I happened to meet a former acquaintance who knew I was a Buraku girl. She showed in an exaggerated manner her surprise at the fact that my husband was a factory supervisor. I felt disgusted at the expression on her face, but I did not realize fully that the woman thought it was simply too much for a Buraku girl like me to be married to a factory supervisor. About ten days later, my husband came home sullen and morose. . . . From that night on my husband became a changed person. . . . He said, finally, that I was from a Buraku, and that it was all wrong. It may sound too naive, but until that time I had not fully realized what it meant to be a Burakumin to those who are not. I had never been told very clearly that I was a Buraku woman, and was therefore the subject of discrimination. I later discovered that my old acquaintance had told everyone at the factory that I was from a Buraku. My husband finally forced me to leave his house. By that time, my previous intense love toward him changed into hatred.

"I received a letter from my husband's brother telling me to sign a divorce paper so that my husband could marry someone else. I wrote back a letter that I would not consent to the divorce unless I was fully persuaded it was best for me. I went to my husband's house anyway to pick up my belongings. . . . There I found my bedding thrown into the garden like some objects of filth. While married, I had made for us bedding of the finest quality, but only the poorest set was given back to me. We also found two suitcases in the garden, which had been filled with the things I had used before my

marriage. I could not meet with my husband; he was out. I had been thrown out of the house, like filth. I trembled with anger and returned to my sister's home, angry, sad, and exhausted.

"My husband and his brother still insisted that I sign the divorce document. I hated them and had no intention of remaining his wife. And yet, I did not like to consent to a divorce, because the stated reasons for divorce . . . were all untrue. I did not believe that my husband had had any feelings of discontent before his discovery of my identity.

"I had an opportunity to meet the man who was secretary of the Kaiho Domei. He told me that discrimination against Burakumin would never end unless Burakumin themselves fought back. He said I should overcome my own depression and fight for all the Burakumin, who were sufferers from discrimination. Also, one of my sisters, married to a non-Buraku man, wanted to keep our background hidden from her husband. If I stood up to fight, my sister's marriage would probably be threatened. I talked with the secretary of the Domei several times, and being ashamed of my indecisive attitude, I still cannot make up my mind. I know that eventually I will have to get over this conflict in myself and stand up and fight [pp. 255–256]."

SOME FINAL COMMENTS ON JAPAN'S "INVISIBLE RACE"

First, it is interesting to note the origin of the DeVos and Wagatsuma study. They were impressed by the high delinquency rate among Negro youth in the U.S. Would they find an analogous relationship in Japan between, on the one hand, the status of a minority group segregated by caste barriers and barred from easy assimilation into its modern industrial society and delinquency on the other hand? Evidence from their inquiry showed a positive relationship between boys' residence in a Buraku ghetto and joblessness, school absenteeism, dropout, low IQ, and a rate of delinquency which was three times that of non-Buraku boys (pp. 258–272). A direct parallel existed in these respects between Buraku youth in Japan, on the one hand, and American-Negro and American-Mexican youth on the other.

Within the context of our discussion, the crucial question is: What is the psychological significance of the black skin of the American Negro? Apparently the kinds of sociopathologies and psychopathologies connected with crime and other forms of deviance do not demand skin color or any other discriminable anatomical factor; in the two groups compared, the latter is present in the United States but absent in Japan. Is it not a mere coincidence that skin color is a badge of the Negro's caste status and that the Burakumin simply wear nonanatomical but equally visible badges? The common factors related to social deviance in both groups appear to be registry of birth in a certain locality, their residence in common ghettos, lack of social, educational, and occupational opportunity, discrimination and other barriers to their involvement in the full life of the community.

The fundamental question that the reader must answer for himself is this: How does "race" enter into our understanding of a person's psychological nature? What does the individual's skin color, hair texture, limb-to-body-height ratio or any other hereditary, anatomical characteristic have to do with his or her attainment of excellence as a Metropolitan Opera star, an atomic scientist, a chemist, violinist, conductor, composer, military strategist, or poet? Today the evidence for high attainment is occurring on a global basis, irrespective of continent, nationality, religion, or "race."

A Spanish-speaking student attending a junior high school in San Antonio, Texas, in 1963 was "caught" speaking his native language among his friends between classes. Since, in this school, Spanish was not allowed to be spoken except, one assumes, in Spanish class, the student was required to write an essay on the topic "Why I Should Speak English." The essay he did write, "Why I speack spanich," is reproduced below (along with his teacher's rather halfhearted corrections of spelling and grammar). His homeroom teacher submitted the essay to the editors of The Texas Foreign Language Bulletin, who published it as the lead article in their December 1963 issue. As a psychologist wrote in that issue, the essay "poignantly expresses the dilemma of a child caught between two cultures." Since then things have changed. It is now official policy throughout the San Antonio Independent School District to encourage the use of Spanish in the schools.

Why I speack spanish

I speack spanich because my mother Can't speack English. I forget how to speack English because We always speack spanich in may Home. But I have forget that I was in school. What why I speack spanich. But I hope I won't forget how to speack in Class. My father no how to speack English. But we speack spanich because my mother don't understand. When we have Visiter we Always speack spanich. My big sister Always speack English. But I speack spanich because my mother don't no. my brother speack spanich with her. And When my Grandmother Come to see use she speack spanich with Us she can't speack English with Us. so that why. I forget how to speack English. When I am speack English my friend speack with me they speack spanich with me And

I have to speack spanich with them. What that's
Why I`am in school I forget how to
speack English.
And wend my mother speack to me I have
to speack spanich with her. And wend I
I go to my Grandmother I have to
speack spanich with her. And my Uncle
And my littil little cousin. But I promise
I won't speack spanich no more.
am ~~to~~ sorry I catch ~~get caught~~ speack spanich.
Hope I won't do it again.

YOU ARE WHAT YOU SAY

"Women's language" is that pleasant (dainty?), euphemistic, never-aggressive way of talking we learned as little girls. Cultural bias was built into the language we were allowed to speak, the subjects we were allowed to speak about, and the ways we were spoken of. Having learned our linguistic lesson well, we go out in the world, only to discover that we are communicative cripples—damned if we do, and damned if we don't.

If we refuse to talk "like a lady," we are ridiculed and criticized for being unfeminine. ("She thinks like a man" is, at best, a left-handed compliment.) If we do learn all the fuzzy-headed, unassertive language of our sex, we are ridiculed for being unable to think clearly, unable to take part in a serious discussion, and therefore unfit to hold a position of power.

It doesn't take much of this for a woman to begin feeling she deserves such treatment because of inadequacies in her own intelligence and education.

. . .

In the area of syntax, . . . there is one construction, in particular, that women use conversationally far more than men: the tag question. A tag is midway between an outright statement and a yes-no question; it is less assertive than the former, but more confident than the latter.

A *flat statement* indicates confidence in the speaker's knowledge and is fairly certain to be believed; a *question* indicates a lack of knowledge on some point and implies that the gap in the speaker's knowledge can and will be remedied by an answer. For example, if, at a Little League game, I have had my glasses off, I can legitimately ask someone else: "Was the player out at third?" A *tag question*, being intermediate between statement and question, is

used when the speaker is stating a claim, but lacks full confidence in the truth of that claim. So if I say, "Is Joan here?" I will probably not be surprised if my respondent answers "no"; but if I say, "Joan is here, isn't she?" instead, chances are I am already biased in favor of a positive answer, wanting only confirmation. I still want a response, but I have enough knowledge (or think I have) to predict that response. A tag question, then, might be thought of as a statement that doesn't demand to be believed by anyone but the speaker, a way of giving leeway, of not forcing the addressee to go along with the views of the speaker.

Another common use of the tag question is in small talk when the speaker is trying to elicit conversation: "Sure is hot here, isn't it?"

But in discussing personal feelings or opinions, only the speaker normally has any way of knowing the correct answer. Sentences such as "I have a headache, don't I?" are clearly ridiculous. But there are other examples where it is the speaker's opinions, rather than perceptions, for which corroboration is sought, as in "The situation in Southeast Asia is terrible, isn't it?"

While there are, of course, other possible interpretations of a sentence like this, one possibility is that the speaker has a particular answer in mind—"yes" or "no"—but is reluctant to state it baldly. This sort of tag question is much more apt to be used by women than by men in conversation. Why is this the case?

The tag question allows a speaker to avoid commitment, and thereby avoid conflict with the addressee. The problem is that, by so doing, speakers may also give the impression of not really being sure of themselves, or looking to the addressee for confirmation of their views. This uncertainty is reinforced in more subliminal ways, too. There is a peculiar sentence intonation-pattern, used almost exclusively by women, as far as I know, which changes a declarative answer into a question. The effect of using the rising inflection typical of a yes-no question is to imply that the speaker is seeking confirmation, even though the speaker is clearly the only one who has the requisite information, which is why the question was put to her in the first place:

(Q) When will dinner be ready?

(A) Oh . . . around six o'clock . . .

It is as though the second speaker were saying, "Six o'clock—if that's okay with you, if you agree." The person being addressed is put in the position of having to provide confirmation. One likely consequence of this sort of speech-pattern in a woman is that, often unbeknownst to herself, the speaker builds a reputation of tentativeness, and others will refrain from taking her seriously or trusting her with any real responsibilities, since she "can't make up her mind," and "isn't sure of herself."

Such idiosyncrasies may explain why women's language sounds much more "polite" than men's. It is polite to leave a decision open, not impose your mind, or views, or claims, on anyone else. So a tag question is a kind of polite statement, in that it does not force agreement or belief on the addressee. In the same way a request is a polite command, in that it does not force obedience on the addressee, but rather suggests something be done as a favor to the speaker. A clearly stated order implies a threat of certain consequences if it is not followed, and—even more impolite—implies that the speaker is in a superior position and able to enforce the order. By couching wishes in the form of a request, on the other hand, a speaker implies that if the request is not carried out, only the speaker will suffer; noncompliance cannot harm the addressee. So the decision is really left up to addressee. The distinction becomes clear in these examples:

Close the door.

Please close the door.

Will you please close the door?

Won't you close the door?

SEXISM SPRINGS ETERNAL . . . IN THE *READER'S DIGEST*

PHILIP G. ZIMBARDO and WENDY MEADOW

Suppose that a white male college student decided to room or set up a bachelor apartment with a black male friend. Surely the typical white student would not blithely assume that his black roommate was to handle all the domestic chores. Nor would his conscience allow him to do so even in the unlikely event that his roommate would say "That's okay. I like doing housework." But change this hypothetical black roommate to a female marriage partner and somehow the student's conscience goes to sleep. At most it is quickly tranquilized by the comforting thought that "she is happiest when she is ironing for her loved one." Such is the power of an unconscious ideology. Of course, it may well be that she *is* happiest when she is ironing for her loved one. Such indeed is the power of an unconscious ideology (Bem & Bem, 1970, p. 99).

The "unconscious ideology" that Bem and Bem are referring to consists of those sexual prejudices that have become the implicit assumptions shaping and, often quite literally, determining roles of both males and females. That ideology is reflected, for example, in the experience of the bright and attractive *woman whose mathematics instructor treats her as a "dumb blonde," even though her grades are consistently the best in the class, or the highly qualified and experienced woman who is denied a job as a counselor because she is judged "immature" and "lacking in appropriate authority" on the basis of her youthful, "cute" appearance.*

In "Sexism Springs Eternal—in the Reader's Digest," Zimbardo and Meadow demonstrate that the content of jokes is one of the most insidious ways in which unconscious sex prejudice is perpetuated.

Once formed, sexism, like all prejudice, is difficult to change. In trying to understand why prejudiced attitudes are so hardy and resistant to counterforces, social psychologists have tended to emphasize their emotional, motivational component, as well as the irrational elements that somehow become central in the personality dynamics of the prejudiced person.

Such thinking extends the fatherly wisdom we note in Lord Chesterfield's *Letters to his Son* (April 13, 1752): "Our prejudices are our mistresses; reason is at best our wife, very often heard indeed, but seldom minded." It has also characterized several decades of research on the authoritarian personality. Psychologists who witnessed the mass conversion of an entire nation's beliefs and values to Nazism sought to explain such phenomena in terms of child-rearing patterns that created repressed hostility and sexuality in particular types of individuals.

This is a typical research strategy of many psychologists: namely, to observe a social movement—a complex, interacting system supported by economics, law, politics, history, and coercive forces—and then to ignore the forest in search of the individual tree responsible for the problem." In doing so, they have inadvertently become part of the repressive machinery of the state that seeks the solution for its problems by identifying the "problem people" responsible for them. Such has been the way psychologists have used IQ tests to root out the feeble-minded among us, to identify those aliens who threaten the status quo by appearing to be different, and then to recommend legislation to restrict their immigration or to sterilize them to prevent proliferation of their "problem children." Thus, we have been blinded to the power of social systems that define reality, relevance, and appropriateness for all of us because we have put the behavior of *individuals*

under our analytic microscope in pursuit of scientific psychology.

Prejudices among young children are as easily modified by new information as they are formed. But this is not so among adults. Along with Sandra Bem and Daryl Bem (1970), we believe that the basis for sexism and many other prejudices is a set of assumptions and beliefs about the way the world and people "really" are. This nonconscious ideology starts, not as a malicious intention to harm others, but as a set of rational propositions about the nature of reality. For example, everyone "knows" that men are generally taller than women, that women can bear children and men cannot. But people also "know" that women are less logical and more emotional than men and that they are also likely to be bad drivers, nags, catty, and spendthrifts. The evidence for the set of beliefs about biological differences comes from empirically validated observations, but so does the "evidence" for the second set of beliefs, which we would all consider prejudiced.

The child learns about these sex-role differences from observing otherwise reliable cultural sources of information, including parents, textbooks, television, newspapers, and magazines. If the message transmitted across all these diverse channels of communication is consistent, then there is no reason to question that it is a statement of *"fact,"* not of opinion or biased perspective. As evidence of reality, it goes unchallenged, becoming part of an ideology that selectively guides subsequent processing of relevant information to accommodate it to these established "truths" or schemata. The more extensive the support for such beliefs is in one's society, the more they become part of a person's basic cognitive orientation to processing additional information. The bias is in the way we distort such information to conform to the cognitive set we have established about the issue. Such beliefs are resistant to change precisely because they are perceived, not as attitudes, opinions, or personal preferences, but as cognitive dimensions of reality.

Paper presented at Western Psychological Association Meeting, San Francisco, April 1974. Reprinted by permission of the authors.

We may differ in our opinions about whether a red shirt is appropriate to wear to an academic convention, and we may recognize each other's right to a personal preference on the matter. But what if you were told that the person wore that shirt because *blue* was his or her favorite color? You could not tolerate that disagreement because it would mean that if the other person was correct, some of your thinking, perception, or labeling process must be wrong. You assume that you know what blue is and what red is and that you can distinguish between them, and it is important to do so—not because of your personality dynamics or some motivational constellation, but because your construction of reality is threatened by such a disagreement.

This, we believe, is the way sexism and racism operate once they have been inculcated by those who control our informational inputs. TV commercials present a view of housebound women obsessed by the need to have their husbands' shirts whiter than white, their families' underarms kissing sweet, and everyone's delicate skin caressed by two-ply toilet tissue. With these pressing demands to attend to, how could they be expected to be concerned about war, politics, civil rights, economic recessions, or other problems with which the menfolk have to deal? The often zany heroine of TV serials proves how incompetent and foolish she is whenever she ventures forth into the real world of business. She does so at the risk of destroying her marriage or being unloved. And if she is happy, then she is unsuccessful in business. The message that comes across the TV tube is well reinforced by the message that comes across in the textbooks a child must read in school: Men build, create, control, roam, seek, achieve, and receive societal acclaim; girls and women have little freedom of choice or action, being merely passive foils for male action. It could be argued that textbooks only describe the social reality available in the child's world, that girls are being prepared for the future *reality* of being housewives and mothers. But instead of being prepared for their future reality of becoming used-car salesmen, mail clerks, and janitors, boys are portrayed in these texts as risking their lives in exciting adventures and engaging in heroic exploits that their real-life parents would never allow.

It is remarkable how blatantly distorted reality becomes in the hands of the textbook writer. For example, a sixth-grade text, *Into New Worlds*, shows one female and three male scientists. The men's work requires originality and tremendous mental effort. But what about the woman's? According to U'Ren (1971):

> The project the young woman is working on is not her own idea. She was assigned to work on it. . . . As an employee working on someone else's idea, she is typical of thousands of scientists working in industry today.

In these educational readers, which, as we have noted, help children construct their socially approved views of reality, when a story is humorous, the female is typically the butt of the joke. The shrill, nagging wife of an inventor is dumped into the garbage by one of his robots; the fat, selfish queen stuffs herself with ice cream while the skinny king gets none; a man who accidentally makes money from having unintentionally killed his wife inspires his fellow townsmen to also "bump off their old wives."

After the children have grown up, they are no longer dominated by their textbooks; they are free to read and see anything they want. What happens when the biased attitudes that they learned face the test of reality? The answer is simple: As adults, people get more of the same misrepresentation from a variety of sources. *However, it is when sexism comes dressed as humor that it may be most effective.* The joke, by its very nature, is not intended to be taken seriously, so one becomes boorish for criticizing its social commentary. It is usually told in a friendly context with the intention of creating a positive emotional response, laughter, in the listener. One becomes a wet blanket for refusing to laugh simply because the butt of the joke happens to be a woman or an ethnic type. If a joke is funny, it is disseminated rapidly both by word of mouth and by being reprinted in the press, thus reaching an unbelievably wide audience. Also contributing to its effectiveness as an agent of bigotry is the likelihood that the recipient of a good joke will then become the sender in a joke-telling chain. It is not uncommon to hear Jews telling anti-Semitic jokes, Poles telling anti-Polish jokes, Newfoundlanders telling anti-Newfie jokes, women telling anti-woman jokes, and black comedians putting down blacks.

We believe that one potent source of informational input to the creation and maintenance of the nonconscious ideology of sexism comes from the portrayal of women as the butt of humor in our mass media. In this preliminary investigation, we wanted to establish the extent to which sexist humor abounds in our mass media, its variation over the recent decades, and the portrait of the average woman that emerges from a content analysis of jokes about women.

We therefore turned to the *Reader's Digest* as our sexist source book. Because the *Digest* has humor columns that it has featured regularly for several decades, it is possible to analyze historical changes in the prevalence of anti-woman jokes. All its humor pieces are drawn from other mass media sources. Thus, evidence of sexism would reflect not only bias in selection on the part of the *Digest*'s editors but also the prejudices of writers and editors of magazines and newspapers throughout the country that feed their bigotry to the *Reader's Digest*.

With its remarkable readership of over 29 million, the *Digest* reaches into the homes of Middle America, the blind (with its Braille edition), and even the foreign-born, with its thirteen foreign-language editions. Its formula of presenting a potpourri of articles and special features that are "not too heavy, not too light, just right" puts readers in a rather receptive mood to attend to, but not be too critical of, its contents. In short, if there is a significant percentage of anti-women jokes in the *Reader's Digest,* we can be sure that a great many people have been affected by them both in their original format and as retold in the *Digest.*

Over 1,000 jokes were analyzed for the existence of anti-women and anti-men humor in two humor columns of the *Digest:* "Laughter, the Best Medicine" and "Cartoon Quips," for the years 1947–1948, 1957–1958, and 1967–1968 (see Table 1). Two independent scorers showed high reliability in being able to sort a sample of 500 jokes into anti-men, -women, or neuter categories according to our explicit scoring rules. An anti-woman joke was defined as one in which (1) the way women (as a class) act, feel, or think is portrayed in stereotyped, derogatory ways; (2) the impact of the joke depends entirely upon its subject being a woman and substituting a man would make it less funny or not funny at all; (3) the subject is explicitly identified as female; (4) the punch line or main thrust of the joke, rather than some peripheral aspect of it, involves the negative characterization; (5) the subject is not a child (to avoid confounding with jokes relying on assumptions about children); and (6) the stereotyped attitude expressed is attributed to the subject's being a woman, not to special situational circumstances or membership in other reference groups (except wife or mother). The reason for this last qualification is to make the criterion for inclusion

TABLE 1. SEXIST HUMOR IN *READER'S DIGEST*

YEAR	TOTAL JOKES	PERCENT ANTI-WOMEN	PERCENT ANTI-MEN
Feature: "Cartoon Quips"			
1947–1948	59	37	4.00
1957–1958	160	11	4.00
1967–1968	184	10	2.00
Total	403	15	3.00
Feature: "Laughter, the Best Medicine"			
1947–1948	138	24	4.00
1957–1958	242	10	1.00
1967–1968	286	4	0.04
Total	666	10	1.00
Total, both features	1,069	12	2.00

relatively specific to just being a woman, not, for example, to being a woman of a given ethnic group or a woman under extreme emotional tension or excitement.

In the process of establishing scoring rules and representative instances of each qualification, it became clear that there were also some jokes that could be classified as anti-male according to these same general rules; for example, "One woman to another: 'my husband is absolutely no good at fixing anything, so everything in our house works,'" and, "Wife, pointing to husband stretched out in hammock, explains to friend, 'Jack's hobby is letting birds watch *him*.'"

The major finding from this analysis is that six times as many anti-women as anti-men jokes appeared in the *Reader's Digest* over the past three decades. In "Cartoon Quips," 15 percent of all the humor was anti-women, and 3 percent was anti-men. In "Laughter Is the Best Medicine," the percentages were 10 to 1 against women.

More remarkable is that in the period after World War II, 37 percent of all the jokes in one of these features and nearly a quarter of all those in the other were attacks on the intelligence, capability, integrity, and motivation of women. Thus, a reader would find internal consistency in going from the humor in "Cartoon Quips" to the humor in "Laughter Is the Best Medicine," a consistency provided by accepting assumptions about the inadequacies, if not the inferiority, of women.

However, the historical trend also clearly reveals the steadily *declining* percentage of total jokes that reflect anti-woman sentiments. The lowered absolute level of sexism is an encouraging trend, to be sure; but even in the late 1960s, 10 percent of the humor in "Cartoon Quips" still involved negative female stereotypes, and an unfavorable ratio of anti-female to anti-male jokes was still being maintained.

Just what *is* the portrait of the average woman that a visitor from outer space would get from reading the *Reader's Digest?* Over all years sampled, the rank ordering of the frequency (from most to least frequent) of negative traits attributed to women has remained the same:

1. Stupid, incompetent, foolish: "Sweet young thing to husband: 'Of course, I know what's going on in the world! I just don't understand any of it, that's all.'"

2. Domineering men, getting their own way: "A woman was helping her husband pick out a new suit. After much disagreement, she finally said, 'Well, go ahead and please yourself. After all, you're the one who will wear the suit!' 'Well, dear,' said the man meekly, 'I figure I'll probably be wearing the coat and vest, anyway.'"

3. Exploiting men for their money: "Woman trying on hat to salesgirl: 'It's nice, but, it's a little less than he can afford.'"

4. Jealous of and catty about other woman: "At a party, one woman called across the room to another: 'I have been wondering, my dear, why you weren't invited to the Asterbilts last week?' The other woman smiled: 'Isn't that a coincidence?' she said. 'I was just wondering why you were.'"

5. Spendthrift or irresponsible with money: "Husband to guest: 'The decor is Helen's own blend of traditional, modern and twenty-five hundred dollars.'"

6. Spreading gossip, nagging: "One woman to another: 'I like her. She just gives you the straight gossip, without slanting or editorializing.'"

7. Manhunting, overanxious to marry: "A young innocent was asked by a professor why she had selected the college she did. 'Well,' she said, 'I came here to get went with, but I ain't yet.'"

8. Miscellaneous, other (such as weak, sentimental, overemotional, irrational, overly enthusiastic, poor sense of organization).

Curiously, the portrait is filled with contradictions so far as female-male relationships are concerned. Dumb, incompetent, irresponsible women who need men to put a light bulb in a socket or to park their cars dominate the male of the species, exploit him, and lead him meekly off to the altar. It may be that these stereotyped contradictions also tell us something about the real confusion surrounding the prevailing conception of what a woman's role in society should be; but it may also be that the contradictory stereotypes perpetuated in this sexist humor contribute directly to the confusion that appears to exist. Nevertheless, we must recognize that such prejudiced beliefs came packaged for us by the men in the most powerful positions we know, those who control the mass media information to which we are exposed.

Sources such as the *Digest* cater to whatever their readership appears to want; they even include women's lib articles. Right below a recent excerpt on the women's rights movement, there was a supposedly innocuous filler item, interestingly titled, "*Eyewitness*"; "One father doubts that his teen-age daughter's tour of Europe impressed her much: 'All she remembers is that Mona Lisa needed more eye shadow'" (July 1970, p. 118).

It is time psychologists took a new look at the power structure that defines right and wrong for us. Then they might stop following Lord Chesterfield's advice and heed the wisdom of Thomas Paine, who reminds us in *The Rights of Man* (1791): "No man is prejudiced in favor of a thing knowing it to be wrong. He is attached to it on the belief of its being right."

REFERENCES

Bem, S. L., & Bem, D. J., Case study of a nonconscious ideology: Training the woman to know her place. In D. J. Bem, *Beliefs, attitudes and human affairs.* Belmont, Calif.: Brooks/Cole, 1970, pp. 89–99.

U'Ren, M. B. The image of woman in textbooks, In V. Gornick & B. K. Moran (Eds.), *Woman in sexist society.* New York: Basic Books, 1971, Pp. 218–225.

PREJUDICE AND FOLKLORE

. . . Ever since the coining of the term "stereotype" by journalist Walter Lippmann in his book *Public Opinion* in 1922, social psychologists among others have actively sought to refine the concept and to document its existence and influence. Attention has been given both to stereotypes of self and to stereotypes of others. In addition, there have been special studies concerned with the relationship between stereotypes and prejudice. It seems clear that stereotypes do contribute materially to the formation and perpetuation of deep-seated prejudices.

Yet, in examining the extensive national character and stereotype scholarship, one finds surprisingly little reference to the materials of folklore. Stereotypes are described almost solely on the basis of questionnaires or interviews in which an a priori set of adjectives, such as "honest" or "stingy," are assigned by informants to national or ethnic groups. One wonders, methodologically speaking, just how the researcher selects the initial list of adjectives and whether or not his personal bias in making up the list does not partially invalidate the results. What psychologists and others fail to realize is that folklore represents an important and virtually untapped source of information for students of national character, stereotypes, and prejudice. The folk have been making national character studies (that is, folk national character studies) for centuries. People A have numerous traditions about the character of People B as do People B about People A. And it is precisely these traditions that transmit stereotypes from one generation to another. The stereotypes are

Reproduced by permission of American Folklore Society and the author from Alan Dundes, "A Study of Ethnic Slurs: The Jew and the Polack in the United States," *Journal of American Folklore,* 84 (332): 186–187, 190, and 203, 1971.

thus "already recorded" and would presumably be free from the inevitable investigator bias found in the unduly leading questionnaires.

. . .

The inadequacy of the term "ethnic slur" concerns essentially the definition of "folk" itself. Some folk groups are ethnic groups, and in such cases the label ethnic slur seems to be very appropriate; however, there are many folk groups which are not ethnic, and in such cases the term seems inappropriate. This is clear if one accepts the modern, flexible definition of "folk" as meaning not a peasant society but any group whatsoever sharing at least one common factor.[1] The linking factor could be ethnicity, but it could just as well be political or religious affiliation, geographical location, or occupation. Any group is potentially both producer and victim of slurs. Some slurs are very much in-group traditions; some are strictly out-group traditions; some are used as often by the in-group as by the out-group. One reasonably empirical and eminently practical way of determining whether a given group does have a "folk" identity separate from the general culture surrounding it is to determine if that group has, or is the subject of, slurs. In medicine, general practitioners have jokes about proctologists, such as calling them "rear admirals." In academic life, university professors have jokes about deans, "Old deans never die, they just lose their faculties." Within Catholicism, one finds jokes about Jesuits, often commenting upon their intellectual rather than mystical approach to life and religion, for example, "There was a meeting of three clergymen, and the three were in a room. There was a Dominican, a Franciscan, and a Jesuit. In the middle of the meeting, the lights go out. Undeterred by the darkness,

[1]Dundes, *The Study of Folklore,* 2.

the Dominican stands up and says, 'Let us consider the nature of light and of darkness, and their meaning.' The Franciscan begins to sing a hymn in honor of our Little Sister Darkness. The Jesuit goes out and replaces the fuse." It is sometimes difficult to collect such in-group traditions inasmuch as the subgroups may close ranks when confronted by what they take to be a threatening outsider who is only posing as a harmless folklorist-collector.

In using the term "ethnic" or "national slur," then, one needs to keep in mind that it is a functional rather than generic category and also that there are slurs having nothing to do with ethnicity. The ethnic slur depends upon an alleged national or ethnic trait. More often than not, the trait or traits are mocked and demeaned. What is of primary interest here is determining precisely the trait or set of traits the folk has singled out for emphasis.

. . .

No doubt some will argue that the study of ethnic slurs may serve no other purpose than to increase the circulation of such slurs and by so doing unwittingly assist the rise of further ethnic and racial prejudice. However, a more realistic view would be that the slurs are used by the folk whether the folklorist studies them or not. Most children in the United States hear these slurs fairly early in their public school careers. I would maintain therefore that an open discussion of the slurs and an objective analysis of the stereotypes contained therein could do no harm and might possibly do a great deal of good in fighting bigotry and prejudice. Only by knowing and recognizing folk stereotypes can children be taught to guard against them so that they may have a better chance of succeeding in judging individuals on an individual basis.

PROJECTS

Name _____

Date _____

4.1: BEM SEX ROLE INVENTORY

The following exercise is to be carried out in the field and then discussed and evaluated in the classroom. Its goal is to give you some data on the ways in which men and women evaluate themselves. Some will rate themselves as either masculine or feminine, while others will consider themselves to be a combination of both (androgynous). Pick two people you know and consider to be either highly sex-typed or not. (They may, of course, be of either sex.) Give them the Bem Sex Role Inventory (called "Attitude Questionnaire" here), and record their answers. After you have completed the interviews, write down any other comments you may have about the scale, the interviewees, and your own feelings and attitudes.

INTERVIEW COMMENTS

Interview A: _____

_____

_____

_____

_____

_____

_____

_____

_____

_____

Interview B: _____

_____

_____

_____

_____

_____

_____

_____

_____

_____

_____

THE BEM SEX ROLE INVENTORY
EXPLAINED

Note: The number preceding each item reflects the position of each adjective as it actually appears on the Inventory. A subject indicates how well each item describes himself or herself on the following scale: (1) never or almost never true; (2) usually not true; (3) sometimes but infrequently true; (4) occasionally true; (5) often true: (6) usually true; (7) always or almost always true.

Masculine items	Feminine items	Neutral items
____ 49. acts as a leader	____ 11. affectionate	____ 51. adaptable
____ 46. aggressive	____ 5. cheerful	____ 36. conceited
____ 58. ambitious	____ 50. childlike	____ 9. conscientious
____ 22. analytical	____ 32. compassionate	____ 60. conventional
____ 13. assertive	____ 53. does not use harsh	____ 45. friendly
____ 10. athletic	language	____ 15. happy
____ 55. competitive	____ 35. eager to soothe hurt	____ 3. helpful
____ 4. defends own beliefs	feelings	____ 48. inefficient
____ 37. dominant	____ 20. feminine	____ 24. jealous
____ 19. forceful	____ 14. flatterable	____ 39. likable
____ 25. has leadership abilities	____ 59. gentle	____ 6. moody
____ 7. independent	____ 47. gullible	____ 21. reliable
____ 52. individualistic	____ 56. loves children	____ 30. secretive
____ 31. makes decisions easily	____ 17. loyal	____ 33. sincere
____ 40. masculine	____ 26. sensitive to the needs of	____ 42. solemn
____ 1. self-reliant	others	____ 57. tactful
____ 34. self-sufficient	____ 8. shy	____ 12. theatrical
____ 16. strong personality	____ 38. soft spoken	____ 27. truthful
____ 43. willing to take a stand	____ 23. sympathetic	____ 18. unpredictable
____ 28. willing to take risks	____ 44. tender	____ 54. unsystematic
	____ 29. understanding	
	____ 41. warm	
	____ 2. yielding	

Scoring:

1. Add up the ratings for items 2, 5, 8, 11, 14, 17, 20, 23, 26, 29, 32, 35, 38, 41, 44, 47, 50, 53, 56, and 59, and divide the sum by twenty. This is the person's Femininity Score.

2. Add up the ratings for items 1, 4, 7, 10, 13, 16, 19, 22, 25, 28, 31, 34, 37, 40, 43, 46, 49, 52, 55, and 58, and divide the sum by twenty. This is the person's Masculinity Score.

3. Subtract the Masculinity Score from the Femininity Score, and multiply the result by 2.322. (This approximates the score derived by more complicated statistical procedures.) If the result is greater than 2.025, the person is sex-typed in the feminine direction. If it is smaller than −2.025, the person is sex-typed in the masculine direction. Bem considers a score between 1 and 2.025 to be "near feminine" and a score between −2.025 and −1 to be "near masculine." A score between −1 and 1 means the person is not sex-typed in either direction: he or she is androgynous.

Age _____

Sex _____

ATTITUDE QUESTIONNAIRE

Instructions: Indicate on a scale of 1-7 how well each of the following characteristics describes you using the following scale: (1) never or almost never true; (2) usually not true; (3) sometimes but infrequently true; (4) occasionally true; (5) often true; (6) usually true; (7) always or almost always true.

_____ 1. self-reliant
_____ 2. yielding
_____ 3. helpful
_____ 4. defends own beliefs
_____ 5. cheerful
_____ 6. moody
_____ 7. independent
_____ 8. shy
_____ 9. conscientious
_____ 10. athletic
_____ 11. affectionate
_____ 12. theatrical
_____ 13. assertive
_____ 14. flatterable
_____ 15. happy
_____ 16. strong personality
_____ 17. loyal
_____ 18. unpredictable
_____ 19. forceful
_____ 20. feminine

_____ 21. reliable
_____ 22. analytical
_____ 23. sympathetic
_____ 24. jealous
_____ 25. has leadership abilities
_____ 26. sensitive to the needs of others
_____ 27. truthful
_____ 28. willing to take risks
_____ 29. understanding
_____ 30. secretive
_____ 31. makes decisions easily
_____ 32. compassionate
_____ 33. sincere
_____ 34. self-sufficient
_____ 35. eager to soothe hurt feelings
_____ 36. conceited
_____ 37. dominant
_____ 38. soft spoken
_____ 39. likable
_____ 40. masculine

_____ 41. warm
_____ 42. solemn
_____ 43. willing to take a stand
_____ 44. tender
_____ 45. friendly
_____ 46. aggressive
_____ 47. gullible
_____ 48. inefficient
_____ 49. acts as a leader
_____ 50. childlike
_____ 51. adaptable
_____ 52. individualistic
_____ 53. does not use harsh language
_____ 54. unsystematic
_____ 55. competitive
_____ 56. loves children
_____ 57. tactful
_____ 58. ambitious
_____ 59. gentle
_____ 60. conventional

Age _____
Sex _____

ATTITUDE QUESTIONNAIRE

Instructions: Indicate on a scale of 1–7 how well each of the following characteristics describes you using the following scale: (1) never or almost never true; (2) usually not true; (3) sometimes but infrequently true; (4) occasionally true; (5) often true; (6) usually true; (7) always or almost always true.

_____ 1. self-reliant
_____ 2. yielding
_____ 3. helpful
_____ 4. defends own beliefs
_____ 5. cheerful
_____ 6. moody
_____ 7. independent
_____ 8. shy
_____ 9. conscientious
_____ 10. athletic
_____ 11. affectionate
_____ 12. theatrical
_____ 13. assertive
_____ 14. flatterable
_____ 15. happy
_____ 16. strong personality
_____ 17. loyal
_____ 18. unpredictable
_____ 19. forceful
_____ 20. feminine

_____ 21. reliable
_____ 22. analytical
_____ 23. sympathetic
_____ 24. jealous
_____ 25. has leadership abilities
_____ 26. sensitive to the needs of others
_____ 27. truthful
_____ 28. willing to take risks
_____ 29. understanding
_____ 30. secretive
_____ 31. makes decisions easily
_____ 32. compassionate
_____ 33. sincere
_____ 34. self-sufficient
_____ 35. eager to soothe hurt feelings
_____ 36. conceited
_____ 37. dominant
_____ 38. soft spoken
_____ 39. likable
_____ 40. masculine

_____ 41. warm
_____ 42. solemn
_____ 43. willing to take a stand
_____ 44. tender
_____ 45. friendly
_____ 46. aggressive
_____ 47. gullible
_____ 48. inefficient
_____ 49. acts as a leader
_____ 50. childlike
_____ 51. adaptable
_____ 52. individualistic
_____ 53. does not use harsh language
_____ 54. unsystematic
_____ 55. competitive
_____ 56. loves children
_____ 57. tactful
_____ 58. ambitious
_____ 59. gentle
_____ 60. conventional

Name _____

Date _____

4.2: CONFRONTATION THROUGH ROLE PLAYING

The goal of the following exercise is to demonstrate, through role playing techniques, some of the issues discussed in this chapter. Familiarize yourself with the background information and the issues presented below until you feel you could comfortably play either role in a confrontation between the principal and the superintendent. You will then be prepared to proceed with the exercise. The roles of principal and superintendent will be assigned by your instructor, who will explain the circumstances of the confrontation.

BACKGROUND INFORMATION

COMMUNITY: About 60,000 people. Conservative values with respect to education. A typical community for its size.

SUPERINTENDENT: Has doctorate in school administration. Twenty years in public education. On present job for five years; came from outside of state. Has made progress improving schools, but moves cautiously.

JUNIOR HIGH SCHOOL PRINCIPAL: Has master's degree in school administration. Second principalship. Total of five years in school administration; nine years in public education. On present job for two years. Came from another state. Predecessor retired after thirty-five years as teacher and principal (fifteen years as principal of the school in question).

SCHOOL: Three years old; modern construction; modern equipment; traditional curriculum.

FACULTY: About equally divided according to age, experience, philosophy, methodology, and so on.

ISSUES

VANDALISM: Apparently increasing. Maintenance staff reports repeated calls for service to ceiling tiles, lavatory partitions, mirrors, marks on walls, blocked sinks, broken faucets.

DISCIPLINE: Disciplinary referrals are running high (there are usually two or three students waiting for the assistant principal). The secretaries complain about the noise; parents are upset when they come into school. Fighting occurs every few days. In addition, food is thrown in cafeteria, and cafeteria workers say students complain rudely about food and are generally impolite.

FACULTY: Older faculty complain about "permissiveness"; they say that the school was run better by former principal, that students knew where they stood. They question need to promote more classroom discussions, student projects, and the like. Young faculty want to move ahead; they enjoy the freedom of the school. Their classrooms tend to be noisier than those of most of the staff veterans because they encourage a greater number of discussions and projects.

PARENTS: There have been several letters to the editor in the local paper in recent months regarding disciplining of students and apparent lack of firmness; the letter writers want less talking to students and more action. Some parents complain that the veteran teachers are frequently unfair in dealing with students; they like most of the young staff and its methods but are quick to criticize its weaknesses.

5

AFFILIATION

One of the basic assumptions of social psychology is that people are "social animals." That is, they live with other people, interact with others, influence others, and are affected by others. John Donne eloquently stated this principle: "No man is an island, entire of itself; every man is a piece of the continent. . . ."

Clearly, all of us are social beings. But why is this so? What do we get from other people that we could not get from ourselves? Why do we seem to need others so much? To begin with, other people are necessary for our basic survival. As infants or young children, we cannot care for ourselves. Furthermore, we need people to teach us language, as well as intellectual and motor skills. We turn to other people for information about the world and for help and guidance in dealing with it. We achieve self-knowledge through other people's reactions to us—that is, how we see ourselves is to a large extent determined by whether we are loved or neglected, approved of or disapproved of, encouraged or discouraged by others. Although we may feel that we could do without particular people, we cannot do without them all. Everyone in the world needs people, and the most fortunate may be those who recognize those needs and satisfy them successfully.

WHEN BELIEF CREATES REALITY: THE SELF-FULFILLING IMPACT OF FIRST IMPRESSIONS ON SOCIAL INTERACTION

MARK SNYDER

How do you come to know and like another person? Presumably, it is a fairly straightforward process in which you observe what the other person is like and then decide whether you are attracted to him or her. However, the assumption that you are the passive observer of another person's inherent charms and foibles may be quite erroneous. According to Snyder in "When Belief Creates Reality," you are more likely to be the active creator of the person you think you see. That is, your initial impression of what a person is "really" like will determine how you behave toward him or her, and your behavior will, in turn, shape the person's responses in ways that confirm

99

your initial expectations. The lesson to be learned from this process is that what you find beautiful or ugly about another person often reflects what is beautiful or ugly about yourself.

For the social psychologist, there may be no processes more complex and intriguing than those by which strangers become friends. How do we form first impressions of those we encounter in our lives? How do we become acquainted with each other? When does an acquaintance become a friend? Why do some relationships develop and withstand the test of time and other equally promising relationships flounder and fall by the wayside? It is to these and similar concerns that my colleagues and I have addressed ourselves in our attempts to chart the unfolding dynamics of social interaction and interpersonal relationships. In doing so, we chose—not surprisingly—to begin at the beginning. Specifically, we have been studying the ways in which first impressions channel and influence subsequent social interaction and acquaintance processes.

When we first meet others, we cannot help but notice certain highly visible and distinctive characteristics such as their sex, age, race, and bodily appearance. Try as we may to avoid it, our first impressions are often molded and influenced by these pieces of information. Consider the case of physical attractiveness. A widely held stereotype in this culture suggests that attractive people are assumed to possess more socially desirable personalities and are expected to lead better personal, social, and occupational lives than their unattractive counterparts. For example, Dion, Berscheid, and Walster (1972) had men and women judge photographs of either men or women who varied in physical attractiveness. Attractive stimulus persons of either sex were perceived to have virtually every character trait that pretesting

© 1977 by Mark Snyder.

This research was supported in part by National Science Foundation Grant SOC 75-13872, "Cognition and Behavior: When Belief Creates Reality," to Mark Snyder. For a more detailed description of the background and rationale, procedures and results, implications and consequences of this investigation, see M. Snyder, E. D. Tanke, & E. Berscheid, Social perception and interpersonal behavior: On the self-fulfilling nature of social stereotypes. *Journal of Personality and Social Psychology*, 1977. For related research on behavioral confirmation in social interaction, see M. Snyder & W. B. Swann, Jr., Behavioral confirmation in social interaction: From social perception to social reality. *Journal of Experimental Social Psychology*, 1978.

had indicated was socially desirable to that participant population: "Physically attractive people, for example, were perceived to be more sexually warm and responsive, sensitive, kind, interesting, strong, poised, modest, sociable, and outgoing than persons of lesser physical attractiveness" (Berscheid & Walster, 1974, p. 169). This powerful stereotype was found for male and female judges and for male and female stimulus persons. In addition, attractive people were predicted to have happier social, professional, and personal lives in store for them than were their less attractive counterparts. (For an excellent and comprehensive review, see Berscheid & Walster, 1974.)

What of the validity of the physical attractiveness stereotype? Are the physically attractive actually more likable, friendly, sensitive, and confident than the unattractive? Are they more successful socially and professionally? Clearly, the physically attractive are more often and more eagerly sought out for social dates. And well they should be, for the stereotype implies that they should be perceived as more desirable social partners than the physically unattractive. Thus, it should come as little surprise that, among young adults, the physically attractive have more friends of the other sex, engage in more sexual activity, report themselves in love more often, and express less anxiety about dating than unattractive individuals do. But the effect is even more general than this. Even as early as nursery school age, physical attractiveness appears to channel social interaction: The physically attractive are chosen and the unattractive are rejected in sociometric choices.

A differential amount of interaction with the attractive and unattractive clearly helps the stereotype persevere because it limits the chances for learning whether the two types of individuals differ in the traits associated with the stereotype. But the point I wish to focus on here is that the stereotype may also channel interaction so as to confirm itself *behaviorally*. Individuals appear to have different patterns and styles of interaction for those whom they perceive to be physically attractive and for those whom they consider unattractive. These differences in self-presentation and interaction style may, in turn, elicit and nurture behaviors from the target person that are in accord with the stereotype. That is, the physically attractive may actually come to behave in a friendly, likable, sociable manner, not because they necessarily possess these dispositions, but because the behavior of others elicits and maintains behaviors taken to be manifestations of such traits.

In our empirical research, we have attempted to demonstrate that stereotypes may create their own social reality by channeling social interaction in ways that cause the stereotyped individual to behave in ways that confirm another person's stereotyped impressions of him or her. In our initial investigation, Elizabeth Decker Tanke, Ellen Berscheid, and I sought to demonstrate the self-fulfilling nature of the physical attractiveness stereotype in a social interaction context designed to mirror as faithfully as possible the spontaneous generation of first impressions in everyday social interaction and the subsequent channeling influences of these impressions on social interaction. In order to do so, pairs of previously unacquainted individuals (designated for our purposes as a *perceiver* and a *target*) interacted in a getting-acquainted situation constructed to allow us to control the information that one member of the dyad (the male perceiver) received about the physical attractiveness of the other individual (the female target). In this way, it was possible to evaluate separately the effects of actual and perceived physical attractiveness on the display of self-presentational and expressive behaviors associated with the stereotype that links beauty and goodness. In order to measure the extent to which the self-presentation of the target individual matched the perceiver's stereotype, naïve observer-judges who were unaware of the actual or perceived physical attractiveness of either participant listened to and evaluated tape recordings of the interaction.

Fifty-one male and fifty-one female undergraduates at the University of Minnesota participated, for extra course credit, in what had been described as a study of the "processes by which people become acquainted with each other." These individuals interacted in male-female dyads in a getting-acquainted situation in which they could hear but not see each other (a telephone conversation). Before initiating the conversation, the male member of each dyad received a Polaroid snapshot of his female interaction partner. These photographs, which had been prepared in advance and assigned at random to dyads, identified the target as either physically attractive (attractive-target condition) or physically unattractive (unattractive-target condition). Each dyad engaged in a ten-minute unstructured telephone conversation that was tape-recorded. Each partici-

pant's voice was recorded on a separate channel of the tape.

In order to assess the extent to which the actions of the female targets provided behavioral confirmation of the male perceivers' stereotypes, twelve observer-judges listened to the tape recordings of the getting-acquainted conversations. The observer-judges were unaware of the experimental hypotheses and knew nothing of the actual or perceived physical attractiveness of the individual whom they heard on the tapes. They heard only those tape tracks containing the female participants' voices. Nine other observer-judges listened to and rated only the male perceivers' voices. (For further details of the experimental procedures, see Snyder, Tanke, & Berscheid, 1977.)

In order to chart the process of behavioral confirmation of stereotype-based attributions in these dyadic social interactions, we examined the effects of our manipulation of the target's apparent physical attractiveness on both the male perceivers' initial impressions of their female targets and the females' behavioral self-presentation during their interactions, as measured by the observer-judges' ratings of the tape recordings of their voices.

The male perceivers clearly formed their initial impressions of their female targets on the basis of general stereotypes that associate physical attractiveness with socially desirable personality characteristics. On the basis of measures of first impressions that were collected after the perceivers had been given access to their partners' photographs but before the initiation of the getting-acquainted conversations, it was clear that (as dictated by the physical attractiveness stereotype) males who anticipated physically attractive partners expected to interact with comparatively cordial, poised, humorous, and socially adept individuals. By contrast, males faced with the prospect of getting acquainted with relatively unattractive partners fashioned images of rather withdrawn, awkward, serious, and socially inept creatures.

Not only did our perceivers fashion their images of their discussion partners on the basis of their stereotyped intuitions about the links between beauty and goodness of character, but the stereotype-based attributions initiated a chain of events that resulted in the behavioral confirmation of these initially erroneous inferences. Analysis of the observer-judges' ratings of the tape recordings of the conversations indicated that female targets who (unbeknown to them) were perceived to be physically attractive (as a consequence of random assignment to the attractive-target experimental condition) actually came to behave in a friendly, likable, and sociable manner. This behavioral confirmation was discernible even by outside observer-judges who knew nothing of the actual or perceived physical attractiveness of the target individuals. In this demonstration of behavioral confirmation in social interaction, the "beautiful" people became "good" people, not because they necessarily possessed the socially valued dispositions that had been attributed to them, but because the actions of the perceivers, which were based on their stereotyped beliefs, had erroneously confirmed and validated these attributions.

Confident in our demonstration of the self-fulfilling nature of this particular social stereotype, we then attempted to chart the process of behavioral confirmation. Specifically, we searched for evidence of the behavioral implications of the perceivers' stereotypes. Did the male perceivers present themselves differently to the target women whom they assumed to be physically attractive or unattractive? An examination of the observer-judges' ratings of the tapes of only the males' contributions to the conversations provided clear evidence that our perceivers did have different interactional styles with targets of different physical attractiveness.

Men who interacted with women whom they believed to be physically attractive appeared . . . to be more cordial, sexually warm, interesting, independent, sexually permissive, bold, outgoing, humorous, obvious, and socially adept than their counterparts in the unattractive-target condition. Moreover, these same men were seen by the judges to be more attractive, more confident, and more animated in their conversation than their counterparts. They were also considered by the observer-judges to be more comfortable in conversation, to enjoy themselves more, to like their partners more, to take the initiative more often, to use their voices more effectively, to see their women partners as more attractive, and finally, to be seen as more attractive by their partners than men in the unattractive-target condition.

It appears, then, that differences in the expressive self-presentation of sociability by the male perceivers may have been a key factor in the process of bringing out those reciprocal patterns of expression in the target women that constitute behavioral confirmation of the attributions from which the perceivers' self-presentation had been generated. One reason that target women who had been labeled attractive may have reciprocated this sociable self-presentation is that they regarded their partners' images of them as more accurate and their style of interaction to be more typical of the way men generally treated them than women in the unattractive-target condition did. Perhaps, these latter individuals rejected their partners' treatment of them as unrepresentative and defensively adopted more cool and aloof postures to cope with their situations.

Our research points to the powerful but often unnoticed consequences of social stereotypes. In our demonstration, first impressions and expectations that were based on common cultural stereotypes about physical attractiveness channeled the unfolding dynamics of social interaction and acquaintance processes in ways that actually made those stereotyped first impressions come true. In our investigation, pairs of individuals got acquainted with each other in a situation that allowed us to control the information that one member of the dyad (the perceiver) received about the physical attractiveness of the other person (the target). Our perceivers . . . fashioned erroneous images of their specific partners that reflected their general stereotypes about physical attractiveness. Moreover, our perceivers had very different patterns and styles of interaction for those whom they perceived to be physically attractive and to be unattractive. These differences in self-presentation and interaction style, in turn, elicited and nurtured behaviors of the targets that were consistent with the perceivers' initial stereotypes. Targets who (unbeknown to them) were perceived to be physically attractive actually came to behave in a friendly, likable, and sociable manner. The perceivers' attributions about their targets based on their stereotyped intuitions about the world had initiated a process that produced behavioral confirmation of those attributions. The initially erroneous impressions of the perceivers had become real. The stereotype had truly functioned as a self-fulfilling prophecy:

> The self-fulfilling prophecy is, in the beginning, a *false* definition of the situation evoking a new behavior which makes the originally false conception come *true*. The specious validity of the self-fulfilling prophecy perpetuates a reign of error. For the prophet will cite the actual course of events as proof that he was right from the very beginning. . . . Such are the perversities of social logic. [Merton 1948, p. 195]

True to Merton's script, our "prophets," in the beginning, created false definitions of their situations. That is, they erroneously labeled their targets as sociable or unsociable persons on the basis of their physical attractiveness. But these mistakes in first impressions quickly became self-erasing mistakes because the perceivers' false definitions evoked new behaviors that made their originally false conceptions come true: They treated their targets as sociable or unsociable persons, and, indeed, these targets came to behave in a sociable or unsociable fashion. Our prophets also cited the actual course of events as proof that they had been right all along. That is, after their getting-acquainted conversations, the men confidently pointed to the sociable or unsociable behavior of their target women as evidence of their sociable or unsociable natures. Such is the power of stereotypes: Belief had created reality!

Might not other important and widespread social stereotypes—particularly those concerning sex, race, social class, and ethnicity—also channel social interaction in ways that create their own social reality? For example, will the common stereotype that women are more conforming and less independent than men . . . influence interaction so that . . . targets believed to be female will actually conform more, be more dependent,

and be more successfully manipulated than targets believed to be male? At least one empirical investigation has pointed to the possible self-fulfilling nature of apparent sex differences in self-presentation (Zanna & Pack, 1975).

Any self-fulfilling influences of social stereotypes may have compelling and pervasive societal consequences. Social observers have for decades commented on and demonstrated the ways in which stigmatized social groups and outsiders may fall victim to self-fulfilling cultural stereotypes. Consider Scott's (1969) observations about the blind:

> When, for example, sighted people continually insist that a blind man is helpless because he is blind, their subsequent treatment of him may preclude his own exercising the kinds of skills that would enable him to be independent. It is in this sense that stereotypic beliefs are self-actualized. [P. 9]

All too often, it is the victims who are blamed for their own plight . . . rather than the social expectations that have constrained their behavioral options.

REFERENCES

Berscheid, E., & Walster, E. Physical attractiveness. In L. Berkowitz (Ed.), *Advances in Experimental Social Psychology.* Vol. 7. New York: Academic Press, 1974.

Dion, K. K., Berscheid, E., & Walster, E. What is good is beautiful. *Journal of Personality and Social Psychology,* 1972, *24,* 285–290.

Merton, R. K. The self-fulfilling prophecy. *Antioch Review,* 1948, *8,* 193–210.

Scott, R. A. *The Making of Blind Men.* New York: Russell Sage, 1969.

Snyder, M., Tanke, E. D., & Berscheid, E. Social perception and interpersonal behavior: On the self-fulfilling nature of social stereotypes. *Journal of Personality and Social Psychology,* 1977, *35,* 656–666.

Zanna, M. P., & Pack, S. J. On the self-fulfilling nature of apparent sex differences in behavior. *Journal of Experimental Social Psychology,* 1975, *11,* 583–591.

"THE VOICE"

Safe in the magic of my woods
   I lay, and watched the dying light.
Faint in the pale high solitudes,
   And washed with rain and veiled
     by night,
Silver and blue and green were show-
     ing.

And the dark woods grew darker
   still;
And birds were hushed; and peace
   was growing;
And quietness crept up the hill;

And no wind was blowing

Were one together, and I should find
Soon in the silence the hidden key
Of all that had hurt and puzzled me—
Why you were you, and the night
   was kind,
And the woods were part of the heart
   of me.

And I knew
That this was the hour of knowing,
And the night and the woods and
   you

And there I waited breathlessly,
Alone; and slowly the holy three,
The three that I loved, together grew
One, in the hour of knowing,

Night, and the woods, and you——
And suddenly
There was an uproar in my woods,

The noise of a fool in mock distress,
Crashing and laughing and blindly
    going,
Of ignorant feet and a swishing dress,
And a Voice profaning the solitudes.

The spell was broken, the key denied
    me
And at length your flat clear voice
    beside me
Mouthed cheerful clear flat platitudes.

You came and quacked beside me
    in the wood.
You said, "The view from here is very
    good!"

You said, "It's nice to be alone a
    bit!"
And, "How the days are drawing
    out!" you said.
You said, "The sunset's pretty, isn't
    it?"

* * *

By God! I wish—I wish that you were
    dead!

PSYCHOLOGISTS AND LOVE

Let's take a one-item test. February's most popular date will be (A) Feb. 2 (Groundhog day), (B) Feb. 12 (Lincoln's Birthday), (C) Feb. 18 (start of the Chinese New Year), (D) Feb. 22 (Washington's Birthday), or (E) None of the above.

The answer is as plain as the nose on Cyrano de Bergerac's face, at least to those who know that *love is sweeping the country* because *what the world needs now is love. Love makes the world go round,* both for the teenager who's *younger than springtime* and the octogenarian who claims that even though *my heart stood still . . . it's never too late to love.* Make no mistake about it, it is love love love, and it is neither chance nor high camp that has kept alive for *sweethearts forever* that cloyingly sentimental ballad, *Indian love call* ("When I'm calling you-oo-oo-oo-oo-oo-oo-oo, will you answer too-oo-oo-oo-oo-oo-oo?").

Give yourself a perfect score if you selected (E), none of the above, because far and away the most beloved date in February, and possibly in the entire year as well, is Feb. 14, St. Valentine's Day. No more proof of this is needed than the torrent of long distance calls lovers make on that day, not to mention lovers' trysts over candlelight dinners seasoned *tenderly* with soft music while *dancing cheek*

to cheek. And don't forget the tons of candy, truckloads of flowers and bales of valentine cards whose sales gorge February's cash registers from coast to coast.

The paradox of all this is that so few psychologists are into love, with the notable exceptions (1) of Harry Harlow's celebrated studies probing the nature of love in monkeys and (2) of scientific voyeurs like Ellen Berscheid, Donn Byrne, Zick Rubin and Elaine Walster, who muse whether *I love you truly* loads more on the *I can't stop loving you* factor than on the factor tentatively identified as *I got it bad and that ain't good.* Although *they say that falling in love is wonderful,* Zick and Donn and Elaine and Ellen constitute a chillingly bare minority of psychologists willing to observe love in the field, or manipulate it in the laboratory.

The power of love to generate seminal hypotheses and to impact upon society is enormous. Freud, for example, realized early on that for most people it is a base canard that *it doesn't cost you anything to dream.* Scientific concepts of love and its correlates have inspired popular songs. A case in point is Freud's Electra complex, which sparked the hit tune, *My heart belongs to daddy,* while research by developmental psychologists analyzing infant behavior triggered such money-makers as *I'll be your baby tonight* and *I can't give you anything but love, baby.*

Although a handful of psychologists—exemplified by trailblazers Zick and Donn and Elaine and

Ellen—are *lucky in love* because they have been *doin' what comes naturally,* psychologists have generally avoided love like *the devil and the deep blue sea.* This is documented in Fred McKinney's "Fifty Years of Psychology" (*American Psychologist,* December 1976), where terms like learning, set, temperament, cognition, meaning and symbolism are in abundance, but, oh, Fred, I ask you, Fred, *where is love? Where is love?* When I discovered that psychology has been bereft of love lo these past 50 years, *zing! went the strings of my heart.* I wondered *what kind of fool am I* to identify with a learned discipline which tells love *I hate you, darling.* As *bewitched, bothered and bewildered am I* by a loveless psychology as by thought of a rockless geology, a numberless mathematics or a matterless physics.

Psychologists who study love use impotent terms like "affiliation," "dependency," "mate selection," "penetration (social)," "romance," "relationships (meaningful)" and "self-esteem." Yet, in *Bartlett's Familiar Quotations* the foregoing words average less than one inch of space, whereas to "love" a whopping 139 inches is allocated! While lovers adjure one another in plain and endearing language to *light my fire, love me tender* and *love me tonight,* all that we psychologists can prattle about is—ugh!—attraction, courtship, involvement, popularity and romantic choices. But *where is love?* Poets, lyricists, balladeers, troubadors, and copywriters caress us with

From Robert Perloff, "Standard Deviations," *APA Monitor,* 8(2):3, 1977. Copyright 1977 by the American Psychological Association. Reprinted by permission.

streams and dreams, lips and trips, thrills and chills, charms and arms, trees and bees, and June and moon and spoon. No offense, Zick and Donn and Elaine and Ellen, but better you should deluge us with more of your streams and dreams and lips and trips, and skip all that jazz about body image, satisfaction, personality, likableness and assertiveness. Let us not pooh-pooh the fact that lovers are turned on by the words and music of Irving Berlin (to whom President Ford awarded the Medal of Freedom on Jan. 10), Bob Dylan, the Jefferson Airplane, Jerome Kern, Cole Porter and The Who.

MEASUREMENT OF ROMANTIC LOVE

ZICK RUBIN

It is likely that more has been written about love than about any other human experience. Given this overwhelming preoccupation, it is somewhat surprising to discover that love has not been a major topic of study by social psychologists. Indeed, it is only within the last ten years that they have taken a systematic look at love, and the article that follows, "Measurement of Romantic Love," reports one of the first of these research projects.

Why have psychologists paid so little attention to love? There are several possible answers. The behaviorist tradition in psychology has led researchers to focus on observable external behavior. Because love is considered an internal emotion, it may have been regarded as not particularly susceptible to scientific study. Furthermore, the popular view of love is that it is a mystical, ineffable state that cannot be precisely defined or described, only experienced. To the extent that psychologists agreed with this viewpoint, they may not have considered studying love, at least not until the recent development of research on various states of consciousness. Another explanation is that there is a general bias in psychology toward studying pathologies. In other words, more attention is focused on such things as mental illness, prejudice, and aggression, all of which cause some form of personal and social suffering and demand immediate solutions. Because love is not considered to be a problem in the same sense, there has been no comparable sense of an urgent need to study it. Finally, there is the popular belief that the scientific study of something as mysterious as love will only destroy it in some way, and thus there is the recurring admonition to scientists to leave well enough alone. Some of these attitudes were reflected in Senator William Proxmire's recent criticism of federally funded research on love and attraction, to which he gave a "Golden Fleece Award" for apparently absurd expenditures of taxpayers' money. These attitudes also occur with some regularity in springtime newspaper editorials decrying any attempt to objectify love (see the boxed excerpt "Psychologists and Love").

The research described by Rubin has itself been criticized on these grounds. Some people have felt that it is absurd to use a scale to measure love. Others have taken a "So, what else is new?" attitude about his findings. Nevertheless, this research is important for breaking new theoretical ground and for helping to open the doors to a new area of scientific concern. And in view of the enormous problems in and failures of love relationships (as reflected in divorce statistics, the numbers of people who seek outside help for their love problems, articles in print about such problems, and so on), it would serve the cause of greater human happiness and well-being to give serious study to the subject.

Love is generally regarded to be the deepest and most meaningful of sentiments. It has occupied a preeminent position in the art and literature of every age, and it is presumably experienced, at least occasionally, by the vast majority of people. In Western culture, moreover, the association between love and marriage gives it a unique status as a link between the individual and the structure of society.

In view of these considerations, it is surprising to discover that social psychologists have devoted virtually no attention to love. Although interpersonal attraction has been a major focus of social-psychological theory and research, workers in this area have not attempted to conceptualize love as an independent entity. For Heider (1958), for example, "loving" is merely intense liking—there is no discussion of possible qualitative differences between the two. Newcomb (1960) does not include love on his list of the "varieties of interpersonal attraction." Even in experiments directed specifically at "romantic" attraction . . . , the dependent measure is simply a verbal report of "liking."

The present research was predicated on the assumption that love may be independently conceptualized and measured. In keeping with a strategy of construct validation, the attempts to define love, to measure it, and to assess its relationships to other variables are all seen as parts of a single endeavor. An initial assumption in this enterprise is that love is an *attitude* held by a person toward a particular other person, involving predispositions to think, feel, and behave in certain ways toward that other person. This assumption places love in the mainstream of social-psychological approaches to interpersonal attraction, alongside such other varieties of attraction as liking, admiration, and respect.

The view of love as a multifaceted attitude implies a broader perspective than that held by those theorists who view love as an "emotion," a "need," or a set of behaviors. On the other hand, its linkage to a particular target implies a more restricted view than that held by those who regard love as an aspect of the individual's personality or experience which transcends particular persons and situations. As Orlinsky (1972) has suggested,

there may well be important common elements among different varieties of "love" (e.g., filial love, marital love, love of God). The focus of the present research, however, was restricted to *romantic love*, which may be defined simply as love between unmarried opposite-sex peers, of the sort which could possibly lead to marriage.

The research had three major phases. First, a paper-and-pencil love scale was developed. Second, the love scale was employed in a questionnaire study of student dating couples. Third, the predictive validity of the love scale was assessed in a laboratory experiment.

DEVELOPING A LOVE SCALE

The development of a love scale was guided by several considerations:

1. Inasmuch as the content of the scale would constitute the initial conceptual definition of romantic love, its items must be grounded in existing theoretical and popular conceptions of love.

2. Responses to these items, if they are tapping a single underlying attitude, must be highly intercorrelated.

3. In order to establish the discriminant validity of the love scale, it was constructed in conjunction with a parallel scale of liking. The goal was to develop internally consistent scales of love and of liking which would be conceptually distinct from one another and which would, in practice, be only moderately intercorrelated.

The first step in this procedure was the assembling of a large pool of questionnaire items referring to a respondent's attitude toward a particular other person (the "target person"). Half of these items were suggested by a wide range of speculations about the nature of love. These items referred to physical attraction, idealization, a predisposition to help, the desire to share emotions and experiences, feelings of exclusiveness and absorption, felt affiliative and dependent needs, the holding of ambivalent feelings, and the relative unimportance of universalistic norms in the relationship. The other half of the items were suggested by the existing theoretical and empirical literature on interpersonal attraction (or liking). They included references to the desire to affiliate with the target in various settings, evaluation of the target on several dimensions, the salience of norms of responsibility and equity, feelings of respect and trust, and the perception that the target is similar to oneself. . . .

To provide some degree of consensual validation for this initial categorization of items, two successive panels of student and faculty judges sorted the items into love and liking categories, relying simply on their personal understanding of the connotations of the two labels. Following this screening procedure, a revised set of 70 items was administered to 198 introductory psychology students during their regular class sessions. Each respondent completed the items with reference to his girlfriend or boyfriend (if he had one), and also with reference to a nonromantically viewed "platonic friend" of the opposite sex. The scales of love and of liking which were employed in the subsequent phases of the research were arrived at through factor analyses of these responses. . . . There was a general factor accounting for a large proportion of the total variance. The items loading highest on this general factor, particularly for lovers, were almost exclusively those which had previously been categorized as love items. These high-loading items defined the more circumscribed conception of love adopted. The items forming the liking scale were based on those which loaded highly on the second factor with respect to platonic friends. . . .

1. *Affiliative and dependent need*—for example, "If I could never be with———, I would feel miserable"; "It would be hard for me to get along without———."

2. *Predisposition to help*—for example, "If——— were feeling badly, my first duty would be to cheer him (her) up"; "I would do almost anything for ———."

3. *Exclusiveness and absorption*—for example, "I feel very possessive toward———"; "I feel that I can confide in———about virtually everything."

The emerging conception of romantic love, as defined by the content of the scale, has an eclectic flavor. The affiliative and dependent need component evokes both Freud's (1955) view of love as sublimated sexuality and Harlow's (1958) equation of love with attachment behavior. The predisposition to help is congruent with Fromm's (1956) analysis of the components of love, which he identifies as care, responsibility, respect, and knowledge. Absorption in a single other person

is the aspect of love which is pointed to most directly by Slater's (1963) analysis of the social-structural implications of dyadic intimacy. The conception of liking, as defined by the liking-scale items, includes components of favorable evaluation and respect for the target person, as well as the perception that the target is similar to oneself. It is in reasonably close accord with measures of "attraction" employed in previous research.

QUESTIONNAIRE STUDY

The 13-item love and liking scales, with their component items interspersed, were included in a questionnaire administered in October 1968 to 158 dating (but non-engaged) couples at the University of Michigan, recruited by means of posters and newspaper ads. In addition to the love and liking scales, completed first with respect to one's dating partner and later with respect to a close, same-sex friend, the questionnaire contained several personality scales and requests for background information about the dating relationship. Each partner completed the questionnaire individually and was paid $1 for taking part. The modal couple consisted of a junior man and a sophomore or junior woman who had been dating for about 1 year. . . .

The love scale had high internal consistency and, as desired, was only moderately correlated with the liking scale. The finding that love and liking were more highly correlated among men than among women was unexpected. It provides at least suggestive support for the notion that women discriminate more sharply between the two sentiments than men do. . . .

The love scores of men (for their girlfriends) and women (for their boyfriends) were almost identical. Women *liked* their boyfriends somewhat more than they were liked in return, however. Inspection of the item means in Table 1 indicates that this sex difference may be attributed to the higher ratings given by women to their boyfriends on such "task-related" dimensions as intelligence, good judgment, and leadership potential. To the extent that these items accurately represent the construct of liking, men may indeed tend to be more "likable" (but not more "lovable") than women. There was no such sex difference with respect to the respondents' liking for their same-sex friends. The mean liking-for-friend scores for the two sexes were virtually identical. Thus, the data do not support the conclusion that men are generally more likable than women, but only that they are liked more in the context of the dating relationship.

Women tended to *love* their same-sex friends more than men did. This result is in accord with cultural stereotypes concerning male and female friendships. It is more socially acceptable for female than for male friends to speak of themselves as "loving" one another, and it has been reported that women tend to confide in same-sex friends more than men do (Jourard & Lasakow, 1958). Finally, . . . whereas both women and men *liked* their dating partners only slightly more than they liked their same-sex friends, they *loved* their dating partners much more than their friends. . . .

Although love scores were highly related to perceived marriage probability, these variables may be distinguished from one another on empirical as well as conceptual grounds. The length of time that the couple had been dating was unrelated to love scores among men, and only slightly related among women. In contrast, the respondents' perceptions of their closeness to marriage were significantly correlated with length of dating among both men and women. These results are in keeping with the common observations that although love may develop rather quickly, progress toward marriage typically occurs only over a longer period of time. . . .

LABORATORY EXPERIMENT: LOVE AND GAZING

Although the questionnaire results provided evidence for the construct validity of the emerging conception of romantic love, it remained to be determined whether love-scale scores could be used to predict behavior outside the realm of questionnaire responses. The notion that romantic love includes a component of exclusiveness and absorption led to the prediction that in an unstructured laboratory situation, dating partners who loved each other a great deal would gaze into one another's eyes more than would partners who loved each other to a lesser degree.

The test of the prediction involved a comparison between "strong-love" and "weak-love" couples, as categorized by their scores on the love scale. To control for the possibility that "strong" and "weak" lovers differ from one another in their more general interpersonal orientations, additional groups were included in which subjects were paired with opposite-sex strangers. The love scores of subjects in these "apart" groups were equated with those of the subjects who were paired

with their own dating partners (the "together" groups). In contrast to the prediction for the together groups, no difference in the amount of eye contact engaged in by the strong-apart and weak-apart groups was expected.

METHOD

Subjects

Two pools of subjects were established from among the couples who completed the questionnaire. Those couples in which both partners scored above the median on the love scale (92 or higher) were designated strong-love couples, and those in which both partners scored below the median were designated weak-love couples. Couples in which one partner scored above and the other below the median were not included in the experiment. Within each of the two pools, the couples were divided into two subgroups with approximately equal love scores. One subgroup in each pool was randomly designated as a together group, the other as an apart group. Subjects in the together group were invited to take part in the experiment together with their boyfriends or girlfriends. Subjects in the apart groups were requested to appear at the experimental session individually, where they would be paired with other people's boyfriends or girlfriends. Pairings in the apart conditions were made on the basis of scheduling convenience, with the additional guideline that women should not be paired with men who were younger than themselves. In this way, four experimental groups were created: strong together (19 pairs), weak together (19 pairs), strong apart (21 pairs), and weak apart (20 pairs). Only 5 of the couples contacted (not included in the above cell sizes) refused to participate—2 who had been preassigned to the strong together group, 2 to the weak together group, and 1 to the strong apart group. No changes in the preassignment of subjects to groups were requested or permitted. As desired, none of the pairs of subjects created in the apart groups were previously acquainted. Each subject was paid $1.25 for his participation.

Sessions

When both members of a scheduled pair had arrived at the laboratory, they were seated across a 52-inch table from one another in an observation room. The experimenter, a male graduate student, explained that the experiment was part of a study of communication among dating and unacquainted couples. The subjects were then asked to read a paragraph about "a couple contemplating marriage." They were told that they would subsequently discuss the case, and that their discussion would be tape recorded. The experimenter told the pair that it would take a few minutes for him to set up the tape recorder, and that meanwhile they could talk about anything except the case to be discussed. He then left the room. After 1 minute had elapsed (to allow the subjects to adapt themselves to the situation), their visual behavior was observed for a 3-minute period.

Measurement

The subjects' visual behavior was recorded by two observers stationed behind a one-way mirror, one facing each subject. Each observer pressed a button, which was connected to a cumulative clock, whenever the subject he was watching was looking across the table at his partner's face. The readings on these clocks provided measures of *individual gazing*. In addition, a third clock was activated whenever the two observers were pressing their buttons simultaneously. The reading on this clock provided a measure of *mutual gazing*. The mean percentage of agreement between pairs of observers in 12 reliability trials, interspersed among the experimental sessions, was 92.8. The observers never knew whether a pair of subjects was in a strong-love or weak-love group. They were sometimes able to infer whether the pair was in the together or the apart condition, however. Each observer's assignment alternated between watching the woman and watching the man in successive sessions.

RESULTS

Table 1 reveals that as predicted, there was a tendency for strong-together couples to engage in more mutual gazing (or "eye contact") than weak-together couples. Although there was also a tendency for strong-apart couples to make more eye contact than weak-apart couples, it was not a reliable one.

Another approach toward assessing the couples' visual behavior is to consider the percentage of "total gazing" time (i.e., the amount of time during which at least one of the partners was looking at the other) which was occupied by mutual gazing. This measure, to be referred to as *mutual focus*, differs from mutual gazing in that it specifi-

TABLE 1. MUTUAL GAZING (IN SECONDS)

GROUP	$\bar{X}$
Strong together	56.2
Weak together	44.7
Strong apart	46.7
Weak apart	40.0

TABLE 2. MUTUAL FOCUS

GROUP	$\bar{X}$
Strong together	44.0
Weak together	34.7
Strong apart	35.3
Weak apart	32.5

TABLE 3. INDIVIDUAL GAZING (IN SECONDS)

	WOMEN	MEN
GROUP	$\bar{X}$	$\bar{X}$
Strong together	98.7	83.7
Weak together	87.4	77.7
Strong apart	94.5	75.0
Weak apart	96.8	64.0

cally takes into account the individual gazing tendencies of the two partners. It is possible, for example, that neither member of a particular pair gazed very much at his partner, but that when they did gaze, they did so simultaneously. Such a pair would have a low mutual gazing score, but a high mutual focus score. Within certain limits, the converse of this situation is also possible. Using this measure (see Table 2), the difference between the strong-together and the weak-together groups was more striking than it was in the case of mutual gazing. The difference between the strong-apart and weak-apart groups was clearly not significant.

Finally, the individual gazing scores of subjects in the four experimental groups are presented in Table 3. The only significant finding was that in all groups, the women spent much more time looking at the men than the men spent looking at the women. Although there was a tendency for strong-together subjects of both sexes to look at their partners more than weak-together subjects, these comparisons did not approach significance.

DISCUSSION

The main prediction of the experiment was confirmed. Couples who were strongly in love, as categorized by their scores on the love scale, spent more time gazing into one another's eyes than did couples who were only weakly in love. With respect to the measure of individual gazing, however, the tendency for strong-together subjects to devote more time than the weak-together subjects to looking at their partners was not substantial for either women or men. This finding suggests that the obtained difference in mutual gazing between these two groups must be attributed to differences in the *simultaneousness*, rather than in the sheer quantity, of gazing. This conclusion is bolstered by the fact that the clearest difference between the strong-together and weak-together groups emerged on the percentage measure of mutual focus.

This pattern of results is in accord with the assumption that gazing is a manifestation of the exclusive and absorptive component of romantic love. Freud (1955) maintained that "The more [two people] are in love, the more completely they suffice for each other (p. 140)." More recently, Slater (1963) has linked Freud's theory of love to the popular concept of "the oblivious lovers, who are 'all wrapped up in each other,' and somewhat careless of their social obligations (p. 349)." One way in which this oblivious absorption may be manifested is through eye contact. As the popular song has it, "Millions of people go by, but they all disappear from view—'cause I only have eyes for you."

Another possible explanation for the findings is that people who are in love (or who complete attitude scales in such a way as to indicate that they are in love) are also the sort of people who are most predisposed to make eye contact with others, regardless of whether or not those others are the people they are in love with. The inclusion of the apart groups helped to rule out this possibility, however. Although there was a slight tendency for strong-apart couples to engage in more eye contact than weak-apart couples (see Table 2), it fell far short of significance. Moreover, when the percentage measure of mutual focus was employed (see Table 3), this difference virtually disappeared. It should be noted that no predictions were made concerning the comparisons between strong-together and strong-apart couples or between weak-together and weak-apart couples. It seemed plausible that unacquainted couples might make use of a relatively large amount of eye contact as a means of getting acquainted. The results indicate, in fact, that subjects in the apart groups typically engaged in as much eye contact as those in the weak-together group, with the strong-together subjects outgazing the other three groups. Future studies which systematically vary the extent to which partners are acquainted would be useful in specifying the acquaintance-seeking functions of eye contact.

The finding that in all experimental groups, women spent more time looking at men than vice versa may reflect the frequently reported tendency of women to specialize in the "social-emotional" aspects of interaction. Gazing may serve as a vehicle of emotional expression for women and, in addition, may allow women to obtain cues from their male partners concerning the appropriateness of their behavior. The present result is in accord with earlier findings that women tend to make more eye contact than men in same-sex groups and in an interview situation, regardless of the sex of the interviewer.

CONCLUSION

"So far as love or affection is concerned," Harlow wrote in 1958, "psychologists have failed in their mission. The little we know about love does not transcend simple observation, and the little we write about it has been written better by poets and novelists (p. 673)." The research reported in this paper represents an attempt to improve this situation by introducing and validating a preliminary social-psychological conception of romantic love. A distinction was drawn between love and liking, and its reasonableness was attested to by the results of the questionnaire study. It was found, for example, that respondents' estimates of the likelihood that they would marry their partners were more highly related to their love than to their liking for their partners. In light of the culturally prescribed association between love and marriage (but not necessarily between liking and marriage), this pattern of correlations seems appropriate. Other findings of the questionnaire study . . . point to the value of a measurable construct of romantic love as a link between the individual and social-structural levels of analysis of social behavior.

Although the present investigation was aimed at developing a unitary conception of romantic love, a promising direction for future research is the attempt to distinguish among patterns of romantic love relationships. One theoretical basis for such distinctions is the nature of the interpersonal rewards exchanged between partners. The attitudes and behaviors of romantic love may differ, for example, depending on whether the most salient rewards exchanged are those of security or those of stimulation. Some of the behavioral variables which might be focused on in the attempt to distinguish among such patterns are in the areas of sexual behavior, helping, and self-disclosure.

REFERENCES

Freud, S. Group psychology and the analysis of the ego. In *The standard edition of the complete psychological works of Sigmund Freud*, Vol. 18. London: Hogarth, 1955.

Fromm, E. *The art of loving*. New York: Harper, 1956.

Harlow, H. F. The nature of love. *American Psychologist*, 1958, *13*, 673–685.

Heider, F. *The psychology of interpersonal relations*. New York: Wiley, 1958.

Jourard, S. M., & Lasakov, P. Some factors in self-disclosure. *Journal of Abnormal and Social Psychology*, 1958, *56*, 91–98.

Newcomb, T. M. The varieties of interpersonal attraction. In D. Cartwright & A. Zander (Eds.), *Group dynamics*. (2nd ed.) Evanston: Row, Peterson, 1960.

Orlinsky, D. E. Love relationships in the life cycle: A developmental interpersonal perspective. In H. A. Otto (Ed.), *Love today: A new exploration*. New York: Association Press, 1972.

Slater, P. E. On social regression. *American Sociological Review*, 1963, *28*, 339–364.

PROJECTS

Name _____

Date _____

5.1: HOW DID YOU KNOW IT WAS LOVE?

The goal of this project is to identify the different dimensions of the experience of love through an introspective look at your first "real" love. Try to recall as much as you can about that love, focusing on your own experience of love, rather than on the unique characteristics of the loved person. How did you know it was love? Once you have described the variables that made up your love experience, compare your answers with those of the other people in your class. Is there any agreement among you about what constitutes love? If so, what is it?

FILL IN THE BLANKS IN THIRD COLUMN

Dimensions	Possible Variables	Personal Experience
Physical symptoms	What did you experience physically in the presence of your loved one (e.g., pounding heart, blushing, great excitement)?	_____ _____ _____ _____
Changed perceptions	How did you perceive your loved one? What attributes made him or her worthy of your love (e.g., good looks, intelligence, poise, kindness, sexiness)?	_____ _____ _____ _____
Behavioral symptoms	What unusual behaviors made you realize you were in love (e.g., thought about him or her all the time, started to stammer when talking to him or her)?	_____ _____ _____ _____

113

Name _____

Date _____

5.2: NONVERBAL COMMUNICATION OF AFFILIATION

People approach what they like and avoid what they dislike. That principle allows us to infer feelings from observations of people's movements toward or away from people, things, and even ideas. Scientists who study nonverbal communication have found that greater liking is conveyed by standing close instead of far, leaning forward instead of back while seated, facing directly instead of turning to one side, touching, having mutual gaze or eye contact, extending bodily contact as during handshake, prolonging goodbyes, and using gestures during a greeting which imply a reaching out toward the other person who is at a distance. [Albert Mehrabian, *Silent Messages* (Belmont, Calif.: Wadsworth), 1971, p 22.]

Through this project you will be studying nonverbal communication more systematically by doing two observational tasks in a social setting such as a restaurant, a classroom, or a park. The observations are to focus on two male-female dyads. One couple should be chosen because they appear to be close friends or lovers (high affiliation); the other dyad should involve two people who appear to be strangers and who have just met (low affiliation). Observe the nonverbal communication between the members of each dyad and record your observations on the data sheet. Then compare your ratings, and describe the similarities and/or differences in this form of communication that existed between the two couples.

NONVERBAL COMMUNICATION OF AFFILIATION

Nonverbal Behavior	High-Affiliation Dyad	Low-Affiliation Dyad	Comments on Similarities and Differences
1. Mutual eye contact			
2. Distance between dyad members			
3. Touching			
4. Posture			
5. Body orientation (facing forward or sideways, leaning)			
6. Facial expressions			
7. Hand gestures			
8. (Other) _____			

6

AGGRESSION

It is commonly said that we are living in violent times. There are wars all around the world, and in the United States the incidence of such violent crimes as murder, rape, and assault is clearly on the rise. The statistics on battered wives and abused children are alarming testimony to the fact that the home is as violent as the street. Violence is an integral part of many sports, such as hockey and football, which are sometimes accompanied by spectator violence as well. Furthermore, violence is increasingly being depicted in the mass media both as entertainment and as information. News reports routinely feature graphic representations and discussions of wars, terrorist events, and sensational crimes. Children's cartoons have long been known for the number and variety of aggressive acts they depict, and adult television programs and films are filled with every imaginable type of interpersonal violence. Meanwhile more and more research has demonstrated that exposure to violence fosters aggressiveness in the viewers. Media executives often respond that violence sells and that they, after all, are only giving the public what it wants. Yet even these notions are being disputed by recent research and by some effective consumer boycotts of the products of advertisers who sponsor violent shows.

The long history of widespread aggression and the seriousness of its consequences have prompted extensive study, by psychologists and others, of the causes of violent behavior. (Paradoxically, such positive social behaviors as love and altruism have only recently become legitimate topics for study by psychologists.) Several different theories of aggression have emerged. Some, such as Freudian and ethological theories, maintain that the source of aggression is within the individual, either as an aggressive instinct or as particular physiological factors or personality characteristics. Other theories focus on causes of aggression found in the external environment. How a person reacts to frustration and certain stimuli associated with aggression is given special emphasis in frustration-aggression models of aggressive behavior. Social learning theory has pointed to the ways in which aggression is learned in our society, and researchers working within this framework have studied the impact of aggressive models, the importance of reinforcements for aggressive behavior, and the pervasiveness of social norms that sanction aggression (such as the norm for males to "be a man and use your fists"). The causes of aggressive behavior are clearly multiple and complex, and it is equally clear that any solutions proposed for the problems of violence must take all of these factors into account.

THE STORY OF CAIN AND ABEL, FROM GENESIS 4:1-12

And the man knew Eve his wife; and she conceived and bore Cain, and said: 'I have gotten a man with the help of the LORD.' And again she bore his brother Abel. And Abel was a keeper of sheep, but Cain was a tiller of the ground. And in process of time it came to pass, that Cain brought of the fruit of the ground an offering unto the LORD. And Abel, he also brought of the firstlings of his flock and of the fat thereof. And the LORD had respect unto Abel and to his offering; but unto Cain and to his offering He had not respect. And Cain was very wroth, and his countenance fell. And the LORD said unto Cain: 'Why art thou wroth? and why is thy countenance fallen? If thou doest well, shall it not be lifted up? and if thou doest not well, sin coucheth at the door; and unto thee is its desire, but thou mayest rule over it.' And Cain spoke unto Abel his brother. And it came to pass, when they were in the field, that Cain rose up against Abel his brother, and slew him.

> And the LORD said unto Cain: 'Where is Abel thy brother?' And he said: 'I know not; am I my brother's keeper?' And He said: 'What hast thou done? the voice of thy brother's blood crieth unto Me from the ground. And now cursed art thou from the ground, which hath opened her mouth to receive thy brother's blood from thy hand. When thou tillest the ground, it shall not henceforth yield unto thee her strength; a fugitive and a wanderer shalt thou be in the earth.'

BATTERED WIVES

DEL MARTIN

An aspect of aggression that frequently goes unmentioned is the relationship between love and violence, between intimacy and aggression. Cain's murder of Abel, perhaps the most famous murder in Western history, is highly representative of homicide today. As police records show, less than 30 percent of all murder victims are strangers to the killer. Slightly more than 30 percent are family members or lovers. In the remaining cases, the victim is a friend, neighbor, or casual acquaintance. About one-fourth of all murders occur within the family. Half of these involve parents and children or other close relatives. The other half involves spouses, and most of these victims are women. Martin's article, "Battered Wives," addresses this form of aggression, which until recently was not even acknowledged. She discusses the various forms of wife abuse, which may result in death, their incredible frequency in contemporary American society, and the attitudes that ignore or even sanction them.

Violent solutions to social problems have been incorporated into the mainstream culture of the United States. Violence is not the only reaction; nor is it the most common one. But, whether or not violent behavior is illegal, certain situations exist in which it is expected and almost inevitably occurs. One terrifying aspect of this fact of American life is that both the expectation and the incidence of violent behavior increase every year.

In 1974, serious crime rose 17 percent across the nation—the sharpest annual increase since the Federal Bureau of Investigation started recording crime statistics in 1930.[1] In the final three months of 1974, crime increased at a 19 percent rate; compare this rate to 16 percent in the first nine months and 6 percent for the whole of 1973. Many families have moved to the suburbs and to rural areas to escape the savage environment of the cities, but emigration from the inner city no longer guarantees safety. Crime was up 20 percent in suburban areas and 21 percent in rural districts in 1974.

During the five-year period from 1968 to 1973, murders per year in the United States jumped from 13,720 to 19,510. Some 100,020 persons were killed during that period—twice the number of Americans killed in the Vietnam War.[2] Nearly half of all American households have at least one gun—a pistol, shotgun, or rifle.[3] These types of firearms are used in 67 percent of all murders committed in the United States.[4] Guns in the home may give some people a sense of security, but the danger exists that family members will use them on each other during a heated quarrel. An alarming number of them do.

Descriptions or enactments of violent acts intrude into the American home many times each day by way of newspapers and television. Surveys show that acts of aggression take place every three and one-half minutes on children's Saturday morning shows.[5] The Federal Communications Commission has made moves to regulate the sexual content of family prime-time programming, but claims it has no jurisdiction over other content. As long as portrayals of violence remain popular, advertisers will continue to sponsor violent programs. As the situation stands now, during the prime-time evening hours Americans have their choice of endless depictions of death on the operating table or death on the streets.

Advertisers' use of violence is getting more subtle and thus more insidious. For example, the December 1975 issue of *Vogue* carried a fashion layout in which a couple was shown alternately fighting and caressing each other. In one photograph the male model had just walloped the female model (his arm was raised in the follow-through) and her face was twisted in pain. The caption made no mention of the sadomasochistic theme of the photographs. It merely noted that the woman's jumpsuit could "really take the heat."[6] And, reported in the "No Comment" section of the July 1973 *Ms.* magazine was this ad for a bowling alley in Michigan: "Have some fun. Beat your wife tonight. Then celebrate with some good food and drink with your friends."

Because of the increase in the crime of rape (62 percent in the five-year period ending in 1973),[7] American women are often advised to "stay at home where they won't get hurt." But people who would impose such a curfew on women's freedom of movement might change their tune if they had access to local police reports on domestic violence, which suggest that women may be even less safe in their homes than they are in the streets.

THE INCIDENCE OF DOMESTIC VIOLENCE

Accurately determining the incidence of wife-beating per se is impossible at this time. Obvious sources of information are police reports, court rosters, and emergency hospital admittance files, but wife-abuse is not an official category on such records. Information on the subject gets buried in other, more general categories. Calls to the police for help in marital violence, for instance, are usually reported as "domestic disturbance calls," or DDs. If the police respond to these calls but decide that everything is under control, they may not file a report. If serious injury has been sustained by a wife, or if a wife has been killed by her husband, the incident is reported as assault and battery, aggravated assault, or homicide; wife-abuse is not necessarily specified. Sometimes written complaints registered by wives against their husbands are the only source of statistics available. But who is to say how many abused women do not register complaints?

Emergency rooms in hospitals are not reliable sources of statistics either. For a variety of reasons, women are often reluctant to tell the truth about how they sustained their injuries. Doctors often accept explanations such as "I ran into a door" or "I accidentally fell down the stairs." Even if they suspect that a woman's injuries are due to a beating, they seldom want to risk personal involvement by asking questions.

Statistical evidence on wife-battering must therefore be culled from the more general statistics available on domestic disturbance calls, complaints, hospital emergency rosters, and crime reports. Here follows a random sample of such information from some American cities:

- In Chicago, a police survey conducted between September 1965 and March 1966 demonstrated that 46.1 percent of all the major crimes except murder perpetrated against women took place at home.[8] The study also revealed that police response to domestic disturbance calls exceeded total response for murder, rape, aggravated assault, and other serious crimes.[9]

- A study in Oakland, California, in 1970 showed that police there responded to more than 16,000 family disturbance calls during a six-month period.[10]

- The 46,137 domestic disturbance calls received by Kansas City, Missouri, police represented 82 percent of all disturbance calls received by them in 1972.[11]

- In Detroit, 4,900 wife-assault complaints were filed in 1972.[12]

- In New York, 14,167 wife-abuse complaints were handled in Family Court throughout the state during the judicial year 1972–73.[13] "Legal experts think that wife-abuse is one of the most underreported crimes in the country—even more underreported than rape, which the FBI estimates is ten times more frequent than statistics indicate. A conservative estimate puts the number of battered wives nationwide at well over a million," states Karen Durbin.[14] Using the New York court statistics and the "ten times" formula to account for the cases that dropped by the wayside or were never reported, 141,670 wife-beatings could have occurred in New York State alone. If we can take this kind of guesswork a step further and consider that wife-battering is probably even more underreported than rape, and that there are fifty states in the Union, Durbin's estimate of "well over a million" could be conservative.

- In 1974, Boston police responded to 11,081 family disturbance calls, most of which involved physical violence.[15] At the end of the first quarter of 1975, 5,589 such calls were received—half the previous year's figure in one-quarter the time. (As an aside to these figures, Boston City Hospital reports that approximately 70 percent of the assault victims received in its emergency room are known to be women who have been attacked in their homes, usually by a husband or lover.[16])

- In Atlanta, Georgia, 60 percent of all police calls on the night shift are domestic disputes.[17]

- The Citizen's Complaint Center in the District of Columbia receives between 7,500 and 10,000 complaints of marital violence each year. Approximately 75 percent of the complainants are women.[18]

- In New Hampshire, for his study *The Violent Home,* Richard Gelles interviewed forty neighbors of known violent families as a means of establishing a nonviolent control group with which the violent group could be compared.[19] Of these supposedly nonviolent neighboring families, 37 percent had experienced at least one incident of violence, and for 12 percent violence was a regular occurrence.[20]

- Trends in domestic violence are similar in city after city. But the problem is not just an urban one; it is to be found in rural areas as well. For example, the police chief in a small Washtenaw County (Michigan) town of 6,000 reports that family assault calls come in every day.[21] And another police official with extensive rural experience estimates that police calls for "family fights" are exceeded only by calls relating to automobile accidents.[22]

The figures cited here were randomly selected from a variety of sources. No attempt has been made to adjust them with respect to population or to compare them and discern regional trends. The point here is that a great many domestic-violence cases come to the attention of the authorities. The raw numbers themselves make it obvious that domestic violence is a social problem,

and a serious one. Just how serious is anyone's guess, since no one knows how many cases of domestic violence go unreported.

Still, the terms "domestic violence" or "domestic disturbance" are not synonymous with "wife-battering." But you don't need a degree in criminology to realize that the police are not called into a domestic situation unless the weaker person(s) involved need help or are perceived to need help by witnesses. If the involved parties could control and resolve a domestic disturbance, no doubt they would do so without inviting the police to interfere. It can be assumed that someone in most reported cases of domestic disturbance was being overpowered or, at the very least, frightened, or that neighbors or passersby thought that was the case.

Two other commonsense factors will help clarify the relationship between domestic-disturbance figures and wife-battering. First, many households are composed of conventional heterosexual marriages or relationships; and second, in most such relationships the woman is physically weaker than the man. We can assume that a good many of the domestic disturbance calls that do not involve juveniles concern women being intimidated, frightened, or assaulted by men to the point where someone decides that help is needed from the police. This assumption is borne out by statistics. Of the figures available on complaints, 82 percent in New York,[23] 75 percent in Washington, D.C.,[24] 85.4 percent in Detroit,[25] and 95 percent in Montgomery County, Maryland,[26] were filed by female victims.

By looking at another random sampling of police statistics, we can get an idea of just how serious a "domestic disturbance" can be:

- In 1971, Kansas City police found that one-third of the aggravated assaults reported were due to domestic disturbance.[27] Police had been called previously at least once in 90 percent of these cases and five or more times in over half of them.[28] Also during 1971, 40 percent of all homicides in Kansas City were cases of spouse killing spouse.[29] In almost 50 percent of these cases, police had been summoned five or more times within a two-year period before the murder occurred.[30]

- Almost one-third of all female homicide victims in California in 1971 were murdered by their husbands.[31]

- Nationwide in 1973, according to the FBI, one-fourth of all murders occurred within the family, and one-half of these were husband-wife killings. In assault cases wives are predominantly the victims, but in homicides husbands are the victims almost as often as wives (48 percent compared with 52 percent in 1973).[32] This phenomenon is partially explained by the fact that, according to a report made to a government commission on violence, women who commit murder are motivated by self-defense almost seven times as often as male offenders.[33]

- In 1974, 25 percent of all murders in San Francisco involved legally married or cohabiting mates.[34]

- Domestic violence not only endangers the lives of family members and marital partners, it accounts for a high percentage of the deaths of and injuries sustained by police officers who answer the calls. According to the FBI, 132 police officers were killed in the nation in 1974.[35] Twenty-nine of them died while responding to domestic-disturbance calls—that is, one out of every five police officers killed in the line of duty in 1974 died while trying to break up a family fight.

It is worthwhile mentioning here that divorce statistics are not a reliable gauge of the frequency of wife-abuse, since mention of marital violence can be negotiated out of the record before the trial or because the wife was unable to produce medical and police records to prove it occurred. However, a survey conducted by George Levinger of 600 applicants for divorce in the Cleveland area revealed that 37 percent of the wives suing for divorce cited "physical abuse" as one of their complaints.[36] And a Wayne County (Michigan) judge stated that approximately 16,000 divorces are initiated in the county annually, and in 80 percent of those coming before him, beating is alleged. Commenting on another aspect of the problem, this judge estimated that fifty to sixty hearings are held in the Third Judicial Circuit Court each month on wives' claims that their estranged husbands have violated injunctions restraining them from physically abusing the wives.[37]

WIFE-ABUSE: THE SKELETON IN THE CLOSET

Common sense tells us that statistics relating to domestic violence reflect, to some extent, the incidence of wife-beating. "Wife-beating has been so prevalent that all of us must have been aware of its existence—if not in our own lives, at least in the lives of others, or when a wife-beating case that resulted in death was reported in the press," states Betsy Warrior.[38] But, although governmental agencies and social scientists have begun to concentrate on social violence in recent years, wife-battering has merited no special attention in those quarters. Nor has it aroused the shocked indignation it should have from the women's movement until very recently. The fact is, the issue has been buried so deeply that no real data exist on the incidence of wife-beating.

The news media have often treated wife-abuse as a bizarre and relatively rare phenomenon—as occasional fodder for sensationalistic reporting—but rarely as a social issue worthy of thorough investigation. *Time* magazine demonstrated the news media's head-in-the-sand attitude in 1974 when it ran an article on Erin Pizzey's Chiswick Center, but carried it only in the European edition. Apparently the *Time* editors thought that wife-battering would not interest Americans.

In *Violence and the Family*, Suzanne Steinmetz and Murray Straus surveyed various kinds of literature in an effort to discern trends in the treatment of wife-beating. In their review of four hundred items, they located little material on husband-wife violence other than murder, even in novels. They were particularly puzzled by the fact that anthropologists had not uncovered evidence of marital violence in their studies of other cultures. But Paul Bohannon suggested to one of their colleagues two possible reasons: (1) middle-class anthropologists share the middle-class horror of violence, and (2) people in cultures under anthropological investigation do not necessarily conduct their family quarrels in the presence of anthropologists; nor do they talk about the violent episodes that might characterize their private lives.[39]

Occasionally, psychiatrists admit to coming across cases of marital violence in their clinical practices, but therapy-prone professionals tend to treat such incidents as exceptions and to see them in terms of the individual's pathology. Psychological studies of family dynamics tend to overlook the physical conflicts between husband and wife; they usually concentrate on the causes of tension within families, not on the means by which it is expressed.

An example of how social scientists skirt the issue of wife-battering is in the otherwise well-researched book by Eleanor Emmons Maccoby and Carol Nagy Jacklin, *The Psychology of Sex Dif-*

ferences. Commenting on an article on wife-beating that appeared in the *Manchester Guardian,* these writers state, "Although incidents of this kind exist as an ugly aspect of marital relations in an unknown number of cases . . . there can be little doubt that direct force is rare in modern marriages. Male behavior such as that described above would be considered pathological in any human (or animal!) society, and, if widespread, would endanger a species."[40]

The wishful thinking demonstrated in this passage—that "direct force is rare in modern marriages"—even in its mildest form has done its share to keep information on wife-beating from surfacing. The fact that such information is all but lost in the tangle of police statistics on domestic disturbances substantiates the suspicions of those who think—and would like to go on thinking—that wife-beating is not a significant problem and does not deserve attention. But Pizzey's experience at the Chiswick Center has proved these Pollyannas to be wrong. When she opened a refuge for women, many abused wives showed up. Their very existence raises the issue of wife-battering.

In *Scream Quietly or the Neighbors Will Hear,* Pizzey points out that people try to ignore violence inside the home and within the family. Many abused wives who came to Chiswick Center told Pizzey that their neighbors knew very well what was going on but went to great lengths to pretend ignorance. They would cross the street to avoid witnessing an incident of domestic violence. Some would even turn up the television to block out the shouts, screams, and sobs coming from next door.[41]

From one point of view, the battered wife in her secrecy conspires with the media, the police, the social scientists, the social reformers, and the social workers to keep the issue hushed up. We can picture a very thick door locked shut. On the inside is a woman trying hard not to cry out for help. On the other side are those who could and should be helping, but instead are going about their business as if she weren't there.

THE GREAT AMERICAN FAMILY

The door behind which the battered wife is trapped is the door to the family home. The white-picket-fence stereotype of the American family home still persists from the days of Andy Hardy. The privacy of the home supposedly protects a comfortable space within which intimate and affectionate relationships among spouses, parents and children, and siblings become richer and deeper with each passing year. Loyalty, constancy, and protectiveness are demonstrated by the parents and learned by the children. If you modernize the picture by adding some self-deprecating humor gleaned from television's situation comedies, the image of the ideal American family will be complete.

In one sense, the family home is supposed to provide refuge from the stormy turbulence of the outside world. In another, it is a family factory, designed to perpetuate its own values and to produce two or three replicas of itself as the children in the family marry—whether or not they are ready for or suited for marriage. The nuclear family is the building block of American society, and the social, religious, educational, and economic institutions of society are designed to maintain, support, and strengthen family ties even if the people involved can't stand the sight of one another.

Until very recently, no acceptable alternatives to the family home existed in the United States. People who chose to live alone or to share their homes with non-relatives, those who chose to set up same-sex households, or who married but chose not to have children—all were seen as outcasts, failures, or deviants. This attitude is changing, albeit very slowly, possibly more as a result of overpopulation than of growing openmindedness and tolerance. But even now, the stereotype of the happy, harmonious family persists in American society. Compared with this ideal, most actual families composed of real people appear to be tragic failures, and in many cases they are.

In reality, the glowing image of the American family is a myth. The privacy that protects the family can also muffle the blows and stifle the yells of a violent home. People who would not otherwise consider striking anyone sometimes act as if establishing a household together gives them the right to abuse each other. "From our interviews," Richard Gelles says in *The Violent Home,* "we are still convinced that in most cases a marriage license also functions as a hitting license."[42] In his research, which admittedly was limited to eighty subjects who were legally married, Gelles found that numerous incidents of violence between married partners were considered by them to be normal, routine, and generally acceptable.[43] He also found a high incidence of violence in his control group and only one instance in which violence had occurred before the couple married. Furthermore, in the case of two couples in his sample who dated, married, divorced, dated again, and remarried, violence occurred *only* when these couples were *legally* married. These findings indicate to Gelles the possibility that violence between a couple is considered acceptable within, but not outside of, marriage.[44]

Unmarried women who have been beaten by their mates undoubtedly would take exception to Gelles's interpretation. It may well be that the shared home, not the marriage vow, is the key element here. Some men may feel that they have the right to exercise power over the women they live with whether or not they are legally married to them.

Our patriarchal system allows a man the right of ownership to some degree over the property *and* people that comprise his household. A feminist friend learned this lesson in an incident in Oakland, California. She witnessed a street fight in which a husband was hitting his pregnant wife in the stomach (a recurring theme in stories of wife-abuse). She saw the fight as she was driving by, stopped her car, and jumped out to help the woman. When she tried to intervene, the male bystanders who stood idly by watching the spectacle shouted at her, "You can't do that! She's his wife!" and "You shouldn't interfere; it's none of your business." Although the wife had begged the gathered crowd to call the police, no one did so until my friend was struck by the furious husband. (I have heard of a similar incident where a man interfered and *he* was the one who was arrested and charged with assault!)

Sociologist Howard Erlanger of the University of Wisconsin found that 25 percent of his sample of American adults actually approved of husband-wife battles. What is more surprising was that the greater the educational level, the greater was the acceptance of marital violence. Approval ranged from 17 percent of grade-school graduates to 32 percent of college postgraduate students, with a slightly lower 30 percent for those who had completed just four years of college. The study also showed that, contrary to popular belief, low-income respondents were no more prone to nor more readily accepting of violence in the home than were middle- or upper-income respondents.[45]

The popular assumption by the middle class that marital violence occurs more frequently in the ghetto and among lower-class families reflects the inability of middle-class investigators to face the universality of the problem. Evidence of wife-beating exists wherever one cares to look for it. Fairfax County, Virginia, for instance, is a suburb of the District of Columbia and considered to be one of the wealthiest counties in the United States.

Police there received 4,073 family disturbance calls in 1974. They estimated that thirty assault warrants are sought by Fairfax County wives each week.[46]

Morton Bard's study of New York's 30th Precinct, a West Harlem community of about 85,000 people, is another example. This socially stable residential community consists mostly of working-class Blacks, with a sprinkling of Latin Americans (8 percent) and whites (2 percent).[47] Bard found that the number of wife-abuse cases reported in the 30th Precinct was roughly the same as that reported in another study conducted in Norwalk, Connecticut—a white, upper-middle-class area with approximately the same population.[48]

A survey conducted for the National Commission on the Causes and Prevention of Violence by Louis Harris and Associates bears out Erlanger's conclusions that a great many people approve of husband-wife battles. The Harris poll in October 1968, consisting of 1,176 interviews with a representative national sample of American adults, showed that one-fifth approved of slapping one's spouse on "appropriate" occasions. In this survey, 16 percent of those with eight years of schooling or less approved, and 25 percent of college-educated people approved of a husband slapping his wife.[49]

Rodney Stark and James McEvoy III further analyzed the Harris data and found that 25 percent of the Blacks, 20 percent of the whites, 25 percent of the males, and 16 percent of the females interviewed "could approve of a husband's slapping his wife's face." The percentage points rose in all of these categories (from 1 to 3 percent) when the question was reversed and subjects were asked if they "could approve of a wife's slapping her husband's face." Analyzed by regions of the country, persons from the West rated highest and the South lowest in approval of either action. Those with an income of $5,000 or less were considerably less approving than those in other income brackets. Persons under thirty years old were most approving, and those sixty-five years or older were least approving of husband-wife slappings.[50]

A slap in the face could be construed as a fairly innocent gesture compared with a full-fledged beating. But a friend of mine told me this story. Three months after her mother and stepfather were married, they had an argument and he gave her a sound "slapping." A few months later he "slapped" her again; this time the woman wound up in the hospital with her jaws wired together. When she came home from the hospital, her husband was contrite and conciliatory. He did his best to please her so that she wouldn't leave him. The woman stayed, though she never really forgave her husband. They still had their fights, but he never laid a hand on her again. However, two years later, when the couple got into a particularly heated argument in the kitchen, he grabbed a knife and killed her.

Later, my daughter was slapped by a friend's violent husband when she responded to the wife's call for help. He just slapped her on the cheek, but with such force that her head snapped back and pain shot through her head to the top of her skull. He struck her twice in this heavy-handed manner. Her face was sore for several days, though there were no bruises; she also suffered the effects of a minor whiplash. "I didn't think he would hit *me*. He was my friend," she said. "And I certainly didn't realize that a man could exert so much force with his open hand. It was just a short slap. He didn't need to take a long swing."

In the Harris poll cited above, if the word had been "hit" instead of "slap" would the results of the poll have been the same? Would 25 percent of the males and 16 percent of the females interviewed approve of a husband hitting his wife in the face? The answer to that question is anybody's guess. But there is a good chance that the interviewees would have considered the question an invasion of privacy had the word been "hit" rather than "slap." I cite this possibility to underscore the subtlety of the problem and the difficulty of interpreting the significance of the data.

Even agreeing on a definition of "violence" may be a problem for some people. Police, for instance, seem to think that few domestic disturbances are really violent. They tend to define violence in terms of its effect. Unless blood is drawn and injuries are visible, they are apt to discount the report of violence and call the incident merely a "family spat." To me, any physical attack by one person upon another is a violent act and an instance of illegal aggression, even if no visible injury results. Still, Gelles noted that after the bruises had healed, some of his subjects called even the most severe beatings they received "nonviolent."[51]

However the terms are defined, though, sufficient evidence of serious injury and homicide exists to show that domestic violence is a critical problem. In *The Violent Home*, Gelles determined where and when violence is most likely to occur. The "typical location of family violence was the kitchen. The bedroom and the living room are the next most likely scenes of violence. Some respondents are unable to pinpoint exact locations because their battles begin in one room and progress through the house. The *only* room in the house where there was *no violence* was the bathroom."[52]

Alex D. Pokorny says that murder seldom occurs in public places. The usual site is the home, though the car is the setting in a fair number of cases.[53] Other studies of homicides show that the bedroom is the deadliest room in the house and that the victims there are usually female.[54] The next most likely place for family murders is the kitchen; in those cases the women are more frequently the offenders.[55]

According to Gelles, couples get into violent fights most often after dinner, between 8 and 11:30 p.m. The second most frequent time is during dinner (5 to 8 p.m.), and the third is late evening to early morning.[56] The same timetable applies to those acts of violence that result in death.[57] Also, violence of either variety occurs most frequently on weekends.[58] Kansas City police cite Monday as another day of reckoning.[59]

THE CHILDREN

If the American-family dream is a nightmare for spouses involved in domestic violence, it is even more so for their children. They suffer the consequences of their parents' battles simply because they exist. When violence becomes a pattern in the household it can take many forms. In her desperation, the battered wife may strike out at the children, scapegoating them as she has been scapegoated by a violent husband. And the man who beats his wife may also beat his children. In J. J. Gayford's survey of one hundred battered women in England, 37 percent of the women admitted taking their own frustrations out on the children, and 54 percent claimed their husbands committed acts of violence against the children.[60] The breaking point for many of these women came when the children were made into victims too. At that point many of the women resolved, or tried, to leave.[61]

Children who "merely" witness physical violence between their parents suffer emotional trauma. They react with shock, fear, and guilt. This fact was brought home to me when my eight-year-old grandson witnessed his friend's drunk father hit my daughter, who had rushed to the aid of the man's wife. The incident happened in front of the house. The husband jumped down from the roof to confront my daughter and grandson. Terrified, my grandson ran for the car and locked himself in. While he was in the car, he saw the man give his mother a couple of hard slaps. Later, when my daughter and the child arrived at my house, my grandson flung himself on the couch. He was emotionally devastated. He could only mumble, "It was horrible!" When he was able to talk about it, he blurted out that if his older sister had been there "she would have done something!" He had been scared; he hadn't known what to do and felt guilty about that. Not until we started discussing self-defense tactics did the little boy perk up. He wanted to form a plan of action so that he would know how to react in the future.

In Bard's study of the 30th Precinct in New York City, children were present in 41 percent of the domestic-disturbance cases in which police intervened. "If this is typical, one can only speculate on the modeling effects of parental aggression on such children—not to speak of the effects of a variety of police behaviors on the perception of children in such situations," he said.[62] The behavior of police officers is bound to have a strong effect on children. If the police identify with the father and treat the incident lightly, they will be reinforcing the role models of violent male and female victim. But if police efficiently calm down the angry parents and effectively communicate the attitude that violent behavior is not to be excused or tolerated, the children will be receiving healthier signals.

Gelles's research shows that people who as children had observed their parents engaging in physical violence were more likely to engage in the same sort of activity with their own spouses than those who never saw their parents fight.[63] He found, too, that adults who were hit frequently as children were more likely to be violent with their mates than people who had never been hit as children. "Not only does the family expose individuals to violence and techniques of violence," Gelles concludes, "the family teaches approval for the use of violence."[64]

Pizzey agrees with Gelles on this point, basing her opinion on her impressions of violent husbands gleaned from interviews with women who had come to Chiswick Women's Aid. "A man who batters is a child who was battered that nobody helped," Pizzey says. "If we look at the histories of these men, they are either beaten children or actually watched it. . . . so the violence goes from one generation to the next. It becomes the norm."[65]

In an article for *Trans-action* on battered children, Serapio R. Zalba estimated (conservatively, he says) that between 200,000 and 250,000 children in the United States need protective services, and that 30,000 to 37,500 children may be badly hurt by their parents each year.[66] And according to Dr. C. Henry Kempe, who conducted the first national study on battered children for the U.S. Department of Health, Education and Welfare, more than one million children suffer abuse and neglect.[67] These figures are certainly horrifying in themselves, but in the light of Pizzey's and Gelles's conclusions as to the perpetuation of domestic violence, they are nothing short of mind-boggling.

Hidden behind the stereotyped image of the nuclear family, then, we find not only isolated instances of domestic violence, but also the potential for ever-increasing patterns of violence as, in literally millions of homes around the world, the children of battling parents establish their own families. If the building block of American society, the modern nuclear family, is ever more frequently wracked by physical brutality, what hope can we have for society as a whole? Past president of the National Council on Family Relations Murray A. Straus declares, "I don't think we are going to understand violence in American society until we understand violence in the family. . . . The home is where violence primarily occurs."[68]

We must stop protecting our myths and lies, and stop teaching our children to strike out blindly with their fists. If there is battering to be done, let it be directed against that sacred front door to the family home.

NOTES

1. All figures in this paragraph from the *San Francisco Chronicle* (April 1, 1975), p. 12.

2. Mary Ann Kuhn, "There's No Place Like Home for Beatings," *Washington Star* (November 11, 1975), p. 1.

3. George Gallup, "Guns Found in 44% of Homes," *San Francisco Chronicle* (July 7, 1975), p. 2.

4. Kuhn, p. A-14.

5. John Harris, "Networks Claim They've Been Toned Down but . . . , *National Enquirer* (August 19, 1975), p. 14.

6. Beth Pombeiro (Knight News Service), "Decadence Is Back—in Vogue," *San Francisco Examiner* (De-

cember 7, 1975), pp. 1, 28, and *Vogue* (December 1975), p. 149.

7. Federal Bureau of Investigation, *Uniform Crime Reports* (1973), p. 14.

8. Letty Cottin Pogrebin, "Do Women Make Men Violent?" *Ms.* (November 1974), p. 55.

9. Raymond Parnas, "The Police Response to Domestic Disturbances," *Wisconsin Law Review* (1967), p. 914, n. 2.

10. Raymond Parnas, "Police Discretion and Diversion of Incidents of Intra-Family Violence," *Law and Contemporary Problems*, Vol. 36, No. 4 (Autumn 1971), p. 54, n. 1.

11. Northeast Patrol Division Task Force, Kansas City Police Department, "Conflict Management: Analysis/Resolution." Taken from first draft, p. 58 (hereinafter called Kansas City Police report).

12. Commander James D. Bannon, from a speech delivered before a conference of the American Bar Association in Montreal, 1975.

13. J. C. Barden, "Wife Beaters: Few of Them Ever Appear Before a Court of Law," *The New York Times* (October 21, 1974), Sec. 2, p. 38. Figures reported as 17,277 family violence cases, of which the wife was plaintiff in 82 percent.

14. Karen Durbin, "Wife-Beating," *Ladies Home Journal* (June 1974), p. 64.

15. Laura White, "Women Organize to Protect Wives from Abusive Husbands," *Boston Herald-American* (Sunday edition, June [22 or 29] 1975).

16. Betsy Warrior, "Battered Lives," *Houseworker's Handbook* (Spring 1975), p. 25.

17. Ibid., p. 25.

18. Lois Yankowski, "Battered Women: A Study of the Situation in the District of Columbia," unpublished (1975), pp. 2-3.

19. Richard Gelles, *The Violent Home* (Beverly Hills: Sage, 1972), p. 36.

20. Ibid., p. 50.

21. Sue Eisenberg and Patricia Micklow, "The Assaulted Wife: 'Catch 22' Revisited," unpublished (University of Michigan, Ann Arbor, 1974), p. 18. A version of this study will be published by *Women's Rights Law Reporter* in 1976.

22. Morton Bard, *Training Police As Specialists in Family Crisis Intervention* (Washington: U.S. Government Printing Office, 1970), p. 1.

23. Barden, p. 38.

24. Yankowski, p. 3.

25. Eisenberg and Micklow, p. 16.

26. Montgomery County Council, Maryland, "A Report by the Task Force to Study a Haven for Physically Abused Persons" (1975), p. 17.

27. Kanas City Police report.

28. Ibid.

29. Ibid.

30. Ibid.

31. *California Homicides*, 1971.

32. Federal Bureau of Investigation, *Uniform Crime Reports*, 1973.

33. *Crimes of Violence*, a staff report to the National Commission on the Causes and Prevention of Violence (Washington, D.C.: U.S. Government Printing Office, 1969), p. 360.

34. San Francisco Police Department, Homicide Bureau. Statistics reviewed and evaluated with respect to marital cases by Susan Jackson and Marta Ashley.

35. Robert B. Murphy, Ed McKay, Jeffrey A. Schwartz, and Donald A. Liebman, "Training Patrolmen As Crisis Intervention Instructors," unpublished, p. 1.

36. George Levinger, "Source of Marital Dissatisfaction among Applicants for Divorce," *American Journal of Orthopsychiatry* (October 1966), pp. 804-06.

37. Eisenberg and Micklow, p. 18.

38. Warrior, p. 25.

39. Suzanne K. Steinmetz and Murray A. Straus, eds., *Violence in the Family* (New York: Dodd, Mead, 1975), p. v.

40. Eleanor Emmons Maccoby and Carol Nagy Jacklin, *The Psychology of Sex Differences* (Stanford: Stanford University Press, 1974), p. 264.

41. Erin Pizzey, "Scream Quietly or the Neighbors Will Hear," *Manchester Daily Express* (October 29, 1974), p. 11.

42. Gelles, p. 153.

43. Ibid., p. 58.

44. Ibid., p. 136.

45. Joyce Brothers, "A Quiz on Crime," *San Francisco Sunday Examiner and Chronicle* (June 22, 1975), Sunday Scene, p. 6.

46. Bill Peterson, "System Frustrates Battered Wives," *Washington Post* (November 2, 1974), p. 18.

47. Morton Bard, "The Study and Modification of Intra-Familial Violence," *The Control of Aggression and Violence: Cognitive and Psychological* (New York: Academic Press, 1971), p. 154.

48. Sally Johnson, "What About Battered Women?" *Majority Report* (February 8, 1975), p. 4.

49. Rodney Stark and James McEvoy III, "Middle-Class Violence," *Psychology Today* (November 1970), pp. 30-31.

50. Ibid., p. 32.

51. Gelles, p. 25.

52. Ibid., pp. 95-96.

53. Alex D. Pokorny, "Human Violence: A Comparison of Homicide, Aggravated Assault, Suicide, and Attempted Suicide," *Journal of Criminal Law, Criminology and Police Science* 56 (1965), pp. 488–97.

54. Marvin E. Wolfgang, *Patterns in Criminal Homicide* (New York: John Wiley, 1958), p. 125.

55. Ibid., p. 126.

56. Gelles, p. 100.

57. Wolfgang, p. 108.

58. Gelles, pp. 104–05. D. J. Pittman and W. Handy, "Patterns in Criminal Aggravated Assault," *Journal of Criminal Law, Criminology and Police Science* 55 (1964), p. 463.

59. Kansas City Police report.

60. J. J. Gayford, "Wife Battering: A Preliminary Survey on 100 Cases," *British Medical Journal* (January 25, 1975), p. 196.

61. Ibid., p. 195.

62. Bard, "The Study and Modification of Intra-Familial Violence," p. 161.

63. Gelles, p. 173.

64. Ibid., p. 171.

65. Quoted by Judith Weinraub, "The Battered Wives of England: A Place to Heal Their Wounds," *The New York Times* (November 29, 1975), p. C-17.

66. Serapio R. Zalba, "Battered Children," *Trans-Action* (July/August, 1971), p. 59.

67. C. Henry Kempe, *Eyewitness News*, CBS Television, December 1, 1975.

68. Quoted in Kuhn, p. A-14.

A LETTER FROM A BATTERED WIFE

I am in my thirties and so is my husband. I have a high school diploma and am presently attending a local college, trying to obtain the additional education I need. My husband is a college graduate and a professional in his field. We are both attractive and, for the most part, respected and well-liked. We have four children and live in a middle-class home with all the comforts we could possibly want.

I have everything, except life without fear.

For most of my married life I have been periodically beaten by my husband. What do I mean by "beaten"? I mean that parts of my body have been hit violently and repeatedly, and that painful bruises, swelling, bleeding wounds, unconsciousness, and combinations of these things have resulted.

Beating should be distinguished from all other kinds of physical abuse—including being hit and shoved around. When I say my husband threatens me with abuse I do not mean he warns me that he may lose control. I mean that he shakes a fist against my face or nose, makes punching-bag jabs at my shoulder, or makes similar gestures which may quickly turn into a full-fledged beating.

I have had glasses thrown at me. I have been kicked in the abdomen when I was visibly pregnant. I have been kicked off the bed and hit while lying on the floor—again, while I was pregnant. I have been whipped, kicked and thrown, picked up again and thrown down again. I have been punched and kicked in the head, chest, face, and abdomen more times than I can count.

I have been slapped for saying something about politics, for having a different view about religion, for swearing, for crying, for wanting to have intercourse.

I have been threatened when I wouldn't do something he told me to do. I have been threatened when he's had a bad day and when he's had a good day.

I have been threatened, slapped, and beaten after stating bitterly that I didn't like what he was doing with another woman.

After each beating my husband has left the house and remained away for days.

Few people have ever seen my black and blue face or swollen lips because I have always stayed indoors afterwards, feeling ashamed. I was never able to drive following one of these beatings, so I could not get myself to a hospital for care. I could never have left my young children alone, even if I could have driven a car.

Hysteria inevitably sets in after a beating. This hysteria—the shaking and crying and mumbling—is not accepted by anyone, so there has never been anyone to call.

My husband on a few occasions did phone a day or so later so we could agree on the excuse I would use for returning to work, the grocery store, the dentist appointment, and so on. I used the excuses—a car accident, oral surgery, things like that.

Now, the first response to this story, which I myself think of, will be "Why didn't you seek help?"

I did. Early in our marriage I went to a clergyman who, after a few visits, told me that my husband meant no real harm, that he was just confused and felt insecure. I was encouraged to be more tolerant and understanding. Most important, I was told to forgive him the beatings just as Christ had forgiven me from the cross. I did that, too.

Things continued. Next time I

turned to a doctor. I was given little pills to relax me and told to take things a little easier. I was just too nervous.

I turned to a friend, and when her husband found out, he accused me of either making things up or exaggerating the situation. She was told to stay away from me. She didn't, but she could no longer really help me. Just by believing me she was made to feel disloyal.

I turned to a professional family guidance agency. I was told there that my husband needed help and that I should find a way to control the incidents. I couldn't control the beatings—that was the whole point of my seeking help. At the agency I found I had to defend myself against the suspicion that I wanted to be hit, that I invited the beatings. Good God! Did the Jews invite themselves to be slaughtered in Germany?

I did go to two more doctors. One asked me what I had done to provoke my husband. The other asked if we had made up yet.

I called the police one time. They not only did not respond to the call, they called several hours later to ask if things had "settled down." I could have been dead by then!

I have nowhere to go if it happens again. No one wants to take in a woman with four children. Even if there were someone kind enough to care, no one wants to become involved in what is commonly referred to as a "domestic situation."

Everyone I have gone to for help has somehow wanted to blame me and vindicate my husband. I can see it lying there between their words and at the end of their sentences. The clergymen, the doctor, the counselor, my friend's husband, the police—all of them have found a way to vindicate my husband.

No one has to "provoke" a wife-beater. He will strike out when he's ready and for whatever reason he has at the moment.

I may be his excuse, but I have never been the reason.

I know that I do not want to be hit. I know, too, that I will be beaten again unless I can find a way out for myself and my children. I am terrified for them also.

As a married woman I have no recourse but to remain in the situation which is causing me to be painfully abused. I have suffered physical and emotional battering and spiritual rape because the social structure of my world says I cannot do anything about a man who wants to beat me. . . . But staying with my husband means that my children must be subjected to the emotional battering caused when they see their mother's beaten face or hear her screams in the middle of the night.

I know that I have to get out. But when you have nowhere to go, you know that you must go on your own and expect no support. I have to be ready for that. I have to be ready to support myself and the children completely, and still provide a decent environment for them. I pray that I can do that before I am murdered in my own home.

I have learned that no one believes me and that I cannot depend upon any outside help. All I have left is the hope that I can get away before it is too late.

I have learned also that the doctors, the police, the clergy, and my friends will excuse my husband for distorting my face, but won't forgive me for looking bruised and broken. The greatest tragedy is that I am still praying, and there is not a human person to listen.

Being beaten is a terrible thing; it is most terrible of all if you are not equipped to fight back. I recall an occasion when I tried to defend myself and actually tore my husband's shirt. Later, he showed it to a relative as proof that I had done something terribly wrong. The fact that at that moment I had several raised spots on my head hidden by my hair, a swollen lip that was bleeding, and a severely damaged cheek with a blood clot that caused a permanent dimple didn't matter to him. What mattered was that I tore his shirt! That I tore it in self-defense didn't mean anything to him.

My situation is so untenable I would guess that anyone who has not experienced one like it would find it incomprehensible. I find it difficult to believe myself.

It must be pointed out that while a husband can beat, slap, or threaten his wife, there are "good days." These days tend to wear away the effects of the beating. They tend to cause the wife to put aside the traumas and look to the good—first, because there is nothing else to do; second, because there is nowhere and no one to turn to; and third, because the defeat is the beating and the hope is that it will not happen again. A loving woman like myself always hopes that it will not happen again. When it does, she simply hopes again, until it becomes obvious after a third beating that there is no hope. That is when she turns outward for help to find an answer. When that help is denied, she either resigns herself to the situation she is in or pulls herself together and starts making plans for a future life that includes only herself and her children.

For many the third beating may be too late. Several of the times I have been abused I have been amazed that I have remained alive. Imagine that I have been thrown to a very hard slate floor several times, kicked in the abdomen, the head, and the chest, and still remained alive!

What determines who is lucky and who isn't? I could have been dead a long time ago had I been hit the wrong way. My baby could have been killed or deformed had I been kicked the wrong way. What saved me?

I don't know. I only know that it has happened and that each night I dread the final blow that will kill me and leave my children motherless. I hope I can hang on until I complete my education, get a good job, and become self-sufficient enough to care for my children on my own.

PREDICTING ATTITUDES TOWARD VIOLENCE

MONICA D. BLUMENTHAL

Although there is widespread agreement that American society is fairly violent, there is less agreement about the values Americans place on violence. Some people are opposed to all forms of violent behavior, but many feel that violence can have beneficial consequences in at least some situations. For example, a positive value is placed on aggression for self-defense or for the protection of others (such as one's children). In wartime, aggressive acts are sanctioned for a special class of people, soldiers, who are expected to follow orders to kill the enemy. However, even in war, there are norms that limit the scope of violence and classify some aggressive actions as wrong. The massacre at My Lai during the Vietnam War is such an act. Violence is sometimes approved for obtaining social change. The American Revolution, for example, is considered an appropriate use of violence. In other cases, violence is justified if it is used to maintain the status quo. Thus, violent police action against rioters is socially approved.

If people's attitudes toward violence reflect the types of behavior that they will either engage in or approve of, it becomes important to gain a better understanding of these attitudes. In "Predicting Attitudes Toward Violence," Blumenthal presents the results of an extensive survey study on American men's views of violence, in which these attitudes were related to the individual's personal values and to the individual's views concerning the people involved in violent acts.

Violence has been a conspicuous part of American life during the last few years (*1*). Assassinations (*2*), riots (*3*), student disruption (*4*), and violent crime, which is increasing in proportion to the population (*5*), have all contributed to the aura of violence in this decade. Moreover, there has historically been a great deal of violence in American life (*6*). Indeed, some authors contend that most major social movements in the United States have been accompanied by violence. When violence is considered in its historical perspective, it is clearly of the utmost importance to develop and test a theoretical model capable of predicting violent behaviors.

As a first step in this quest, a model designed to predict attitudes toward violence was developed and tested. It was assumed that attitudes are likely to be reflected by behaviors, and that a model capable of predicting attitudes toward

violence could later be modified to explain part of the variance in predicting behavior. To test this model, a survey was taken of attitudes toward violence in a representative random sample of 1374 American men between the ages of 16 and 64 (*7*). The men were interviewed in the coterminous United States in the summer of 1969, and the final response rate was 80 percent. Black men were sampled at a higher rate than others, thus the final sample included 303 blacks.

Measuring attitudes toward violence is an important venture in its own right. One of the characteristics of contemporary American life is the extent to which the mass media expose us to violence. For example, the question of whether or not television increases aggressive and violent behaviors was considered so crucial by the surgeon general that he established a major committee to investigate the problem (*8*), even though the staff of the National Commission on the Causes and Prevention of Violence had already published an extensive monograph on the subject (*9*). If the mass media can influence people to act more aggressively and violently, as may be the case, one must ask how such influence is exerted. Do the media simply serve as a model for imitation (*10*), or do the messages they project modify fundamental social values that inhibit or facilitate violent behaviors?

Many people think of violence as primarily expressive actions generated by frustration and fueled by anger, possibly because much of the work on aggression by social psychologists has developed along this line, beginning with the studies of Dollard *et al.* (*11*). . . . However, as Berkowitz (*12*) points out, violence may be primarily instrumental—neither directly related to frustration, nor accompanied by anger. Instrumental violence can be used as a tool for achieving a variety of goals, some of which are political (*13*). For example, it may be used to force a change in the distribution of power in situations where persuasion and influence cannot be used successfully (*14*), or it may be used as a tool to maintain the status quo. Instrumental violence can also be used for purely individual purposes, such as gaining money by committing robbery.

Clearly, individuals might hold quite different attitudes toward different kinds of violence. One would not expect the same person to approve of both violence to maintain the status quo and violence to produce revolutionary change. Consequently, the model developed to explain attitudes toward violence specified that types of violence must be differentiated. The survey focused mainly on measuring attitudes toward violence for social change and violence for social control.

THE MODEL

For any particular set of circumstances and for any particular person, the level of violence considered to be justifiable may be regarded as the resultant of opposing forces, some of which tend to drive the level down until no violent act is perceived as justifiable and others of which tend to drive the level up until acts of extreme violence become justifiable. Among these forces are the following.

1) *Basic cultural values against violence.* The Judeo-Christian ethic, which is widely espoused in this country, states that "Thou shalt not kill." In addition, a prominent theme in the New Testament is the notion of the golden rule—that is, that one ought to treat one's neighbors as one would like to be treated oneself. Both of these injunctions seem directly related to the problem of violence, and both

should act to mitigate the justification of violent behaviors.

2) *Basic cultural values in favor of violence.* The Bible, in addition to its gentler moods, also provides the basis for the development of values that are more sanguineous than loving. "Eye for eye, tooth for tooth, hand for hand, foot for foot" provides grounds for a good deal of violence of one kind or another. Moreover, this country has traditionally glorified the hard-riding, straight-shooting frontiersman, who settled arguments with the action end of his gun in calm disregard of legal prescriptions and processes (*15*). This aspect of our heritage has been widely popularized by the mass media (*9*). In addition, some concepts of masculinity imply positive attitudes toward violence, not to mention the positive attitudes that are implicit in long-established traditions of self-defense. To the extent that an individual cleaves to such values, he should be likely to justify the higher levels of violence.

3) *Identification with the person or group committing the aggression.* The extent to which the individual perceives himself to be allied with the membership, motives, and goals of the aggressor can act to determine the extent to which he will perceive a particular act of violence as justifiable. For example, if the individual perceives the aggressor in negative terms, he is less likely to justify the aggressor's violent behavior than that of a neutral party or an aggressor with whom he feels allied. Thus, negative identification with the aggressor will act as a force to make violence appear less justified.

4) *Identification with the victims of aggression.* The person or group that is a victim of violence is also the object of identification that can range from quite positive to negative. The more positively an individual identifies with the victim of a violent action, the less likely he is to justify violence committed against that group or person. Conversely, categorizing members of a group as aliens or out of the range of identification can be used as a justification for violence (*16*). For example, some Southerners have regarded blacks as a lower form of life, and other ethnic or social groups may be perceived similarly. Taylor (*17*) has suggested that thinking of Vietnamese citizens as "gooks" or "dinks" makes it easier to justify brutal treatment of both prisoners and civilians. Similarly, during World War II, Americans

were horrified when Hitler killed several thousand Allied civilians by bombing Rotterdam, but expressed little concern when over 100,000 enemy civilians were killed in the Allied fire bombing of Dresden (18). In short, it seems reasonable to suggest that negative identification with the victim of a violent action serves to increase the level of violence that is seen as justifiable.

5) *Definition of violent behavior.* To the extent that a behavior, however forceful and destructive, is not regarded as violence, it will not be necessary for the individual to justify the action in the terms listed above.

Attitudes Toward Violence

One of the first tasks in the survey was to develop scales to measure attitudes justifying violence for social control and attitudes justifying violence for social change. The former scale was developed from a set of five questions, repeated three times during the interview. Each time the respondent was asked how much force the police should use. The first scenario was one in which hoodlum gangs destroyed property and terrified citizens; the second specified a campus disturbance in which there was "a lot of property damage"; the third was a ghetto disturbance. In each case the respondent was asked whether the police should "let it go," "make arrests without using clubs or guns," "use clubs but not guns," "shoot but not to kill," or "shoot to kill." For every item the recommendation could be made to use a given method "almost always," "sometimes," "hardly ever," or "never."

Table 1 gives the percentage distribution of responses to the questions asking how the respondents felt the police should handle ghetto riots and campus disturbances. There are interesting patterns in these statistics. The respondents'

"center of gravity" is toward minimal rather than maximal force, arrest, or use of clubs without guns. But a substantial majority support the use of guns at least sometimes. The largest break is between the percentage of respondents who felt that shooting but not killing is appropriate and the percentage who felt the police should shoot to kill "almost always" or "sometimes." It is known that the use of firearms in any kind of assault greatly increases the probability of death (19); it may be that respondents who felt that the police should shoot but not kill anyone in the process might have a somewhat optimistic notion about the accuracy with which guns can be used.

Opinions referring to how much force the police should use in the three scenarios were combined into a scale—the violence for social control index. The higher the score on this index, the more police force the respondent justifies.

Also developed in the survey were scales measuring attitudes toward how much property damage and personal injury the respondents felt was necessary to bring about social change. Specifically, the respondents were asked how much violence is necessary to bring about changes of the type needed by students, needed by blacks, and needed in general. Table 2, which shows the amount of violence American men typically think necessary to produce social change, gives the responses to the question of how much violence is necessary to bring about changes needed by blacks. By far the majority of Americans agree that changes can be made fast enough without property damage or injury, but sizable minorities think some violence is necessary to bring about changes fast enough.

Responses to the three sets of questions about how much property damage and personal injury are necessary to bring about social changes "fast enough" were combined into a scale—the violence for social change index. The higher the score on this index, the more the respondent thinks

TABLE 1. HOW SHOULD POLICE HANDLE STUDENT DISTURBANCES? (N = 1374).

RESPONSE	ALMOST ALWAYS (%)	SOMETIMES (%)	HARDLY EVER (%)	NEVER (%)	TOTAL (%)
The police should let it go, not do anything.	4	12	14	70	100
Police should make arrests without using clubs or guns.	38	49	6	7	100
Police should use clubs, but not guns.	16	60	15	9	100
The police should shoot, but not to kill.	16	32	25	27	100
The police should shoot to kill.	3	16	19	62	100

TABLE 2. HOW MUCH VIOLENCE IS NECESSARY TO PRODUCE CHANGE NEEDED BY BLACKS? (N = 1374).

RESPONSE	AGREE A GREAT DEAL (%)	AGREE SOMEWHAT (%)	DISAGREE SOMEWHAT (%)	DISAGREE A GREAT DEAL (%)	TOTAL (%)
Changes can be made fast enough without action involving property damage or injury.	58	24	12	6	100
Protest in which some people are hurt is necessary for changes to come fast enough.	6	17	22	55	100
Protest in which there is *some* property damage is necessary for changes to be brought about fast enough.	6	19	22	53	100
Protest in which there is much property damage is necessary before changes can be brought about fast enough.	4	6	16	74	100
Protest in which some people are killed is necessary before changes will take place fast enough.	4	5	7	84	100

property damage and personal injury are necessary to bring about change fast enough.

It should be noted that the phrasing of the question is such that agreement with the statement does not necessarily mean that the respondent himself endorses or would participate in violence to bring about social change, merely that the respondent feels changes will not occur at a reasonably rapid rate without violence. One interpretation of the violence for social change index is that it is a measure of the cynicism with which American men regard the ability or willingness of the society to remedy its problems.

Violence for social control, as reflected in the index, appears to be everybody's business. Although there were some differences associated with the demographic characteristics of the respondents, no one group had a corner on justifying such attitudes. There is a tendency for the more educated and the young to recommend less stringent measures, but differences in attitudes associated with demographic characteristics tend to be small. Race is the one exception to this dictum; black men recommend lower levels of violence on the violence for social control index than do white men.

In the case of the violence for social change index, there is also a slight tendency for the better educated to see less necessity for the use of violence. However, there is a substantial difference between blacks and whites, black men agreeing more often that protest involving property damage or bodily injury is necessary to bring about changes fast enough. In contrast to 25 percent of American men generally, 49 percent of black men think some property damage is necessary to bring about social change for blacks fast enough, and 27 percent of black men, in contrast to 9 percent of men generally, think protest involving some deaths is necessary to bring about change of this type.

VALUES IN RELATION TO ATTITUDES TOWARD VIOLENCE

. . .

In studying the tendencies of American men to justify violence, it is important to understand the effects of values, both those that condone and those that condemn violent acts. Specifically, five values were studied: retributive justice, kindness, self-defense, the worth of people relative to property, and humanistic ideals relative to more conservative-materialistic attitudes. All of these values are related to the justification of violence, although two of them are more strongly related than the others. These two values, both of which have a great deal of support among American men, are retributive justice and self-defense. The exact items presented to the respondents and the percentage distribution of the responses are given in Tables 3 and 4. The five items shown in Table

TABLE 3. RESPONSES TO ITEMS MEASURING RETRIBUTIVE JUSTICE (N =1374).

RESPONSE	STRONGLY AGREE (%)	AGREE SOMEWHAT (%)	DISAGREE SOMEWHAT (%)	STRONGLY DISAGREE (%)	TOTAL (%)
People who commit murder deserve capital punishment.	43	28	14	15	100
When someone does wrong, he should be paid back for it.	23	44	22	11	100
It is often necessary to use violence to prevent it.	19	45	20	16	100
Violence deserves violence.	17	27	26	30	100
"An eye for an eye and a tooth for a tooth" is a good rule for living.	9	15	29	47	100

TABLE 4. RESPONSES TO ITEMS MEASURING SELF-DEFENSE (N = 1374).

RESPONSE	STRONGLY AGREE (%)	AGREE SOMEWHAT (%)	DISAGREE SOMEWHAT (%)	STRONGLY DISAGREE (%)	TOTAL (%)
A man has a right to kill another man in a case of self-defense.	60	29	6	5	100
A man has a right to kill a person to defend his family.	69	24	4	3	100
A man has a right to kill a person to defend his house.	23	35	25	17	100

3 were combined into the retributive justice index; the higher the score on this index, the more retributive the individual. The three items shown in Table 4 were combined into the self-defense index. The higher the score on this index, the more the respondent believed in the right to defend himself.

The retributive justice index is related to how much force an individual feels the police should use. The more retributive the individual, the higher the levels of police force he is likely to recommend. Among black men, the retributive justice index is related to opinions about how much property damage and personal injury are necessary to bring about social change fast enough. The more retributive the black man, the more likely he is to consider violence necessary for producing social change.

Similarly, the greater the belief in self-defense, the more positively the respondent views violence. Among the consistent respondents, such beliefs are associated with recommendations for higher levels of police force. Among black men, such attitudes are associated with higher scores on the violence for social change index.

Three other values were measured in the survey: the extent to which the individual ranks freedom, equality, and human dignity above respect for law, respect for property, and financial security (the humanism index); the extent to which the individual values people over property (the person-property index); and the degree to which the individual agrees with the principle of the golden rule (the kindness index).

The more the respondents value freedom, equality, and human dignity over respect for law, respect for property, and financial security, the less likely they are to advocate high levels of violence on the violence for social control index. Among blacks, there is no clear relation between the humanism index and the violence for social change index. The more the individual values property over persons, the more likely he is to advocate high levels of police force. Among blacks, the more the individual values persons over property, the more likely he is to justify high levels of violence on the violence for social change index. At first glance this may appear to be a contradiction. If human life is seen as valuable, then it would seem to follow that one would be less likely to advocate anything that might injure or destroy people. However, it is not difficult to imagine that a black man who is concerned with the value of people, particularly black people, might be inclined to view problems such as poverty and discrimination as issues requiring urgent action. Such individuals might be more inclined to feel that social change will not take place fast enough without violence. Hence the apparent contradiction is resolved.

. . .

Of the five values studied, the kindness index showed the least relation with the violence for social control index—not because there was lack of variance in the measure, but simply because belief in the golden rule is not greatly related to beliefs about whether police should beat, shoot, and kill. This finding is not true for blacks. Among black men, the more the individual professes to believe in the golden rule, the less likely he is to feel violence is necessary to produce social change. Nevertheless, one must ask why a value that ought to say so much about how people treat each other has so little relation to attitudes toward violence.

IDENTIFICATION WITH GROUPS INVOLVED IN VIOLENCE

. . .

[I]n general, American men are inclined to view the police positively, while regarding white student demonstrators and black protesters negatively. Such feelings about the contenders in the violent scenarios relate to attitudes toward violence in substantial ways. In each case, attitudes toward the contenders are related to attitudes toward violence, as predicted by the model specified earlier. In the case of the violence for social control index, the police may be regarded as the protagonists or the aggressors in the action, while white student demonstrators and black protesters are the opponents. According to the model, one would expect that the more the individual identified with the police and the less the individual identified with the dissidents, the higher the level of violence he would justify on the violence for social control index. The data demonstrate that such is the case. The more the respondent finds student demonstrators and black protesters looking for trouble, untrustworthy, hostile, and likely to change life for the worse, the higher the level of violence he advocates on the violence for social control index. On the other hand, the more the individual finds the police untrustworthy, hostile, looking for trouble, and likely to change life for the worse, the lower the level of violence he justifies on the violence for social control index.

As one would expect, diametrically opposite relations hold in the case of the violence for social change index. Here the respondent was asked how much property damage and personal injury were necessary to bring about changes needed by blacks and students. Such questions place the white student demonstrator and the black protester in the position of protagonist or aggressor, while placing the police, by implication, in the position of opponent. The more the individual finds white student demonstrators and black protesters untrustworthy, looking for trouble, hostile, and likely to change life for the worse, the lower the level of violence he justifies on the violence for social change index. The more the police are seen as having these undesirable characteristics, the higher the level of violence seen as necessary to produce social change.

RHETORIC AND ATTITUDES TOWARD VIOLENCE

The last topic to be discussed is the relation between the rhetoric of violence and attitudes toward violence. During the course of the interview the respondent was told: "Here is a list of nine things that have been in the news. Tell me if you think about these as violence. I don't mean if they lead to violence, but if you think about them *as violence in themselves.* Do you think of *student protest* as violence?" The respondent was then asked each of the items shown in Table 5. (The table is arranged according to the frequency with which the respondents labeled these acts as violence.)

It is interesting that 58 percent of American men think that burning a draft card is violence, in and of itself; 38 percent think student protest is violence; and 22 percent feel sit-ins are violence. Clearly, many Americans consider acts of dissent, per se, to be violent.

According to Webster's (*20*), violence is the exertion of physical force so as to injure or abuse. If one has something like this definition in mind one must conclude that acts such as "police beating students" or "shooting looters" are violent. After all, even if one does not consider a beaten student or a shot looter abused, both are likely to be injured. In view of the dictionary definition of the word, it is curious that only 35 percent of American men define "police shooting looters" as violence, and only 56 percent define "police beating students" in this manner. Of the behaviors inquired about, these two involve the

TABLE 5. ACTS DEFINED AS VIOLENCE (RESPONSES TO THE QUESTION OF WHETHER A GIVEN ACT IS VIOLENT) (*N* = 1374).

ITEMS	YES (%)	BOTH (%)	NO (%)	TOTAL (%)
Do you think of looting as violence?	85	3	12	100
Do you think of burglary as violence?	65	5	30	100
Do you think of draftcard burning as violence?	58	4	38	100
Do you think of police beating students as violence?	56	14	30	100
Do you think of not letting people have their civil rights as violence?	49	8	43	100
Do you think of student protest as violence?	38	15	47	100
Do you think of police shooting looters as violence?	35	8	57	100
Do you think of sit-ins as violence?	22	9	69	100
Do you think of police stopping to frisk people as violence?	16	10	74	100

most force and are most likely to lead to injury, yet they are not the acts most likely to be called violence.

Since agreement on what acts are considered violence is far from universal, one can ask whether the way in which language is used is related to attitudes toward violence. To facilitate answering this question, responses to the three items involving dissent were combined into the "Is protest violence?" index, and the responses to the three items dealing with police acts were combined into the "Are police acts violence?" index. The higher the score on an index, the more the respondent believes those items to be violence.

The more the respondent considers dissent to be violence, the more likely he is to favor the use of maximal force by the police. On the other hand, the less he considers police actions such as shooting looters and beating students to be violence, the less likely he is to advocate high levels of police force. It is as if, by labeling dissent "violence" and violent police actions "not violence," the American man is able to rationalize police behaviors that might not be so easily justified if the language were used differently.

Whether or not dissent is called violence relates only minimally to attitudes on the violence for social change index. One might speculate that those who think violence necessary to produce social change hold such beliefs consciously and therefore are not much affected by the rhetoric. On the other hand, those who believe violence for social control is necessary have not consciously recognized that it is violence which they advocate—hence the necessity of "bending" the language a bit to allow them to deny the nature of the acts they advocate. If such were the case, it

would account for the strong relation between what acts a person defines as violence and his attitudes on the violence for social control index.

· · ·

DISCUSSION

The data presented indicate that, to a very substantial degree, attitudes toward violence are related to values and attitudes toward the contenders in the violence. Moreover, the same values that enable one to justify the use of police force in an effort to maintain social control enable one to justify the use of violence as a means of producing social change. The two values that are most closely related to attitudes toward violence are retributive justice and self-defense. Both are positively oriented toward violence, and both are beliefs to which American men subscribe heavily. In addition, both have been greatly popularized by the mass media—it is not difficult to pick out the theme of retribution or self-defense in the average Western or other television adventure story. Nor is it difficult to identify these themes in the texts that are used to teach American history in many secondary school systems. The relation of these two values to attitudes toward violence and the ease with which they can apparently be used to justify violence of different types should raise some question about the extent to which such values cause positive attitudes toward violence. In addition, one must ask to what extent such values are excessively reinforced by contemporary life.

Attitudes toward violence also vary directly with beliefs about the contenders in disturbances. The more negatively those against whom violence is directed are viewed, the higher the level of force likely to be justified against them. This is equally true of those situations in which the recipients of violence are student demonstrators or black protesters, and of those in which the recipients are police. It seems likely that further research will demonstrate that the level of force felt necessary to deal with a particular situation will be a direct function of the degree to which the recipient of that force is viewed negatively. If such is the case, serious questions must be raised.

It is clear that police and other law enforcement agents should use the minimum amount of force necessary to accomplish specific objectives. The President's Commission on Campus Unrest (4) commented on this point in respect to the disaster at Kent State University. The commission reviewed the Ohio State Guard rules that apply to the use of lethal weapons. These rules state that rifles will be used only when all other means, including gun butt, bayonet, and chemicals have failed. In addition, the rules require that only single shots at confirmed targets (snipers) are to be fired unless human life is endangered by the forcible, violent acts of a rioter, or when rioters cannot be dispersed by any other reasonable means. These criteria are not predicated on notions of the trustworthiness or helpfulness of those at whom the force is directed; rather, they are based directly on the tactical requirements of the situation. Under the judicial system of this country, an individual is presumed innocent until proven guilty, is assured the right to a trial, and is protected from punishment without such a trial. To support the use of police force on the basis of the presumed attributes of the recipients of that force is to short-circuit the system of justice and to place the right to punish in the hands of the police on a spur-of-the-moment basis. The results of shooting often involve permanent injury, if not death, thus precluding the possibility of a fair trial and true justice.

It is, of course, equally unreasonable for radical proponents of social change, on the basis of negative beliefs about members of the "establishment," to resort to property damage and death to promulgate their cause. One cannot, however, control the actions of such people by policy statements. Serious legal sanctions against such behaviors already exist. What can be changed is the example set by the government, in terms of how much violence it is willing to condone in the pursuit of its proper purposes.

The last set of attitudes discussed is what the respondent defines as violence. Many Americans believe that acts of dissent are violence in and of themselves. The right to dissent is guaranteed by the Constitution, and freedom of speech has been vigorously upheld by the presidential commissions that have investigated problems of violence. The President's Commission on Campus Unrest, for example, asserted that student protest, per se, is not a problem and that vigorous debate on current issues should be an integral part of the university's function. The commission clearly and repeatedly distinguished among protest, defined as organized expression of dissent; disruption, or interference with organized activities; and violence, defined as willful property damage and injury to persons.

A good many Americans, however, do not make such distinctions. As the data clearly show, large numbers are convinced that protest is violence in and of itself. This is not merely a semantic issue. When an action is labeled "violence," the level of police force recommended to control that action is escalated.

"Inflammatory rhetoric" is a cliché that contains a considerable amount of truth. Rhetoric does inflame. When an action is called violent, irrespective of its intrinsic harmfulness or lack of harmfulness, the public becomes more willing to control that action with measures that are literally violent—that is, with police acts that will lead to substantial injury or death. Although I do not have the data to prove the point, I can easily imagine that labeling nonviolent actions of government officials and agencies violent would escalate the level of violence justified against them. One can argue from these data that the time has come for us to lower our voices and that it is irresponsible, especially for people in public life, to label behaviors that are not destructive of property or persons as violent. Such rhetoric escalates the level of violence that is justified as retaliation.

It appears from the data that attitudes toward violence are strongly related to basic values, attitudes toward others, and the language used to describe events. The fact that the levels of violence considered to be justified can be predicted (at least in the statistical sense) from a model based on values and beliefs about others implies that violence is not an aberrant or asocial phenomenon, but an integral part of the culture in which we live. If such is the case, positive attitudes toward violence will not be changed before reorientations in other areas of American life take place.

REFERENCES AND NOTES

1. *To Establish Justice, to Insure Domestic Tranquility,* final report of the National Commission on the Causes and Prevention of Violence (Government Printing Office, Washington, D.C., 1969).

2. *Assassination and Political Violence,* staff report to the National Commission on the Causes and Prevention of Violence (Government Printing Office, Washington, D.C., 1969).

3. *Report of the National Advisory Commission on Civil Disorders* (Bantam, New York, 1968).

4. *Report of the President's Commission on Campus Unrest* (Government Printing Office, Washington, D.C., 1970).

5. F. T. Graham, in *Violence in America: Historical and Comparative Perspectives,* H. D. Graham and T. R. Gurr, Eds., staff report to the National Commission on the Causes and Prevention of Violence (Government Printing Office, Washington, D.C., 1969), vol. 2, pp. 371–385.

6. R. M. Brown, in *ibid.,* vol. 1, 35–64.

7. M. D. Blumenthal. R. L. Kahn, F. M. Andrews, K. B. Head, *Justifying Violence: Attitudes of American Men* (Institute for Social Research, Ann Arbor, Mich., 1972).

8. *Television and Growing Up: The Impact of Televised Violence,* report to the Surgeon General, United States Public Health Service, from the Surgeon General's Scientific Advisory Committee on Television and Social Behavior (Government Printing Office, Washington, D.C., 1972).

9. D. L. Lange, R. K. Baker, S. J. Ball, *Mass Media and Violence,* staff report to the National Commission on the Causes and Prevention of Violence (Government Printing Office, Washington, D.C., 1969), vol. 11.

10. A. Bandura, in *The Young Child: Reviews of Research,* W. W. Hartup and N. L. Smothergill, Eds. (National Association for the Education of Young Children, Washington, D.C., 1967), pp. 42–58.

11. J. Dollard, L. Doob, N. Miller, O. Mowrer, R. Sears, *Frustration and Aggression* (Yale Univ. Press, New Haven, Conn., 1939).

12. L. Berkowitz, *Aggression: A Social Psychological Analysis* (McGraw-Hill, New York, 1962).

13. T. R. Gurr, *Why Men Rebel* (Princeton Univ. Press, Princeton, N.J., 1970).

14. W. A. Gamson, *Power and Discontent* (Dorsey, Homewood. Ill., 1968); C. Tilly, unpublished manuscript.

15. J. B. Frantz, in *Violence in America: Historical and Comparative Perspectives,* H. D. Graham and T. R. Gurr, Eds., staff report to the National Commission on the Causes and Prevention of Violence (Government Printing Office, Washington, D.C., 1969), vol. 1, pp. 101–120.

16. T. Duster, in *Sanctions for Evil,* N. Sanford, C. Comstock & Associates, Eds. (Jossey-Bass, San Francisco. 1971), pp. 25–36; V. W. Bernard, P. Ottenberg, F. Redl, *ibid.,* pp. 102–124; N. J. Smelser, *Theory of Collective Behavior* (Free Press, New York, 1962).

17. T. Taylor, *Nuremberg and Vietnam: An American Tragedy* (Random House, Quadrangle Books, Chicago, 1970).

18. H. Zinn, in *Violence in America,* T. Rose, Ed. (Random House, New York, 1969), pp. 57–69.

19. J. C. Gillen and F. M. Ochberg, in *Violence and the Struggle for Existence,* D. N. Daniels, M. F. Gilula, F. M. Ochberg, Eds. (Little, Brown, Boston, 1970), pp. 241–256.

20. *Webster's Seventh New Collegiate Dictionary* (Merriam, Springfield, Mass., 1969).

PROJECTS

Name _____

Date _____

6.1: AGGRESSION? SAYS WHO?

Psychologists have suggested a variety of definitions of aggression. For example: a response that delivers noxious stimuli to another organism; a response having for its goal the injury of a living organism; and behavior that results in personal injury and/or destruction of property (the injury may be psychological as well as physical). But the definitions do not always agree on what constitutes an aggressive behavior. The goal of this project is to stimulate you to examine your own definition of aggression more closely.

A. Listed below are a number of different actions that a person might engage in. Rate each act according to your opinion of its degree of aggressiveness. Circle the appropriate rating number.

PERSONAL RATINGS OF AGGRESSION

ACTION		RATING			
	Highly Aggressive				Not at All Aggressive
1. A baseball pitcher strikes a batter during a game.	5	4	3	2	1
2. A man slaps his wife during an argument.	5	4	3	2	1
3. A soldier shoots an enemy soldier during an attack in wartime.	5	4	3	2	1
4. A mother slaps a child who misbehaved.	5	4	3	2	1
5. A teacher disciplines a student who did not do his homework.	5	4	3	2	1
6. A woman kills her rapist.	5	4	3	2	3
7. A group of revolutionaries sets off a bomb at night in a bank as part of a political protest.	5	4	3	2	1
8. A disenchanted citizen decides not to vote.	5	4	3	2	1
9. Two young children fantasize about the horrible ways in which they will get back at their enemies.	5	4	3	2	1
10. A prison warden executes a convicted criminal.	5	4	3	2	1
11. During an argument a woman slaps her husband.	5	4	3	2	1
12. While watching a particularly bloody scene on television, a child bursts out laughing.	5	4	3	2	1
13. A person draws graffiti on the walls of a bathroom.	5	4	3	2	1
14. A person accidentally knocks a flowerpot off a ledge, which hits and injures a pedestrian.	5	4	3	2	1
15. Two people in a bar get upset and start yelling at each other.	5	4	3	2	1
16. Two policemen restrain and handcuff a demonstrator.	5	4	3	2	1

B. Ask another person to rate the same set of behaviors on the rating sheet on page 141. Try to select someone whose attitudes or political philosophy is different from your own. Compare your ratings with that person's and with the ratings of other people in your class.

C. Do your ratings of aggressiveness agree or disagree with the ratings of the person you selected to fill out the second rating sheet?

D. If there is disagreement, for what rated behaviors does it occur?

E. What is the reason for the disagreement? That is, how does your basic definition of aggression seem to differ from the other person's?

Name _____

Date _____

RATINGS OF AGGRESSION BY _____

ACTION	RATING				
	Highly Aggressive				*Not at All Aggressive*
1. A baseball pitcher strikes a batter during a game.	5	4	3	2	1
2. A man slaps his wife during an argument.	5	4	3	2	1
3. A soldier shoots an enemy soldier during an attack in wartime.	5	4	3	2	1
4. A mother slaps a child who misbehaved.	5	4	3	2	1
5. A teacher disciplines a student who did not do his homework.	5	4	3	2	1
6. A woman kills her rapist.	5	4	3	2	1
7. A group of revolutionaries sets off a bomb at night in a bank as part of a political protest.	5	4	3	2	1
8. A disenchanted citizen decides not to vote.	5	4	3	2	1
9. Two young children fantasize about the horrible ways in which they will get back at their enemies.	5	4	3	2	1
10. A prison warden executes a convicted criminal.	5	4	3	2	1
11. During an argument, a woman slaps her husband.	5	4	3	2	1
12. While watching a particularly bloody scene on television, a child bursts out laughing.	5	4	3	2	1
13. A person draws graffiti on the walls of a bathroom.	5	4	3	2	1
14. A person accidentally knocks a flowerpot off a ledge, which hits and injures a pedestrian.	5	4	3	2	1
15. Two people in a bar get upset and start yelling at each other.	5	4	3	2	1
16. Two policemen restrain and handcuff a demonstrator.	5	4	3	2	1

Name _____

Date _____

F. Rate the same actions according to each of the three definitions of aggression. Circle either "yes" or "no."

RATING AGGRESSION BY DEFINITION

ACTION	DEFINITION 1 "A response that delivers noxious stimuli to another organism"		DEFINITION 2 "A response having for its goal the injury of a living organism"		DEFINITION 3 "Behavior that results in personal injury and/or destruction of property; the injury may be psychological as well as physical"	
1. A baseball pitcher strikes a batter during a game.	yes	no	yes	no	yes	no
2. A man slaps his wife during an argument.	yes	no	yes	no	yes	no
3. A soldier shoots an enemy soldier during an attack in wartime.	yes	no	yes	no	yes	no
4. A mother slaps a child who misbehaved.	yes	no	yes	no	yes	no
5. A teacher disciplines a student who did not do his homework.	yes	no	yes	no	yes	no
6. A woman kills her rapist.	yes	no	yes	no	yes	no
7. A group of revolutionaries sets off a bomb at night in a bank as part of a political protest.	yes	no	yes	no	yes	no
8. A disenchanted citizen decides not to vote.	yes	no	yes	no	yes	no
9. Two young children fantasize about the horrible ways in which they will get back at their enemies.	yes	no	yes	no	yes	no
10. A prison warden executes a convicted criminal.	yes	no	yes	no	yes	no
11. During an argument, a woman slaps her husband.	yes	no	yes	no	yes	no
12. While watching a particularly bloody scene on television, a child bursts out laughing.	yes	no	yes	no	yes	no
13. A person draws graffiti on the walls of a bathroom.	yes	no	yes	no	yes	no
14. A person accidentally knocks a flowerpot off a ledge, which hits and injures a pedestrian.	yes	no	yes	no	yes	no

15. Two people in a bar get
    upset and start yelling at
    each other.   yes   no   yes   no   yes   no
16. Two policemen restrain
    and handcuff a
    demonstrator.   yes   no   yes   no   yes   no

Name _____

Date _____

6.2: A Case of Violence in Search of a Theory

THE LEEVILLE LYNCHING

This is the story of one of the twenty-one lynchings that occurred in 1930. The Southern Commission on the Study of Lynching (1931) investigated all twenty-one and the Leeville lynching is one of only eight in which the Southern Commission thought it fairly likely that the lynching victim had been actually guilty of the crime of which he was accused. The description that follows is based on an account by Cantril (1941).

One Saturday morning in the spring of 1930 a Negro laborer on a white man's farm near Leeville, Texas, dropped by the farmer's house to pick up the week's wages due him. The farmer's wife told him that her husband was away from the house and had not left the money. The Negro, feeling disgruntled, left the house but came back a short time later with a shotgun and demanded his money. The farmer's wife ordered him out of the house but he backed her into the bedroom and assaulted her sexually several times. Then he fled the house. The woman ran to a neighbor who phoned the sheriff. The Negro was soon captured; he confessed, agreed to plead guilty, and for safekeeping was taken to jail some miles from Leeville.

The above is the version that was commonly accepted by the white population of Leeville, but investigators listening to gossip heard other versions. Negroes in the area, for the most part, believed that the whole story was a frame-up to permit cheating the Negro laborer of his wages. Some of the white farmers said, in private, that they suspected the farmer's wife had invited the Negro to have intercourse with her and then had been frightened into a lie, possibly because her five-year-old child had interrupted the pair. A medical record showed only that intercourse had occurred; it was possible that the Negro was guilty of rape and possible that he was not. In others of the twenty-one lynchings of 1930 it was much less likely that the victim had been guilty.

In spite of the threatening mood of the Leeville community the judge insisted on holding the trial in that town, but he had four Texas Rangers detailed to preserve order. The Rangers brought the Negro into the courtroom early in the morning before any crowd had gathered. That day a large number of people came into Leeville from the farms outside of town. During the morning a crowd gathered in the courtyard and the crowd grew increasingly belligerent. At this critical juncture a rumor developed that the governor of the state had ordered the Rangers not to fire on the crowd in their efforts to protect the accused. The rumor was not true, but it was believed and it lifted the major restraint on the crowd.

About one o'clock the farmer's wife, the presumed rapist's victim, was brought from the hospital by ambulance to give testimony at the trial. When the presumably assaulted woman was carried in on a stretcher the crowd went wild. At first the Rangers kept them back with tear gas and the Negro was taken from the courtroom to a fireproof vault room. Later in the afternoon the mob burned down the courthouse and that night they used an acetylene torch to make a hole in the vault. They inserted dynamite and blew a large enough hole to permit one *man to crawl into the vault. A few minutes after disappearing he tossed out the dead body of the Negro.*

The corpse was raised with a rope to an elm tree in the courthouse yard so that every one might see it. Then it was tied to a Ford car and dragged through the town; five thousand howling people paraded behind. Finally the body was chained to a tree in the Negro section of Leeville and burned. The Leeville lynching turned into prolonged terrorization of the Negro population and it took several hundred members of the National Guard to restore order. [From Roger Brown, Social Psychology (New York: Free Press), 1965. Copyright © 1965 by The Free Press. Reprinted by permission.]

After reading the preceding description of the Leeville lynching, answer the following questions, which relate various theories of aggression to the incidents that took place in Leeville.

1. How would a Freudian theory of aggression explain this case?

2. How would frustration-aggression theory explain the Leeville lynching?

3. How would social learning theory explain it?

4. What aspects of the Leeville case (if any) cannot be adequately explained by these three theories?

7

ALTRUISM

The rates of crime and violence are rising in American society, and there is increased concern for personal safety and protection. One answer to this intensifying problem is greater individual and community involvement through helping people who are in danger. Surely you would want someone to help you if you were in need. Why not extend help to others? The solution seems clear-cut.

But in recent years, people have shown considerable reluctance to become involved and to help others. This has stimulated many expressions of shock and concern in the media and from ordinary citizens. The most celebrated case of bystander apathy was the murder of Kitty Genovese, who was stalked and killed by her assailant near an apartment building where over thirty-eight residents heard her cries but did nothing to help. In the aftermath of the Genovese incident, social psychologists conducted a series of experiments on helping behavior in an effort to determine the circumstances under which someone will assume the role of the Good Samaritan and come to the aid of a fellow human being in distress.

"FROM JERUSALEM TO JERICHO": A STUDY OF SITUATIONAL AND DISPOSITIONAL VARIABLES IN HELPING BEHAVIOR

JOHN M. DARLEY and C. DANIEL BATSON

In the parable of the Good Samaritan, a priest and a Levite fail to help a robbery victim. In contrast, the Samaritan stops to take care of the injured man. What is responsible for this difference in behavior? Was the Samaritan an inherently more moral and responsible individual? Or was there some situational constraint that might explain the lack of altruism displayed by the men of religion?

In "From Jerusalem to Jericho," Darley and Batson recount an experiment designed to analyze the parable. They conclude that helping behavior may be affected by time—more precisely, by too little of it. Their study suggests that the pressures of daily life that are so important to each of us may prevent us from paying attention to the needs of others. The person who asks for help is perceived as an obstacle in our path, hindering the successful completion of our tasks.

Helping other people in distress is, among other things, an ethical act. That is, it is an act governed by ethical norms and precepts taught to children at home, in school, and in church. From Freudian and other personality theories, one would expect individual differences in internalization of these standards that would lead to differences between individuals in the likelihood with which they would help others. But recent research on bystander intervention in emergency situations . . . has had bad luck in finding personality determinants of helping behavior. Although personality variables that one might expect to correlate with helping behavior have been measured (Machiavellianism, authoritarianism, social desirability, alienation, and social responsibility), these were not predictive of helping. Nor was this due to a generalized lack of predictability in the helping situation examined, since variations in the experimental situation, such as the availability of other people who might also help, produced marked changes in rates of helping behavior. These findings are reminiscent of Hartshorne and May's (1928) discovery that resistance to temptation, another ethically relevant act, did not seem to be a fixed characteristic of an individual. That is, a person who was likely to be honest in one situation was not particularly likely to be honest in the next (but see also Burton, 1963).

The rather disappointing correlation between the social psychologist's traditional set of personality variables and helping behavior in emergency situations suggests the need for a fresh perspective on possible predictors of helping and possible situations in which to test them. Therefore, for inspiration we turned to the Bible, to what is perhaps the classical helping story in the Judeo-Christian tradition, the parable of the Good Samaritan. The parable proved of value in suggesting both personality and situational variables relevant to helping.

"And who is my neighbor?" Jesus replied. "A man was going down from Jerusalem to Jericho, and he fell among robbers, who stripped him and beat him,

From *Journal of Personality and Social Psychology*, 1973, *27*, 100–108. Copyright © 1973 by The American Psychological Association. Reprinted by permission of the authors and The American Psychological Association.

and departed, leaving him half dead. Now by chance a priest was going down the road; and when he saw him he passed by on the other side. So likewise a Levite, when he came to the place and saw him, passed by on the other side. But a Samaritan, as he journeyed, came to where he was; and when he saw him, he had compassion, and went to him and bound his wounds, pouring on oil and wine; then he set him on his own beast and brought him to an inn, and took care of him. And the next day he took out two dennarii and gave them to the innkeeper, saying, "Take care of him; and whatever more you spend, I will repay you when I come back." Which of these three, do you think, proved neighbor to him who fell among the robbers? He said, "The one who showed mercy on him." And Jesus said to him, "Go and do likewise." [Luke 10: 29–37 RSV]

To psychologists who reflect on the parable, it seems to suggest situational and personality differences between the nonhelpful priest and Levite and the helpful Samaritan. What might each have been thinking and doing when he came upon the robbery victim on that desolate road? What sort of persons were they?

One can speculate on differences in thought. Both the priest and the Levite were religious functionaries who could be expected to have their minds occupied with religious matters. The priest's role in religious activities is obvious. The Levite's role, although less obvious, is equally important: The Levites were necessary participants in temple ceremonies. Much less can be said with any confidence about what the Samaritan might have been thinking, but, in contrast to the others, it was most likely not of a religious nature, for Samaritans were religious outcasts.

Not only was the Samaritan most likely thinking about more mundane matters than the priest and Levite, but, because he was socially less important, it seems likely that he was operating on a quite different time schedule. One can imagine the priest and Levite, prominent public figures, hurrying along with little black books full of meetings and appointments, glancing furtively at their sundials. In contrast, the Samaritan would likely have far fewer and less important people counting on him to be at a particular place at a particular time, and therefore might be expected to be in less of a hurry than the prominent priest or Levite.

In addition to these situational variables, one

finds personality factors suggested as well. Central among these, and apparently basic to the point that Jesus was trying to make, is a distinction between types of religiosity. Both the priest and Levite are extremely "religious." But it seems to be precisely their type of religiosity that the parable challenges. At issue is the motivation for one's religion and ethical behavior. Jesus seems to feel that the religious leaders of his time, though certainly respected and upstanding citizens, may be "virtuous" for what it will get them, both in terms of the admiration of their fellowmen and in the eyes of God. New Testament scholar R. W. Funk (1966) noted that the Samaritan is at the other end of the spectrum:

> The Samaritan does not love with side glances at God. The need of neighbor alone is made self-evident, and the Samaritan responds without other motivation [pp. 218–219].

That is, the Samaritan is interpreted as responding spontaneously to the situation, not as being preoccupied with the abstract ethical or organizational do's and don'ts of religion as the priest and Levite would seem to be. This is not to say that the Samaritan is portrayed as irreligious. A major intent of the parable would seem to be to present the Samaritan as a religious and ethical example, but at the same time to contrast his type of religiosity with the more common conception of religiosity that the priest and Levite represent.

To summarize the variables suggested as affecting helping behavior by the parable, the situational variables include the content of one's thinking and the amount of hurry in one's journey. The major dispositional variable seems to be differing types of religiosity. Certainly these variables do not exhaust the list that could be elicited from the parable, but they do suggest several research hypotheses.

Hypothesis 1. The parable implies that people who encounter a situation possibly calling for a helping response while thinking religious and ethical thoughts will be no more likely to offer aid than persons thinking about something else. Such a hypothesis seems to run counter to a theory that focuses on norms as determining helping behavior because a normative account would predict that the increased salience of helping norms produced by thinking about religious and ethical examples would increase helping behavior.

Hypothesis 2. Persons encountering a possible helping situation when they are in a hurry will

be less likely to offer aid than persons not in a hurry.

Hypothesis 3. Concerning types of religiosity, persons who are religious in a Samaritanlike fashion will help more frequently than those religious in a priest or Levite fashion.

Obviously, this last hypothesis is hardly operationalized as stated. Prior research by one of the investigators on types of religiosity . . . , however, led us to differentiate three distinct ways of being religious: (a) for what it will gain one . . . , (b) for its own intrinsic value . . . , and (c) as a response to and quest for meaning in one's everyday life. . . . Both of the latter conceptions would be proposed by their exponents as related to the more Samaritanlike "true" religiosity. Therefore, depending on the theorist one follows, the third hypothesis may be stated like this: People (a) who are religious for intrinsic reasons . . . or (b) whose religion emerges out of questioning the meaning of their everyday lives . . . will be more likely to stop to offer help to the victim.

The parable of the Good Samaritan also suggested how we would measure people's helping behavior—their response to a stranger slumped by the side of one's path. The victim should appear somewhat ambiguous—ill-dressed, possibly in need of help, but also possibly drunk or even potentially dangerous.

Further, the parable suggests a means by which the incident could be perceived as a real one rather than part of a psychological experiment in which one's behavior was under surveillance and might be shaped by demand characteristics . . . , evaluation apprehension . . . , or other potentially artifactual determinants of helping behavior. The victim should be encountered not in the experimental context but on the road between various tasks.

METHOD

In order to examine the influence of these variables on helping behavior, seminary students were asked to participate in a study on religious education and vocations. In the first testing session, personality questionnaires concerning types of religiosity were administered. In a second individual session, the subject began experimental procedures in one building and was asked to report to another building for later procedures. While in transit, the subject passed a slumped "victim" planted in an alleyway. The dependent variable was whether and how the subject helped the victim. The independent variables were the degree to which the subject was told to hurry in reaching the other building and the talk he was to give when he arrived there. Some subjects were to give a talk on the jobs in which seminary students would be most effective, others, on the parable of the Good Samaritan.

Subjects

The subjects for the questionnaire administration were 67 students at Princeton Theological Seminary. Forty-seven of them, those who could be reached by telephone, were scheduled for the experiment. Of the 47, 7 subjects' data were not included in the analyses—3 because of contamination of the experimental procedures during their testing and 4 due to suspicion of the experimental situation. Each subject was paid $1 for the questionnaire session and $1.50 for the experimental session.

Personality Measures

Detailed discussion of the personality scales used may be found elsewhere (Batson, 1971), so the present discussion will be brief. The general personality construct under examination was religiosity. Various conceptions of religiosity have been offered in recent years based on different psychometric scales. The conception seeming to generate the most interest is the Allport and Ross (1967) distinction between "intrinsic" versus "extrinsic" religiosity. . . . This bipolar conception of religiosity has been questioned by Brown (1964) and Batson (1971), who suggested three-dimensional analyses instead. Therefore, in the present research, types of religiosity were measured with three instruments which together provided six separate scales: (a) a *doctrinal orthodoxy* (D-O) scale patterned after that used by Glock and Stark (1966), scaling agreement with classic doctrines of Protestant theology; (b) the Allport-Ross *extrinsic* (AR-E) scale, measuring the use of religion as a means to an end rather than as an end in itself; (c) the Allport-Ross *intrinsic* (AR-I) scale, measuring the use of religion as an end in itself; (d) the *extrinsic external* scale of Batson's Religious Life Inventory (RELI-EE), designed to measure the influence of significant others and situations in generating one's religiosity; (e) the *extrinsic internal* scale of the Religious Life Inventory (RELI-EI), designed to measure the degree of "driveness" in one's religiosity; and (f) the *intrinsic* scale of the Religious Life Inventory (RELI-I),

designed to measure the degree to which one's religiosity involves a questioning of the meaning of life arising out of one's interactions with his social environment. The order of presentation of the scales in the questionnaire was RELI, AR, D-O.

Scheduling of Experimental Study

Since the incident requiring a helping response was staged outdoors, the entire experimental study was run in 3 days, December 14–16, 1970, between 10 A.M. and 4 P.M. A tight schedule was used in an attempt to maintain reasonably consistent weather and light conditions. Temperature fluctuation according to the *New York Times* for the 3 days during these hours was not more than 5 degrees Fahrenheit. No rain or snow fell, although the third day was cloudy, whereas the first two were sunny. Within days the subjects were randomly assigned to experimental conditions.

Procedure

When a subject appeared for the experiment, an assistant (who was blind with respect to the personality scores) asked him to read a brief statement which explained that he was participating in a study of the vocational careers of seminary students. After developing the rationale for the study, the statement read:

> What we have called you in for today is to provide us with some additional material which will give us a clearer picture of how you think than does the questionnaire material we have gathered thus far. Questionnaires are helpful, but tend to be somewhat oversimplified. Therefore, we would like to record a 3–5-minute talk you give based on the following passage. . . .

Variable 1: Message. In the task-relevant condition the passage read,

> With increasing frequency the question is being asked: What jobs or professions do seminary students subsequently enjoy most, and in what jobs are they most effective? The answer to this question used to be so obvious that the question was not even asked. Seminary students were being trained for the ministry, and since both society at large and the seminary student himself had a relatively clear understanding of what made a "good" minister, there was no need even to raise the question of for what

other jobs seminary experience seems to be an asset. Today, however, neither society nor many seminaries have a very clearly defined conception of what a "good" minister is or of what sorts of jobs and professions are the best context in which to minister. Many seminary students, apparently genuinely concerned with "ministering," seem to feel that it is impossible to minister in the professional clergy. Other students, no less concerned, find the clergy the most viable profession for ministry. But are there other jobs and/or professions for which seminary experience is an asset? And, indeed, how much of an asset is it for the professional ministry? Or, even more broadly, can one minister through an "establishment" job at all?

In the helping-relevant condition, the subject was given the parable of the Good Samaritan exactly as printed earlier in this article. Next, regardless of condition, all subjects were told,

> You can say whatever you wish based on the passage. Because we are interested in how you think on your feet, you will not be allowed to use notes in giving the talk. Do you understand what you are to do? If not, the assistant will be glad to answer questions.

After a few minutes the assistant returned, asked if there were any questions, and then said:

> Since they're rather tight on space in this building, we're using a free office in the building next door for recording the talks. Let me show you how to get there [draws and explains map on 3 × 5 card]. This is where Professor Steiner's laboratory is. If you go in this door [points at map], there's a secretary right here, and she'll direct you to the office we're using for recording. Another of Professor Steiner's assistants will set you up for recording your talk. Is the map clear?

Variable 2: Hurry. In the high-hurry condition the assistant then looked at his watch and said, "Oh, you're late. They were expecting you a few minutes ago. We'd better get moving. The assistant should be waiting for you so you'd better hurry. It shouldn't take but just a minute." In the intermediate-hurry condition he said, "The assistant is ready for you, so please go right over." In the low-hurry condition he said, "It'll be a few minutes before they're ready for you, but you might as well head on over. If you have to wait over there, it shouldn't be long."

The incident. When the subject passed through the alley, the victim was sitting slumped in a doorway, head down, eyes closed, not moving. As the subject went by, the victim coughed twice and groaned, keeping his head down. If the subject stopped and asked if something was wrong or offered to help, the victim, startled and somewhat groggy, said, "Oh, thank you [cough]. . . . No, it's all right. [Pause] I've got this respiratory condition [cough]. . . . The doctor's given me these pills to take, and I just took one. . . . If I just sit and rest for a few minutes I'll be O.K. . . . Thanks very much for stopping though [smiles weakly]." If the subject persisted, insisting on taking the victim inside the building, the victim allowed him to do so and thanked him.

Helping ratings. The victim rated each subject on a scale of helping behavior as follows:

> 0 = failed to notice the victim as possibly in need at all; 1 = perceived the victim as possibly in need but did not offer aid; 2 = did not stop but helped indirectly (e.g., by telling Steiner's assistant about the victim); 3 = stopped and asked if victim needed help; 4 = after stopping, insisted on taking the victim inside and then left him.

The victim was blind to the personality scale scores and experimental conditions of all subjects. At the suggestion of the victim, another category was added to the rating scales, based on his observations of pilot subjects' behavior:

> 5 = after stopping, refused to leave the victim (after 3–5 minutes) and/or insisted on taking him somewhere outside experimental context (e.g., for coffee or to the infirmary).

(In some cases it was necessary to distinguish Category 0 from Category 1 by the postexperimental questionnaire and Category 2 from Category 1 on the report of the experimental assistant.)

This 6-point scale of helping behavior and a description of the victim were given to a panel of 10 judges (unacquainted with the research) who were asked to rank order the (unnumbered) categories in terms of "the amount of helping behavior displayed toward the person in the doorway." Of the 10, 1 judge reversed the order of Categories 0 and 1. Otherwise there was complete agreement with the ranking implied in the presentation of the scale above.

The speech. After passing through the alley and entering the door marked on the map, the subject entered a secretary's office. She introduced him to the assistant who gave the subject time to prepare and privately record his talk.

Helping behavior questionnaire. After recording the talk, the subject was sent to another experimenter, who administered "an exploratory questionnaire on personal and social ethics." The questionnaire contained several initial questions about the interrelationship between social and personal ethics, and then asked three key questions: (a) "When was the last time you saw a person who seemed to be in need of help?" (b) "When was the last time you stopped to help someone in need?" (c) "Have you had experience helping persons in need? If so, outline briefly." These data were collected as a check on the victim's ratings of whether subjects who did not stop perceived the situation in the alley as one possibly involving need or not.

When he returned, the experimenter reviewed the subject's questionnaire, and, if no mention was made of the situation in the alley, probed for reactions to it and then phased into an elaborate debriefing and discussion session.

Debriefing

In the debriefing, the subject was told the exact nature of the study, including the deception involved, and the reasons for the deception were explained. The subject's reactions to the victim and to the study in general were discussed. The role of situational determinants of helping behavior was explained in relation to this particular incident and to other experiences of the subject. All subjects seemed readily to understand the necessity for the deception, and none indicated any resentment of it. After debriefing, the subject was thanked for his time and paid, then he left.

RESULTS AND DISCUSSION

Overall Helping Behavior

The average amount of help that a subject offered the victim, by condition, is shown in Table 1. The unequal-N analysis of variance indicates that while the hurry variable was significantly ($F = 3.56$, $df = 2/34$, $p < .05$) related to helping behavior, the message variable was not. Subjects in a hurry were likely to offer less help than were subjects not in a hurry. Whether the subject was going to give a speech on the parable of the Good Samaritan or not did not significantly affect his helping behavior on this analysis.

TABLE 1: MEANS AND ANALYSIS OF VARIANCE OF GRADED HELPING RESPONSES

		M		
		HURRY		
MESSAGE	LOW	MEDIUM	HIGH	SUMMARY
Helping relevant	3.800	2.000	1.000	2.263
Task relevant	1.667	1.667	.500	1.333
Summary	3.000	1.818	.700	

Analysis of Variance

SOURCE	SS	df	MS	F
Message (A)	7.766	1	7.766	2.65
Hurry (B)	20.884	2	10.442	3.56*
A × B	5.237	2	2.619	.89
Error	99.633	34	2.930	

Note: N = 40.
*p < .05.

Other studies have focused on the question of whether a person initiates helping action or not, rather than on scaled kinds of helping. The data from the present study can also be analyzed on the following terms: Of the 40 subjects, 16 (40%) offered some form of direct or indirect aid to the victim (Coding Categories 2–5), 24 (60%) did not (Coding Categories 0 and 1). The percentages of subjects who offered aid by situational variable were, for low hurry, 63% offered help, intermediate hurry 45%, and high hurry 10%; for helping-relevant message 53%, task-relevant message 29%. With regard to this more general question of whether help was offered or not, an unequal-N analysis of variance . . . indicated that again only the hurry main effect was significantly ($F = 5.22$, $p < .05$) related to helping behavior; the subjects in a hurry were more likely to pass by the victim than were those in less of a hurry.

Reviewing the predictions in the light of these results, the second hypothesis, that the degree of hurry a person is in determines his helping behavior, was supported. The prediction involved in the first hypothesis concerning the message content was based on the parable. The parable itself seemed to suggest that thinking pious thoughts would not increase helping. Another and conflicting prediction might be produced by a norm salience theory. Thinking about the parable should make norms for helping salient and therefore produce more helping. The data, as hypothesized, are more congruent with the prediction drawn from the parable. A person going to speak on the parable of the Good Samaritan is not significantly more likely to stop to help a person by the side of the road than is a person going to talk about possible occupations for seminary graduates.

. . .

Notice also that neither form of the third hypothesis, that types of religiosity will predict helping, received support from these data. No correlation between the various measures of religiosity and any form of the dependent measure ever came near statistical significance. . . .

. . .

CONCLUSION AND IMPLICATIONS

A person not in a hurry may stop and offer help to a person in distress. A person in a hurry is likely to keep going. Ironically, he is likely to keep going even if he is hurrying to speak on the parable of the Good Samaritan, thus inadvertently confirming the point of the parable. (Indeed, on several occasions, a seminary student going to give his talk on the parable of the Good Samaritan literally stepped over the victim as he hurried on his way!)

Although the degree to which a person was in a hurry had a clearly significant effect on his likelihood of offering the victim help, whether he was going to give a sermon on the parable or on possible vocational roles of ministers did not. This lack of effect of sermon topic raises certain difficulties for an explanation of helping behavior involving helping norms and their salience. It is hard to think of a context in which norms concerning helping those in distress are more salient than for a person thinking about the Good Samaritan, and yet it did not significantly increase helping behavior. The results were in the direction suggested by the norm salience hypothesis, but they were not significant. The most accurate conclusion seems to be that salience of helping norms is a less strong determinant of

behavior in the present situation than many, including the present authors, would expect.

Thinking about the Good Samaritan did not increase helping behavior, but being in a hurry decreased it. It is difficult not to conclude from this that the frequently cited explanation that ethics becomes a luxury as the speed of our daily lives increases is at least an accurate description. The picture that this explanation conveys is of a person seeing another, consciously noting his distress, and consciously choosing to leave him in distress. But perhaps this is not entirely accurate, for, when a person is in a hurry, something seems to happen that is akin to Tolman's (1948) concept of the "narrowing of the cognitive map." Our seminarians in a hurry noticed the victim in that in the postexperiment interview almost all mentioned him as, on reflection, possibly in need of help. But it seems that they often had not worked this out when they were near the victim. Either the interpretation of [the] visual picture as a person in distress or the empathic reactions usually associated with that interpretation had been deferred because they were hurrying. According to the reflections of some of the subjects, it would be inaccurate to say that they realized the victim's possible distress, then chose to ignore it; instead, because of the time pressures, they did not perceive the scene in the alley as an occasion for an ethical decision.

For other subjects it seems more accurate to conclude that they decided not to stop. They appeared aroused and anxious after the encounter in the alley. For these subjects, what were the elements of the choice that they were making? Why were the seminarians hurrying? Because the experimenter, *whom the subject was helping,* was depending on him to get to a particular place quickly. In other words, he was in conflict between stopping to help the victim and continuing on his way to help the experimenter. And this is often true of people in a hurry; they hurry because somebody depends on their being somewhere. Conflict, rather than callousness, can explain their failure to stop.

. . .

REFERENCES

Allport, G. W., & Ross, J. M. Personal religious orientation and prejudice. *Journal of Personality and Social Psychology,* 1967, 5, 432–443.

Batson, C. D. Creativity and religious development: Toward a structural-functional psychology of religion. Unpublished doctoral dissertation, Princeton Theological Seminary, 1971.

Brown, L. B. Classifications of religious orientation. *Journal for the Scientific Study of Religion,* 1964, 4, 91–99.

Burton, R. V. The generality of honesty reconsidered. *Psychological Review*, 1963, 70, 481–499.

Funk, R. W. *Language, hermeneutic, and word of God.* New York: Harper & Row, 1966.

Glock, C. Y., & Stark, R. *Christian beliefs and anti-Semitism.* New York: Harper & Row, 1966.

Hartshorne, H., & May, M. A. *Studies in the nature of character.* Vol. 1. *Studies in deceit.* New York: Macmillan, 1928.

Tolman, E. C. Cognitive maps in rats and men. *Psychological Review*, 1948, 55, 189–208.

WHY DO WE CALL THE GOOD SAMARITAN GOOD?

1. The Good Samaritan was traveling. We assume that there was a place to which he had to go. Nevertheless, he stopped and gave of his time to help the victim.

2. He gave his own money. When someone gives his own money freely, we tend to attribute a pure motive to that person.

3. Besides actually giving his own money, he offered to pay more if it was needed.

4. He took upon himself some personal responsibility for the victim's health. He said that he would stop at the inn on his return trip so that he could assess the victim's condition as well as pay any extra costs.

5. He helped voluntarily, without coercion or social pressure.

6. He did something that exceeded social mores; that is, his actions exceeded what was expected of a despised Samaritan. The Samaritans were the outgroup of the first century. Nobody would expect one of them to do a good deed.

7. The Good Samaritan's helping behavior is vividly contrasted with that of the priest and Levite, two people who, according to the standards of the society, ought to have helped.

The Good Samaritan performed a prosocial act without external justification, contrary to social mores, and at personal cost. Because of this cluster of factors, we attribute to him a pure altruistic motive. The attribution of goodness is to the person rather than to the context.

Adapted from Raymond F. Paloutzian, *Religious Belief and Behavior* (Scottsdale, Arizona: Christian Academic Publications), 1978.

"I'm sorry. My responsibility doesn't go beyond this bubble."

• • •

Drawing by David Pascal; © 1976 The New Yorker Magazine, Inc.

GOOD SAMARITANISM: AN UNDERGROUND PHENOMENON?

IRVING M. PILIAVIN, JUDITH RODIN, and JANE ALLYN PILIAVIN

Among the factors that may contribute to the decision to come to the aid of a person in distress are the characteristics of the victim and the nature of his or her plight. If helping the victim would involve some sort of risk, or if the victim's problem is a distasteful one (such as public drunkenness), people may be reluctant to lend a helping hand. Another variable involves the social impact of models. Are people more or less likely to help a person if they see someone else doing so? In "Good Samaritanism: An Underground Phenomenon," Piliavin, Rodin, and Piliavin describe responses to a help-requiring situation staged in the real-life world of New York City's subways.

Since the murder of Kitty Genovese in Queens, a rapidly increasing number of social scientists have turned their attentions to the study of the good Samaritan's act and an associated phenomenon, the evaluation of victims by bystanders and agents. Some of the findings of this research have been provocative and nonobvious. For example, there is evidence that agents, and even bystanders, will sometimes derogate the character of the victims of misfortune, instead of feeling compassion. . . . Furthermore, recent findings indicate that under certain circumstances there is not "safety in numbers," but rather "diffusion of responsibility." Darley and Latané (1968) have reported that among bystanders hearing an epileptic seizure over earphones, those who believed other witnesses were present were less likely to seek assistance for the victim than were bystanders who believed they were alone. Subsequent research by Latané and Rodin (1969) on response to the victim of a fall confirmed this finding and suggested further that assistance from a group of bystanders was less likely to come if the group members were strangers than if they were prior acquaintances. The field experiments of Bryan and Test (1967), on the other hand, provide interesting findings that fit common sense expectations; namely, one is more likely to be a good Samaritan if one has just observed another individual performing a helpful act.

From *Journal of Personality and Social Psychology*, 1969, *13*, 289–299. Copyright 1969 by The American Psychological Association, and reprinted with permission.

Much of the work on victimization to date has been performed in the laboratory. It is commonly argued that the ideal research strategy over the long haul is to move back and forth between the laboratory, with its advantage of greater control, and the field, with its advantage of greater reality. The present study was designed to provide more information from the latter setting.

The primary focus of the study was on the effect of type of victim (drunk or ill) and race of victim (black or white) on speed of responding, frequency of responding, and the race of the helper. On the basis of the large body of research on similarity and liking as well as that on race and social distance, it was assumed that an individual would be more inclined to help someone of his race than a person of another race. The expectation regarding type of victim was that help would be accorded more frequently and rapidly to the apparently ill victim. This expectation was derived from two considerations. First, it was assumed that people who are regarded as partly responsible for their plight would receive less sympathy and consequently less help than people seen as not responsible for their circumstances. . . .

Secondly, it was assumed that whatever sympathy individuals may experience when they observe a drunk collapse, their inclination to help hm will be dampened by the realization that the victim may become disgusting, embarrassing, and/or violent. This realization may, in fact, not only constrain helping but also lead observers to turn away from the victim—that is, to leave the scene of the emergency.

Aside from examining the effects of race and type of victim, the present research sought to investigate the impact of modeling in emergency situations. Several investigators have found that an individual's actions in a given situation lead others in that situation to engage in similar actions. This modeling phenomenon has been observed in a variety of contexts including those involving good Samaritanism. . . . It was expected that the phenomenon would be observed as well in the present study. A final concern of the study was to examine the relationship between size of group and frequency and latency of the helping response, with a victim who was both seen and heard. In previous laboratory studies . . . increases in group size led to decreases in frequency and increases in latency of responding. In these studies, however, the emergency was only heard, not seen. Since visual cues are likely to make an emergency much more arousing for the observer, it is not clear that, given these cues, such considerations as crowd size will be relevant determinants of the observer's response to the emergency. Visual cues also provide clear information as to whether anyone has yet helped the victim or if he has been able to help himself. Thus, in the laboratory studies, observers lacking visual cues could rationalize not helping by assuming assistance was no longer needed when the victim ceased calling for help. Staging emergencies in full view of observers eliminates the possibility of such rationalization.

To conduct a field investigation of the above questions under the desired conditions required a setting which would allow the repeated staging of emergencies in the midst of reasonably large groups which remained fairly similar in composition from incident to incident. It was also desirable that each group retain the same composition over the course of the incident and that a reasonable amount of time be available after the emergency occurred for good Samaritans to act. To meet these requirements, the emergencies were staged during the approximately 7½-minute express run between the 59th Street and 125th Street stations of the Eighth Avenue Independent (IND) branch of the New York subways.

METHOD

Subjects

About 4,450 men and women who traveled on the 8th Avenue IND in New York City, weekdays

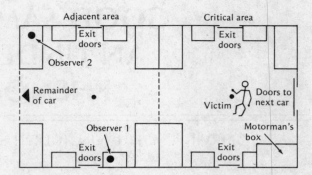

FIGURE 1 Layout of adjacent and critical areas of subway car.

between the hours of 11:00 A.M. and 3:00 P.M. during the period from April 15 to June 26, 1968, were the unsolicited participants in this study. The racial composition of a typical train, which travels through Harlem to the Bronx, was about 45% black and 55% white. The mean number of people per car during these hours was 43; the mean number of people in the "critical area," in which the staged incident took place, was 8.5.

Field situation. The A and D trains of the 8th Avenue IND were selected because they make no stops between 59th Street and 125th Street. Thus, for about 7½ minutes there was a captive audience who, after the first 70 seconds of their ride, became bystanders to an emergency situation. A single trial was a nonstop ride between 59th and 125th Streets, going in either direction. All trials were run only on the old New York subway cars which serviced the 8th Avenue line since they had two-person seats in group arrangement rather than extended seats. The designated experimental or critical area was that end section of any car whose doors led to the next car. There are 13 seats and some standing room in this area on all trains (see Fig. 1).

Procedure

On each trial a team of four Columbia General Studies students, two males and two females, boarded the train using different doors. Four different teams, whose members always worked together, were used to collect data for 103 trials. Each team varied the location of the experimental car from trial to trial. The female confederates took seats outside the critical area and recorded data as unobtrusively as possible for the duration of the ride, while the male model and victim remained standing. The victim always stood next to a pole in the center of the critical area (see Fig. 1). As the train passed the first station (approximately 70 seconds after departing) the victim staggered forward and collapsed. Until receiving help, the victim remained supine on the floor looking at the ceiling. If the victim received no assistance by the time the train slowed to a stop, the model helped him to his feet. At the stop, the team disembarked and waited separately until other riders had left the station. They then proceeded to another platform to board a train going in the opposite direction for the next trial. From 6 to 8 trials were run on a given day. All trials on a given day were in the same "victim condition."

Victim: The four victims (one from each team) were males between the ages of 26 and 35. Three were white and one was black. All were identically dressed in Eisenhower jackets, old slacks, and no tie. On 38 trials the victims smelled of liquor and carried a liquor bottle wrapped tightly in a brown bag (drunk condition), while on the remaining 65 trials they appeared sober and carried a black cane (cane condition). In all other aspects, victims dressed and behaved identically in the two conditions. Each victim participated in drunk and cane trials.[1]

Model: Four white males between the ages of 24 and 29 assumed the roles of model in each team. All models wore informal clothes, although they were not identically attired. There were four different model conditions used across both victim conditions (drunk or cane).

1. *Critical area—early.* Model stood in critical area and waited until passing fourth station to assist victim (approximately 70 seconds after collapse).

2. *Critical area—late.* Model stood in critical area and waited until passing sixth station to assist victim (approximately 150 seconds after collapse).

3. *Adjacent area—early.* Model stood in middle of car in area adjacent to critical area and waited until passing fourth station.

4. *Adjacent area—late.* Model stood in adjacent area and waited until passing sixth station.

When the model provided assistance, he raised the victim to a sitting position and stayed with him for the remainder of the trial. An equal number of trials in the no-model condition and in each of the four model conditions were preprogrammed by a random number table and assigned to each team.

Measures: On each trial one observer noted the race, sex, and location of every rider seated or standing in the critical area. In addition, she counted the total number of individuals in the car and the total number of individuals who came to the victim's assistance. She also recorded the race, sex, and location of every helper. A second observer coded the race, sex, and location of all persons in the adjacent area. She also recorded the latency of the first helper's arrival after the victim had fallen and on appropriate trials, the latency of the first helper's arrival after the programmed model had arrived. Both observers recorded comments spontaneously made by nearby passengers and attempted to elicit comments from a rider sitting next to them.

RESULTS AND DISCUSSION

As can be seen in Table 1, the frequency of help received by the victims was impressive, at least as compared to earlier laboratory results. The victim with the cane received spontaneous help, that is, before the model acted, on 62 of the 65 trials. Even the drunk received spontaneous help on 19 of 38 trials. The difference is not explicable on the basis of gross differences in the numbers of potential helpers in the cars. (Mean number of passengers in the car on cane trials was 45; on drunk trials, 40. Total range was 15–120.)

On the basis of past research, relatively long latencies of spontaneous helping were expected; thus, it was assumed that models would have time to help, and their effects could be assessed. However, in all but three of the cane trials planned to be model trials, the victim received help before the model was scheduled to offer assistance. This was less likely to happen with the drunk victim. In many cases, the early model was able to intervene, and in a few, even the delayed model could act (see Table 1 for frequencies).

---

[1]It will be noted later that not only were there more cane trials than drunk trials, they were also distributed unevenly across black and white victims. The reason for this is easier to explain than to correct. Teams 1 and 2 (both white victims) started the first day in the cane condition. Teams 3 (black) and 4 (white) began in the drunk condition. Teams were told to alternate the conditions across days. They arranged their running days to fit their schedules. On their fourth day, Team 2 violated the instruction and ran cane trials when they should have run drunk trials; the victim "didn't like" playing the drunk! Then the Columbia student strike occurred, the teams disbanded, and the study of necessity was over. At this point, Teams 1 and 3 had run on only 3 days each, while 2 and 4 had run on 4 days each.

TABLE 1: PERCENTAGE OF TRIALS ON WHICH HELP WAS GIVEN, BY RACE AND CONDITION OF VICTIM, AND TOTAL NUMBER OF TRIALS RUN IN EACH CONDITION

TRIALS	WHITE VICTIMS		BLACK VICTIM	
	CANE	DRUNK	CANE	DRUNK
No model	100%	100%	100%	73%
Number of trials run	54	11	8	11
Model trials	100%	77%	—	67%
Number of trials run	3	13	0	3
Total number of trials	57	24	8	14

Note: Distribution of model trials for the drunk was as follows: critical area: early, 4; late, 4; adjacent area: early, 5; late, 3. The three model trials completed for the cane victim were all early, with 2 from the critical area and 1 from the adjacent area.

A direct comparison between the latency of response in the drunk and cane conditions might be misleading, since on model trials one does not know how long it might have taken for a helper to arrive without the stimulus of the model. Omitting the model trials, however, would reduce the number of drunk trials drastically. In order to get around these problems the trials have been dichotomized into a group in which someone helped *before* 70 seconds (the time at which the early model was programmed to help) and a group in which no one had helped by this time. The second group includes some trials in which people helped the model and a very few in which no one helped at all. It is quite clear from the first section of Table 2 that there was more immediate, spontaneous helping of the victim with the cane than of the drunk. The effect seems to be essentially the same for the black victim and for the white victims.

What of the total number of people who helped? On 60% of the 81 trials on which the victim received help, he received it not from one good Samaritan but from two, three, or even more.[2] There are no significant differences between black

[2]The data from the model trials are not included in this analysis because the model was programmed to behave rather differently from the way in which most real helpers behaved. That is, his role was to raise the victim to a sitting position and then appear to need assistance. Most real helpers managed to drag the victim to a seat or to a standing position on their own. Thus the programmed model received somewhat more help than did real first helpers.

and white victims, or between cane and drunk victims, in the number of helpers subsequent to the first who came to his aid. Seemingly, then, the presence of the first helper has important implications which override whatever cognitive and emotional differences were initially engendered among observers by the characteristics of the victim. It may be that the victim's uniformly passive response to the individual trying to assist him reduced observers' fear about possible unpleasantness in the drunk conditions. Another possibility is that the key factor in the decisions of second and third helpers to offer assistance was the first helper. That is, perhaps assistance was being offered primarily to him rather than to the victim. Unfortunately the data do not permit adequate assessment of these or other possible explanations.

Characteristics of Spontaneous First Helpers

Having discovered that people do, in fact, help with rather high frequency, the next question is, "Who helps?" The effect of two variables, sex and race, can be examined. On the average, 60% of the people in the critical area were males. Yet, of the 81 spontaneous first helpers, 90% were males. In this situation, then, men are considerably more likely to help than are women ($\chi^2 = 30.63$; $p < .001$).

Turning now to the race variable, of the 81 first helpers, 64% were white. This percentage does not differ significantly from the expected percentage of 55% based on racial distribution in the cars. Since both black and white victims were used, it is also possible to see whether blacks and whites are more likely to help a member of their own race. On the 65 trials on which spontaneous help was offered to the white victims, 68% of the helpers were white. This proportion differs from the expected 55% at the .05 level ($\chi^2 = 4.23$). On the 16 trials on which spontaneous help was offered to the black victim, half of the first helpers were white. While this proportion does not differ from chance expectation, we again see a slight tendency toward "same-race" helping.

When race of helper is examined separately for cane and drunk victims, an interesting although nonsignificant trend emerges (see Table 3). With both the black and white cane victims, the proportion of helpers of each race was in accord with the expected 55%–45% split. With the drunk, on the other hand, it was mainly members of his own race who came to his aid.

This interesting tendency toward same-race helping only in the case of the drunk victim may

TABLE 2: TIME AND RESPONSES TO THE INCIDENT

TRIALS ON WHICH HELP WAS OFFERED:	TOTAL NUMBER OF TRIALS		% OF TRIALS ON WHICH 1 + PERSONS LEFT CRITICAL AREA[b]		% OF TRIALS ON WHICH 1 + COMMENTS WERE RECORDED[b]		MEAN NUMBER OF COMMENTS	
	WHITE VICTIMS	BLACK VICTIM	WHITE VICTIMS	BLACK VICTIM	WHITE VICTIMS	BLACK VICTIM	WHITE VICTIMS	BLACK VICTIM
Before 70 sec.								
Cane	52	7	4%	14%	21%	0%	.27	.00
Drunk	5	4	20%	0%	80%	50%	1.00	.50
Total	57	11	5%	9%	26%	18%	.33	.18
After 70 sec.								
Cane	5	1	40%	—	60%	—	.80	—
Drunk	19	10	42%	60%	100%	70%	2.00	.90
Total	24	11	42%	64%	96%	64%	1.75	.82
χ^2	36.83	[a]	χ^2 time = 23.19		χ^2 time = 31.45			
p	< .001	< .03	$p < .001$		$p < .001$			
			χ^2 cane-drunk = 11.71		χ^2 cane-drunk = 37.95			
			$p < .001$		$p < .001$			

Note: Percentage and means not calculated for *n*'s less than 4.
[a]Fisher's exact test, estimate of two-tailed probability.
[b]Black and white victims are combined for the analyses of these data.

reflect more empathy, sympathy, and trust toward victims of one's own racial group. In the case of an innocent victim (e.g., the cane victim), when sympathy, though differentially experienced, is relatively uncomplicated by other emotions, assistance can readily cut across group lines. In the case of the drunk (and potentially dangerous) victim, complications are present, probably blame, fear, and disgust. When the victim is a member of one's own group—when the conditions for empathy and trust are more favorable—assistance is more likely to be offered. As we have seen, however, this does not happen without the passing of time to think things over.

. . .

Other Responses to the Incident

What other responses do observers make to the incident? Do the passengers leave the car, move out of the area, make comments about the inci-

dent? No one left the car on any of the trials. However, on 21 of the 103 trials, a total of 34 people did leave the critical area. The second section of Table 2 presents the percentage of trials on which someone left the critical area as a function of three variables: type of victim, race of victim, and time to receipt of help (before or after 70 seconds). People left the area on a higher proportion of trials with the drunk than with the cane victim. They also were far more likely to leave on trials on which help was not offered by 70 seconds, as compared to trials on which help was received before that time. The frequencies are too small to make comparisons with each of the variables held constant.

Each observer spoke to the person seated next to her after the incident took place. She also noted spontaneous comments and actions by those around her. A content analysis of these data was performed, with little in the way of interesting

TABLE 3: SPONTANEOUS HELPING OF CANE AND DRUNK BY RACE OF HELPER AND RACE OF VICTIM

RACE OF HELPER	WHITE VICTIMS			BLACK VICTIM			ALL VICTIMS		
	CANE	DRUNK	TOTAL	CANE	DRUNK	TOTAL	CANE	DRUNK	TOTAL
Same as victim	34	10	44	2	6	8	36	16	52
Different from victim	20	1	21	6	2	8	26	3	29
Total	54	11	65	8	8	16	62	19	81

Note: Chi-squares are corrected for continuity. White victims, $\chi^2 = 2.11$, $p = .16$; black victim, $p = .16$ (two-tailed estimate from Fisher's exact probabilities test); all victims, $\chi^2 = 3.26$, $p = .08$.

findings. The distribution of number of comments over different sorts of trials, however, did prove interesting (see Section 3 of Table 2). Far more comments were obtained on drunk trials than on cane trials. Similarly, most of the comments were obtained on trials in which no one helped until after 70 seconds. The discomfort observers felt in sitting inactive in the presence of the victim may have led them to talk about the incident, perhaps hoping others would confirm the fact that inaction was appropriate. Many women, for example, made comments such as, "It's for men to help him," or "I wish I could help him—I'm not strong enough," "I never saw this kind of thing before—I don't know where to look," "You feel so bad that you don't know what to do."

A Test of the Diffusion of Responsibility Hypothesis

In the Darley and Latané experiment it was predicted and found that as the number of bystanders increased, the likelihood that any individual would help decreased and the latency of response increased. Their study involved bystanders who could not see each other or the victim. In the Latané and Rodin study, the effect was again found, with bystanders who were face to face, but with the victim still only heard. In the present study, bystanders saw both the victim and each other. Will the diffusion of responsibility finding still occur in this situation?

In order to check this hypothesis, two analyses were performed. First, all nonmodel trials were separated into three groups according to the number of males in the critical area (the assumed reference group for spontaneous first helpers). Mean and median latencies of response were then calculated for each group, separately by type and race of victim. . . . There is no evidence in these data for diffusion of responsibility; in fact, response times, using either measure, are consistently faster for the 7 or more groups compared to the 1 to 3 groups.

As Darley and Latané pointed out, however, different-size real groups cannot be meaningfully compared to one another, since as group size increases the likelihood that one or more persons will help also increases. A second analysis as similar as possible to that used by those authors was therefore performed, comparing latencies actually obtained for each size group with a base line of hypothetical groups of the same size made up by combining smaller groups. . . .

As can be seen in . . . Figure 2, the cumulative

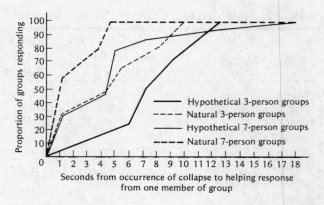

FIGURE 2 Cumulative proportion of groups producing a helper over time (cane trials, white victims, male helpers from inside critical area).

helping response curves for the hypothetical groups of both sizes are lower than those for the corresponding real groups. That is, members of real groups responded more rapidly than would be expected on the basis of the faster of the two scores obtained from the combined smaller groups. While these results . . . do not necessarily contradict the diffusion of responsibility hypothesis, they do not follow the pattern of findings obtained by Darley and Latané and are clearly at variance with the tentative conclusion of those investigators that "a victim may be more likely to receive help . . . the fewer people there are to take action [Latané & Darley, 1968, p. 221]."

Two explanations can be suggested to account for the disparity between the findings of . . . Fig. 2 and those of Darley and Latané and Rodin. As indicated earlier in this paper, the conditions of the present study were quite different from those in previous investigations. First, the fact that observers in the present study could see the victim may not only have constrained observers' abilities to conclude there was no emergency, but may also have overwhelmed with other considerations any tendency to diffuse responsibility. Second, the present findings may indicate that even if diffusion of responsibility *is* experienced by people who can actually see an emergency, when groups are larger than two the increment in deterrence to action resulting from increasing the number of observers may be less than the increase in probability that within a given time interval at least one of the observers will take action to assist the victim. Clearly, more work is needed in both natural and laboratory settings before an understanding is reached of the conditions under which diffusion of responsibility will or will not occur.

CONCLUSIONS

In this field study, a personal emergency occurred in which escape for the bystander was virtually impossible. It was a public, face-to-face situation, and in this respect differed from previous lab studies. Moreover, since generalizations from field studies to lab research must be made with caution, few comparisons will be drawn. However, several conclusions may be put forth:

1. An individual who appears to be ill is more likely to receive aid than is one who appears to be drunk, even when the immediate help needed is of the same kind.
2. Given mixed groups of men and women, and a male victim, men are more likely to help than are women.
3. Given mixed racial groups, there is some tendency for same-race helping to be more frequent. This tendency is increased when the victim is drunk as compared to apparently ill.
4. There is no strong relationship between number of bystanders and speed of helping; the expected increased "diffusion of responsibility" with a greater number of bystanders was not obtained for groups of these sizes. That is, help is not less frequent or slower in coming from larger as compared to smaller groups of bystanders; what effect there is, is in the opposite direction.
5. The longer the emergency continues without help being offered (a) the less impact a model has on the helping behavior of observers; (b) the more likely it is that individuals will leave the immediate area; that is, they appear to move purposively to another area in order to avoid the situation; (c) the more likely it is that observers will discuss the incident and its implications for their behavior.

A model of response to emergency situations consistent with the previous findings is currently being developed by the authors. It is briefly presented here as a possible heuristic device. The model includes the following assumptions: Observation of an emergency creates an emotional arousal state in the bystander. This state will be differently interpreted in different situations . . . as fear, disgust, sympathy, etc., and possibly a combination of these. This state of arousal is higher (a) the more one can empathize with the victim. . . , (b) the closer one is to the emergency, and (c) the longer the state of emergency continues without the intervention of a helper. It can be reduced by one of a number of possible responses:

(a) helping directly, (b) going to get help, (c) leaving the scene of the emergency, and (d) rejecting the victim as undeserving of help. . . . The response that will be chosen is a function of a cost-reward matrix that includes costs associated with helping (e.g., effort, embarrassment, possible disgusting or distasteful experiences, possible physical harm, etc.), costs associated with not helping (mainly self-blame and perceived censure from others), rewards associated with helping (mainly praise from self, victim, and others), and rewards associated with not helping (mainly those stemming from continuation of other activities). Note that the major motivation implied in the model is not a positive "altruistic" one, but rather a selfish desire to rid oneself of an unpleasant emotional state.

In terms of this model, the following after-the-fact interpretations can be made of the findings obtained:

1. The drunk is helped less because costs for helping are higher (greater disgust) and costs for not helping are lower (less self-blame and censure because he is in part responsible for his own victimization).
2. Women help less because costs for helping are higher in this situation (effort, mainly) and costs for not helping are lower (less censure from others; it is not her role).
3. Same-race helping, particularly of the drunk, can be explained by differential costs for not helping (less censure if one is of opposite race) and, with the drunk, differential costs for helping (more fear if of different race).
4. Diffusion of responsibility is not found on cane trials because costs for helping in general are low and costs for not helping are high (more self-blame because of possible severity of problem). That is, the suggestion is made that the diffusion of responsibility effect will increase as costs for helping increase and costs for not helping decrease. This interpretation is consistent with the well-known public incidents, in which possible bodily harm to a helper is almost always involved, and thus costs for helping are very high, and also with previous research done with nonvisible victims in which either (a) it was easy to assume someone had already helped and thus costs for not helping were reduced (Darley & Latané) or (b) it was possible to think that the emergency was minor, which also reduces the costs for not helping (Latané & Rodin).

5. All of the effects of time are also consistent with the model. The longer the emergency continues, the more likely it is that observers will be aroused and therefore will have chosen among the possible responses. Thus, (a) a late model will elicit less helping, since people have already reduced their arousal by one of the other methods; (b) unless arousal is reduced by other methods, people will leave more as time goes on, because arousal is still increasing; and (c) observers will discuss the incident in an attempt to reduce self-blame and arrive at the fourth resolution, namely a justification for not helping based on rejection of the victim.

. . .

REFERENCES

Bryan, J. H., & Test, M. A. Models and helping: Naturalistic studies in aiding behavior. *Journal of Personality and Social Psychology*, 1967, 6, 400–407.

Darley, J., & Latané, B. Bystander intervention in emergencies: Diffusion of responsibility. *Journal of Personality and Social Psychology*, 1968, 8, 377–383.

Latané, B., & Darley, J. Group inhibition of bystander intervention in emergencies. *Journal of Personality and Social Psychology*, 1968, 10, 215–221.

Latané, B., & Rodin, J. A lady in distress: Inhibiting effects of friends and strangers on bystander intervention. *Journal of Experimental Social Psychology*, 1969, 5, 189–202.

THEY WERE BOUND, GAGGED, AND IGNORED

Two San Francisco State University journalism students yesterday presented evidence that victims of kidnaping, rape and brutality can expect little or no help, and hardly any sympathy from San Francisco onlookers.

The students, Judith Nielsen and Ron Patrick, posed as victims last week in places in the city where they would be noticed by hundreds of citizens. The result they proclaimed yesterday in a banner headline in The Phoenix:

"DAMNED FEW GOOD SAMARITANS"

The Phoenix is the prize-winning weekly of the campus' journalism department.

One of their experiments was carried out in Union Square, where Patrick was gagged and tied to a bench near the corner of Post and Stockton streets.

Miss Nielsen took up a position on a nearby bench, pretending to read a book. She reported that:

Patrick remained in his "plight" for 15 minutes, during which 42 men and women walked within five feet of him.

One man, on a seat two benches away, spooned strawberry yogurt and watched intently.

"Oh, look, he's tied up," a middle-aged woman said to her well-dressed male companion.

A man later identified as a scientist from Washington, D.C., asked Miss Nielsen, "Does he come like that or did someone tie him up?"

Later he told her, "You see so many crazy things in San Francisco—I was afraid that whoever tied him up might be hiding in the bushes waiting to attack me if I helped."

An older man surveyed the crowded square and sat down on the bench next to Patrick, who was groaning and shaking the bench in his plea for help. The man moved to another bench.

In a second experiment, Miss Nielsen was the "victim." With hair disheveled and scantily clad, she writhed against a pole on Portola drive near Laguna Honda boulevard.

Sixty-seven cars passed by, the writers reported, but none stopped. Most drivers gawked, pointed, and resumed their trips.

Then a car with two women in the front seat stopped and one woman asked, "Are you all right?"

After another 33 cars passed by, the team reported, two policemen arrived and reported a lady had phoned from a phone booth about the young woman in distress.

The next day, Miss Neilsen took her turn gagged and tied on a Union Square bench. Patrick reported her muffled pleas were ignored by 65 persons within 16 minutes.

A businessman approached her several times, but finally retreated behind a trash can. He told Patrick later:

"I thought maybe she was on a trip or something. I didn't ask her if she needed help because she would have had a hard time answering through the gag."

At the corner of Mission and 16th streets the two set themselves up in the back seat of a Volkswagen, both bound and gagged. They reported that:

Two young women approached the car, peered through the window, watched the "hostages" squirm and pound their heads against the window, then turned their backs to windowshop.

Two women in a Ford pulled into the red zone behind the VW. Miss Nielsen and Patrick rapped their heads against the rear window.

The women in the Ford looked away—they only wanted the parking space.

PROJECTS

Name _____

Date _____

7.1: WHEN DO PEOPLE HELP?

Research on altruism has tried to isolate both the personal and the situational factors that influence one person's tendency to help another. Studies have looked at the effect of the helper's mood and personality, various characteristics of the recipients, the type of aid requested, the presence of other people, and so on.

This project involves a field experiment in which you are to collect data on people's responses to an individual in need of help. The stimulus person will be obviously lost and in need of directions. The extent to which this person makes a direct or indirect request for aid may determine whether such aid will be forthcoming. Therefore, with half the subjects, this person will specifically ask for directions (direct request); with the remaining subjects, the person will make the need salient but will not specifically ask for help (indirect request). Your data should include the sex of the stimulus person and the sex of the subjects.

HYPOTHESES

1. Subjects will be more likely to help someone who makes a direct request for aid than someone who makes an indirect request.

2. Subjects will be more likely to help females than males.

3. The sex of the stimulus person and of the subjects will have an effect on stimulus-subject interaction. Most helping will occur when male subjects see a female stimulus person; least helping will occur when female subjects see a male stimulus person.

Would you propose any additional hypotheses? Would you propose any alternative hypotheses? State your hypotheses and the reasoning behind them.

PROCEDURE

The best way to handle this project is to work in teams of two. One of you will be the stimulus person; the other will be the experimenter and therefore responsible for the random assignment of subjects and for observing the subjects' responses. (You and your partner should alternate these roles periodically, so that each of you spends an equal amount of time as subject and as experimenter-observer.) Choose several areas of the campus or surrounding community where a lot of people are likely to pass by and where (if possible) there are benches on which people often sit.

In this setting, the stimulus person (who will be perusing a map and looking obviously lost) will sit down on a bench near the subject designated by the experimenter. In the indirect-request condition, the stimulus person will search briefly through the map, look around in a bewildered way, and then mumble something like, "Boy, I don't know *where* that is." The stimulus person will then wait one minute. If help is not forthcoming, he or she will then leave. In the direct-request condition, the stimulus person will go through the same sequence of actions; but after the mumbled statement, he or she will turn to the subject and say, "Excuse me. Can you tell me how to get to *X*?" In either condition, if the subject does offer help, he or she is to be thanked by the stimulus person, who then leaves.

In both conditions, the subjects' responses will be noted on the data sheet (p. 167) by both the stimulus person and the experimenter (who should remain standing inconspicuously nearby). Each subject's response can be coded in one of several categories: ignores stimulus person, looks at stimulus person but says nothing, says that he or she doesn't know where *X* is, tells stimulus person where *X* is, or gives stimulus person some suggestion for finding *X*. In addition, the subject's facial expression and posture can be rated by both the stimulus person and the experimenter for the degree of friendliness or hostility that was conveyed.

In addition to selecting the subjects, the experimenter will specify what request condition is to be run and will record the data. The request condition can easily be determined by the flip of a coin. Deciding at random who among many passers-by is to be the subject is a more difficult task. However, if the experimenter does not use a systematic procedure, he or she runs the risk of biasing the sample in some way (e.g., by picking only friendly-looking people as subjects). In such a field situation, it is often best to develop a "sort of random" procedure for selecting subjects. For example, the experimenter might choose some arbitrary starting point (the edge of a plaza, a row of benches) and then use a random numbers table to determine who will be the subject. If the random number 5 appeared, it would mean that the fifth person who crossed the edge of the plaza (after the experimenter had started counting) or the fifth person sitting along the row of benches would be the subject. If unforseen circumstances make it impossible for you to use the chosen subject (e.g., the subject gets up from the bench and leaves just as the stimulus person sits down), you and your partner should wait awhile, then leave, and return a little later to do another trial. After successfully testing a subject, you and your partner should also leave the setting for a short period of time before coming back to test another subject. If you do not leave, the stimulus person's behavior will look suspicious. If you have chosen several possible locations for your study, you can move from one to another after running each trial.

Name _____

Date _____

DATA SHEET

Subjects	Sex of Stimulus Person	Sex of Subject	Condition (DR/IR)	Response No				Expression Hostile (1) to Friendly (7)
				Ignores	Looks	Information	Helps	
1								
2								
3								
4								
5								
6								
7								
8								
9								
10								
11								
12								
13								
14								
15								
16								
17								
18								
19								
20								

ANALYSIS

Look at the pattern of your own findings, and then compare it with those of the other teams in the class.

1. Did your data support or refute the hypotheses? Explain.

2. Do your results suggest alternative hypotheses? If so, what are they?

3. Were there any confounding variables or other problems that might account for your findings? For example, might your prior knowledge of the hypotheses and the experimental condition (or your partner's prior knowledge) have affected your results?

Name _____

Date _____

7.2: GOOD AND BAD NEWS

There are many ways to assess the prevalence of prosocial or altruistic behaviors in a society, including direct observation and interviews. In a society that is so dependent on mass media, one very effective way to study the prevalence of prosocial behavior, compared with the prevalence of antisocial behavior, is to tabulate its coverage in the news media. Analyze the contents of your favorite television news program for a one-week period, and record the number of prosocial and antisocial events that are reported, as well as the number of neutral events, on the following data sheet. Prosocial items would include acts of helping or kindness, awards, donations, and success stories. Antisocial news stories would include coverage of war, murder, rape, vandalism, and verbal attacks. Neutral news events would include stock market reports, weather forecasts, sports scores, announcements of new laws or food prices, and similar information. Specify the items in detail, especially those that do not obviously fit any of the categories, so that you can discuss them in class.

TV Station _____ Local or National News _____

	Neutral	
Monday	Prosocial	
	Antisocial	
	Neutral	
Tuesday	Prosocial	
	Antisocial	
	Neutral	
Wednesday	Prosocial	
	Antisocial	
	Neutral	
Thursday	Prosocial	
	Antisocial	
	Neutral	
Friday	Prosocial	
	Antisocial	

	Neutral	
Saturday	*Prosocial*	
	Antisocial	
	Neutral	
Sunday	*Prosocial*	
	Antisocial	

1. How many prosocial events did you count? _____ Antisocial? _____ Neutral? _____

2. What do the results suggest?

3. Does the frequency of occurrence of prosocial events in the news truly reflect the frequency of their occurrence in real life?

8
PERSON PERCEPTION

You have heard the old saying, "Beauty is in the eye of the beholder." That is, our judgments of beauty are based on the way we think about things. There are no universal, hard-and-fast characteristics of people or objects that are beautiful in and of themselves. Psychologists extend this argument to say that most of *reality* is in the eye—and mind—of the beholder. What we see in the world around us is as much the product of our personal biases, thoughts, and feelings as it is of what physically exists. Our perceptions are not a passive reflection of the environment; rather, they are the result of an active process of selecting, organizing, and interpreting various bits of information. We actually shape and create our reality, although we are often not aware of how much we do so. (Optical illusions provide one way of exploring the nature of this active, creative process. See, for example, the box on this topic, which begins this chapter.) As Lewis Mumford said, "What was once called the objective world is a sort of Rorschach ink blot, into which each culture, each system of science and religion, each type of personality, reads a meaning only remotely derived from the shape and color of the blot itself" ("Orientation to Life," *The Conduct of Life,* 1951).

Social psychologists are particularly interested in people's perceptions of other people. We all make judgments about others and have different attitudes and feelings toward them. But where do these judgments come from? How do we know that a person is kind, aggressive, aloof, or trustworthy? How can we tell whether a person's compliment is sincere or merely currying favor? What is the basis for the good or bad feelings that we have about different people? We tend to assume that our reactions reflect what these people are really like. But in fact, they indicate a lot about what *we* are like. Our own expectations and attitudes bias what we see of other people and lead us to make certain interpretations about their behavior. We often see what we are prepared to see, either by focusing on particular characteristics of the person and ignoring others or by distorting what we remember about him or her. Nevertheless, these perceptual biases are also very valuable because they help us to organize and make sense of the chaotic mass of information that constantly bombards us.

OPTICAL ILLUSIONS

Perception, whether of people, objects, or events, concerns the way we interpret information received from the environment and then organize it into meaningful patterns. This process of information gathering and analysis forms the basis of all our agreed-upon knowledge of the universe, yet most of the time we take it for granted. Indeed, we usually pay attention to our perceptual processes only when our senses are jarred by unexpected or ambiguous features of the objects and events we encounter, as indicated in the common expression of surprise, "I can't believe my eyes."

Three different types of optical illusions are shown on p. 173. All three examples contain elements that play tricks on the perceiver. It is through such devices as these simple illusions that scientists have come to a better understanding of how our perceptual processes work under normal conditions. One thing is clear—our expectations of the way things are supposed to be can make it difficult, if not impossible, for us to experience things as they really are; and so, what our eyes witness and transmit to the brain may be quite unreliable

information. In order to grasp what is going on in the figures and sentences that follow, you probably should not believe your eyes.
(For an explanation of the illusions, see p. 174).

THE EYE OF THE UMPIRE

Three baseball umpires were comparing notes on how they called balls and strikes. Because the outcome of a game may depend upon a single decision by the umpire, the question arose of how objective such decisions are.

"Well," said the first umpire, "I crouch in real tight behind the catcher, keep my eyes fixed on the ball at all times, and then when the ball is thrown, *I call it as it is.*"

"No, that's not right," replied the second ump. "I do what you do until the pitcher throws the ball, and then *I call it as I see it.*"

The third ump smiled. "You guys are both wrong," he said. "I crouch down and keep my eye on the ball, too. But after the pitch, *it ain't nothing until I call it.*"

PSYCHOLOGY OF THE EYEWITNESS

ROBERT BUCKHOUT

The creative aspect of the perceptual process can be valuable, but it can also be detrimental. In a situation in which a premium is placed on completely accurate observation, perceptual biases can cause problems. The courtroom presents just such a situation. There, the goal is to determine "the truth, the whole truth, and nothing but the truth." To accomplish that goal, witnesses are called to testify under oath about the facts of a case. There is often conflicting testimony about those facts, but that is not necessarily the result of deliberate misrepresentation. Even with the best of intentions to be completely objective, witnesses are not, and cannot be, infallible. Just as, in the famous parable, three blind men gave totally different (but "truthful") descriptions of an elephant, many witnesses may give differing accounts of an incident as a function of the way in which they perceived it. Their personal biases and expectations may lead them to make different judgments about a person or recall different aspects of the event. They are being truthful in their reports, but it is the truth as they saw it. The subjective and creative qualities of their perceptions and memories may have distorted the content of that report.

In "Psychology of the Eyewitness," Buckhout presents a thorough analysis of the limitations and possible pitfalls of courtroom evidence. He draws on a wide variety of studies to demonstrate the applicability of person perception research to the real-life situation of legal proceedings. Although there is as yet no adequate alternative to eyewitness testimony, a recognition and understanding of the errors that an eyewitness may make would surely aid in making the justice system more sensitive to its human frailty.

If you see an auto accident or witness a murder, and are then asked to describe what you saw, there is no one who can create an instant replay in slow motion for you. You depend upon your memory with all its limitations—a fact which may be of minor importance in your ordinary daily activities. If you are unreliable, if you shade the truth in describing what you saw, it matters little.

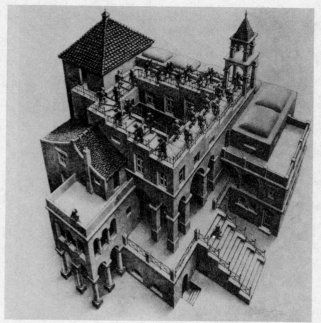

(1)

Can you find the end of the top staircase?

(2)

Can you read this sentence out loud correctly?

A BIRD IN THE
THE HAND IS WORTHLESS.

Using only your eye, count the number of F's in the sentence below.

Fascinating fairytales of faraway lands are the fertilizer for the fructification of the creative minds of the future.

(3)

(1) M. C. Escher, *Ascending and Descending*, lithograph, 1960, 35 × 28.5 cm., courtesy of Vorpal Galleries, San Francisco, California. Reproduced with permission of the Escher Foundation, Haags Gemeentemuseum, The Hague, The Netherlands.

(2–6) Reproduced by permission of the publisher from *Optricks: A Book of Optical Illusions* by Melinda Wentzell and D. K. Holland. © 1973 Troubador Press, San Francisco, California.

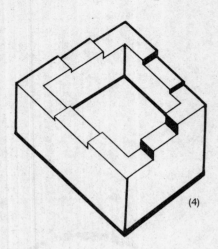

(4)

In the lithograph (1), M. C. Escher used a classic example of an irrational figure (4) to form the staircase on the top of the building. Though most of the monks in the picture are climbing stairs endlessly, there are two who refuse to take part in this meaningless exercise. Escher said that sooner or later they would be brought to see the error of their nonconformity and would join their fellow monks.

(5)

By duplicating the eyes and mouth on the faces (2), a "conflict" of grouping is created. At first glance you probably saw only a normal number of features, since the eye finds it difficult to interpret unfamiliar repetitions in familiar figures.

(6)

The tricky phrase that makes up the first part of the third illusion (3) contains the word "the" twice, one after the other. But because the two "thes" appear on separate lines, the lazy eye ignores the second one and rushes to finish the sentence. Seeing the word "worthless" (instead of the familiar ending to this phrase) confuses some people so much that even on second glance the illusion goes undiscovered.

The second deceptive sentence contains eleven F's. If you counted only eight, you probably skipped the word "of," which appears three times. We read "of" as "ov" and thus tend to overlook the "f" in the word.

But when you are called in as a witness to a crime, the situation escalates in importance. A person's life or an institution's reputation may be at stake. You may be asked to report what you saw in excruciating detail as if you were a videotape recorder.

In court, the written transcript contains your replay of the events. The prosecutor will attempt to show that you have perfect recall; the defense attorney will try to show, by cross-examining you vigorously, that your "tape recorder" is defective. The stakes are high because in modern courts eyewitness testimony is more highly valued than alibi testimony or "circumstantial" evidence. Uncritical acceptance of eyewitness testimony seems to be based on the fallacious notion that the human observer is a perfect recording device—that everything that passes before his or her eyes is recorded and can be "pulled out" by sharp questioning or "refreshing one's memory." In a categorical statement, which psychologists rarely make, I argue that this is *impossible*—human perception and memory function effectively by being selective. A human being has no particular need for perfect recall; perception and memory are decision-making processes affected by the totality of a person's abilities, background, environment, attitudes, motives, and beliefs, and by the methods used in testing recollection of people and events.

As I work in criminal courts, I'm aware of a fundamental clash of conceptions—the nineteenth-century vs. the twentieth-century view of a person. The nineteenth-century view—embodied in psychophysics—asserted a scientific parallel between the mechanisms of the physical world and the mechanisms of the brain. The courts in the United States accept this nineteenth-century thinking quite readily—as does much of the public. However, modern psychologists have developed a conception of a whole human being with an information processing mechanism which is far more complex than the one in the nineteenth-century model. Unfortunately, research psychologists, who began by studying practical problems (functionalism), have become more esoteric in their research and less visible in the real world.

I regard the human observer as an active rather than a passive observer of the environment; motivated by (a) a desire to be accurate in extracting meaning from the overabundance of information which affects the senses; and (b) a desire to live up to the expectations of others and stay in their good graces, a factor which makes the eye, the ear, and other senses social as well as physical organs.

In our laboratory experiments on the physical capabilities of the eye and the ear, we speak of an "ideal observer," by which we mean a subject who would respond cooperatively to lights and tones with unbiased ears and eyes much like a machine. However, the ideal observer does not exist. In other words, the "ideal observer" is a convenient fiction. Great effort and expense are put into the design of laboratories to provide an "ideal physical environment" free of distractions to enable the observer to concentrate. Such ideal environments can be approached only in a laboratory; in the real world they are seldom, if ever, found. The nonmachine-like human observer copes reasonably effectively in uncontrolled environments with a perceptual capability which fits the nature of a social being. The witness to a crime is engaged in what can be described as "one-shot perception."

In a machine we would expect that what comes out (the report) would be a direct function of what goes in (the input or stimulus). However, human perception can be characterized in terms of the phrase: "The whole is greater than the sum of the parts." This characterization reflects the ability of the human observer to take the fragments of information to which he or she has time to pay attention (i.e., actively reduce the information), and to reach conclusions based on his or her prior experience, familiarity, biases, expectancy, faith, desire to appear certain, etc. Most human observers, for example, look at the moon and see a sphere—despite their inability to verify the shape of the unseen side. The conclusion, in psychological terms, is a decision efficiently arrived at and independent of the physical evidence which is incomplete.

As an eyewitness to crime, the fallible human observer is usually in a less than ideal environment. He or she is subject to factors which I believe inherently limit a person's ability to give a complete account of what took place or to identify the persons involved with complete accuracy.

The thrust of my research has been to learn about and describe (in a form useful to the criminal justice system) those factors which affect both the *recall* of events by a witness and his or her subsequent ability to make an *identification*. I've ventured into the courtroom in some 30 criminal trials discussing the following factors as they relate to eye-witness accounts.

STRESS

"I could never forget what he looked like!" This common statement expresses the faith that people have in their memory—even under stress. When a person's life or well-being is threatened, a stress pattern known as the General Adaptional Syndrome (GAS) can be expected to occur in varying degrees. . . . This pattern is due to an increase in adrenaline levels and involves increased heart-rate, breathing rate, and higher blood pressure. The end result is a dramatic increase in available energy, making the person capable of running fast, fighting, lifting enormous weight—taking the steps necessary to ensure safety or survival.

But, if you are under extreme stress, you will be a less reliable witness than you would be normally. Research shows that observers are less capable of remembering details, less accurate in reading dials, less accurate in detecting signals when under stress. They are paying more attention to their own well-being and safety than to nonessential elements in the environment. My research with trained Air Force flight crew members confirms that even highly trained people became poorer observers when under stress. They never can forget the stress and what hit them; the events, being highly significant at the time, can be remembered. But memory for details, clothing worn, colors, etc., is not as clear. Time estimates are especially exaggerated under stress.

You might test this idea by asking a few people where they were in 1963 when they first heard the news of the assassination of President John F. Kennedy. Chances are they will recall vividly where they were and who they were with. But can they describe what they or the persons with them were wearing? Can those who witnessed the killing of Lee Harvey Oswald on television describe the people next to the killer? These are logical questions—seemingly trivial—but if you were asking them in court, would you be willing to agree that the witnesses might have been too concerned with more important things to pay attention?

PRIOR CONDITIONING AND EXPERIENCE

Psychologists have done extensive research on how *set*, or expectancy, is used by the human observer to make judgments more efficiently. In a classic experiment done in the 1930's, observers were shown a display of playing cards for a few seconds and asked to report the number of aces of spades in the display.[1] Most observers reported only three, when actually there were five. Two of the aces of spades were colored red instead of the more familiar black color. The interpretation was given that since people were so familiar with black aces of spades, they did not waste time looking carefully at the display. Thus efficiency, in this case, led to unreliable observation. In many criminal cases, the prior conditioning of the witness may enable him to report facts or events which were not present but which should have been. Our research also indicates that white observers show better recognition of white people than of black people in a lineup. Recent research supports the proposition that observers have better recognition of people of their own race.

PERSONAL BIASES AND STEREOTYPES

Expectancy in its least palatable form can be found in the case of biases or prejudices held by a witness. A victim of a mugging may initially report being attacked by "niggers," and may, because of limited experience as well as prejudice, be unable to tell one black man from another ("they all look alike to me"). In a classic study of this phenomenon, observers were asked to take a brief look at a drawing of several people on a subway train.[2] In the picture, a black man was seated and a white man was standing with a knife in his hand. When questioned later, observers tended to report having seen the knife in the hand of the black man.

Prejudices may be racial, religious, or based on physical characteristics such as long hair, dirty clothes, status, etc. All human beings have some stereotypes upon which they base perceptual judgments; stereotypes which lead not only to prejudice but are a means of making decisions more efficiently. A witness to an auto accident may save thinking time by reporting his well-ingrained stereotype about "woman drivers." But these shortcuts to thinking may be erroneously reported and expanded upon by an eyewitness

[1] J. S. Bruner and L. J. Postman, On the perception of incongruity: A paradigm, *Journal of Personality* 18 (1949): 206–223.
[2] G. W. Allport and L. J. Postman, in *Transactions of the New York Academy of Sciences* 8 (1945): 66.

who is unaware that he or she is describing a stereotype rather than the events which actually took place. If the witness's biases are shared by the investigator taking the statement, the report may reflect their mutual biases rather than what was actually seen.

UNFAIR TEST CONSTRUCTION

The lineup and the array of photographs used in testing the eyewitness's ability to identify a suspect can be analyzed as fair or unfair on the basis of criteria which most psychologists can agree on. A fair test should be designed carefully so that, first, all items have an equal chance of being selected by a person who didn't see the suspect; second, the items are similar enough to each other and to the original description of the suspect to be confusing to a person who is merely guessing; and last, the test is conducted without leading questions or suggestions from the test giver.

All too frequently, I have found that lineups or photographic arrays are carelessly assembled or even rigged in such a way as to make the eyewitness identification test completely unreliable. If, for example, you present five pictures, the chance should be only 1 in 5 (20%) that any one picture will be chosen on the basis of guessing; but frequently, a single picture of a suspect may stand out. In the Angela Davis case, one set of nine pictures used to check identification contained three pictures of the defendant taken at an outdoor rally, two mug shots of other women showing their names, one of a 55-year-old woman, etc. It was so easy for a witness to rule out five pictures as ridiculous choices, that the "test" was reduced to four pictures—including three of Davis. This means that witnesses had a 75 percent chance of picking out her picture, whether they had seen her or not. Such a "test" is meaningless to a psychologist and probably tainted as an item of evidence in court.

Research on memory has also shown that if one item in the array of photos is uniquely different (in dress, race, height, sex, photographic quality, etc.), it is more likely to be picked out and attended to. A teacher making up a multiple-choice test designs several answers which sound or look alike to make it difficult for a person who doesn't know the right answer to succeed. Police lineups and photo layouts are also multiple-choice tests. If the rules for designing fair tests are ignored by authorities, the tests become unreliable.

So far I've presented the research framework on which I've built my testimony in court as an expert witness. The framework is built on the work of the past, much of which is familiar to a working psychologist, but is hardly the day-to-day conversation of adult Americans who become jurors. Some of the earliest psychologists, notably Münsterberg . . . , had written the essence of this analysis as far back as the beginning of this century. But there was a nagging gap between the controlled research settings which yield data on basic perceptual processes and some very important questions about perception in the less well controlled, but real world. Thus our laboratory and field studies are designed to evaluate eyewitness accuracy and reliability after seeing simulated crimes where we have a good record of the veridical (real) events for comparison. I began with a more detailed version of an experiment which Münsterberg and others had conducted over 65 years ago.

AN EXPERIMENTAL STUDY OF THE EYEWITNESS

In order to study the effects of eyewitness testimony in a somewhat realistic setting, we staged an assault on a California State University campus, in which a distraught student "attacked" a professor in front of 141 witnesses. We recorded the entire incident on videotape so that we could compare the veridical event with the eyewitness reports. After the attack we took sworn statements from each witness, asking them to describe the suspect, the incident, and the clothes worn (essentially a free recall process). We also asked for a confidence rating (0–100%) in their description. Another outsider, of the same age as the suspect, was on the scene.

Table 1 shows a comparison of the known characteristics of the suspect and the averages of the descriptions given by the witnesses. It is clear that the witnesses gave very inaccurate

TABLE 1: COMPARISON OF AVERAGE DESCRIPTIONS BY 141 EYEWITNESSES WITH ACTUAL DESCRIPTION OF SUSPECT AND EVENTS

	KNOWN CHARACTERISTICS	AVERAGED DESCRIPTIONS
Duration of incident	34 sec	81.1 sec
Height	69.5 in	70.4 in
Weight	155 lb	180 lb
Age	25 yr	22.7 yr
Total accuracy score	28 pts	7.4 pts

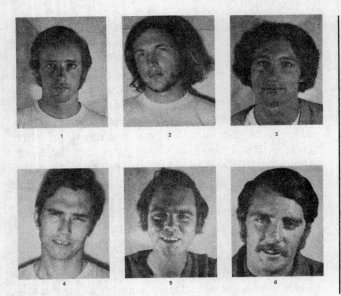

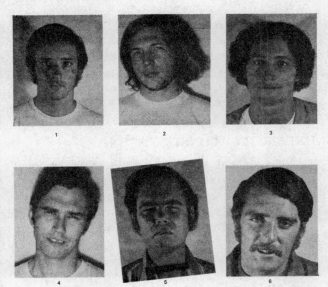

Confidence level

0–10–20–30–40–50–60–70–80–90–100%

FIGURE 1. Example of a reasonably unbiased photo-spread lineup used in testing eyewitnesses to an assault. Number 5 was the perpetrator.

Confidence level

0–10–20–30–40–50–60–70–80–90–100%

FIGURE 2. Example of a biased photo-spread lineup used in testing witnesses to an assault.

descriptions, a fact which has been demonstrated so often in this type of experiment that professors of psychology use this as a demonstration of the unreliability of the eyewitness. People tend to overestimate the passage of time—in this case by a factor of almost 2½ to 1. The weight estimate was 14 percent higher, the age was underestimated, and the accuracy score—made up of points for appearance and dress—was only 25 percent of the maximum possible total score. Only the height estimate was close; but this may be due to the fact that the suspect was of average height. People will often cite known facts about the "average" man when they are uncertain—inaccurate witnesses' weight estimates correlate significantly with their own weight.

We then waited seven weeks and presented a set of six photographs to each witness individually, creating four conditions in order to test the effects of biased instructions and unfair testing on eyewitness identification. There were two kinds of instructions: Low Bias, in which witnesses were asked only if they recognized anybody in the photos; and High Bias, where witnesses were told that we had an idea of who the assailant was, and we made a plea for them to find the attacker in the photos. There were two types of photo spreads, using well-lit frontal views of young men the same age as the suspect. In the nonleading photo spread (Figure 1), all six photos

were neatly set out, with the same expression on all faces and similar clothing worn by all men. In the biased photo spread (Figure 2), the photo of the actual assailant was placed crooked in the array, and the suspect wore different clothing and had a different expression from the other photos. We thus violated good testing practice for the sake of comparison.

The results indicated that overall only 40 percent of the witnesses correctly identified the assailant; 25 percent of the witnesses identified the wrong man—an innocent bystander who had been at the scene of the crime. Even the professor who was attacked picked out the *innocent* man from the photos as his attacker! Of those correctly identifying the assailant, the highest percentage correct was found in the condition where there was a combination of a biased set of photos and biased instructions. In some of our recent research we have tested the same photo spreads with a group of nonwitnesses, who also picked out suspect number 5. We thus demonstrated how the violation of good testing practices could lead to unreliable eyewitness identifications in a fairly realistic setting.

Our conclusions in this study were as follows. First, the reports of over 100 eyewitnesses to a crime were so highly unreliable that if an investigation began to find the person most witnesses described, the likelihood is high that attention would focus on the wrong person. Second, in following police procedures for testing identification through photographs, the presence of biased instructions and leading sets of photos can increase the percentage of witnesses who end up picking the photo toward which the authorities are already biased. Third, if the police are biased toward an innocent man, the presence of biased instructions and a leading set of photos could increase the likelihood that the wrong person would be identified.

Our more recent research is guided by the "signal detection" paradigm. This choice was made because signal detection theory evolved in psychophysics as a means of coping with the empirical fact that the observer's attitude "interferes" with the accurate detecting, processing, and reporting of sensory stimuli. An ideal observer has a clear distinction in mind as to what a signal (stimulus) is and what it is not. The task usually is to say whether a signal (e.g., a tone of a particular frequency) is present or not. The experimenter always presents the subject with some background noise, but only on half the trials will a low strength signal (the tone) also be present. In deciding whether the trial consists of noise alone or contains a signal, the subject employs a criterion which is influenced by individual factors such as personality, experience, anticipated cost or reward, or motivation to please or frustrate. The experimenter keeps track of both hits (correct "yeses") and false alarms (incorrect "yeses"), thus providing a quantitative estimate of the observer's criterion for judging his or her immediate experience. A very cautious person might have very few false alarms and a high number of hits, indicating that "yes" is being used sparingly. A less cautious observer might say "yes" most of the time, increasing the proportion of false alarms to hits.

In our experiment, we presented 20 to 25 statements about the crime which were true and the same number which were false. The witness indicated yes or no and gave a confidence rating as well. We end up with a record of hits and false alarms based on the witness's recall of the crime. These data are combined statistically to produce Receiver Operating Characteristic (ROC) curves as shown in Figure 3. The straight line would be generated by a person or group whose hits and false alarms were equal—indicating that responses have no relationship to the facts. The sharper the curve, the more cautious the observer. The greater the area under the curve, the more sensitive was the witness to the difference between a true and a false statement. Our current studies

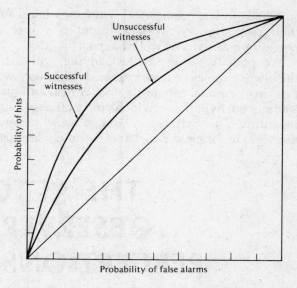

FIGURE 3. Comparison of ROC curves of successful and unsuccessful eyewitnesses where successful $d' = 1.18$ and unsuccessful $d' = 0.74$.

indicate that the witnesses with better ROC curves in the laboratory perform more accurately in recognizing the suspect in a lineup. This observer sensitivity function enables us to test various hypotheses on how environmental conditions, stress, bias in interrogation, sex, and social milieu affect the accuracy and reliability of an eyewitness. Thus, we are on the way toward developing a standardized test of eyewitness sensitivity, accuracy, and reliability.

One basic change has occurred in our research strategy. Instead of staging the crimes "live" in the classroom, we are using color and sound movies of carefully staged crimes. In part, we did this for control, but more importantly, the time of the apathetic bystander to a crime appears to have passed. Staging even an innocuous purse-snatching became dangerous for our "perpetrators" as a number of the (bigger) witnesses began to take off in hot pursuit of the purse-snatcher. No research is worth that much realism (at least my suffering assistants didn't think so)!

With the ROC curve as a measure of the sensitivity of witnesses, we can explore the extent to which biasing factors commonly encountered in court cases affect identifications. In our early studies, we found that witnesses who were ultimately successful in recognizing the suspect in a good lineup had shown high observer sensitivity scores during recall. People with low observer sensitivity scores tended to give height and weight descriptions which correlated with their own stature—confirming our belief that when pressured to give a description, witnesses fabricate their responses in the meaningful way that a perception researcher would expect.

We plan to refine the test, giving witnesses the chance to see several crimes. In this way we can check general reliability of a witness and test a number of hypotheses which police officers hold regarding older witnesses, women as witnesses, members of different racial and economic groups,

etc. Thus, in one sense, we are just beginning a large research program which came from the real world to be absorbed into the laboratory—and changed the laboratory. Soon we hope to emerge from the laboratory and to bring the results back to the real world where they belong—and hopefully to utilize psychological knowledge to make eyewitness identification a more reliable and much fairer element in the judicial process.

THE ACTOR AND THE OBSERVER: DIVERGENT PERCEPTIONS OF THE CAUSES OF BEHAVIOR

EDWARD E. JONES and RICHARD E. NISBETT

Our opinions about people are based not only on what they say and do but on the context in which they act. The situation and the other people present all affect our perception of a particular individual. For example, what would you think about a woman who is sitting very quietly with her eyes lowered? If you saw her in a classroom, where other people were sitting quietly and bending over their notes, you would probably say that she was absorbed in listening to the professor's lecture. However, if you saw her at a party, where other people were talking loudly and dancing, you might conclude that she is shy. In other words, your assessments of the causes of her behavior will be quite different in the two situations, even though her physical behavior is the same. In the first case, you perceive her quietness as caused by the external constraints of classroom etiquette; in the second case, you perceive her quietness as caused by an internal, dispositional trait.

In addition to making causal inferences about other people's behavior, we make similar judgments about ourselves. If we blush and stammer when we speak in front of a group of people, is it because we are shy and easily embarrassed, because the people are hostile toward us, or because of some other reason?

One might expect that the way in which we arrive at causal inferences of behavior is always the same, regardless of whether we are judging ourselves or other people. However, in "The Actor and the Observer" Jones and Nisbett argue that this is not the case. They contend that the perceived causes of our own behavior are often quite different from those of other people's behavior, even if the overt behavior is the same.

When a student who is doing poorly in school discusses his problem with a faculty adviser, there is often a fundamental difference of opinion between the two. The student, in attempting to understand and explain his inadequate performance, is usually able to point to environmental

obstacles such as a particularly onerous course load, to temporary emotional stress such as worry about his draft status, or to a transitory confusion about life goals that is now resolved. The faculty adviser may nod and may wish to believe, but in his heart of hearts he usually disagrees. The adviser is convinced that the poor performance is due neither to the student's environment nor to transient emotional states. He believes instead that the failure is due to enduring qualities of the student—to lack of ability, to irremediable laziness, to neurotic ineptitude.

When Kitty Genovese was murdered in view of thirty-nine witnesses in Queens, social scientists, the press, and the public marveled at the apathy of the residents of New York and, by extension, of urban America. Yet it seems unlikely that the witnesses themselves felt that their failure to intercede on the woman's behalf was due to apathy. At any rate, interviewers were unable to elicit comments from the witnesses on the order of "I really didn't care if she lived or died." Instead, the eyewitnesses reported that they had been upset, but felt that there was nothing they could or needed to do about a situation that in any case was ambiguous to them.

In their autobiographies, former political leaders often report a different perspective on their past acts from that commonly held by the public. Acts perceived by the public to have been wise, planful, courageous, and imaginative on the one hand, or unwise, haphazard, cowardly, or pedestrian on the other, are often seen in quite a different light by the autobiographer. He is likely to emphasize the situational constraints at the time of the action—the role limitations, the conflicting pressures brought to bear, the alternative paths of action that were never open or that were momentarily closed—and to perceive his actions as having been inevitable. "Wise moves" and "blunders" alike are often viewed by the leader as largely inescapable under the circumstances. The public is more inclined to personalize causation for success and failure. There are good leaders who can cope with what the situation brings and bad leaders who cannot.

In each of these instances, the actor's perceptions of the causes of his behavior are at variance with those held by outside observers. The actor's view of his behavior emphasizes the role of environmental conditions at the moment of action. The observer's view emphasizes the causal role of stable dispositional properties of the actor. We wish to argue that *there is a pervasive tendency for actors to attribute their actions to situational requirements, whereas observers tend to attribute*

the same actions to stable personal dispositions. This tendency often stems in part from the actor's need to justify blameworthy action, but may also reflect a variety of other factors having nothing to do with the maintenance of self-esteem. We shall emphasize these other, more cognitive factors but include also a consideration of the role of self-justification.

. . .

EXPERIMENTAL EVIDENCE CONSISTENT WITH THE PROPOSITION

Jones, Rock, Shaver, Goethals, and Ward [1968] compared the attributions made by actor-subjects with those made by observer-subjects in a rigged IQ testing situation. To collect their observer data, Jones et al. asked each subject and an accomplice to take an IQ test "designed to discriminate at the very highest levels of intelligence." The items were quite difficult and some were insoluble. Success and failure feedback for both the accomplice and the subject was reported after each item. The items were ambiguous enough to permit feedback that bore no necessary relation to the performance of the subject. The pattern of "successes" was such that at the end of the series the subject believed he had solved ten of the thirty items, with success scattered randomly throughout the test. In one of the experimental conditions, it was made to appear that the accomplice had solved fifteen randomly scattered problems. In another condition, it was also made to appear that the accomplice solved fifteen problems, but many more of the initial problems were solved than final problems. In a third condition, the accomplice again solved fifteen problems, but he had many more successes at the end than at the beginning. Special pains were taken to assure the subjects that the items were of equal difficulty, and the evidence suggests these assurances were accepted.

Whether the accomplice solved more problems at the beginning of the series (descending condition) or at the end (ascending condition) had a pronounced influence on (a) the subject's recall of the accomplice's performance, (b) the subject's prediction about the number of problems the accomplice would solve on a later, similar series, and (c) the subject's estimate of the accomplice's intelligence. If the accomplice solved a great many problems at the beginning of the series, the subject perceived him as more intelligent, distorted his overall performance on the test in a more favorable direction, and predicted that he would do better on the later series than if the accomplice solved few problems at the beginning. For most of the measures, in most of the variations of the experiment reported by Jones et al., the randomly successful accomplice was judged to be intermediate between the descending and ascending accomplices.

Jones et al. interpreted their data as evidence of a strong primacy effect in the attribution of ability: early information was weighted heavily and later evidence was essentially ignored. . . . For our purposes, the important point is that ability attributions were made at all. This fact serves as the background against which to evaluate the results of a variation in which the tables were turned and the accomplice randomly solved the ten problems while the subject solved fifteen problems, either in random order, in descending order, or in ascending order.

When the feedback patterns were thus reassigned, the results were markedly different. In the descending and ascending conditions it was apparently impossible for the subjects to resist the conclusion, despite the experimenter's initial disclaimer, that the item difficulty had changed over the series. Descending subjects believed that the items got more difficult and ascending subjects believed they got less difficult. These beliefs apparently affected subjects' expectations about their performance on a future series. Ascending subjects predicted they would do better on the later series than did descending subjects, completely reversing the direction of observers' predictions. As would be expected, subjects' judgments about their own intellectual ability were unaffected by the experimental manipulations.

The pattern of attributions is therefore quite different for actor and observer. In identical situations, the actor attributes performance to variations in task difficulty, the observer to variations in ability.

The experiments by Jones et al. present data for actors and observers in identical situations. Another set of experiments, while lacking data on actors themselves, indicates that observers are remarkably inclined to see behavior in dispositional terms. Three experiments were conducted by Jones and Harris [1967]. In the first of these they asked their college student subjects to read essays or listen to speeches presumably written by fellow students. Subjects were asked to give their estimates of the communicator's real opinions. They were told either that the communicator had been assigned one side of the issue or that he had been completely free to choose a side. It is the "no choice" conditions that are of most interest to us here. In one case the impression of no choice was created by telling subjects they

were reading essays written for a political science course in which the instructor had required the students to write, for example, a "short cogent defense of Castro's Cuba." In another experiment subjects believed they were reading the opening statement by a college debater whose adviser had directed him to argue a specified side of the Castro topic. In a third experiment subjects believed they were hearing a tape recording of a subject in a psychology experiment who had been instructed to give a speech favoring or opposing segregation. Questionnaire responses showed that subjects easily distinguished between choice and no choice conditions in the degree of choice available to the communicator.

Despite the fact that the subjects seem to have clearly perceived the heavy constraints on the communicator in the no choice conditions, their estimates of the true opinions of the communicator were markedly affected by the particular position espoused. When subjects read an essay or speech supporting Castro's Cuba, they inferred that the communicator was pro-Castro. If the communication opposed Castro's Cuba, they inferred that the communicator was anti-Castro. Across the three experiments, the effect of taking a pro versus anti stand was a highly significant determinant of attributed attitude in no choice conditions, though the effect of position taken was roughly twice as great when the communicator had complete choice.

These results are extremely interesting if they may be taken as evidence that observers attach insufficient weight to the situational determinants of behavior and attribute it, on slim evidence, to a disposition of the actor. It may be, however, that something about the content of the speeches caused the subjects to infer that the communicator actually held the opinion he was advocating. If the communications were quite eloquent and drew on esoteric sources of knowledge, it would not be surprising to learn that observers inferred that the communicator held the opinion he was delivering. This does not seem to be the proper explanation of the results, however, in view of the following facts: (a) the communications were designed to be "neither polished nor crude"; "of a C+ quality" in the case of the political science essay; (b) in each experiment it was made clear that subjects had access to study materials to help them formulate their arguments; (c) in a later series of experiments, Snyder (unpublished data) found that when the communications used were the actual products of students under no choice conditions, the same effects found by Jones and Harris were obtained. A crucial feature of Snyder's experiments was that each subject wrote a no choice essay himself, to be delivered to another subject. Thus the subjects should have been clearly aware of the constraints involved and of the ease or difficulty of generating arguments for a position opposite to that privately held.

The Jones and Harris experiment provides evidence, then, that observers are willing to take behavior more or less at "face value," as reflecting a stable disposition, even when it is made clear that the actor's behavior is under severe external constraints. These results have been replicated both by Snyder and more recently by Jones, Worchel, Goethals, and Grumet [1971] with "legalization of marijuana" as the issue.

A second study providing data for observers only has been performed by McArthur [1970]. Her study is quite relevant to our proposition if one is willing to lean heavily on intuitions about the causal attributions that would be expected of actors. Subjects were given a simple, one-sentence description of an action, such as "George translates the sentence incorrectly," "While dancing, Ralph trips over Jane's feet," "Steve puts a bumper sticker advocating improved automobile safety on his car." They were then asked why this action probably occurred: Whether it was something about the *person* that caused him to act this way ("Something about *George* probably caused him to translate the sentence incorrectly"), or something about the *stimulus* ("Something about the *sentence* probably caused George to translate it incorrectly"), or something about the *situation* ("Something about the *particular circumstances* probably caused George to translate it incorrectly"). If subjects found none of these simple explanations to be the likely one, they were allowed to give whatever explanation they thought necessary to account for the behavior. These were then coded into complex explanations involving both person and stimulus, both person and circumstances, both stimulus and circumstances, or all three. (As it happened, only the person-stimulus combination was resorted to with very great frequency.)

It seems likely that if one were to ask a random sample of people who had mistranslated sentences, tripped over feet, or placed bumper stickers on their cars why they had performed their various actions, a rather high fraction of explanations would be pure stimulus attributions or mixed stimulus-circumstance attributions. We would expect answers such as "That sentence was difficult to translate," "It was dark and Jane doesn't cha-cha the way I do," "The AAA sent me this catchy bumper sticker in the mail." For McArthur's vicarious observers, however, such reasons were extremely infrequent, amounting to only 4 per cent of the total attributions. By far the greatest proportion of reasons given—44 per cent for each of these particular actions—were pure *person* attributions: George translates the sentence incorrectly because he is rather poor at translating sentences and Steve is the sort who puts bumper stickers on his car.

McArthur also presented her subjects with statements about emotional experiences, such as "John laughs at the comedian," "Sue is afraid of the dog," "Tom is enthralled by the painting." One would expect that in a random sample of people found laughing at comedians, being frightened by dogs, or being enthralled by paintings, most of the actors would explain their experiences in pure stimulus terms: The comedian is funny; the dog is scary; the painting is beautiful. For McArthur's observers, however, only 19 per cent of the attributions were pure stimulus attributions and the most frequent attributions (45 per cent of the total) were *person-stimulus interactions:* "Sue tends to be afraid of dogs and this is a very large one." Interestingly, one of the emotion items did produce a very high proportion (52 per cent) of pure stimulus attributions: "Mary is angered by the psychology experiment." Since subjects were at that moment participating in a psychology experiment, it is tempting to conclude that they were responding as actors rather than as observers.

It is possible that some unintended feature of McArthur's highly artificial situation forced attributions away from the stimulus and toward the person. Perhaps a different sample of statements or a more extended account of the behavior would yield different results. Nevertheless, the willingness of her subjects to invoke explanations involving dispositions of the person seems striking. One's strong intuition is that the actors themselves in real-life situations of the type described to McArthur's subjects would rarely interpret their behavior in dispositional terms.

McArthur [1970] completed a second experiment that is less open to criticism on methodological grounds. Subjects were induced to perform a particular act and a written account of the actor and the surrounding circumstances was presented to observers. It was then possible to compare the attributions made by the actor-subjects with the later attributions made by observer-subjects. McArthur obtained the consent of subjects to participate in a survey concerning interpersonal relationships and then asked the subjects why they had agreed to participate. As we would expect, subjects were inclined to attribute their participation to the importance of the survey and were not likely to attribute their participation to a general disposition to take part in such surveys. Observers exactly reversed this pattern, attributing subjects' participation primarily to a personal inclination to take part in surveys and only secondarily to the value of the survey.

McArthur's study comes very close to being a direct test of the proposition that actors attribute cause to situations while observers attribute cause to dispositions. It suffers, however, from the interpretive difficulty that information about the actor's behavior was given to observers only in printed, verbal form. Two studies by Nisbett and his colleagues avoided this problem by examining situations where more nearly equivalent forms of information were available to actors and observers.

In the first of these studies, Nisbett and Caputo [1971] asked college students to write a brief paragraph stating why they had chosen their major field of concentration and why they liked the girl they dated most frequently. Subjects were asked to write similar brief paragraphs explaining why their best friends had chosen their majors and girl friends. It proved possible to code all of the answers, à la McArthur, into either stimulus attributions ("Chemistry is a high-paying field," "She's a very warm person") or person attributions ("I want to make a lot of money," "I like warm girls"). When answering for himself, the average subject listed roughly the same number of stimulus and person reasons for choosing his major and twice as many stimulus as person reasons for choosing his girl friend. When answering for his best friend, subjects listed approximately three times as many person as stimulus reasons for choosing the major and roughly the same number of stimulus as person reasons for choosing the girl friend. Thus, when describing either choice of a major or choice of a girl friend, subjects were more likely to use dispositional language for their best friends than for themselves.

In a final study, Nisbett, Legant, and Marecek [1971] allowed observer subjects to watch actor-subjects in a controlled laboratory setting. Subjects were Yale coeds. Those designated as actors believed they were to participate in a study on decision making. Subjects designated as observers believed their task would be to watch the subject make decisions and then make judgments about the subject's reasons for making her decisions. Prior to the fictitious decision-making study, the experimenter met with the actor and two confederates who presumably also were going to be subjects in the decision-making study. The observer sat in the background, with instructions simply to observe the (real) target subject. The experimenter, after some introductions and throat-clearing, said, "Before we begin the study, I happen to have sort of a real decision for you to make." The experimenter explained that the "Human Development Institute" at Yale would be sponsoring a weekend for the corporate board and some of their prospective financial backers. The wives of these men would need entertainment and campus tours for the weekend. As a consequence, the Institute had asked the psychology department to recruit students to help with this chore. After elaborating on details of time, place, and specific activities, the experimenter solicited the help of the two confederates and the actor. The confederates were always asked first, and, in order to boost compliance rates on the part of actors, always willingly volunteered.

The amount of money offered to volunteers was manipulated—either $.50 per hour or $1.50 per hour—with very large effects on compliance rates. Only about a fifth of the low-payment actors volunteered, while two-thirds of the high-payment actors volunteered. Volunteers' rates were thus determined in a major way by a purely extrinsic factor: the amount of money offered for compliance.

Actor and observer were then led to separate rooms where they were asked detailed questions concerning the actor's reasons for volunteering or not volunteering. The questions included an item designed to tap the extent to which the actor's behavior was considered an expression of a general disposition to volunteer or not volunteer for worthy activities: "How likely do you think it is that you (or the subject) would also volunteer to canvass for the United Fund?" Observers of volunteering actors thought that the actors would be more likely to volunteer for the United Fund than observers of nonvolunteering actors. Actors themselves did not think they were any more likely to help the United Fund if they were volunteers than if they were nonvolunteers. Thus, in this experimental situation, observers infer dispositions from observation of the actor's behavior, while actors themselves do not.

. . .

THE INFORMATION AVAILABLE TO ACTOR AND OBSERVER

It is a truism that the meaning of an action can be judged only in relation to its context. It is central to our argument that the context data are often quite different for actor and observer and that these differing data prompt differing attributions. The kinds of data available for the attribution process may be conveniently broken down into effect data and cause data. Effect data are of three broad types: data about the nature of the act itself (what was done), data about the environmental outcomes of the act (success or failure, reaction of the recipient of action, and so on), and data about the actor's experiences (pleasure, anger, embarrassment). Cause data are of two broad types: environmental causes (incentives, task difficulty) and intention data (what the actor meant to do, how hard he was working to do it). This categorization is useful for pinpointing the areas where discrepancies are likely to occur in the information available to actor and observer.

Effect Data

Under the category of effect data, it seems clear that actor and observer can have equivalent information about the nature of the act and about environmental outcomes. The observer may know that the actor has delivered an insult and that the recipient is angered. The observer can, however, have no direct knowledge of the experiential accompaniments of the act for the actor. The observer's knowledge about the actor's feelings is limited to inferences of two types: attempts to read inner experience from physiognomic and gestural cues, and judgments based on the observer's knowledge of what others and he himself have felt in similar situations. The observer may infer from the actor's flushed face that he spoke in anger, or he may guess that an insult of the type delivered would probably only be spoken by someone in a great rage. Of course, expressive behavior may not be witnessed by the observer at all. If it is not, then he simply has no information on this score. If it is, his knowledge of the experience of the actor may range from superior in rare cases—a parent may know better than his child that the child is disappointed over a failure or frightened of moving to a strange city—to quite inferior or utterly wrong. In many circumstances actors are motivated to conceal their inner feelings. In others, misperceptions derive from unrecognized individual differences in expressive style. Knowledge of the actor's feeling states is therefore never direct, usually sketchy, and sometimes wrong.

Cause Data

Under the category of perceived causes, it seems clear that there can be equal or nearly equal knowledge of the . . . environmental stimuli operating on the actor. The observer, for example, may know that the recipient of the actor's insult had previously taunted the actor. In principle such knowledge can be as complete for the observer as for the actor. In practice such completeness is probably rarely approximated, if only because of the likelihood that the actor is responding to events more extended in time than those available to the observer. The particular taunt that triggered the actor's outburst may have been the straw that broke the camel's back—the latest in a series of frustrations. The observer is more likely to work instead with the data from one slice of time. . . .

Like the actor's feeling states, his intentions can never be directly known to the observer. In attempting to determine whether the insult was a spontaneous outburst produced by rage or a calculated move to embarrass and motivate the recipient, the observer may infer intentions from the actor's expressive behavior or from the "logic" of the situation. But, as with feeling states, knowledge of intentions is indirect, usually quite inferior, and highly subject to error.

Historical Data   . . .

Because the actor knows his past, he is often diverted from making a dispositional attribution. If the actor insults someone, an observer, who may assume that this is a typical sample of behavior, may infer that the actor is hostile. The actor, on the other hand, may believe that the sample is anything but typical. He may recall very few other instances when he insulted anyone and may believe that in most of these instances he was sharply provoked. The actor's knowledge about the variability of his previous conduct—associated, in his mind, with different situational requirements—often preempts the possibility of a dispositional attribution. We suspect that because of the differences in the availability of personal history data, actors and observers evaluate each act along a different scale of comparison. . . .

There is, in summary, good reason to believe that actors and observers often bring different information to bear on their inferences about the actor and his environment. Typically, the actor has more, and more precise, information than the observer about his own emotional state and his intentions. (We say "typically" rather than "obviously" because there are occasions when the actor might be defensively unaware of his own motives, motives that are readily discernible to the observer.) Moreover, in the absence of precise knowledge of the actor's history, the observer is compelled to deal with him as a modal case and to ignore his unique history and orientation.

The difference in information available to actor and observer probably plays an important role in producing differential attributions, but this is not the whole story. There are good reasons for believing that the same information is differentially processed by actors and observers.

DIFFERENCES IN INFORMATION PROCESSING

While it hardly seems debatable that actors and observers operate much of the time with different background data, the contention that actors and observers differ fundamentally in the *processing* of available data is bound to be more controversial. We believe that important information-processing differences do exist for the basic reason that *different aspects of the available information are salient for actors and observers and this differential salience affects the course and outcome of the attribution process.*

The actor and the observer are both reaching for interpretations of behavior that are sufficient for their own decision-making purposes. With unlimited time, and using the kinds of probes that emphasize a full deterministic picture of an action sequence, observers can probably reach attributional conclusions very similar to those of the actor. In the heat of the interaction moment, however, the purposes of actor and observer are apt to be different enough to start the inference process along distinctive tracks. Conceptualization of this problem depends to some extent on the kind of action-observation situation we are considering. Two extreme cases are the mutual contingency interaction . . . , where each actor observes and is affected by the other, and the asymmetrical case of passive observation, where running behavioral decisions are thrust exclusively upon the actor while the observer's only task is to record and interpret—as if from behind a one-way screen.

We shall later examine the differences between these two situations, but a very important feature is common to both: the action itself—its topography, rhythm, style, and content—is more salient to the observer than to the actor. . . . We may begin with the observation that action involves perceptible movement and change (by definition) and it is always to some extent unpredictable. While the environment is stable and contextual from the observer's point of view, action is figural and dynamic. The actor, however, is less likely to focus his attention on his behavior than on the environmental cues that evoke and shape it. . . . In short, the actor need not and in some ways cannot observe his behavior very closely. Instead, his attention is directed outward, toward the environment with its constantly shifting demands and opportunities.

These attentional differences should result in differences in causal perception. The actor should perceive his behavior to be a response to environmental cues that trigger, guide, and terminate it. But for the observer the focal, commanding stimulus is the actor's behavior, and situational cues are to a degree ignored. This leaves the actor as the likely causal candidate, and the observer will account for the actor's responses in terms of attributed dispositions.

The effect of these differential attribution tendencies is amplified by bias from another source, the tendency to regard one's reactions to entities as based on accurate perceptions of them. Rather than humbly regarding our impressions of the world as interpretations of it, we see them as understandings or correct apprehensions of it. . . .

. . .

It is now time to return to the distinction between passive and active observers, and to consider the implications of this distinction for our discussion. By definition the passive observer is not in a position to respond to the actor and the actor is unaware of his specific presence. The observer may be affected by the actor, but the actor cannot be affected by the observer—there is asymmetrical contingency. This is the situation of the moviegoer, the TV watcher, and the concealed observer behind a one-way screen. The passive observer may have any of a number of purposes that make him more attentive to certain kinds of information than others. . . . It is possible to affect the amount of empathy shown by the observer for the actor by simple variations in observational instructions. Presumably, the more the observer is set to empathize with the actor, the more similar their attributional perspectives will be. Unless the observer has a strong empathy set, however, we would expect him to show the general observer tendency to underestimate the role of the environment, if only because of the differential salience of behavioral and situational information.

For the observer who is at the same time an actor, the tendency toward heightened salience of action should become more pronounced for several reasons. The fact that the observer is also caught up in action suggests that he will not be in a position to make leisurely appraisals of the setting and its contributions to unfolding behavior. Rather than being in a set to understand and evaluate the relative contributions of person and environment, the actor-observer will be tuned to process those cues that are particularly pertinent for his own next responses. Short-run behavior prediction is of paramount importance to the observer who is preparing his next act, and we suggest that the actor's behavior is more likely to seem pertinent for such predictions than the situational context evoking it. . . .

A second consideration arises from the fact that the observer's presence and behavior may affect the actor's responses in ways not discerned by the observer. It is difficult for the active observer to evaluate the significance of his own presence because he is not often afforded clear comparative tests—tests that pit the stimulus contributions he generally makes against the stimulus contributions of others. In the situation we are now considering, where the observer is also an actor, the observer is likely to exaggerate the uniqueness and emphasize the dispositional origin of the other's responses to his own actions, actions the observer assumes to be perfectly standard, unexceptional, and unprovocative.

. . .

In summary, the observer and the actor are likely to take different perspectives toward the same information. For the observer, the actor's behavior is the figural stimulus against the ground of the situation. The actor's attention is focused outward toward situational cues rather than inward on his own behavior, and moreover, those situational cues are endowed with intrinsic properties that are seen to cause the actor's behavior toward them. Thus, for the observer the proximal cause of action is the actor; for the actor the proximal cause lies in the compelling qualities of the environment. Finally, the tendency for the observer to attribute action to the actor is probably increased to the extent that the observer is also an actor and to the extent that both the observing and the observed actor are tied together in a mutually contingent interaction.

THE NAIVE PSYCHOLOGY OF OBSERVERS AND ACTORS

The preceding discussion is likely to raise in the reader's mind a question as to who is correct, the actor or the observer. In the typical case, is behavior really caused by the actor or elicited by the environment? Put in these simplified terms, the question is of course unanswerable. All behavior is in one sense caused or produced by the actor. Except perhaps in acts such as the patellar reflex, all action involves some form of explicit or implicit decision process suggesting volition or personal causation.

The more pertinent and answerable question concerns the extent to which a particular setting is likely to evoke the same response across many persons. . . . A situation that evokes a response common to many persons is likely to be seen as causing the behavior. Situations that evoke varied or unique responses are much less likely to be seen as causal. Obversely, when a person acts in a similar fashion on many different occasions, the act is seen to reflect a personal disposition.

It is obviously safer to talk about *phenomenal* causality than to raise any questions concerning accuracy or objective causality. Nevertheless, it is interesting to consider the many occasions on which the observer appears . . . to make a dispositional inference when the data do not allow it. Without insisting that the actor is usually right, we can point to many instances where the observer's interpretation of behavior is simply wrong. The observer is wrong when he infers that an attitude is consistent with an essay written in response to a legitimate request. He is wrong when he thinks the nonintervening bystander is apathetic, or infers that the subject who agrees to help out for a handsome fee is a chronic volunteer. In each of these cases the observer seems to underestimate the power of the situation and to overestimate the uniqueness of the (in fact modal) response.

The Observer's View: Personality as a Trait Package

It is interesting to speculate on the possible implications of the observer's bias for the conception of personality structure held by most people in our society and indeed by most personality psychologists. At bottom this conception is an Aristotelian view of personality as a collection of traits, that is, the most general kind of dispositions. Does this conception err by overemphasizing individual differences at the trait level and slighting the impact of situational variance?

Mischel [1968] argues persuasively that such overemphasis is common. He reviews the evidence on the existence of several dimensions of behavior usually presumed to be manifestations of a trait—honesty, dependency, attitudes toward authority, rigidity or intolerance for ambiguity, persuasibility, and so on. Using the restricted empirical criterion of predictability from one behavior that is presumed to reflect the trait to another such behavior, Mischel finds little evidence that traits exist anywhere but in the cognitive structure of observers. For example, in the early but very sophisticated and ambitious honesty study of Hartshorne and May [1928], children were exposed to a variety of temptations in a variety of settings, including the opportunity to cheat on a test, steal money, and lie to save face. Despite the fact that there was some reliability of behavior. . . , there was very little generality of honesty across settings. . . . Mischel reviewed many other studies attempting to find behavioral generality across settings usually presumed to reflect a given trait. With the rather clear exception of abilities and ability-related traits, no disposition was found to be immune from the indictment of low generality.

The trait concept fares no better when it is examined in terms of attempts to predict behavior from paper and pencil trait measurements. When trait scores are obtained from questionnaire self-reports, they rarely predict with any accuracy behavior that is presumed to tap the trait dimension. . . . Thus, when we ask a person what his position is on a trait or when we infer it from his response to questionnaire items, we learn almost nothing about his actual behavior.

What Sustains the Belief in Traits?

Mischel therefore contends that there is little evidence for the existence of the broad trait concepts that have been such a standard part of our psychological vocabulary for centuries. From our position of lesser expertise, we agree that a conception of personality emphasizing behavior generality is inadequate and misleading. How does it happen, then, that students of personality have persistently embraced a trait construction of behavior? Why has it taken forty years of negative findings on the question for anyone to propose seriously in a textbook on personality that these trait dimensions may not exist? One answer is that the conclusion is based on inadequate data, another, that the traits have not been measured properly, or still a third, that the wrong traits have been examined. Another answer, and this is a conclusion that Mischel and the present writers prefer, is that traits exist more in the eye of the beholder than in the psyche of the actor.

If we are to uphold the position that personality traits are overattributed, then it is incumbent upon us to account for the widespread belief in their existence. . . . If the belief in traits is mistaken, there would have to be very strong forces operating to sustain it. We believe there are such forces

and have already dealt with two of them: (1) the information-processing biases that conspire to make behavior appear as a manifestation or quality of the actor and (2) the informational deficit of the observer, which prevents disconfirmation of the trait inference. We believe there are still other important reasons for the illusion. In discussing these reasons, it will be helpful to categorize them into sources of informational bias, sources of information-processing bias, and sources of linguistic bias. . . .

Informational bias. Most of the people we observe are seen only in a very few roles. Within those already narrow confines, we are likely to see them in a biased sample of situations: when they are at their best or at their worst, when they are at their most harassed or their most relaxed, in their work moods or their play moods, in the morning or in the evening, in the company of people they like or with people they dislike. Those of us who are embedded in a bureaucracy may be especially prone to confuse responses to role requirements with personality dispositions. Bank presidents are usually surprised when the drab, black-suited teller absconds with the funds and is found living it up in Tahiti. To the extent that role and situational factors produce behavior that can be labeled as conforming, hostile, thrifty, brave, clean, or reverent, observers are likely to see the individual as being a conforming, hostile, thrifty, brave, clean, or reverent person.

Beyond the sampling bias produced by roles and situations, one carries with him into a relationship with others a bias in the form of oneself. To the extent that one's own behavior is a restricted sample of possible behaviors, it will evoke a restricted sample from the other person in turn. This point has been anticipated in our previous discussion of the "active observer." . . . One's own behavior may evoke complementary responses in another that one then mistakenly perceives as a manifestation of the other's personality. One may unwittingly shape the other's behavior in a variety of ways: by one's own role- and situation-determined behaviors toward the other, by implicitly communicated expectations and hopes about his behavior, and by a host of personal characteristics such as one's abilities, physical appearance, mannerisms, or social status.

Information-processing bias. Much has been written about the human tendency toward cognitive balance or consistency. Surely the tendency toward consistency must play some role in the observer's assignment of traits. A person who is aggressive in one setting should, to be "consistent," be aggressive in other settings. To see dependence and independence in the same actor may lead to greater subtleties of categorization, or it may lead to misperception of the evidence so that it becomes more consistent. In short, all the cognitive mechanisms of inconsistency reduction can be put to work in the service of dispositional accounts of action. It is not surprising that personal consistency is exaggerated in the eye of the beholder.

. . . Out of his needs to impose structure on the environment, the observer often makes premature commitments to the nature of those entities he is observing. Within certain limits of discrepancy, therefore, inconsistent information will be seen as more consistent than it deserves to be. Even beyond these limits, contradictory data can be treated as anomalous, even as the exception that proves the rule.

. . . The simple fact that another person is physically continuous, always looks more or less the same, and has the same mannerisms, may encourage the impression that there is continuity in his behavior as well. The fact of physical constancy may produce the illusion of behavioral and therefore dispositional consistency.

Linguistic distortions. Language probably facilitates the inference of traits in several ways. Once we have labeled an action as hostile, it is very easy to move to the inference that the perpetrator is a hostile person. Our language allows the same term to be applied to behavior and to the underlying disposition it reflects. . . .

It may also be noted that our vocabulary is rich in dispositional or trait terms (the Allport-Ogbert list includes over 18,000 terms) and quite impoverished when it comes to describing the situation. . . .

. . .

The rarity of disconfirmation. Informational bias, processing bias, and linguistic bias all operate, therefore, in such a way as to generate trait inferences where there may be no traits. Are there no mechanisms that can curtail and reverse the errors? There probably are. Certainly the better we know someone, the more restraints there are against facile trait ascription. There are probably sharp limits, however, to the power of additional information to disconfirm a trait ascription. Once we have decided that a person is hostile or dependent, a wide variety of behaviors can be construed as support for this supposition, including even behaviors commonly taken as implying the opposite of the trait ascription. A kind behavior

on the part of a "hostile" person may be perceived as insincere, manipulative, or condescending. We are probably all rather adept at the maintenance of a trait inference in the face of disconfirmatory evidence. When practiced by some psychoanalytic writers, the maneuvering can be truly breathtaking.

It might be argued that discussion with others provides ample opportunity for disconfirmation of a trait inference. The individual may find in such discussion that his trait inferences are not shared. This is undoubtedly true. We can all think of instances where our beliefs about another person have been altered by hearing about someone else's experiences with that person. There are good reasons to expect that our erroneous trait inferences will more often receive consensual validation, however. To the extent that another person resembles oneself in role, status, personal and physical characteristics, he is likely to have the same sorts of experiences with a given person that one has had oneself, and therefore to have made the same trait inferences. It seems likely, moreover, that the more similar two people are the more probable it is that they will discuss the personality of someone they know mutually. The chairman of a department does not often exchange opinions with graduate students on the intelligence or warmth of assistant professors. Finally, when one's trait inferences are flatly contradicted by another person, everything we have said implies that one is likely to explain the contradiction in terms of the dispositions of the person who is contradicting him: "I wonder why John is unable to see the essential kindness of Mary."

In summary, the observer . . . is apt to conceive of the personalities of others as a collection of broad dispositions or traits, despite the scant empirical evidence for their existence. This conception appears to result from deficits and biases in the information available to the observer and to a variety of biases in the processing of information at the perceptual, cognitive, and linguistic levels. It should be noted, however, that the low empirical validity of the trait concept may be of importance only to the psychologist. The observer, in his daily life, may achieve fairly high predictability using trait inferences that the psychologist can show to be erroneous. If the observer is habitually insulted by a given actor, it may make little difference to the observer whether the reason for this consistent behavior is the hostility of the actor, the actor's dislike of the observer, or the fact that the observer sees the actor only in the early morning when the actor is always grouchy.

. . .

PERSONALITY TRAITS ARE THINGS OTHER PEOPLE HAVE

If it is true that actors and observers have different conceptions of personality structure along the lines we have discussed, then it should be the case that each individual perceives every other individual to have more stable personality traits than he himself possesses. He should view others as having generalized response dispositions but himself as acting in accord with the demands and opportunities inherent in each new situation. In order to test this proposition, Nisbett and Caputo [1971] constructed a variant of the standard trait description questionnaire. A list of twenty polar adjectives ("reserved–emotionally expressive"; "lenient–firm") was presented to subjects, along with the option, for each dimension, "depends on the situation." Each of the male college student subjects was asked to check one of the three alternatives for each trait dimension for each of five people: himself, his best friend, an age peer whom the subject liked but did not know well, his father, and (to fill in the remaining cell of the young–old, familiar–unfamiliar matrix) the television commentator Walter Cronkite. In line with anticipations, subjects were likely to use the "depends on the situation" category for themselves but quite willing to assign traits to the other stimulus persons. Neither degree of acquaintance nor similarity in age was a very potent determinant of the willingness to ascribe traits to others: subjects assigned traits in about equal numbers to each of the other stimulus persons.

. . .

SUMMARY AND CONCLUSIONS

Actors tend to attribute the causes of their behavior to stimuli inherent in the situation, while observers tend to attribute behavior to stable dispositions of the actor. This is due in part to the actor's more detailed knowledge of his circumstances, history, motives, and experiences. Perhaps more importantly, the tendency is a result of the differential salience of the information available to both actor and observer. For the observer behavior is figural against the ground of the situation. For the actor it is the situational cues that are figural and that are seen to elicit behavior. Moreover, the actor is inclined to think of his judgments about the situational cues as being perceptions or accurate readings of them. These cues are therefore more "real" as well as more salient than they are for the observer. Behavior is thus seen by the observer to be a manifestation of the actor and seen by the actor to be a response to the situation.

The observer often errs by overattributing dispositions, including the broadest kind of dispositions—personality traits. The evidence for personality traits as commonly conceived is sparse. The widespread belief in their existence appears to be due to the observer's failure to realize that the samples of behavior that he sees are not random, as well as to the observer's tendency to see behavior as a manifestation of the actor rather than a response to situational cues. A variety of additional perceptual, cognitive, and linguistic processes help to sustain the belief in traits.

. . .

BIBLIOGRAPHY

H. Hartshorne and Mark A. May, *Studies in the Nature of Character*, Vol. I. *Studies in Deceit.* Macmillan, 1928.

Edward E. Jones and Victor A. Harris, "The Attribution of Attitudes." *Journal of Experimental Social Psychology*, 1967, 3:1–24.

Edward E. Jones, Leslie Rock, Kelly G. Shaver, George R. Goethals, and Lawrence M. Ward, "Pattern of Performance and Ability Attribution: An Unexpected Primacy Effect." *Journal of Personality and Social Psychology*, 1968, 10:317–340.

Edward E. Jones, Stephen Worchel, George R. Goethals, and Judy Grumet, "Prior Expectancy and Behavioral Extremity as Determinants of Attitude Attribution." *Journal of Experimental Social Psychology*, 1971, 7: 59–80.

Leslie Z. McArthur, "The How and What of Why: Some Determinants and Consequences of Causal Attribution." Unpublished Ph.D. dissertation, Yale University, 1970.

Richard E. Nisbett and G. Craig Caputo, "Personality Traits: Why Other People Do the Things They Do." Unpublished manuscript. Yale University, 1971.

Richard E. Nisbett, Patricia Legant, and Jeanne Marecek, "The Causes of Behavior as Seen by Actor and Observer." Unpublished manuscript, Yale University, 1971.

PROJECTS

Name _____

Date _____

8.1: PERCEPTION OF MOTIVATIONS

This project is intended to give you an opportunity to evaluate fellow students and then to compare your evaluations with theirs. It lists several possible reasons why students decide to attend a particular college. Use the following scale to rate how important you think each of these reasons was in his or her choice of school: Rate one or two people (whose names will be given to you by your instructor) on 1 = not at all important, 2 = slightly important, 3 = moderately important, 4 = quite important, and 5 = extremely important.

Person being evaluated _____

Reason for choosing this college	Importance of reason (1–5)
Parental wishes	
Desire to get away from home	
Good scholastic reputation	
Good location	
Desire to find a marriage partner	
Good social life	
Ease of getting admitted	

Person being evaluated _____

Reason for choosing this college   Importance of reason (1-5)

Parental wishes

Desire to get away from home

Good scholastic reputation

Good location

Desire to find a marriage partner

Good social life

Ease of getting admitted

Name _____

Date _____

8.2: ACTOR AND OBSERVER

According to Jones and Nisbett, people tend to see their own behavior as caused by external situational factors but to attribute the behavior of others to internal personality traits. This exercise is designed to gather some data in order to test the validity of that proposition.

Collect a series of ratings from several people (students from another class, roommates), and record their responses on the data sheet. These ratings are evaluations of the characteristic behaviors of two other people and a self-evaluation. Each of the behaviors ("assertive," "calm," and so on) should be rated as follows: "yes" (this behavior is definitely characteristic of this person), "no" (this behavior is definitely *not* characteristic of this person), and "depends" (sometimes "yes," sometimes "no"—it depends on the situation). For ease of recording, use the abbreviations Y, N, and D.

First, have your subjects rate someone that they like very much. Ask them to think of that person and then to rate him or her on the set of behaviors, indicating how characteristic (or uncharacteristic) each is. It is easiest if you read off the behaviors one by one and mark down the subjects' responses. Then ask the subjects to think of someone that they dislike very much. Repeat the procedure. Finally, ask the subjects to rate themselves.

Now recode your data so that you can compare the frequency of trait responses (Y + N) with the frequency of situation responses (D). If the Jones-Nisbett hypothesis is correct, you should have found that subjects gave more trait responses for themselves. If there are exceptions to this pattern, how do you account for them? For example, what types of behavior did the subjects attribute to their own personalities rather than to the situations?

DATA SHEET

INDIVIDUAL RATINGS

	Assertive	Calm	Talkative	Impulsive	Kind	Optimistic	Cynical	Self-confident
S_1 Liked other								
Disliked other								
Self								
S_2 Liked other								
Disliked other								
Self								
S_3 Liked other								
Disliked other								
Self								
S_4 Liked other								
Disliked other								
Self								

COMBINED RATINGS

Other (liked and disliked)		
No. trait ratings (Y and D)		
No. situation ratings (D)		
Self		
No. trait ratings (Y and N)		
No. situation ratings (D)		

9
GROUP PROCESSES

The group is essential to human survival because without other people, the individual cannot function and develop. As we noted in our introduction to Chapter 5, people need each other for a variety of reasons, and it is through various kinds of groups that one person gains access to others. Whether it is small or large, informal or formal, each group to which a person belongs can have a tremendous impact on his or her life.

Groups can increase the individual's chances for survival, promote his or her welfare, protect the individual's rights, and establish a basis for validation of an individual's beliefs. However, membership in a group can also make the individual susceptible to social influences that encourage irrational or destructive behavior. The group pressures that cause us to obey the command to "love thy neighbor" are intimately related to the pressures that prompt us to reject those who are different from ourselves. Clearly, groups have the potential for both good and ill. That theme is reflected in the readings in this chapter.

GROUPTHINK

IRVING L. JANIS

When difficult or even critical decisions need to be made, it is often helpful to have several people involved in this process. As the old adage says, "Two heads are better than one." Different people can bring a variety of viewpoints to a problem, propose more ideas, and help each other to think in new and creative ways. But there is another adage that tells us: "Too many cooks spoil the broth." Obviously, it is important to learn how to recognize the circumstances when one of these statements is more likely to be true than the other. In his article "Groupthink," Janis offers an analysis based on historical reports of group meetings that precipitated fiascos in American foreign policy. He identifies the factors that can cause group decision making to go wrong, a pattern of group behavior that he calls groupthink.

"How could we have been so stupid?" President John F. Kennedy asked after he and a close group of advisers had blundered into the Bay of Pigs invasion. For the last two years I have been studying that question, as it applies not only to

Reprinted from *Psychology Today*, Nov. 1971, pp. 43 ff. Copyright © 1971 by Ziff-Davis Publishing Company. Reprinted by permission of *Psychology Today Magazine*.

the Bay of Pigs decision-makers but also to those who led the United States into such other major fiascos as the failure to be prepared for the attack on Pearl Harbor, the Korean War stalemate and the escalation of the Vietnam War.

Stupidity certainly is not the explanation. The men who participated in making the Bay of Pigs decision, for instance, comprised one of the greatest arrays of intellectual talent in the history of American Government—Dean Rusk, Robert Mc-

Namara, Douglas Dillon, Robert Kennedy, Mc-George Bundy, Arthur Schlesinger, Jr., Allen Dulles and others.

It also seemed to me that explanations were incomplete if they concentrated only on disturbances in the behavior of each individual within a decision-making body: temporary emotional states of elation, fear, or anger that reduce a man's mental efficiency, for example, or chronic blind spots arising from a man's social prejudices or idiosyncratic biases.

I preferred to broaden the picture by looking at the fiascos from the standpoint of group dynamics as it has been explored over the past three decades, first by the great social psychologist Kurt Lewin and later in many experimental situations by myself and other behavioral scientists. My conclusion after poring over hundreds of relevant documents—historical reports about formal group meetings and informal conversations among the members—is that the groups that committed the fiascos were victims of what I call "groupthink."

"GROUPY"

In each case study, I was surprised to discover the extent to which each group displayed the typical phenomena of social conformity that are regularly encountered in studies of group dynamics among ordinary citizens. For example, some of the phenomena appear to be completely in line with findings from social-psychological experiments showing that powerful social pressures are brought to bear by the members of a cohesive group whenever a dissident begins to voice his objections to a group consensus. Other phenomena are reminiscent of the shared illusions observed in encounter groups and friendship cliques when the members simultaneously reach a peak of "groupy" feelings.

Above all, there are numerous indications pointing to the development of group norms that bolster morale at the expense of critical thinking. One of the most common norms appears to be that of remaining loyal to the group by sticking with the policies to which the group has already committed itself, even when those policies are obviously working out badly and have unintended consequences that disturb the conscience of each member. This is one of the key characteristics of groupthink.

1984

I use the term groupthink as a quick and easy way to refer to the mode of thinking that persons engage in when *concurrence-seeking* becomes so dominant in a cohesive ingroup that it tends to override realistic appraisal of alternative courses of action. Groupthink is a term of the same order as the words in the newspeak vocabulary George Orwell used in his dismaying world of *1984*. In that context, groupthink takes on an invidious connotation. Exactly such a connotation is intended, since the term refers to a deterioration in mental efficiency, reality testing and moral judgments as a result of group pressures.

The symptoms of groupthink arise when the members of decision-making groups become motivated to avoid being too harsh in their judgments of their leaders' or their colleagues' ideas. They adopt a soft line of criticism, even in their own thinking. At their meetings, all the members are amiable and seek complete concurrence on every important issue, with no bickering or conflict to spoil the cozy, "we-feeling" atmosphere.

KILL

Paradoxically, soft-headed groups are often hard-hearted when it comes to dealing with outgroups or enemies. They find it relatively easy to resort to dehumanizing solutions—they will readily authorize bombing attacks that kill large numbers of civilians in the name of the noble cause of persuading an unfriendly government to negotiate at the peace table. They are unlikely to pursue the more difficult and controversial issues that arise when alternatives to a harsh military solution come up for discussion. Nor are they inclined to raise ethical issues that carry the implication that *this fine group of ours, with its humanitarianism and its high-minded principles, might be capable of adopting a course of action that is inhumane and immoral.*

NORMS

There is evidence from a number of social-psychological studies that as the members of a group feel more accepted by the others, which is a central feature of increased group cohesiveness, they display less overt conformity to group norms. Thus we would expect that the more cohesive a group becomes, the less the members will feel constrained to censor what they say out of fear of being socially punished for antagonizing the leader or any of their fellow members.

In contrast, the groupthink type of conformity tends to increase as group cohesiveness increases.

Groupthink involves nondeliberate suppression of critical thoughts as a result of internalization of the group's norms, which is quite different from deliberate suppression on the basis of external threats of social punishment. The more cohesive the group, the greater the inner compulsion on the part of each member to avoid creating disunity, which inclines him to believe in the soundness of whatever proposals are promoted by the leader or by a majority of the group's members.

In a cohesive group, the danger is not so much that each individual will fail to reveal his objections to what the others propose but that he will think the proposal is a good one, without attempting to carry out a careful, critical scrutiny of the pros and cons of the alternatives. When groupthink becomes dominant, there also is considerable suppression of deviant thoughts, but it takes the form of each person's deciding that his misgivings are not relevant and should be set aside, that the benefit of the doubt regarding any lingering uncertainties should be given to the group consensus.

STRESS

I do not mean to imply that all cohesive groups necessarily suffer from groupthink. All ingroups may have a mild tendency toward groupthink, displaying one or another of the symptoms from time to time, but it need not be so dominant as to influence the quality of the group's final decision. Neither do I mean to imply that there is anything necessarily inefficient or harmful about group decisions in general. On the contrary, a group whose members have properly defined roles, with traditions concerning the procedures to follow in pursuing a critical inquiry, probably is capable of making better decisions than any individual group member working alone.

The problem is that the advantages of having decisions made by groups are often lost because of powerful psychological pressures that arise when the members work closely together, share the same set of values and, above all, face a crisis situation that puts everyone under intense stress.

The main principle of groupthink, which I offer in the spirit of Parkinson's Law, is this: *The more amiability and esprit de corps there is among the members of a policy-making ingroup, the greater the danger that independent critical thinking will be replaced by groupthink, which is likely to result in irrational and dehumanizing actions directed against outgroups.*

SYMPTOMS

In my studies of high-level governmental decision-makers, both civilian and military, I have found eight main symptoms of groupthink.

1. Invulnerability

Most or all of the members of the ingroup share an *illusion* of invulnerability that provides for them some degree of reassurance about obvious dangers and leads them to become over-optimistic and willing to take extraordinary risks. It also causes them to fail to respond to clear warnings of danger.

The Kennedy ingroup, which uncritically accepted the Central Intelligence Agency's disastrous Bay of Pigs plan, operated on the false assumption that they could keep secret the fact that the United States was responsible for the invasion of Cuba. Even after news of the plan began to leak out, their belief remained unshaken. They failed even to consider the danger that awaited them: a worldwide revulsion against the U.S.

A similar attitude appeared among the members of President Lyndon B. Johnson's ingroup, the "Tuesday Cabinet," which kept escalating the Vietnam War despite repeated setbacks and failures. "There was a belief," Bill Moyers commented after he resigned, "that if we indicated a willingness to use our power, they [the North Vietnamese] would get the message and back away from an all-out confrontation. . . . There was a confidence—it was never bragged about, it was just there—that when the chips were really down, the other people would fold."

A most poignant example of an illusion of invulnerability involves the ingroup around Admiral H. E. Kimmel, which failed to prepare for the possibility of a Japanese attack on Pearl Harbor despite repeated warnings. Informed by his intelligence chief that radio contact with Japanese aircraft carriers had been lost, Kimmel joked about it: "What, you don't know where the carriers are? Do you mean to say that they could be rounding Diamond Head (at Honolulu) and you wouldn't know it?" The carriers were in fact moving full-steam toward Kimmel's command post at the time. Laughing together about a danger signal, which labels it as a purely laughing matter, is a characteristic manifestation of groupthink.

2. Rationale

As we see, victims of groupthink ignore warnings; they also collectively construct rationalizations in order to discount warnings and other forms of negative feedback that, taken seriously, might lead the group members to reconsider their assumptions each time they recommit themselves to past decisions. Why did the Johnson ingroup avoid reconsidering its escalation policy when time and again the expectations on which they based their decisions turned out to be wrong? James C. Thompson, Jr., a Harvard historian who spent five years as an observing participant in both the State Department and the White House, tells us that the policymakers avoided critical discussion of their prior decisions and continually invented new rationalizations so that they could sincerely recommit themselves to defeating the North Vietnamese.

In the fall of 1964, before the bombing of North Vietnam began, some of the policymakers predicted that six weeks of air strikes would induce the North Vietnamese to seek peace talks. When someone asked, ''What if they don't?'' the answer was that another four weeks certainly would do the trick.

Later, after each setback, the ingroup agreed that by investing just a bit more effort (by stepping up the bomb tonnage a bit, for instance), their course of action would prove to be right. *The Pentagon Papers* bear out these observations.

In *The Limits of Intervention*, Townsend Hoopes, who was acting Secretary of the Air Force under Johnson, says that Walt W. Rostow in particular showed a remarkable capacity for what has been called ''instant rationalization.'' According to Hoopes, Rostow buttressed the group's optimism about being on the road to victory by culling selected scraps of evidence from news reports or, if necessary, by inventing ''plausible'' forecasts that had no basis in evidence at all.

Admiral Kimmel's group rationalized away their warnings, too. Right up to December 7, 1941, they convinced themselves that the Japanese would never dare attempt a full-scale surprise assault against Hawaii because Japan's leaders would realize that it would precipitate an all-out war which the United States would surely win. They made no attempt to look at the situation through the eyes of the Japanese leaders—another manifestation of groupthink.

3. Morality

Victims of groupthink believe unquestioningly in the inherent morality of their ingroup; this belief inclines the members to ignore the ethical or moral consequences of their decisions.

Evidence that this symptom is at work usually is of a negative kind—the things that are left unsaid in group meetings. At least two influential persons had doubts about the morality of the Bay of Pigs adventure. One of them, Arthur Schlesinger, Jr., presented his strong objections in a memorandum to President Kennedy and Secretary of State Rusk but suppressed them when he attended meetings of the Kennedy team. The other, Senator J. William Fulbright, was not a member of the group, but the President invited him to express his misgivings in a speech to the policymakers. However, when Fulbright finished speaking the President moved on to other agenda items without asking for reactions of the group.

David Kraslow and Stuart H. Loory, in *The Secret Search for Peace in Vietnam*, report that during 1966 President Johnson's ingroup was concerned primarily with selecting bomb targets in North Vietnam. They based their selections on four factors—the military advantage, the risk to American aircraft and pilots, the danger of forcing other countries into the fighting, and the danger of heavy civilian casualties. At their regular Tuesday luncheons, they weighed these factors the way school teachers grade examination papers, averaging them out. Though evidence on this point is scant, I suspect that the group's ritualistic adherence to a standardized procedure induced the members to feel morally justified in their destructive way of dealing with the Vietnamese people—after all, the danger of heavy civilian casualties from U.S. air strikes was taken into account on their checklists.

4. Stereotypes

Victims of groupthink hold stereotyped views of the leaders of enemy groups: they are so evil that genuine attempts at negotiating differences with them are unwarranted, or they are too weak or too stupid to deal effectively with whatever attempts the ingroup makes to defeat their purposes, no matter how risky the attempts are.

Kennedy's groupthinkers believed that Premier Fidel Castro's air force was so ineffectual that obsolete B-26s could knock it out completely in a surprise attack before the invasion began. They also believed that Castro's army was so weak that a small Cuban-exile brigade could establish a well-protected beachhead at the Bay of Pigs. In addition, they believed that Castro was not smart enough to put down any possible internal uprisings in support of the exiles. They were wrong on all three assumptions. Though much of the blame was attributable to faulty intelligence, the point is that none of Kennedy's advisers even questioned the CIA planners about these assumptions.

The Johnson advisers' sloganistic thinking about "the Communist apparatus" that was "working all around the world" (as Dean Rusk put it) led them to overlook the powerful nationalistic strivings of the North Vietnamese government and its efforts to ward off Chinese domination. The crudest of all stereotypes used by Johnson's inner circle to justify their policies was the domino theory ("If we don't stop the Reds in South Vietnam, tomorrow they will be in Hawaii and next week they will be in San Francisco," Johnson once said). The group so firmly accepted this stereotype that it became almost impossible for any adviser to introduce a more sophisticated viewpoint.

In the documents on Pearl Harbor, it is clear to see that the Navy commanders stationed in Hawaii had a naive image of Japan as a midget that would not dare to strike a blow against a powerful giant.

5. Pressure

Victims of groupthink apply direct pressure to any individual who momentarily expresses doubts about any of the group's shared illusions or who questions the validity of the arguments supporting a policy alternative favored by the majority. This gambit reinforces the concurrence-seeking norm that loyal members are expected to maintain.

President Kennedy probably was more active than anyone else in raising skeptical questions during the Bay of Pigs meetings, and yet he seems to have encouraged the group's docile, uncritical acceptance of defective arguments in favor of the CIA's plan. At every meeting, he allowed the CIA representatives to dominate the discussion. He permitted them to give their immediate refutations in response to each tentative doubt that one of the others expressed, instead of asking whether anyone shared the doubt or wanted to pursue the implications of the new worrisome issue that had just been raised. And at the most crucial meeting, when he was calling on each member to give his vote for or against the plan, he did not call on Arthur Schlesinger, the one man there who was known by the President to have serious misgivings.

Historian Thompson informs us that whenever a member of Johnson's ingroup began to express doubts, the group used subtle social pressures to "domesticate" him. To start with, the dissenter was made to feel at home, provided that he lived up to two restrictions: 1) that he did not voice his doubts to outsiders, which would play into the hands of the opposition; and 2) that he kept his criticisms within the bounds of acceptable deviation, which meant not challenging any of the fundamental assumptions that went into the group's prior commitments. One such "domesticated dissenter" was Bill Moyers. When Moyers arrived at a meeting, Thompson tells us, the President greeted him with, "Well, here comes Mr. Stop-the-Bombing."

6. Self-censorship

Victims of groupthink avoid deviating from what appears to be group consensus; they keep silent about their misgivings and even minimize to themselves the importance of their doubts.

As we have seen, Schlesinger was not at all hesitant about presenting his strong objections to the Bay of Pigs plan in a memorandum to the President and the Secretary of State. But he became keenly aware of his tendency to suppress objections at the White House meetings. "In the months after the Bay of Pigs I bitterly reproached myself for having kept so silent during those crucial discussions in the cabinet room," Schlesinger writes in *A Thousand Days*. "I can only explain my failure to do more than raise a few timid questions by reporting that one's impulse to blow the whistle on this nonsense was simply undone by the circumstances of the discussion."

7. Unanimity

Victims of groupthink share an *illusion* of unanimity within the group concerning almost all judgments expressed by members who speak in favor of the majority view. This symptom results partly from the preceding one, whose effects are augmented by the false assumption that any individual who remains silent during any part of the discussion is in full accord with what the others are saying.

When a group of persons who respect each other's opinions arrives at a unanimous view, each member is likely to feel that the belief must be true. This reliance on consensual validation within the group tends to replace individual critical thinking and reality testing, unless there are clear-cut disagreements among the members. In contemplating a course of action such as the invasion of Cuba, it is painful for the members to confront disagreements within their group, particularly if it becomes apparent that there are widely divergent views about whether the preferred course of action is too risky to undertake at all. Such disagreements are likely to arouse anxieties about making a serious error. Once the sense of unanimity is shattered, the members no longer can feel complacently confident about the decision they are inclined to make. Each man must then face the annoying realization that there are troublesome uncertainties and he must diligently seek out the best information he can get in order to decide for himself exactly how serious the risks might be. This is one of the unpleasant consequences of being in a group of hardheaded, critical thinkers.

To avoid such an unpleasant state, the members often become inclined, without quite realizing it, to prevent latent disagreements from surfacing when they are about to initiate a risky course of action. The group leader and the members support each other in playing up the areas of convergence in their thinking, at the expense of fully exploring divergencies that might reveal unsettled issues.

"Our meetings took place in a curious atmosphere of assumed consensus," Schlesinger writes. His additional comments clearly show that, curiously, the consensus was an illusion—an illusion that could be maintained only because the major participants did not reveal their own reasoning or discuss their idiosyncratic assumptions and vague reservations. Evidence from several sources makes it clear that even the three principals—President Kennedy, Rusk and McNamara—had widely differing assumptions about the invasion plan.

8. Mindguards

Victims of groupthink sometimes appoint themselves as mindguards to protect the leader and fellow members from adverse information that might break the complacency they shared about the effectiveness and morality of past decisions. At a large birthday party for his wife, Attorney General Robert F. Kennedy, who had been constantly informed about the Cuban invasion plan, took Schlesinger aside and asked him why he was opposed. Kennedy listened coldly and said, "You may be right or you may be wrong, but the President has made his mind up. Don't push it any further. Now is the time for everyone to help him all they can."

Rusk also functioned as a highly effective mindguard by failing to transmit to the group the strong objections of three "outsiders" who had learned of the invasion plan—Undersecretary of State Chester Bowles, USIA Director Edward R. Murrow, and Rusk's intelligence chief, Roger Hilsman. Had Rusk done so, their warnings might have reinforced Schlesinger's memorandum and jolted some of Kennedy's ingroup, if not the President himself, into reconsidering the decision.

PRODUCTS

When a group of executives frequently displays most or all of these interrelated symptoms, a detailed study of their deliberations is likely to reveal a number of immediate consequences. These consequences are, in effect, products of poor decision-making practices because they lead to inadequate solutions to the problems under discussion.

First, the group limits its discussions to a few alternative courses of action (often only two) without an initial survey of all the alternatives that might be worthy of consideration.

Second, the group fails to reexamine the course of action initially preferred by the majority after they learn of risks and drawbacks they had not considered originally.

Third, the members spend little or no time discussing whether there are nonobvious gains they may have overlooked or ways of reducing the seemingly prohibitive costs that made rejected alternatives appear undesirable to them.

Fourth, members make little or no attempt to obtain information from experts within their own organizations who might be able to supply more precise estimates of potential losses and gains.

Fifth, members show positive interest in facts and opinions that support their preferred policy; they tend to ignore facts and opinions that do not.

Sixth, members spend little time deliberating about how the chosen policy might be hindered by bureaucratic inertia, sabotaged by political opponents, or temporarily derailed by common accidents. Consequently, they fail to work out contingency plans to cope with foreseeable setbacks that could endanger the overall success of their chosen course.

SUPPORT

The search for an explanation of why groupthink occurs has led me through a quagmire of complicated theoretical issues in the murky area of human motivation. My belief, based on recent social-psychological research, is that we can best understand the various symptoms of groupthink as a mutual effort among the group members to maintain self-esteem and emotional equanimity by providing social support to each other, especially at times when they share responsibility for making vital decisions.

Even when no important decision is pending, the typical administrator will begin to doubt the wisdom and morality of his past decisions each time he receives information about setbacks, particularly if the information is accompanied by negative feedback from prominent men who originally had been his supporters. It should not be surprising, therefore, to find that individual members strive to develop unanimity and esprit de corps that will help bolster each other's morale, to create an optimistic outlook about the success of pending decisions, and to reaffirm the positive value of past policies to which all of them are committed.

PRIDE

Shared illusions of invulnerability, for example, can reduce anxiety about taking risks. Rationalizations help members believe that the risks are really not so bad after all. The assumption of inherent morality helps the members to avoid feelings of shame or guilt. Negative stereotypes function as stress-reducing devices to enhance a sense of moral righteousness as well as pride in a lofty mission.

The mutual enhancement of self-esteem and morale may have functional value in enabling the members to maintain their capacity to take action, but it has maladaptive consequences insofar as concurrence-seeking tendencies interfere with critical, rational capacities and lead to serious errors of judgment.

While I have limited my study to decision-making bodies in Government, groupthink symptoms appear in business, industry and any other field where small, cohesive groups make the decisions. It is vital, then, for all sorts of people—and especially group leaders—to know what steps they can take to prevent groupthink.

REMEDIES

To counterpoint my case studies of the major fiascos, I have also investigated two highly successful group enterprises, the formulation of the Marshall Plan in the Truman Administration and the handling of the Cuban missile crisis by President Kennedy and his advisers. I have found it instructive to examine the steps Kennedy took to change his group's decision-making processes. These changes ensured that the mistakes made by his Bay of Pigs ingroup were not repeated by the missile-crisis ingroup, even though the membership of both groups was essentially the same.

The following recommendations for preventing groupthink incorporate many of the good practices I discovered to be characteristic of the Marshall Plan and missile-crisis groups:

1. The leader of a policy-forming group should assign the role of critical evaluator to each member, encouraging the group to give high priority to open airing of objections and doubts. This practice needs to be reinforced by the leader's acceptance of criticism of his own judgments in order to discourage members from soft-pedaling their disagreements and from allowing their striving for concurrence to inhibit critical thinking.

2. When the key members of a hierarchy assign a policy-planning mission to any group within their organization, they should adopt an impartial stance instead of stating preferences and expectations at the beginning. This will encourage open inquiry and impartial probing of a wide range of policy alternatives.

3. The organization routinely should set up several outside policy-planning and evaluation groups to work on the same policy question, each deliberating under a different leader. This can prevent the insulation of an ingroup.

4. At intervals before the group reaches a final consensus, the leader should require each member to discuss the group's deliberations with associates in his own unit of the organization—assuming that those associates can be trusted to adhere to the same security regulations that govern the policymakers—and then to report back their reactions to the group.

5. The group should invite one or more outside experts to each meeting on a staggered basis and encourage the experts to challenge the views of the core members.

6. At every general meeting of the group, whenever the agenda calls for an evaluation of policy alternatives, at least one member should play devil's advocate, functioning as a good lawyer in challenging the testimony of those who advocate the majority position.

7. Whenever the policy issue involves relations with a rival nation or organization, the group

should devote a sizable block of time, perhaps an entire session, to a survey of all warning signals from the rivals and should write alternative scenarios on the rivals' intentions.

8. When the group is surveying policy alternatives for feasibility and effectiveness, it should from time to time divide into two or more subgroups to meet separately, under different chairmen, and then come back together to hammer out differences.

9. After reaching a preliminary consensus about what seems to be the best policy, the group should hold a "second-chance" meeting at which every member expresses as vividly as he can all his residual doubts, and rethinks the entire issue before making a definitive choice.

HOW

These recommendations have their disadvantages. To encourage the open airing of objections, for instance, might lead to prolonged and costly debates when a rapidly growing crisis requires immediate solution. It also could cause rejection, depression and anger. A leader's failure to set a norm might create cleavage between leader and members that could develop into a disruptive power struggle if the leader looks on the emerging consensus as anathema. Setting up outside evaluation groups might increase the risk of security leakage. Still, inventive executives who know their way around the organizational maze probably can figure out how to apply one or another of the prescriptions successfully, without harmful side effects.

They also could benefit from the advice of outside experts in the administrative and behavioral sciences. Though these experts have much to offer, they have had few chances to work on policy-making machinery within large organizations. As matters now stand, executives innovate only when they need new procedures to avoid repeating serious errors that have deflated their self-images.

In this era of atomic warheads, urban disorganization and ecocatastrophes, it seems to me that policymakers should collaborate with behavioral scientists and give top priority to preventing groupthink and its attendant fiascos.

ON LEADERS

What is a leader—the controller of history and personal fortune or a pawn of fate, history's slave? Machiavelli and Tolstoy express opposing views on the subject.

HOW FAR HUMAN AFFAIRS ARE GOVERNED BY FORTUNE[1]

I am not unaware that many have held and hold the opinion that events are controlled by fortune and by God in such a way that the prudence of men cannot modify them, indeed, that men have no influence whatsoever. Because of this, they would conclude that there is no point in sweating over things, but that one should submit to the rulings of chance. This opinion has been more widely held in our own times, because of the great changes and variations, beyond human imagining, which we have experienced and experience every day. Sometimes, when thinking of

[1]From The Prince by Niccolò Machiavelli, translated by George Bull (Penguin Classics, 1961), pp. 130–131, 131, 132. Copyright © George Bull, 1961. Reprinted by permission of Penguin Books Ltd.

this, I have myself inclined to this same opinion. Nonetheless, so as not to rule out our free will, I believe that it is probably true that fortune is the arbiter of half the things we do, leaving the other half or so to be controlled by ourselves. I compare fortune to one of those violent rivers which, when they are enraged, flood the plains, tear down trees and buildings, wash soil from one place to deposit it in another. Everyone flees before them, everybody yields to their impetus, there is no possibility of resistance. Yet although such is their nature, it does not follow that when they are flowing quietly one cannot take precautions, constructing dykes and embankments so that when the river is in flood it runs into a canal or else its impetus is less wild and dangerous. So it is with fortune. She shows her power where there is no force to hold her in check; and her impetus is felt where she knows there are no embankments and dykes built to restrain her. . . .

We see that some princes flourish one day and come to grief the next,

without appearing to have changed in character or any other way. This I believe arises, first [because] those princes who are utterly dependent on fortune come to grief when their fortune changes. I also believe that the one who adapts his policy to the times prospers, and likewise that the one whose policy clashes with the demands of the times does not. It can be observed that men use various methods in pursuing their own personal objectives, such as glory and riches. One man proceeds with circumspection, another impetuously; one uses violence, another stratagem; one man goes about things patiently, another does the opposite; and yet everyone, for all this diversity of method, can reach his objective. It can also be observed that with two circumspect men, one will achieve his end, the other not; and likewise two men succeed equally well with different methods, one of them being circumspect and the other impetuous. This results from nothing else except the extent to which their methods are or are not suited to the nature of the times. Thus it happens that, as I have said, two men, working in different ways, can achieve the same end, and of two men working in the same way one gets what he wants and the other does not. This also explains why prosperity is ephemeral; because if a man behaves with patience and circumspection and the time and circumstances are such that this method is called for, he will prosper; but if time and circumstances change he will be ruined because he does not change his policy. Nor do we find any man shrewd enough to know how to adapt his policy in this way; either because he cannot do otherwise than what is in character or because, having always prospered by proceeding one way, he cannot persuade himself to change. Thus a man who is circumspect, when circumstances demand impetuous behaviour, is unequal to the task, and so he comes to grief. If he changed his character according to the time and circumstances, then his fortune would not change.

HISTORY AND GREAT LEADERS[2]
Man lives consciously for himself, but is an unconscious instrument in the

[2]From *War and Peace* by Leo Tolstoy, translated by Ann Dunnigan. Copyright © 1968 by Ann Dunnigan. Reprinted by arrangement with The New American Library, Inc., New York.

attainment of the historic, universal, aims of humanity. A deed done is irrevocable, and its result coinciding in time with the actions of millions of other men assumes an historic significance. The higher a man stands on the social ladder, the more people he is connected with and the more power he has over others, the more evident is the predestination and inevitability of his every action.

"The king's heart is in the hands of the Lord."

A king is history's slave.

History, that is, the unconscious, general, hive life of mankind, uses every moment of the life of kings as a tool for its own purposes.

. . .

Chance, millions of *chances*, give Napoleon power, and all men, as if by agreement, collaborate to confirm that power. *Chance* forms the characters of the rulers of France, who submit to him; *chance* forms the character of Paul I of Russia, who recognizes his power; *chance* puts the Duc d'Enghien in his hands and unexpectedly impels him to assassinate him—thereby convincing the mob by the most cogent of means that he has the right since he has the might. *Chance* contrives that though he bends all his efforts toward an expedition against England (which unquestionably would have ruined

him) he never executes this plan, but fortuitously falls upon Mack and the Austrians, who surrender without a battle. *Chance* and *genius* give him the victory at Austerlitz; and by *chance* all men, not only the French but all Europe, except England, which takes no part in the events about to occur—forget their former horror and detestation of his crimes, and now recognize his authority, the title he had bestowed upon himself, and his ideal of glory and grandeur, which seems splendid and reasonable to them all.

. . .

The invasion courses eastward and reaches its final goal—Moscow. The capital is taken; the Russian army suffers heavier losses than the opposing army suffered at any time during previous wars from Austerlitz to Wagram. But all at once, instead of *chance* and the *genius* that had so consistently led him by an unbroken series of successes to the predestined goal, a succession of counter *chances* occur—from the cold in his head at Borodino to the frosts, and the spark that set fire to Moscow—and instead of *genius*, stupidity and unprecedented baseness are displayed.

The invaders flee, turn back, flee again, and now the *chances* are not for Napoleon but consistently against him.

THE THIRD WAVE

RON JONES

It has often been noted that a group can transcend its individual members and become an entity that may act in ways contrary to the normal individual behavior of those members. This effect may result from the establishment of new norms (combined with the group's power to enforce conformity to them), from diffusion of responsibility, and from feelings of anonymity. "The Third Wave" is a vivid account of a group movement that took on a life of its own, far exceeding the intentions of its creator. A week-long experiment designed to enhance the students' understanding of Nazi Germany quickly became far too real, sucking in almost everyone who came in contact with it. Although Jones has not written a social psychological analysis, his article illustrates a number of group processes at work and shows how they can be simultaneously attractive and destructive.

For years I kept a strange secret. I shared this silence with two hundred students. Yesterday I ran into one of those students. For a brief moment it all rushed back.

Steve Coniglo had been a sophomore student in my world history class. We ran into each other quite by accident. It's one of those occasions experienced by teachers when they least expect. You're walking down the street, eating at a secluded restaurant, or buying some underwear, when all of a sudden an ex-student pops up to say hello. In this case it was Steve running down the street shouting, "Mr. Jones, Mr. Jones." In an embarrassed hug we greet. I had to stop for a minute to remember. Who is this young man hugging me? He calls me Mr. Jones. Must be a former student. What's his name? In the split second of my race back in time Steve sensed my questioning and backed up. Then he smiled and slowly raised a hand in a cupped position. My God. He's a member of the *Third Wave*. It's Steve, Steve Coniglo. He sat in the second row. He was a sensitive and bright student. Played guitar and enjoyed drama.

We just stood there exchanging smiles when, without a conscious command, I raised my hand in curved position. The salute was given. Two comrades had met long after the war. The *Third Wave* was still alive. "Mr. Jones, do you remember the Third Wave?" I sure do; it was one of the most frightening events I ever experienced in the classroom. It was also the genesis of a secret that I and two hundred students would sadly share for the rest of our lives.

We talked and laughed about the Third Wave for the next few hours. Then it was time to part. It's strange: you meet a past student in these chance ways. You catch a few moments of your life, hold them tight, then say good-bye, not knowing when and if you'd ever see each other again. Oh, you make promises to call each other, but it won't happen. Steve will continue to grow and change. I will remain an ageless benchmark in his life, a presence that will not change. I am Mr. Jones. Steve turns and gives a quiet salute, hand raised upward in the shape of a curling wave. Hand curved in a similar fashion, I return the gesture.

The Third Wave. Well at last it can be talked about. Here I've met a student, and we've talked

for hours about this nightmare. The secret must finally be waning. It's taken three years. I can tell you and anyone else about the Third Wave. It's now just a dream, something to remember. No, it's something we tried to forget. That's how it all started. By strange coincidence I think it was Steve who started the Third Wave with a question.

We were studying Nazi Germany, and in the middle of a lecture I was interrupted by the question. How could the German populace claim ignorance of the slaughter of the Jewish people? How could the townspeople, railroad conductors, teachers, doctors, claim they knew nothing about concentration camps and human carnage? How can people who were neighbors and maybe even friends of the Jewish citizen say they weren't there when it happened? It was a good question. I didn't know the answer.

In as much as there were several months still to go in the school year and I was already at World War II, I decided to take a week and explore the question.

STRENGTH THROUGH DISCIPLINE

On Monday, I introduced my sophomore history students to one of the experiences that characterized Nazi Germany: discipline. I lectured about the beauty of discipline. How an athlete feels having worked hard and regularly to be successful at a sport. How a ballet dancer or painter works hard to perfect a movement. The dedicated patience of a scientist in pursuit of an idea. It's discipline, that self-training, control, the power of the will, the exchange of physical hardships for superior mental and physical facilities, the ultimate triumph.

To experience the power of discipline, I invited—no, I commanded—the class to exercise and use a new seating posture. I described how proper sitting posture assists concentration and strengthens the will. In fact I instructed the class in a mandatory sitting posture. This posture started with feet flat on the floor, hands placed flat across the small of the back to force a straight alignment of the spine. "There, can't you breathe more easily? You're more alert. Don't you feel better?"

We practiced this new attention position over and over. I walked up and down the aisles of seated students pointing out small flaws, making improvements. Proper seating became the most important aspect of learning. I would dismiss the

---

From *No Substitute for Madness* by Ron Jones, San Francisco, Calif.: Zephyros. Copyright 1977 by Ron Jones and T.A.T. Communications Company. Reprinted with permission.

class, allowing them to leave their desks, and then call them abruptly back to an attention sitting position. In speed drills the class learned to move from standing position to attention sitting in fifteen seconds. In focus drills I concentrated attention on the feet being parallel and flat, ankles locked, knees bent at ninety-degree angles, hands flat and crossed against the back, spine straight, chin down, head forward. We did noise drills in which talking was allowed only to be shown as a distraction. Following minutes of progressive drill assignments the class could move from standing positions outside the room to attention sitting positions at their desks without making a sound. The maneuver took five seconds.

It was strange how quickly the students took to this uniform code of behavior. I began to wonder just how far they could be pushed. Was this display of obedience a momentary game we were all playing, or was it something else? Was the desire for discipline and uniformity a natural need, a societal instinct we hide within our franchise restaurants and TV programming?

I decided to push the tolerance of the class for regimented action. In the final twenty-five minutes of the class I introduced some new rules. Students must be sitting in class at the attention position before the late bell; all students must carry pencils and paper for note-taking; when asking or answering questions students must stand at the side of their desk; the first words given in answering or asking a question are "Mr. Jones." We practiced short "silent reading" sessions. Students who responded in a sluggish manner were reprimanded and in every case made to repeat their behavior until it was a model of punctuality and respect. The intensity of the response became more important than the content. To accentuate this, I requested answers to be given in three words or less. Students were rewarded for making an effort at answering or asking questions. They were also acknowledged for doing this in a crisp and attentive manner. Soon everyone in the class began popping up with answers and questions. The involvement level in the class moved from the few who always dominated discussions to the entire class. Even stranger was the gradual improvement in the quality of answers. Everyone seemed to be listening more intently. New people were speaking. Answers started to stretch out as students usually hesitant to speak found support for their effort.

As for my part in this exercise, I had nothing but questions. Why hadn't I thought of this technique before? Students seemed intent on the assignment and displayed accurate recitation of facts and concepts. They even seemed to be asking better questions and treating each other with more compassion. How could this be? Here I was enacting an authoritarian learning environment, and it seemed very productive. I now began to ponder not just how far this class could be pushed but how much I would change my basic beliefs toward an open classroom and self-directed learning. Was all my belief in Carl Rogers to shrivel and die? Where was this experiment leading?

STRENGTH THROUGH COMMUNITY

On Tuesday, the second day of the exercise, I entered the classroom to find everyone sitting in silence at the attention position. Some of their faces were relaxed with smiles that come from pleasing the teacher. But most of the students looked straight ahead in earnest concentration, neck muscles rigid, no sign of a smile or a thought or even a question, every fiber strained to perform the deed. To release the tension I went to the chalkboard and wrote in big letters, "STRENGTH THROUGH DISCIPLINE." Below this I wrote a second law, "STRENGTH THROUGH COMMUNITY."

While the class sat in stern silence, I began to talk, lecture, sermonize about the value of community. At this stage of the game I was debating in my own mind whether to stop the experiment or continue. I hadn't planned such intensity or compliance. In fact I was surprised to find the ideas on discipline enacted at all. While debating whether to stop or go on with the experiment, I talked on and on about community. I made up stories from my experiences as an athlete, coach, and historian. It was easy. Community is that bond between individuals who work and struggle together. It's raising a barn with your neighbors; it's feeling that you are a part of something beyond yourself, a movement, a team, *La Raza*, a cause.

It was too late to step back. I now can appreciate why the astronomer turns relentlessly to the telescope. I was probing deeper and deeper into my own perceptions and the motivations for group and individual action. There was much more to see and try to understand. Many questions haunted me. Why did the students accept the authority I was imposing? Where is their curiosity or resistance to this martial behavior? When and how will this end?

Following my description of community I once

again told the class that community, like discipline, must be experienced if it is to be understood. To provide an encounter with community I had the class recite in unison, "Strength through Discipline. Strength through Community." First I would have two students stand and call back our motto, then add two more, until finally the whole class was standing and reciting. It was fun. The students began to look at each other and sense the power of belonging. Everyone was capable and equal. They were doing something together. We worked on this simple act for the entire class period. We would repeat the mottos in a rotating chorus or say them with various degrees of loudness. Always we said them together, emphasizing the proper way to sit, stand, and talk.

I began to think of myself as a part of the experiment. I enjoyed the unified action demonstrated by the students. It was rewarding to see their satisfaction and excitement to do more. I found it harder and harder to extract myself from the momentum and identity that the class was developing. I was following the group dictate as much as I was directing it.

As the class period was ending, and without forethought, I created a class salute. It was for class members only. To make the salute you brought your right hand up toward the right shoulder in a curled position. I called it the Third Wave salute because the hand resembled a wave about to top over. The idea for the three came from beach lore that waves travel in chains, the third wave being the last and largest of each series. Because we had a salute, I made it a rule to salute all class members outside the classroom. When the bell sounded, ending the period, I asked the class for complete silence. With everyone sitting at attention, I slowly raised my arm and with a cupped hand I saluted. It was a silent signal of recognition. They were something special. Without command the entire group of students returned the salute.

Throughout the next few days students in the class would exchange this greeting. You would be walking down the hall when all of a sudden three classmates would turn your way, each flashing a quick salute. In the library or in gym students would be seen giving this strange hand jive. You would hear a crash of cafeteria food only to have it followed by two classmates saluting each other. The mystique of thirty individuals doing this strange gyration soon brought more attention to the class and its experiment into the German personality. Many students outside the class asked if they could join.

STRENGTH THROUGH ACTION

On Wednesday, I decided to issue membership cards to every student that wanted to continue what I now called the experiment. Not a single student elected to leave the room. In this the third day of activity there were forty-three students in the class. Thirteen students had cut other classes to be a part of the experiment. While the class sat at attention, I gave each person a card. I marked three of the cards with a red x and informed the recipients that they had a special assignment to report any students not complying with class rules. I then proceeded to talk about the meaning of action. I explained how discipline and community were meaningless without action. I discussed the beauty of taking full responsibility for one's action, of believing so thoroughly in yourself and your community or family that you will do anything to preserve, protect, and extend that being. I stressed how hard work and allegiance to each other would allow accelerated learning and accomplishment. I reminded students of what it felt like being in classes where competition caused pain and degradation, of situations in which students were pitted against each other in everything from gym to reading, of the feeling of never acting, never being a part of something, never supporting each other.

At this point students stood without prompting and began to give what amounted to testimonials. "Mr. Jones, for the first time I'm learning lots of things." "Mr. Jones, why don't you teach like this all the time." I was shocked! Yes, I had been pushing information at them in an extremely controlled setting, but the fact that they found it comfortable and acceptable was startling. It was equally disconcerting to realize that complex and time-consuming written homework assignments on German life were being completed and even enlarged on by students. Performance in academic skill areas was significantly improving. They were learning more. And they seemed to want more. I began to think that the students might do anything I assigned. I decided to find out.

To allow students the experience of direct action I gave each individual a specific verbal assignment. "It's your task to design a Third Wave banner." "You are responsible for stopping any student that is not a Third Wave member from entering this room." "I want you to remember and be able to recite by tomorrow the name and address of every Third Wave member." "You are assigned the problem of training and convincing at least twenty children in the adjacent elementary school that our sitting posture is necessary for better learning." "It's your job to read this pamphlet and report its entire content to the class before the period ends." "I want each of you to give me the name and address of one reliable friend that you think might want to join the Third Wave. . . ."

To conclude the session on direct action I instructed students in a simple procedure for initiating new members. It went like this: A new member had only to be recommended by an existing member and issued a card by me. Upon receiving this card the new member had to demonstrate knowledge of our rules and pledge obedience to them. My announcement unleashed a fervor of effort.

The school was alive with conjecture and curiosity. It affected everyone. The school cook asked what a Third Wave cookie looked like. I said chocolate chip, of course. Our principal came into an afternoon faculty meeting and gave me the Third Wave salute. I saluted back. The librarian thanked me for the thirty-foot banner on learning that she placed above the library entrance. By the end of the day over two hundred students were admitted into the order. I felt very alone and a little scared.

Most of my fear emanated from the incidence of tattling. Although I formally appointed only three students to report deviate behavior, approximately twenty students came to me with reports about how Allan didn't salute or Georgene was talking critically about our experiment. This incidence of monitoring meant that half the class now considered it their duty to observe and report on members of their class. Within this avalanche of reporting one legitimate conspiracy did seem under way.

Three women in the class had told their parents all about our classroom activities. These three young women were by far the most intelligent students in the class. As friends they chummed together. They possessed a silent confidence and took pleasure in a school setting that gave them academic and leadership opportunity. During the days of the experiment I was curious how they would respond to the equalitarian and physical reshaping of the class. The rewards they were accustomed to winning just didn't exist in the experiment. The intellectual skills of questioning and reasoning were nonexistent. In the martial atmosphere of the class they seemed stunned and pensive. Now that I look back, they appeared much like the child with so-called learning disability. They watched the activities and participated in

a mechanical fashion. Whereas others jumped in, they held back, watching.

In telling their parents of the experiment they set up a brief chain of events. The rabbi for one of the parents called me at home. He was polite and condescending. I told him we were merely studying the German personality. He seemed delighted and told me not to worry, he would talk to the parents and calm their concern. In concluding this conversation I envisioned similar conversations throughout history in which the clergy accepted and apologized for untenable conditions. If only he had raged in anger or simply investigated the situation, I could point the students to an example of righteous rebellion. But no. The rabbi became a part of the experiment. In remaining ignorant of the oppression in the experiment he became an accomplice and advocate.

By the end of the third day I was exhausted. I was tearing myself apart. The balance between role playing and directed behavior became indistinguishable. Many of the students were completely into being Third Wave members. They demanded strict obedience of the rules from other students and bullied those that took the experiment lightly. Others simply sunk into the activity and took self-assigned roles. I particularly remember Robert. Robert was big for his age and displayed very few academic skills. Oh, he tried harder than anyone I know to be successful. He handed in elaborate weekly reports copied word for word from the reference books in the library. Robert is like so many kids in school that don't excel or cause trouble. They aren't bright, can't make the athletic teams, and don't strike out for attention. They are lost, invisible. The only reason I came to know Robert at all is that I found him eating lunch in my classroom. He always ate lunch alone.

Well, the Third Wave gave Robert a place in school. At last he was equal to everyone. He could do something, take part, be meaningful. That's just what Robert did. Late Wednesday afternoon I found Robert following me and asked what in the world was he doing. He smiled (I don't think I had ever seen him smile) and announced, "Mr. Jones, I'm your bodyguard. I'm afraid something will happen to you. Can I do it, Mr. Jones, please?" Given that assurance and smile I couldn't say no. I had a bodyguard. All day long he opened and closed doors for me. He walked always on my right, just smiling and saluting other class members. He followed me everywhere. In the faculty room (closed to students) he stood at silent attention while I gulped some coffee. When accosted by an English teacher for being a student in the "teachers' room," he just smiled and informed the faculty member that he wasn't a student, he was a bodyguard.

STRENGTH THROUGH PRIDE

On Thursday I began to draw the experiment to a conclusion. I was exhausted and worried. Many students were over the line. The Third Wave had become the center of their existence. I was in pretty bad shape myself. I was now acting instinctively as a dictator. Oh, I was benevolent. And I daily argued with myself on the benefits of the learning experience. By this, the fourth day of the experiment, I was beginning to lose my own arguments. As I spent more time playing the role, I had less time to remember its rational origins and purpose. I found myself sliding into the role even when it wasn't necessary. I wondered if this doesn't happen to lots of people. We get or take an ascribed role and then bend our life to fit the image. Soon the image is the only identity people will accept. So we become the image. The trouble with the situation and role I had created was that I didn't have time to think where it was leading. Events were crushing around me. I worried for students doing things they would regret. I worried for myself.

Once again I faced the thoughts of closing the experiment or letting it go its own course. Both options were unworkable. If I stopped the experiment, a great number of students would be left hanging. They had committed themselves in front of their peers to radical behavior. Emotionally and psychologically they had exposed themselves. If I suddenly jolted them back to classroom reality, I would face a confused student body for the remainder of the year. It would be too painful and demeaning for Robert and the students like him to be twisted back into a seat and told it's just a game. They would take the ridicule from the brighter students that participated in a measured and cautious way. I couldn't let the Roberts lose again.

The other option of just letting the experiment run its course was also out of the question. Things were already getting out of control. Wednesday evening someone had broken into the room and ransacked the place. I later found out it was the father of one of the students. He was a retired air force colonel who had spent time in a German prisoner of war camp. Upon hearing of our activity he simply lost control. Late in the evening he broke into the room and tore it apart. I found

him that morning propped up against the classroom door. He told me about his friends that had been killed in Germany. He was holding onto me and shaking. In staccato words he pleaded that I understand and help him get home. I called his wife and with the help of a neighbor walked him home. We spent hours later talking about what he felt and did, but from that moment on Thursday morning I was more concerned with what might be happening at school.

I was increasingly worried about how our activity was affecting the faculty and other students in the school. The Third Wave was disrupting normal learning. Students were cutting class to participate, and the school counselors were beginning to question every student in the class. The real gestapo in the school was at work. Faced with this experiment exploding in one hundred directions, I decided to try an old basketball strategy. When you're playing against all the odds, the best action to take is to try the unexpected. That's what I did.

By Thursday the class had swollen in size to over eighty students. The only thing that allowed them all to fit was the enforced discipline of sitting in silence at attention. A strange calm is in effect when a room full of people sit in quiet observation and anticipation. It helped me approach them in a deliberate way. I talked about pride. "Pride is more than banners or salutes. Pride is something no one can take from you. Pride is knowing you are the best. . . . It can't be destroyed. . . ."

In the midst of this crescendo I abruptly changed and lowered my voice to announce the real reason for the Third Wave. In slow, methodic tone I explained what was behind the Third Wave. "The Third Wave isn't just an experiment or classroom activity. It's far more important than that. The Third Wave is a nationwide program to find students who are willing to fight for political change in this country. That's right. This activity we have been doing has been practice for the real thing. Across the country teachers like myself have been recruiting and training a youth brigade capable of showing the nation a better society through discipline, community, pride, and action. If we can change the way that school is run, we can change the way that factories, stores, universities and all the other institutions are run. You are a selected group of young people chosen to help in this cause. If you will stand up and display what you have learned in the past four days . . . , we can change the destiny of this nation. We can bring it a new sense of order, community, pride, and action, a new purpose.

Everything rests with you and your willingness to take a stand."

To give validity to the seriousness of my words I turned to the three women in the class who I knew had questioned the Third Wave. I demanded that they leave the room. I explained why I acted and then assigned four guards to escort the women to the library and to keep them from entering the class on Friday. Then in dramatic style I informed the class of a special noon rally to take place on Friday. This would be a rally for Third Wave members only.

It was a wild gamble. I just kept talking, afraid that if I stopped, someone would laugh or ask a question and the grand scheme would dissolve in chaos. I explained how at noon on Friday a national candidate for president would announce the formation of a Third Wave Youth Program. Simultaneous to this announcement over 1,000 youth groups from every part of the country would stand up and display their support for such a movement. I confided that they were the students selected to represent their area. I also questioned if they could make a good showing, because the press had been invited to record the event. No one laughed. There was not a murmur of resistance. Quite the contrary. A fever pitch of excitement swelled across the room. "We can do it!" "Should we wear white shirts?" "Can we bring friends?" "Mr. Jones, have you seen this advertisement in *Time* magazine?"

The clincher came quite by accident. It was a full-page color advertisement in the current issue of *Time* for some lumber products. The advertiser identified his product as the Third Wave. The advertisement proclaimed in big red, white, and blue letters, "The Third Wave is coming." "Is this part of the campaign, Mr. Jones?" "Is it a code or something?"

"Yes. Now listen carefully. It's all set for tomorrow. Be in the small auditorium ten minutes before twelve. Be seated. Be ready to display the discipline, community, and pride you have learned. Don't talk to anyone about this. This rally is for members only."

STRENGTH THROUGH UNDERSTANDING

On Friday, the final day of the exercise, I spent the early morning preparing the auditorium for the rally. At eleven-thirty students began to ant their way into the room; at first a few scouting the way and then more. Row after row began to fill. A hushed silence shrouded the room. Third Wave banners hung like clouds over the assembly.

At twelve o'clock sharp I closed the room and placed guards at each door. Several friends of mine posing as reporters and photographers began to interact with the crowd, taking pictures and jotting frantic descriptive notes. A group photograph was taken. Over two hundred students were crammed into the room. Not a vacant seat could be found. The group seemed to be composed of students from many persuasions. There were the athletes, the socially prominents, the student leaders, the loners, the group of kids that always left school early, the bikers, the pseudo hip, a few representatives of the school's Dadaist clique, and some of the students that hung out at the laundromat. The entire collection, however, looked like one force as they sat in perfect attention. Every person focusing on the TV set I had in the front of the room. No one moved. The room was empty of sound. It was as if we were all witness to a birth. The tension and anticipation were beyond belief.

"Before turning on the national press conference, which begins in five minutes, I want to demonstrate to the press the extent of our training." With that, I gave the salute. It was followed automatically by two hundred arms stabbing a reply. I then said the words "Strength through Discipline." It was followed by a repetitive chorus. We did this again and again. Each time the response was louder. The photographers were circling the ritual, snapping pictures, but by now they were ignored. I reiterated the importance of this event and asked once more for a show of allegiance. It was the last time I would ask anyone to recite. The room rocked with a guttural cry: "Strength through Discipline."

It was 12:05. I turned off the lights in the room and walked quickly to the television set. The air in the room seemed to be drying up. It felt hard to breathe and even harder to talk. It was as if the climax of shouting souls had pushed everything out of the room. I switched the television set on. I was now standing next to the television, directly facing the room full of people. The machine came to life, producing a luminous field of phosphorous light. Robert was at my side. I whispered to him to watch closely and pay attention for the next few minutes. The only light in the room was coming from the television, and it played against the faces in the room. Eyes strained and pulled at the light, but the pattern didn't change. The room stayed deathly still, waiting. There was a mental tug of war between the people in the room and the television. The television won. The white glow of the test pattern didn't snap into the vision of a political candidate. It just whined on. Still the viewers persisted. There must be a program. It must be coming on. Where is it? The trance with the television continued for what seemed like hours. It was 12:07. Nothing. A blank field of white. It's not going to happen. Anticipation turned to anxiety and then frustration. Someone stood up and shouted.

"There isn't any leader, is there?" Everyone turned in shock, first to the despondent student and then back to the television. Their faces held looks of disbelief.

In the confusion of the moment I moved slowly toward the television. I turned it off. I felt air rush back into the room. The room remained in fixed silence, but for the first time I could sense people breathing. Students were withdrawing their arms from behind their chairs. I expected a flood of questions but instead got intense quietness. I began to talk. Every word seemed to be taken and absorbed.

"Listen closely. I have something important to tell you. Sit down. There is no leader! There is no such thing as a national youth movement called the Third Wave. You have been used, manipulated, shoved by your own desires into the place you now find yourself. You are no better or worse than the German Nazi we have been studying.

"You thought that you were the elect, that you were better than those outside this room. You bargained your freedom for the comfort of discipline and superiority. You chose to accept the group's will and the big lie over your own conviction. Oh, you think to youself that you were just going along for the fun, that you could extricate yourself at any moment. But where were you heading? How far would you have gone? Let me show you your future."

With that I switched on a rear screen projector. It quickly illuminated a white drop cloth hanging behind the television. Large numbers appeared in a countdown. The roar of a Nuremberg rally blasted into vision. My heart was pounding. In ghostly images the history of the Third Reich paraded into the room: the discipline; the march of super race; the big lie; arrogance, violence, terror; people being pushed into vans; the visual stench of death camps; faces without eyes; the trials; the plea of ignorance. I was only doing my job, my job. As abruptly as it started, the film froze to a halt on a single written frame: "Everyone must accept the blame. No one can claim that they didn't in some way take part."

The room stayed dark as the final footage of film flapped against the projector. I felt sick to my stomach. The room sweated and smelled like a locker room. No one moved. It was as if everyone wanted to dissect the moment, figure out what had happened. As though awakening from a dream and deep sleep, the entire room of people took one last look back into their consciousness. I waited for several minutes to let everyone catch up. Finally questions began to emerge. All the questions probed at imaginary situations and sought to discover the meaning of this event.

In the still-darkened room I began the explanation. I confessed my feeling of sickness and remorse. I told the assembly that a full explanation would take quite a while. But it was important to start. I sensed myself moving from an introspective participant in the event toward the role of teacher. It's easier being a teacher. In objective terms I began to describe the past events.

"Through the experience of the past week we have all tasted what it was like to live and act in Nazi Germany. We learned what it felt like to create a disciplined social environment, to build a special society, to pledge allegiance to that society, to replace reason with rules. Yes, we would all have made good Germans. We would have put on the uniform, turned our head as friends and neighbors were cursed and then persecuted, pulled the locks shut, worked in the 'defense' plants, burned ideas. Yes, we know in a small way what it feels like to find a hero, to grab quick solutions, to feel strong and in control of destiny. We know the fear of being left out, the pleasure of doing something right and being rewarded, of being number one, of being right. Taken to an extreme we have seen and perhaps felt what these actions will lead to. We each have witnessed something over the past week. We have seen that fascism is not just something those other people did. No, it's right here, in this room, in our own personal habits and way of life. Scratch the surface, and it appears. It is something in all of us. We carry it like a disease. It is the belief that human beings are basically evil and therefore unable to act well toward each other, a belief that demands a strong leader and discipline to preserve social order. And there is something else—the act of apology.

"This is the final lesson to be experienced. This last lesson is perhaps the one of greatest importance. This lesson was the question that started our plunge in studying Nazi life. Do you remember the question? It concerned a bewilderment at the German populace claiming ignorance and noninvolvement in the Nazi movement. If I remember the question, it went something like this: 'How could the German soldier, teacher, railroad conductor, nurse, tax collector, the average citizen, claim at the end of the Third Reich that they knew nothing of what was going on? How can a people be a part of something and then claim at the demise that they were not really involved? What causes people to blank out their own history?' In the next few minutes and perhaps years you will have an opportunity to answer this question.

"If our enactment of the Fascist mentality is complete, not one of you will ever admit to being at this final Third Wave rally. Like the Germans, you will have trouble admitting to yourself that you came this far. You will not allow your friends and parents to know that you were willing to give up individual freedom and power for the dictates of order and unseen leaders. You can't admit to being manipulated, to being a follower, to accepting the Third Wave as a way of life. You won't admit to participating in this madness. You will keep this day and this rally a secret. It's a secret I shall share with you."

I took the film from the cameras of the three photographers in the room and pulled the celluloid into the exposing light. The deed was concluded. The trial was over. The Third Wave had ended.

I glanced over my shoulder. Robert was crying. Students slowly rose from their chairs and without words filed into the outdoor light. I walked over to Robert and threw my arms around him. Robert was sobbing, taking in large, uncontrollable gulps of air. "It's over." "It's all right." In our consoling each other we became a rock in the stream of exiting students. Some swirled back to momentarily hold Robert and me. Others cried openly and then brushed away tears to carry on. Human beings circling and holding each other, moving toward the door and the world outside.

For a week in the middle of a school year we had shared fully in life. And as predicted we also shared a deep secret. In the four years I taught at Cubberley High School no one ever admitted to attending the Third Wave rally. Oh, we talked and studied our actions intently. But the rally itself. No. It was something we all wanted to forget.

PROJECTS

Name _____

Date _____

9.1: MAKING DECISIONS

The goal of this project is to compare the ways in which an individual and a group make decisions. You will be the individual decision maker; you will also be a part of the group, which will be made up of several people in your class. Your instructor will assign people to these small groups.

The decisions concern three different personal dilemmas, which are described on the following pages. The central character in each situation is faced with two possible courses of action. One alternative is more desirable than the other, but it always involves greater risk.

1. Read each situation and determine the *lowest* probability that you consider acceptable for the central character to pursue the more desirable alternative. For example, if you think the alternative should be attempted only if it is sure to work, check the answer "the chances are 10 in 10 that the alternative will succeed." However, if you think the alternative should be tried when the odds are even, check the answer "the chances are 5 in 10." Read each situation, and indicate your own decision.

> Mr. C., a competent chess player, is participating in a national chess tournament. In an early match he draws the top-favored player in the tournament as his opponent. Mr. C. has been given a relatively low ranking in view of his performance in previous tournaments. During the course of his play with the top-favored man, Mr. C. notes the possibility of a deceptive though risky maneuver which might bring him a quick victory. At the same time, if the attempted maneuver should fail, Mr. C. would be left in an exposed position and defeat would almost certainly follow.
>
> Imagine that you are advising Mr. C. Listed are several probabilities or odds that Mr. C's deceptive play would succeed. *Please check the lowest probability that you would consider acceptable for the risky play in question to be attempted.*

_____ The chances are 0 in 10 that the play would succeed (i.e., the play is certain to fail).

_____ The chances are 1 in 10.

_____ The chances are 2 in 10.

_____ The chances are 3 in 10.

_____ The chances are 4 in 10.

_____ The chances are 5 in 10.

_____ The chances are 6 in 10.

_____ The chances are 7 in 10.

_____ The chances are 8 in 10.

_____ The chances are 9 in 10.

_____ The chances are 10 in 10 that the play would succeed (i.e., the play is certain to succeed).

> Ms. G. is currently a college senior who is very eager to pursue graduate study in chemistry leading to the Doctor of Philosophy degree. She has been accepted by both University X and University Y. University X has a world-wide reputation

for excellence in chemistry. While a degree from University X would signify outstanding training in the field, the standards are so rigorous that only a fraction of the degree candidates actually receive the degree. University Y, on the other hand, has a much less prestigious reputation in chemistry, but almost everyone admitted is awarded the Doctor of Philosophy degree, so the degree carries much less esteem than the corresponding degree from University X.

Imagine that you are advising Ms. G. Listed are several probabilities or odds that Ms. G. would be awarded a degree at University X, the one with the greater prestige. *Please check the lowest probability that you would consider acceptable to make it worthwhile for Ms. G. to enroll in University X rather than University Y.*

____The chances are 0 in 10 that Ms. G. would receive a degree from University X.

____The chances are 1 in 10.

____The chances are 2 in 10.

____The chances are 3 in 10.

____The chances are 4 in 10.

____The chances are 5 in 10.

____The chances are 6 in 10.

____The chances are 7 in 10.

____The chances are 8 in 10.

____The chances are 9 in 10.

____The chances are 10 in 10.

Mr. I. is the captain of College X's football team. College X is playing its traditional rival, College Y, in the last game of the season. The game is in its final seconds and Mr. I.'s team, College X, is behind by three points. College X has time to run one more play. Mr. I., the captain, must decide whether it would be best to settle for a tie score with a play which would be almost certain to work or whether he should try a more complicated and risky play which would bring victory if it succeeded, but defeat if it failed.

Imagine that you are advising Mr. I. Listed are several probabilities or odds that the risky play will work. *Please check the lowest probability that you would consider for the play to be attempted.*

____The chances are 0 in 10 that the risky play will work.

____The chances are 1 in 10.

____The chances are 2 in 10.

____The chances are 3 in 10.

____The chances are 4 in 10.

____The chances are 5 in 10.

____The chances are 6 in 10.

____The chances are 7 in 10.

____The chances are 8 in 10.

____The chances are 9 in 10.

____The chances are 10 in 10.

2. After participating in the group discussion and decision making, list the group's decisions. Then list your individual decisions.

	Group	**Individual**	**Riskier decision**
Situation 1			
Situation 2			
Situation 3			

3. In the third column of question 2, indicate whose decision was riskier for each situation (i.e., had the lower probability): group, individual, or no difference. Is there any pattern to these results? For example, was one set of decisions riskier than the other? Compare your own results with those of the other people in class. Do these overall findings suggest a group-individual difference in riskiness?

4. If there is an apparent difference between group and individual decisions, how do you explain it? What sorts of things happened during the group discussion that might have led you to support a decision different from the one you made on your own?

Name _____

Date _____

9.2: THE CLASS PIE

The goal of this exercise is for you to see your class as a small group and to analyze its structure.

Imagine that the circle below is a pie chart representing the members of your discussion group, and divide the pie into slices (one per person). The size of each slice should indicate the amount of each person't contribution to the class. Be sure to include a slice for yourself and for your instructor, and identify each slice by the person's name or initials.

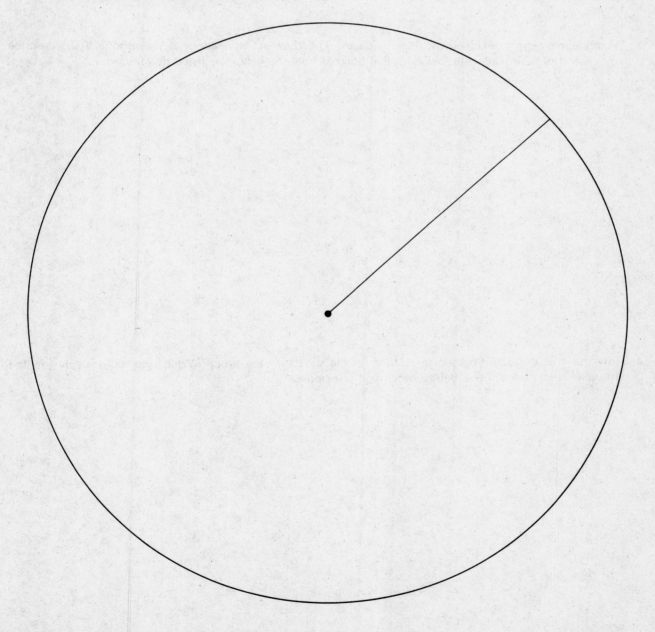

1. What criteria did you use to determine the amount of each person's contribution to the class (e.g., amount of talking, quality of comments, number of interesting questions, influence on others)?

2. Describe the way in which you divided the pie. That is, did you give everyone an equal slice, or did you give some people much larger slices than you gave to others?

3. Which three people received the biggest slices? Did they act as leaders of the group? If so, describe any aspects of their leadership behavior that differed from the behaviors listed in question 1.

4. How did you evaluate yourself in relation to the others in the group? What role did you play in the group? That is, how did you behave in class discussions?

10

THE HUMAN ENVIRONMENT

People have long been aware that their environment has an effect on their feelings and behavior. For example, it is commonly believed that the weather can influence one's moods. We have all heard or made remarks such as "Rainy days get me down" or "I feel happy when the sun is shining." Spring fever and spring madness on college campuses and elsewhere often begin with the first warm days following a cold and dreary winter. Hot temperatures are thought to exacerbate interpersonal aggression, and moonlight has often been linked to mental problems (see the boxed excerpt "The Moon and the Mind"). Work, home, and play environments are also viewed as instrumental to psychological well-being. How many times have you heard someone say, "I hate to work in an inner office without windows" or "Those endless walls of institutional green get me depressed" or "I always feel cheery in a room full of plants"?

In recent years, these presumed connections between the physical environment and personal experience have been subjected to careful study by psychologists and other social scientists. Environmental psychology is now a recognized discipline, with its own division in the American Psychological Association. The exciting new research being done in this area has important implications for shaping and improving the settings in which we live.

THE MOON AND THE MIND

The belief in the effects of the moon on the human mind dates from ancient times and has survived rather obstinately. The following little experience will serve both as a sample and as evidence of how alive this belief is today, in our midst.

Our little party was standing on the terrace of the suburban home, admiring the yellow disk of the moon which was shining bright and full from a cloudless summer night sky. Suddenly our young hostess exclaimed, "Oh dear, I forgot to pull the shades in Tommy's room!" and, explaining, she added, "The poor child has his bed right near the window; the moon must be shining right on his face." Later, when she returned, someone made a skeptical remark as to the alleged harmful effect of the moon on the sleeper, but our hostess stood firm in her conviction, and two or three of the guests, both men and women, spoke up in her defense. "No, it is quite true," said a middle-aged businessman from a midwestern city, "to have the moon shine on your face when you sleep, is bad; particularly for children. It gives them bad dreams and nightmares, and I have heard that some people with a delicate nervous system even become insane."

. . . From the oldest times 'lunacy' (from the Latin luna = moon) was closely associated with the moon, both in etiology and clinical manifestations. The origins of this belief, so widespread and persistent, lose themselves far back in ancient history. Both the Old and the New Testament mention the moon in connection with mental derangement. Later this relation became a commonplace. Plutarch, in the first century, said, "Everybody knows that those who sleep outside under the influence of the moon are not easily awakened, but seem stupid and senseless." Pliny the Elder asserted that the "moon produces drowsiness and stupor in those who sleep under her beams." And even before their time Hippocrates had written, "As often as one is seized with terror and fright and madness during the night, he is said to be suffering from the visitation of Hecate [moon goddess]."

Novelists and poets have also made frequent mention of this belief. Charles Dickens created the term 'a mooner,' signifying "one who wan-

From J. F. Oliven, "Moonlight and Nervous Disorders: A Historical Study," *American Journal of Psychiatry, 99,* 579–584, 1943. Copyright 1943, the American Psychiatric Association. Reprinted by permission.

ders or gazes idly or moodily about as if moonstruck.''. . . Byron, too, used the word 'moon-struck,' T. Adams, English writer of the 17th century, mentions ''a moonsick head,'' and Ben Jonson 'the moonling.' Shelley spoke of 'moon-madness.' Richard Brome, in *Queen and*

Concubine, blamed a 'moon-flaw' for an exalted condition of one of his heroes. . . .

There actually seems to be no country or culture where the belief in the moon's effect upon the human mind has not prevailed at some time or other, and frequently still does. ''It

is dangerous to sleep in the moonlight,'' say the French peasants. Or, ''It is not well to gaze fixedly at the moon,'' goes a saying among the Bedouins, or the German country people think that ''When the moon shines into the window, the maid breaks many pots.''

THE EXPERIENCE OF LIVING IN CITIES: A PSYCHOLOGICAL ANALYSIS

STANLEY MILGRAM

The condition of America's cities is currently the topic of much controversy. The rising costs of municipal services, the increased crime rate, the deterioration in the quality of public education, and the problems of overcrowding and pollution are only some of the difficulties that must be dealt with. New York City's financial crisis is an extreme example of these urban woes, but many other cities are approaching crisis points. City life offers many advantages, such as greater access to the arts, education, and entertainment. But for many people, these advantages are offset by the grave problems that are also part of city life, and they have been relocating to the suburbs and rural areas in increasing numbers, seeking a better life.

But what constitutes "a better life"? In large part, the phrase is used in a psychological sense to refer to a life-style that allows people to feel secure, happy, relaxed, and in control of their destiny. To the extent that the urban life mitigates against these feelings, it is viewed as something from which to escape. In "The Experience of Living in Cities," Milgram analyzes city life from a psychological point of view, examining various factors that distinguish the urban experience from the rural experience and the different behaviors of city dwellers and their small-town counterparts. Rather than agreeing with the cliché that "city slickers" are a different breed of folk, Milgram suggests that the behavior of urban residents reflects a variety of adaptations to the "overload" situations, encounters, and other stimuli that are a part of everyday life in a city.

When I first came to New York it seemed like a nightmare. As soon as I got off the train at Grand Central I was caught up in pushing, shoving crowds on 42nd Street. Sometimes people bumped into me without apology; what really frightened me was to see two people literally engaged

in combat for possession of a cab. Why were they so rushed? Even drunks on the street were bypassed without a glance. People didn't seem to care about each other at all.

This statement represents a common reaction to a great city, but it does not tell the whole story. Obviously, cities have great appeal because of their variety, eventfulness, possibility of choice, and the stimulation of an intense atmosphere that

From *Science*, Vol. 167, pp. 1461–1468 (March 13, 1970). Copyright © 1970 by the American Association for the Advancement of Science. Reprinted by permission.

many individuals find a desirable background to their lives. Where face to face contacts are important, the city is unparalleled in its possibilities. It has been calculated by the Regional Plan Association (1969) that in Nassau county, a suburb of New York City, an official can meet 11,000 others with whom he may do business within 10 minutes of his office by foot or car. In Newark, a moderate-sized city, he could see more than 20,000 persons. But in midtown Manhattan an office worker can meet 220,000 persons within 10 minutes of his desk. There is an order of magnitude increment in the communication possibilities offered by a great city. That is one of the bases of its appeal and, indeed, of its functional necessity. The city provides options that no other social arrangement permits. But there is a negative side also, as we shall see.

Granted that cities are indispensable in a complex society, we may still ask what contribution psychology can make to understanding the experience of living in them. What theories are relevant? How can we extend our knowledge of the psychological aspects of life in cities through empirical inquiry? If empirical inquiry is possible, along what lines should it proceed? In short, where do we start in the construction of urban theory and in laying out lines of research?

Observation is the indispensable starting point. Any observer in the streets of midtown Manhattan will see: (a) large numbers of people, (b) high density, and (c) heterogeneity of population. These three factors need to be at the root of any sociopsychological theory of city life, for they condition all aspects of our experience in the metropolis. Wirth (1938), if not the first to point to these factors, is nonetheless the sociologist who relied most heavily on them in his analysis of the city. Yet, for a psychologist there is something unsatisfactory about Wirth's theoretical variables. *Numbers, density,* and *heterogeneity* are demographic facts, but they are not yet psychological facts. They are external to the individual. Psychology needs an idea that links the individual's *experience* to the demographic circumstances of urban life.

One link is provided by the concept of *overload.* This term, drawn from systems analysis, refers to the inability of a system to process inputs from the environment because there are too many inputs for the system to cope with, or because successive inputs come so fast that Input A cannot be processed when Input B is presented. When overload is present, adaptations occur. The system must set priorities and make choices. Input A may be

processed first while B is kept in abeyance, or one input may be sacrificed altogether. City life, as we experience it, constitutes a continuous set of encounters with adaptations to overload. Overload characteristically deforms daily life on several levels, impinging on *role performance*, evolution of *social norms, cognitive functioning,* and the *use of facilities.*

The concept has been implicit in several theories of urban experience. Simmel (1950) pointed out that since urban dwellers come into contact with vast numbers of people each day, they conserve psychic energy by becoming acquainted with a far smaller proportion of people than their rural counterparts and by maintaining more superficial relationships even with these acquaintances. Wirth (1938) points specifically to "the superficiality, the anonymity, and the transitory character of urban social relations," and to the loss of community that produces "the state of *anomie,* or the social void." Simmel notes as well that the high density of cities encourages inhabitants to create distance in social contacts to counteract the overwhelming pressures of close physical contact. The greater the number and frequency of human contacts the less time, attention, and emotional investment one can give to each of them, thus, the purported blasé and indifferent attitude of city dwellers toward each other.

One adaptive response to overload, therefore, is that *less time is given to each input.* A second adaptive mechanism is that *low priority inputs are disregarded.* Principles of selectivity are formulated so that the investment of time and energy is reserved for carefully defined inputs (e.g., the urbanite disregards a drunk, sick on the street, as he purposefully navigates through the crowd). Third, *boundaries are redrawn in certain social transactions so that the overloaded system can shift the burden to the other party in the exchange;* for example, harried New York bus drivers once made change for customers, but now this responsibility has been shifted to the client who must have the exact fare ready. Fourth, *reception is blocked off prior to entering a system;* city dwellers increasingly use unlisted telephone numbers to prevent individuals from calling them, and a small but growing number resort to keeping the telephone off the hook to prevent incoming calls. More subtly, one blocks inputs by assuming an unfriendly countenance, which discourages others from initiating contact. Additionally, *social screening devices are interposed between the individual and environmental inputs* (in a town of 5,000 anyone can drop in to chat with the mayor, but in the metropolis organizational screening devices deflect inputs to other destinations). Fifth, the *intensity of inputs is diminished by filtering devices* so that only weak and relatively superficial forms of involvement with others are allowed. Sixth, *specialized institutions are created to absorb inputs that would otherwise swamp the individual* (e.g., welfare departments handle the financial needs of a million individuals in New York City, who would otherwise create an army of mendicants continuously importuning the pedestrian). The interposition of institutions between the individual and the social world, a characteristic of all modern society and most acutely present in the large metropolis, has its negative side. It deprives the individual of a sense of direct contact and spontaneous integration in the life around him. It simultaneously protects and estranges the individual from his social environment. . . .

In summary, the observed behavior of the urbanite in a wide range of situations appears to be determined largely by a variety of adaptations to overload. We shall now deal with several specific consequences of responses to overload, which come to create a different tone to city and town.

SOCIAL RESPONSIBILITY

The principal point of interest for a social psychology of the city is that moral and social involvement with individuals is necessarily restricted. This is a direct and necessary function of excess of input over capacity to process. Restriction of involvement runs a broad spectrum from refusal to become involved in the needs of another person, even when the person desperately needs assistance (as in the Kitty Genovese case), through refusal to do favors, to the simple withdrawal of courtesies (such as offering a lady a seat, or saying "sorry" when a pedestrian collision occurs). In any transaction more and more details need to be dropped as the total number of units to be processed increases and assaults an instrument of limited processing capacity. There are myriad specific situations dealing with social responsibility. Specific incidents can be ordered in terms of two dimensions. First, there is the dimension of the importance of the action in question. Clearly, intervening to save someone's life rates higher than tipping one's hat, though both imply a degree of social involvement with others. Second, one may place any specific inci-

dent in terms of its position on a social-anomic continuum. Thus, in regard to courtesy expressions, a person may extend courtesies (the social end of the continuum) or withhold them (the anomic end). Anomic conditions, up and down the spectrum, are said to characterize the metropolis in comparison with the small town.

The ultimate adaptation to an overloaded social environment is to totally disregard the needs, interests, and demands of those whom one does not define as relevant to personal need satisfaction, and to develop optimally efficient means of identifying whether an individual falls into the category of friend or stranger. The disparity in treatment of friends and strangers ought to be greater in cities than towns; the time allotment and willingness to become involved with those who can make no personal claim on one's time will be less in cities than in towns.

Bystander Intervention in Crises

The most striking deficiencies in urban social responsibility occur in crisis situations, such as the Genovese murder in Queens. As is well known, in 1964, Catherine Genovese, coming home from a night job in the early hours of an April morning, was stabbed repeatedly over an extended period of time. Thirty-eight residents of a respectable New York City neighborhood admitted to having witnessed at least part of the attack but none went to her aid or called the police until after she was dead. Milgram and Hollander (1964) analyzed the event in these terms:

Urban friendships and associations are not primarily formed on the basis of physical proximity. A person with numerous close friends in different parts of the city may not know the occupant of an adjacent apartment. This does not mean that a city dweller has fewer friends than does a villager, or knows fewer persons who will come to his aid; however, it does mean that his allies are not constantly at hand. Miss Genovese required immediate aid from those physically present. There is no evidence that the city had deprived Miss Genovese of human associations, but the friends who might have rushed to her side were miles from the scene of her tragedy. Further, it is known that her cries for help were not directed to a specific person; they were general. But only individuals can act, and as the cries were not specifically directed, no particular person felt a special responsibility. The crime and the failure of community response seem absurd to us. At the time, it may well have seemed equally absurd to the Kew Gardens residents that not one of the neighbors would have called the police. A collective paralysis may have developed from the belief of each of the witnesses that someone else must surely have taken that obvious step [p. 602].

. . . More than just callousness prevents bystanders from participating in altercations between people. A rule of urban life is respect for other people's emotional and social privacy, perhaps because physical privacy is so hard to achieve. And in situations for which the standards are heterogeneous, it is much harder to know whether taking an active role is unwarranted meddling or an appropriate response to a critical situation. If a husband and wife are quarreling in public, at which point should a bystander step in? On the one hand, the heterogeneity of the city produces substantially greater tolerance of behavior, dress, and codes of ethics than does the small town, but this diversity also encourages people to withhold aid for fear of antagonizing the participants or crossing an inappropriate and difficult-to-define line.

Moreover, the frequency of demands present in the city gives rise to norms of noninvolvement. There are practical limitations to the Samaritan impulse in a major city. If a citizen attended to every needy person, if he were sensitive to and acted on every altruistic impulse that was evoked in the city, he could scarcely keep his own affairs in order. . . .

Favor Doing Based on Trust

We may now move away from crisis situations to less urgent examples of social responsibility; for it is not only in situations of dramatic need, but in the ordinary, everyday willingness to lend a hand, that the city dweller is said to be deficient relative to his small-town cousin. The comparative method must be employed in any empirical examination of this question. A commonplace social situation is staged both in an urban setting and a small town, a situation to which a subject can respond either by extending help or withholding it. The responses in town and city are then compared.

One factor in the purported unwillingness of urbanites to extend themselves to strangers may well be their heightened sense of physical and emotional vulnerability—a feeling that is supported by urban crime statistics. A key test for distinguishing between city and town behavior,

therefore, is how city dwellers compare with town dwellers in offering aid that increases their personal vulnerability and requires some trust of strangers. Altman, Levine, Nadien, and Villena (1969) devised a study to compare city and town dwellers in this respect. The criterion used in their study was the willingness of householders to allow strangers to enter their homes to use the telephone. Individually the investigators rang doorbells, explained that they had misplaced the address of a friend nearby, and asked to use the phone. The investigators (two males and two females) completed a total of 100 requests for entry in the city and 60 in the small towns. The results gleaned from middle-income housing developments in Manhattan were compared with data gathered in several small towns in Rockland County, outside of New York City (Stony Point, Spring Valley, Ramapo, Nyack, New City, and West Clarkstown).

As Table 1 shows, in all cases there was a sharp increase in the proportion of entries gained by an investigator when he moved from the city to a small town. In the most extreme case the investigator was five times more likely to gain admission to a home in a small town than in Manhattan. Although the female investigators had noticeably higher levels of entry in both cities and towns than the male investigators, all four students did at least twice as well in gaining access to small-town homes than they did to city homes, suggesting that the city-town distinction overrides even the predictably greater fear of male strangers than of female ones.

The lower level of helpfulness by city dwellers

TABLE 1. PERCENTAGE OF ENTRIES BY INVESTIGATORS FOR CITY AND TOWN HOMES

INVESTIGATOR	% ENTRIES	
	CITY (n = 100)	SMALL TOWN (n = 60)
Male		
1	16	40
2	12	60
Female		
1	40	87
2	40	100

seems due in part to recognition of the *dangers* of Manhattan living, rather than to mere indifference or coldness. It is significant that 75% of all city respondents received and answered messages either by shouting through closed doors or by peering through peepholes; in the towns, by contrast, about 75% of the respondents opened the doors, with no barriers between themselves and the investigator.

Supporting the investigators' quantitative results was their general observation that the town dwellers were noticeably more friendly and less suspicious than the city dwellers. Even city dwellers who allowed the investigators to use the phone appeared more ill at ease than their town counterparts; city dwellers often refused to answer the doorbell even when they were at home; and in a few cases city residents called the security police of the housing development. In seeking to explain the sense of psychological vulnerability city dwellers feel, above and beyond differences in actual crime statistics, Altman et al. (1969) point out that for a village resident, if a crime is committed in a neighboring village, he may not perceive it as personally relevant, though the geographic distance may be small. But a criminal act committed anywhere in the city, though miles from the city-dweller's home, is still verbally located within the city, "therefore . . . the inhabitant of the city possesses a larger vulnerable space."

Civilities

Even at the most superficial level of involvement, the exercise of everyday civilities, urbanites are reputedly deficient. Persons bump into each other and frequently do not apologize. They knock over another person's packages, and, as often as not, proceed on their way with a grump, rather than taking the time to help the victim. Such behavior, which many visitors to great cities find distasteful, is less common, we are told, in smaller communities where traditional courtesies are more likely to be maintained.

In some instances it is not simply that in the city traditional courtesies are violated; rather, the cities develop *new norms of noninvolvement*. They are so well defined and so deeply a part of city life that *they* constitute the norms people are reluctant to violate. Men are actually embarrassed to give up a seat on the subway for an old woman; they will mumble, "I was getting off anyway," instead of making the gesture in a straightforward and gracious way. These norms develop because everyone realizes that in situations of high-density people cannot implicate themselves in each other's affairs, for to do so would create conditions of continual distraction that would frustrate purposeful action.

The effects of overload do not imply that at every instant the city dweller is bombarded with an unmanageable number of inputs, and that his responses are determined by the input excess at any given instant. Rather, adaptation occurs in the form of the gradual evolution of norms of behavior. Norms are created in response to frequent discrete experiences of overload; they persist and become generalized modes of responding. They are part of the culture of the metropolis, and even newcomers may adapt to these manners in the course of time.

Overload on Cognitive Capacities: Anonymity

It is a truism that we respond differently toward those whom we know and those who are strangers to us. An eager patron aggressively cuts in front of someone in a long movie line to save time only to confront a friend; he then behaves sheepishly. A man gets into an automobile accident caused by another driver, emerges from his car shouting in rage, then moderates his behavior on discovering a friend driving the other car. The city dweller, when moving through the midtown streets, is in a state of continual anonymity vis à vis the other pedestrians. His ability to know everyone he passes is restricted by inherent limitations of human cognitive capacity. A continual succession of faces briefly appears before him then disappears. Minimal scanning for recognition occurs, but storage in long-term memory is avoided. (No one has yet calculated the number of faces scanned in a day by the typical midtown worker.)

The concept of "anonymity" is a shibboleth of social psychology, but few have defined it precisely or attempted to measure it quantitatively in order to compare cities and towns. Anonymity is part of a continuous spectrum ranging from total anonymity at one end to full acquaintance at the other, and it may well be that measurement of the precise degrees of anonymity in cities and towns would help to explain important distinctions between the quality of life in each. Conditions of full acquaintance, for example, offer security and familiarity, but they may also be stifling because the inhabitant is under continuous scrutiny by people who know him. Conditions of complete anonymity, by contrast, provide freedom from routine social ties, but they may also create feelings of alienation and detachment.

One could investigate empirically the proportion of activities in which the city dweller and town dweller are known by others at given times in their daily lives, and, if known, with what proportion of those the urbanite and town dweller interact. At his job, for instance, the city dweller may know fully as many people as his rural counterpart. While not fulfilling his occupational or family role, however—say, in traveling about the city—the urbanite is doubtlessly more anonymous than his rural counterpart. (One way to measure the difference in degrees of anonymity would be to display the picture of a New York inhabitant at a busy midtown intersection. One could offer a significant reward to any passerby who could identify the person pictured. Calculation of the total number of passersby during a given period, coupled with the proportion who could identify the picture, provides one measure of urban anonymity. Results could then be compared with those gleaned by displaying the picture of a town dweller on the main street in his town. This test could also be used to define a person's "neighborhood boundary," that area within which a high proportion of people could identify the inhabitant's picture.) . . .

Limited laboratory work on anonymity has begun. [An] experiment by Zimbardo (1969) tested whether the social anonymity and impersonality of the big city encourage greater vandalism than found in small towns. . . . Zimbardo arranged for one car to be left for 64 hours near the New York University campus in the Bronx and a counterpart to be left near Stanford University in Palo Alto. The license plates on both cars were removed and the hoods opened, to provide "releaser cues" for potential vandals. The results were as expected: The New York car was stripped of all moveable parts within the first 24 hours, and was left a hunk of metal rubble by the end of three days. Unexpectedly, however, most destruction occurred during daylight hours usually under scrutiny by observers, and was led by well-dressed, white adults. The Palo Alto car was left untouched. . . .

Another direction for empirical study is the investigation of the beneficial effects of anonymity. Impersonality of city life breeds its own tolerance for the private lives of inhabitants. Individuality and even eccentricity, we may assume, can flourish more readily in the metropolis than in the small town. Stigmatized persons may find it easier to lead comfortable lives without the constant scrutiny of neighbors. . . .

Role Behavior in Cities and Towns

Another product of urban "overload" is the adjustment in roles made by urbanites in daily interactions. As Wirth has said: "Urbanites meet one another in highly segmental roles. . . . They are less dependent upon particular persons, and their dependence upon others is confined to a highly fractionalized aspect of the other's round of activity." This tendency is particularly noticeable in transactions between customers and those offering professional or sales services: The owner of a country store has time to become well acquainted with his dozen-or-so daily customers; but the girl at the checkout counter of a busy A & P, handling hundreds of customers a day, barely has time to toss the green stamps into one customer's shopping bag before the next customer has confronted her with his pile of groceries.

In his stimulating analysis of the city, *A Communications Theory of Urban Growth*, Meier (1962) discusses several adaptations a system may make when confronted by inputs that exceed its capacity to process them. Specifically, Meier states that according to the principle of competition for scarce resources the scope and time of the transaction shrinks as customer volume and daily turnover rise. . . . This, in fact, is what is meant by the brusque quality of city life. New standards have developed in cities about what levels of services are appropriate in business transactions. . . .

The research on this subject needs to be guided by unifying theoretical concepts. As this section of the paper has tried to demonstrate, the concept of overload helps to explain a wide variety of contrasts between city and town behavior: (*a*) the differences in *role enactment* (the urban dwellers' tendency to deal with one another in highly segmented, functional terms; the constricted time and services offered customers by sales personnel); (*b*) the evolution of *urban norms* quite different from traditional town values (such as the acceptance of noninvolvement, impersonality, and aloofness in urban life); (*c*) consequences for the urban dweller's *cognitive processes* (his inability to identify most of the people seen daily; his screening of sensory stimuli; his development of blasé attitudes toward deviant or bizarre behavior; and his selectivity in responding to human demands); and (*d*) the far greater competition for scarce *facilities* in the city (the subway rush, the fight for taxis, traffic jams, standing in line to await services). I would suggest that contrasts between city and rural behavior probably reflect the responses of similar people to very different situations, rather than intrinsic differences between rural personalities and city personalities. The city is a situation to which individuals respond adaptively. . . .

REFERENCES

Altman, D., Levine, M., Nadien, M., & Villena, J. "Trust of the stranger in the city and the small town" (unpublished research, Graduate Center, City University of New York, 1969).

Meier, R. L. *A communications theory of urban growth.* Cambridge: MIT Press, 1962.

Milgram, S., & Hollander, P. Paralyzed witnesses: The murder they heard. *The Nation,* 1964, *25,* 602–604.

Regional Plan Association (1969). The second regional plan. *The New York Times,* June 15, 1969, *119,* Section 12.

Simmel, G. The metropolis and mental life. In K. H. Wolff (Ed.), *The sociology of George Simmel.* New York: The Free Press, 1950. (Originally published: *Die Grossstadte und das Geistesleben die Grossstadt.* Dresden: v. Zahn & Jaensch, 1903.)

Wirth, L. Urbanism as a way of life. *American Journal of Sociology,* 1938, *44,* 1–24.

Zimbardo, P. G. The human choice: Individuation, reason and order vs. deindividuation, impulse and chaos. *Nebraska Symposium on Motivation,* Lincoln, Neb.: University of Nebraska Press, 1969.

URBAN GRAFFITI AS TERRITORIAL MARKERS

DAVID LEY and ROMAN CYBRIWSKY

An increasingly common feature of the urban environment is graffiti. Graffiti are inscriptions, slogans, and drawings scratched or scribbled on a wall or other public surface. Some people have analyzed the content of graffiti (the types of humor, the political commentary, the words of wisdom, and the like); others have discussed them as a modern art form. However, very little attention has been paid to the psychological and social functions of graffiti. Ley and Cybriwsky address some of these issues in their article "Urban Graffiti as Territorial Markers." They see graffiti as important indicators of attitudes and social relationships. Their analysis of graffiti in Philadelphia neighborhoods provides intriguing insights into the relationship between the physical and the social environment.

In an era of massive social change and unmitigated erasure of the past, one small feature of man's heritage is making a resurgence—the practice of marking graffiti in public places. Graffiti might

"Urban Graffiti As Territorial Markers" by David Ley and Roman Cybriwsky, from *Annals of the Association of American Geographers,* Vol. 64, No. 4, December, 1974. © 1974 by the Association of American Geographers. Reproduced by permission of the authors and the Association of American Geographers.

be regarded, perhaps, as a rather whimsical element in the sum total of cultural baggage of interest to the social scientist, yet in inner city Philadelphia they provide accurate indicators of local attitudes and social process in areas where more direct measurement is difficult. The quality and location of graffiti display regularities. They manifest the distribution of various social attitudes and intimate subsequent behavior in space; as such, certain types of graffiti forecast both potential and actual behavior. To borrow a current graffito: "Today's graffiti are tomorrow's head-lines."

The contemporary reappearance of graffiti dates from 1965, or perhaps a little earlier. The number of articles and commentaries on graffiti in popular magazines and the *New York Times* increased from only one over the fifteen-year period, 1950–64, to five in 1969, and then to forty in 1972. The rapid increase in 1972 accompanied an "urban epidemic" in East Coast cities.[1] Popular media often are more sensitive to the public mood than are the social sciences, and as yet there is limited indication of scholarly interest in graffiti. During the 1960s articles on graffiti had dealt with fairly traditional forms, the amorous, the erotic, the political, the historic, and the intellectual, but a new trend appeared in 1970. Graffiti writing had spread to the inner city. Almost all of the graffiti reports discovered for 1972 and half of those for 1971 were concerned with the newfound popularity of spray-painting among inner city youth. This rediscovered form of expression will form the basis of our discussion.[2]

Graffiti have not traditionally been regarded as a societal indicator, but rather as a folk symbol in their own right. Consequently, their diagnostic significance has been neglected, and they have been primarily treated in anecdotal and jocular vein in popular magazines. Although it is scarcely surprising that the people's slogans should appear in the people's press, a broader treatment of graffiti is justified. The graffito represents part of "a twilight zone of communication," an outlet for often deeply felt but rarely articulated sentiments and attitudes. Wall inscriptions reveal "developments, trends, and attitudes in man's history . . . little insights, little peepholes into the minds of individuals who are spokesmen not only for themselves but for others like them" (Reisner, 1971, p. 1). . . .

THE GRAFFITI LONER

Perhaps the least geographical inner city inscriptions are the products of single individuals, or pairs of artists. In Philadelphia and New York these inscriptions include the work of graffiti celebrities, the self-proclaimed kings of the walls. The majority are black youngsters who range widely through the city, the downtown, the airport, the inner suburbs, and even beyond. They make little claim to the black residential sections away from the main thoroughfares. Their "territory" is overwhelmingly linear, following the main transport arteries, and their targets are city-wide public structures. Their goal is to leave a mark on exotic space, to make a claim to the world outside the ghetto. They leave inner city residential blocks to the local street gang, which has its own claim to the walls of its turf.

The more brazen the spatial conquest, the greater the status, so that graffiti kings seek to emulate each other in the inaccessibility of locations they invade. Tity Peace Sign sprayed his name in red on an elephant's backside at Philadelphia Zoo; Bobby Kidd sprayed a police car while a friend held the officers' attention; and at the airport Cornbread sprayed a TWA jet which took off to the south bearing his name upon its wings. The signs at the airport read "Cornbread welcomes you to Philadelphia." So esteemed is his reputation as King of the Walls that when a city newspaper carried a false report of his death in a gang fight, a number of "Cornbreads" contacted the press to report they were still alive.

The integral characteristics of the graffiti kings are their nicknames and their signatures. The names they select are revealing; in 1971 leading Philadelphia exhibitors included Dr. Cool No. 1, Cool Earl, Bobby Cool, Kool Kev, Sir Smooth. "Cool" denotes confidence, style, suavity, a mastery of the intricate signal language of street life. A title is a common affectation; another is to paint a crown above the nickname. Nicknames often show considerable creativity and originality; North Philadelphia boasts a Sherlock Holmes and Dr. Watson, and even Baron Eric von Schwenk makes a graceful appearance in a solidly black neighborhood.

The signature is distinctive. It is usually spray-painted from an aerosol can and is highly accentuated, embellished with elegant curves and generous serifs. The letters, like the name itself, convey a message of "style," yet imply frustrated ambition, a bittersweet theme.

The conquest of territory, even in fantasy, is always an act performed for an audience. Locations have a meaning; to claim access to an inaccessible location is to make a claim of primacy for oneself. . . .

---

[1] By the middle of the year the President of the New York City Council was suggesting a monthly Anti-Graffiti Day, much like Earth Day, under the auspices of the Environmental Protection Administration; *The New York Times*, May 21, 1972, p. 66.

[2] Urban graffiti are not new; Philadelphia walls, for example, were heavily inscribed in the 1850s; *Philadelphia Evening Bulletin*, January 12, 1973, p. G-3.

EXPERIENCING SOCIAL PSYCHOLOGY

228

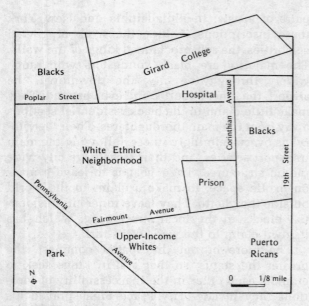

FIGURE 1. Social groups in Fairmount and vicinity.

GRAFFITI OF THE TEENAGE STREET GANG

In contrast to the graffiti kings, who are free-ranging and make temporary claims to space, the street gangs occupy a more fixed and permanent territory. Some gangs can trace a continuous identity over several decades; a few have shown their strength by reforming uptown after urban renewal cleared their original neighborhood. Street gangs are strongly place specific; in Philadelphia most of them take their names from an intersection near the center of their territory. Though the relationship is not as exclusive as it once was, the gang remains a block and neighborhood-based organization. Its sphere of movement, fixed rather than fluid, confined rather than expansive, is a close approximation to the movement patterns of many inner city residents. . . .

In Philadelphia, wall graffiti offer an accurate indicator of turf ownership. As a general rule, the incidence of gang graffiti becomes denser with increasing proximity to the core of a territory. Overwhelmingly graffiti consist of signatures, a nickname, often followed by the gang name. Occasionally, boastful slogans are painted near the core of the turf. . . .

The evidence of the walls gives a good approximation of the extent of each territory. Boundaries compiled from the relative incidence of gang graffiti found a ready acceptance by neighborhood youth as an accurate portrayal of each gang's area of control, and the residences of gang members living in the neighborhood also show close agreement with them. . . .

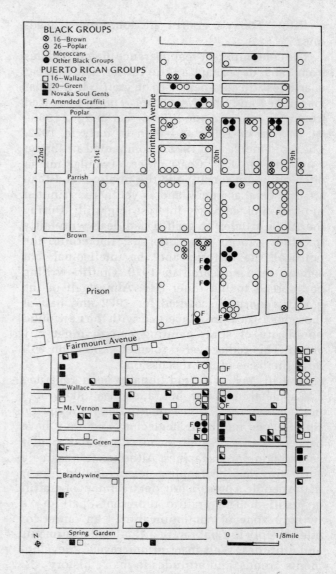

FIGURE 2. Gang graffiti in the eastern portion of Fairmount and vicinity.

We have used graffiti to provide insights into the social and spatial order with equal success in a second Philadelphia neighborhood (Cybriwsky, 1972). Fairmount is a working-class white enclave on the edge of the North Philadelphia ghetto; black residential areas are north and east, a weakening Puerto Rican neighborhood is southeast, and a section of young white professionals, recent in-migrants, is to the south (Figure 1).

The territories of the Puerto Rican groups south of Fairmount Avenue, the Navaka Soul Gents and 20-G, are not well defined (Figure 2). Their territorial claims show considerable overlap. Territorial indistinctness mirrors social weakness; both groups are weak, and neither appears in the files

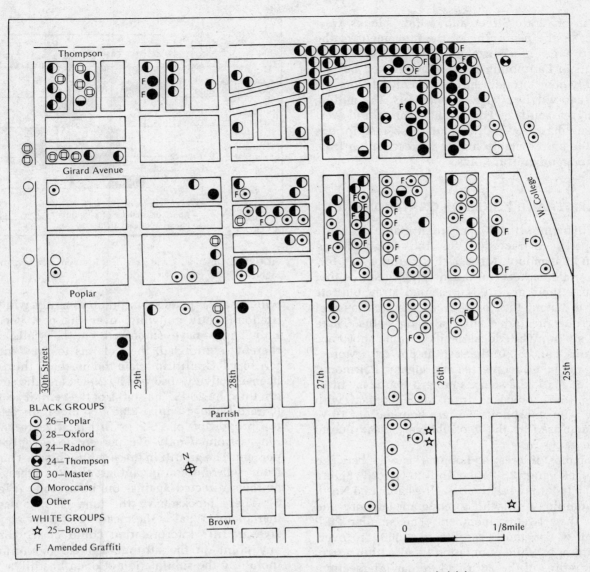

FIGURE 3. Gang graffiti in the northwestern portion of Fairmount and vicinity.

of the City's gang control units.[3] Both are on the western edge of the territory of the powerful 16-W gang; 16-W graffiti are scattered throughout their area, showing that neither 20-G nor the Gents have been able to assert their independence from their more powerful neighbor.

North of Fairmount Avenue, and east of the jail, there is a sharp break from a biracial population to a solidly black neighborhood. Despite a large number of vacant and cleared rubble-strewn lots, the intensity of graffiti increases, for this is part of the territory of the Moroccans, one of

the larger and more violent North Philadelphia gangs.[4] At Corinthian Avenue their territory abuts abruptly against the white neighborhood of Fairmount, and there is very little graffiti transgression across this boundary (Figure 2).

Graffiti again become intense west of 25th and north of Poplar, in an area which has recently become black. Although a number of small or distant groups (including the Moroccans) make a weak claim to parts of this area, the strongest claimants are the powerful 28-Oxford gang, centered four blocks north, and a recent local group taking the name of the 26th and Poplar intersection (Figure 3). The thrust of 26-P graffiti south of

[3]20-G claims to be the main drafting unit for local Puerto Rican youth, and sporadic minor coercion is directed against Puerto Rican teenagers who resist enlistment. The Navaka Soul Gents are unknown to city gang workers.

[4]The Moroccans and 16-Wallace have a long history of feuding, usually just east of the study area on 18th street.

Poplar on 26th Street and a few blocks west indicates the beginning of the movement of the ghetto edge into Fairmount. The distribution of graffiti in Fairmount itself, more limited but extremely concentrated, has been omitted from the map, and will be analyzed separately. The middle class area south of Fairmount Avenue and west of 22nd has few graffiti, and these inscriptions include a predictably higher representation from the nongang graffiti kings.

GRAFFITI AND ZONES OF GANG CONFLICT

Graffiti for more than twenty identifiable nonwhite groups were recorded for the neighborhood around Fairmount. Most of these groups had few territorial markers in the neighborhood, either because their graffiti represented stray outliers from a distant turf, or because the smallness of the group precluded any real gang status. There were six nonwhite local gangs of some substance (Figures 2 and 3). In the east the powerful Moroccan gang had uncontested supremacy; Fairmount Avenue marked a sharp southern boundary insulating the Moroccans from close contact with 16-W. The amorphous western boundary of 16-W was confused by the two relatively weak Puerto Rican gangs.

The most interesting boundaries were between the black gangs 26-Poplar and 28-Oxford (Figure 3). The latter is a relatively well-established North Philadelphia unit with a moderate territory and more than twenty members. The smaller 26-P group is far more recent; in 1960 an overwhelmingly white population lived within a two-block radius of the 26th and Poplar intersection. The emergence of 26-P might be seen as spontaneous once the area contained a majority of nonwhite residents, but the dynamics are complicated; the 28th and Oxford intersection is only seven blocks away, and as one of the more aggressive gangs, 28-Ox might well have expected to expand south following the ghetto edge. Northward expansion was thwarted by powerful neighbors; between 1966 and 1970 eleven serious incidents involving 28-Ox and rival gangs to the north and east were known to city authorities.[5] The appearance of 26-P would clearly have been an obstacle to such southern expansion, and a certain amount of tension between the two groups might be expected.

The area which we might expect to have been contested consists of nine blocks or part-blocks

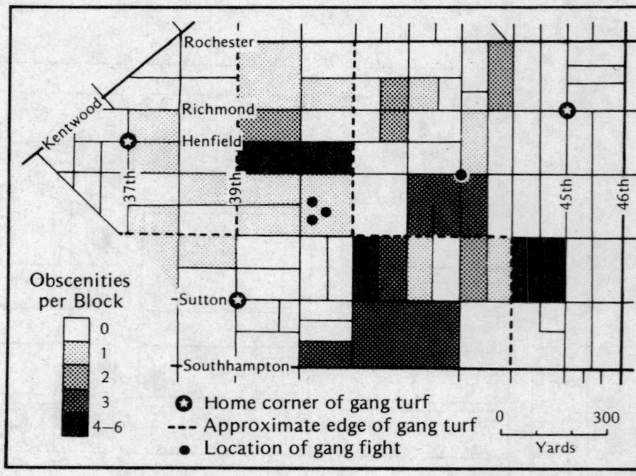

FIGURE 4. Obscenities and gang fight locations in a section of Monroe.

which have tipped from predominantly white to predominantly nonwhite over the past decade. Both gangs have embossed on the walls, and thereby legitimized, their claims to this "virgin territory." Graffiti indicate the northern third has been effectively absorbed by 28-Ox and the southern third by 26-P. The status of the central section (Girard-College-Poplar-28th) is more uncertain; the proportion of 26-P graffiti relative to 28-Ox ranges from twenty-five percent to seventy-five percent. The graffiti in these central blocks change from self-reinforcing autographs to aggressive epithets directed against the other gang (Figure 3). These blocks have the tone of a contested marchland. What is the meaning of these aggressive graffiti? Interpretation could clearly lie at any point on the attitude-behavior continuum, including the sublimation of open hostility.

Evidence from the second inner city study area in North Philadelphia suggest that aggressive graffiti represent more than simply hostile attitudes; they indicate dispositions to overt behavior. There are three street gangs in this neighborhood, and turf boundaries again have the highest incidence of aggressive wall markings (Figure 4). There is a consistent pattern to the victims of aggressive taunts; wall epithets are exchanged between 45-R and 39-S, and between 37-H and 39-S. If graffiti are indicators of behavior we would expect 45-R and 37-H to be common antagonists of 39-S. Behavioral data substantiate this expectation. 39-S is the largest gang with perhaps seventy-five members; 45-R has around sixty adherents and 37-H has thirty-five.[6] On a number

---

[5]Youth Conservation Service, City of Philadelphia.

[6]Official estimates of gang size fluctuate between 85 and 200.

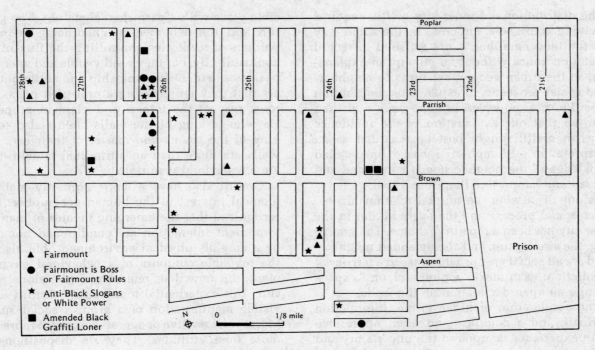

FIGURE 5. The distribution of Fairmount graffiti.

of occasions 45-R and 37-H have formed an alliance against 39-S; in May, 1971, for example, after a week of gang fighting, fifty to sixty boys gathered on 37th Street and carried out a sweep along Sutton Street. This conflict has existed for a number of years. City files record ten serious incidents between 39-S and 45-R between 1966 and 1970, and a further ten between 39-S and 37-H, but no incidents between 45-R and 37-H. The articulation on the walls has indeed found its manifestation in the streets. . . .

GRAFFITI AND THE DEFENDED NEIGHBORHOOD

A third type of inner city graffiti is wall inscriptions and emblems of the defended neighborhood, a neighborhood of some homogeneity, a recognized identity, and with authenticity as a distinct unit in its "foreign relations" with other parts of the city (Suttles, 1972). The wall markings of the defended neighborhood are internally supportive and externally aggressive. They are messages for two audiences. Such graffiti are commonly boundary markers; they delineate an interface, the edge of socially claimed space, a boundary which in the North American city is often ethnic, and commonly racial. Fairmount is a defended neighborhood, a pocket of first and second generation immigrants experiencing encroachment from all quarters; to the north and east from the bursting North Philadelphia black community, and to the

south from a burgeoning population of middle-class townhouse dwellers. The threat from the north and east is most keenly felt in Fairmount; the townhouse dwellers are reluctantly viewed as allies who at best will maintain property prices and the racial structure of the neighborhood.

The visible walls articulate invisible sentiments. In a defended neighborhood fettered by more powerful neighbors, graffiti promote an introspective self-consciousness. "Fairmount Rules," "Fairmount is Boss," or simply "Fairmount," are the self-reinforcing slogans on the walls of a neighborhood with an uncertain identity. Externally directed racial epithets and obscenities are a neighborhood counterpart of aggressive gang graffiti (Figure 5). . . .

At the level of the defended neighborhood, wall graffiti in Fairmount continue to be diagnostic indicators of an invisible environment of attitudes and social processes. They indicate far more than fears, threats, and prejudices; they are a prelude and a directive to open behavior, and clues to the bounds and intensity of a community's control of its territory. In Fairmount, at least, they pinpoint the location where that behavior will occur.

CONCLUSION

The humble graffito is making a resurgence; our analysis of Philadelphia could profitably be extended to other cities in North America and Europe. An understanding of this resurgence and of the distributions of inner city graffiti requires a delving into social process. In the same way that the biogeographer is not satisfied to record vegetation zones without an attempt at explanation, so the urban geographer turns to neighborhood social processes to explain his distribution maps. Process, however, is more equivocal than form, so that our explanation of the incidence of urban graffiti might best be regarded as an interpretation, although it is based on detailed knowledge of the neighborhoods concerned and a broad and supportive literature.

In our discussion the mutual relationship between social process and the spatial order in the inner city has been a repetitive theme. The graffiti king, the street gang, and the defended neighborhood are all social groups which assert a territorial jurisdiction; each makes a public claim to space through an open declaration on the walls.

The acceleration of urban crime, information overload, and a complex and often oppressive urban experience compound the uncertainty and confusion of inner city life. The restoration of some predictability to one's environment is a prescription for a territorial imperative. To define a small space of one's own permits a higher level of social control to be maintained, by surveillance, by restricting entry to recognized friends, and by limiting the range of acceptable behavior within the area. Establishing the territory generates security; maintaining or embellishing it guarantees status.

The graffiti king conquers a place momentarily; maintenance is impossible, hence embellishment is maximized in the capture of an exotic, inaccessible place with a garnished signature. The gang turf and the defended neighborhood are more permanent territories controlling the flux of the confusing city, but they need visible and unequivocal cues to identify ownership and notify outsiders that they are entering a protected place and must respect the integrity of claimed property. He who is king of the walls claims also to be king of the streets and master of their use. The walls are more than an attitudinal tabloid; they are a behavioral manifesto.

Graffiti also have a more explicitly methodological interest to the human geographer. It is recognized that the emerging themes of man-environment interaction are conditioned not only by a tangible physical environment, but also by the invisible contours of a behavioral environment. But how does one identify, let alone measure, this experiential topography? Graffiti are a visible manifestation of a group's social space. Moreover, assertive or aggressive graffiti represent more than attitudes. They are dispositions to behavior, and as such impress a bolder outline on the fuzzy transition between perception and action.

The scholar must be sensitive to the nuances of such native guides as inner city graffiti. If he is unable to interpret the visible, then the invisible meaning of place will be beyond his grasp. We must understand the behavioral environment, the complex of socially and culturally determined beliefs and perceptions, and learn to read its diagnostic indicators if we wish to develop social and behavioral theory.

REFERENCES

Cybriwsky, R. "Social aspects of neighborhood change." *Annals of the Association of American Geographers,* 68 (1), March 1978.

Ley, D. *The black inner city as frontier outpost: images and behavior of a Philadelphia neighborhood.* Washington, D.C.: Association of American Geographers, Monograph Series, No. 7, 1974.

Reisner, R. *Graffiti: two thousand years of wall writing.* New York: Cowles Book Company, 1971.

Suttles, G. *The social construction of communities.* Chicago: University of Chicago Press, 1972.

PROJECTS

Name _____

Date _____

10.1: MENTAL MAPS

Milgram has proposed the concept of "psychological maps" to study people's perceptions of the city environment. You can adapt this technique to gain some insight into your own and others' perceptions of your college campus. Basically, the technique involves drawing a map of the campus. The emphasis should be on representing the campus as the person sees it, not on geographical accuracy. On the first blank work sheet (Mental Map 1), draw your own map of the campus. Select two acquaintances who might have different relationships to the campus (e.g., an athlete and a scholar, a freshman and a senior), and ask each of them to draw a map of the campus. Have them use the second and third work sheets. Do not let them see any of the other maps before they draw their own.

1. Are there certain landmarks or boundaries that are included on all three maps? If so, what are they?

2. Are certain parts of the campus overrepresented on the maps or drawn in more detail than other parts? If so, do these special parts of the maps reflect the interests and activities of the particular map maker? For example, did the scholar note all the libraries; whereas the athlete drew the various playing fields and sports facilities?

3. What aspects of the campus environment are *not* represented on the maps?

4. Aside from omissions, are there any other patterns of distortion in the maps? If so, what are they?

MENTAL MAP 1

Drawn by _____

MENTAL MAP 2

Drawn by _____

MENTAL MAP 3

Drawn by _____

10.2: THE PROFESSORIAL ENVIRONMENT

The physical environment that surrounds a person can, without conscious intent or cognition, influence behavior and social interaction. Such things as the arrangement of furniture can encourage or discourage contact and intimacy and can indicate status differences (e.g., limiting the immediacy of contact is a very effective means of conveying high status). Thus, one professor's office may sometimes look cold and impersonal; whereas another's is friendly and casual, depending on furniture placement. In situations in which it is important to establish good rapport and intimacy, a seating arrangement that encourages immediacy is critical.

The goal of this project is to explore the relationship between the physical layout of various professors' offices and the general friendliness of those professors. In order to do that, you should first establish criteria for evaluating the office environment and the professor's rapport with students. You might consider such variables as the placement of the desk (along the side of the wall or as a barrier between student and professor), the type and placement of chairs, and the amount of open space and such variables as availability (how many office hours the professor has and whether he or she is keeping them), the physical distance between the student's and the professor's chairs, and the amount of eye contact between professor and student. Decide on five criteria for evaluating the office environment and five criteria for evaluating the professor's rapport with students, and list them on the data sheet. Then visit the offices of three different professors (whom you have previously met) to talk about some topic of interest. Rate both the office and the professor's rapport with you according to your set of criteria.

Name _____

Date _____

DATA SHEET

Variables	Professor A	Professor B	Professor C

Environment

1. _____

2. _____

3. _____

4. _____

5. _____

Rapport

1. _____

2. _____

3. _____

4. _____

5. _____

Name _____

Date _____

1. Look at the pattern of ratings, and speculate on possible relationships between environment and behavior (e.g., how the placement of a desk can reduce personal contact).

2. Compare your criteria and your ratings with those of other people in your class. What hypotheses do your collective ratings suggest?

3. According to your own hypotheses, what would be the ideal office environment for promoting student-professor rapport? What would be the ideal environment for hindering it?

11
SOCIAL PATHOLOGY

P eople often turn to the bad seed theory to explain the ills of society. That is, they believe that various antisocial and deviant behaviors are committed by individuals who are evil, weak, defective, sick, or perverted. In psychological terms, people tend to make *dispositional* attributions for these types of behaviors. For example, an individual's criminal actions are attributed to such presumed internal traits as a "psychopathic personality" or a "lack of moral character."

Social psychology has helped bring a new and wider perspective to the consideration of these problems by emphasizing *situational* attributions. That is, it has focused attention on environmental factors, both social and physical, that cause people to act in particular ways. Such an approach does not deny the importance of individual traits and characteristics. Rather, it suggests that human pathology may often have a social basis or component.

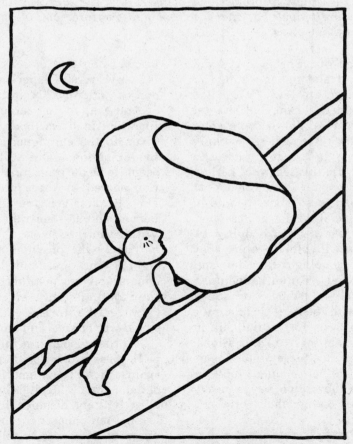

Jan Castle/California Journal

It Doesn't Have to Be an Uphill Battle

BURNOUT: THE LOSS OF HUMAN CARING

CHRISTINA MASLACH and AYALA PINES

In recent years, the number and range of services offered by the helping professions have greatly increased. More and more opportunities exist for people to seek and obtain help, protection, cure, education, or special treatment of some kind for the problems that they face. The professionals they turn to are often highly skilled in such areas as law, medicine, social welfare, and counseling. But more than simple application of skill is expected from these professionals. The people who seek their help expect them to be personally concerned. The helping professionals are asked to be warm and caring, on the one hand, and objective, on the other. If they fail to meet these high expectations and treat their patients or clients in ways that are considered indifferent, rude, or even dehumanizing, people are quick to criticize them and complain about the individuals who staff society's service institutions.

In "Burnout: The Loss of Human Caring," Maslach and Pines look at this problem from the point of view of the professionals. They identify a syndrome of emotional burnout that occurs with considerable frequency among these people. The widespread occurrence of burnout, which Maslach and Pines observed in a variety of professions, suggests that the source of the problem is not the individual but the structure and environment of the helping professions themselves.

Ellen says she is burned out. She is angry and frustrated, feels impotent and incompetent. Her morale and her self-image are low. "I feel like my soul is dying," says Ellen. "I can't look straight in my clients' eyes anymore. I've become cold, uncaring, and no longer interested in working with losers. All I want to do is quit my job, and yet I feel trapped." How did this sensitive, caring, and committed young woman get burned out? And why does it happen to so many people in the various health and social-service professions?

There are many situations in which people work intensely and intimately with other people. They learn about people's psychological, social, and physical problems, and they are often called upon to provide personal help of some kind. Such intense involvement with people occurs on a large-scale, continuous basis for individuals in various health and social-service professions. Hour after hour, day after day, these professionals must *care* about many other people, and our research indicates that they often pay a heavy psychological price for being their brother's

keeper. Constant or repeated emotional arousal is a very stressful experience for any human being and can often be disruptive or incapacitating.

And yet, in the large and steadily growing literature in these fields, very little attention is given to the emotional stresses experienced by the professional. One of the main reasons for this seems to be the traditional client-centered orientation shared by these professions. The focus is almost exclusively the client, the patient, or the person who, in some other way, receives services. Within this framework, the professional is viewed as merely the provider of services, whose role and existence are defined by the presence of the clients and are justified only as long as he or she continues to serve, help, and provide. However, the stresses experienced by the professional are very real and have a tremendous impact.

In order to perform their work efficiently and well, these professionals may defend themselves against their strong emotions through techniques of detachment. Ideally, they try to gain sufficient objectivity and distance from the situation without losing their concern for the person they are working with. However, in all too many cases, they are unable to cope with this continual emotional stress, and *burnout* (a total emotional and physical exhaustion) eventually occurs. They develop negative self-concepts and negative job attitudes, lose all concern or emotional feeling for the people they work with, and come to treat their clients in detached and even dehumanized ways.

Burnout is not an isolated phenomenon that can be attributed to a limited number of individuals. On the contrary, it occurs very frequently for a wide variety of people within many professions. It appears to be a major factor in low worker morale, poor performance, absenteeism, and high job turnover, and it plays a primary role in the poor delivery of health and welfare services to people who are in need of them. It may well be implicated in the increasing number of malpractice suits and thus the soaring costs of insurance for doctors. Furthermore, it is correlated with other negative indexes of personal stress, such as alcoholism, mental illness, and marital conflict. Burnout may vary in severity among different professions and may be called by different names (e.g., some law enforcement groups refer to this suppression of emotion as the *John Wayne syndrome*), but the same basic phenomenon seems to be occurring in a wide variety of work settings.

For the past few years, we have been studying the dynamics of this destructive process with our co-workers at the University of California, Berkeley. We have observed professionals at work, collected extensive questionnaire data, and conducted personal interviews, lectures, seminars, and workshops. Thus far, the professional samples that we have studied include social-welfare workers, social-service workers, psychiatric nurses, poverty lawyers, college teachers, child-care workers, clinical psychologists and psychiatrists in a mental hospital, supervisors of institutions for the mentally retarded, some prison personnel, and physicians. Our research goals have been to identify the interpersonal stresses these professionals face, what distinguishes those work settings in which burnout typically occurs from those in which it is uncommon, what specific techniques can be used to combat burnout, what personal and social consequences result from using such techniques, and what (if any) educational preparation professionals received for coping with these stresses.

Our findings to date show that all these professional groups (and perhaps others that you can think of from your own experience) often find it necessary to cope with their feelings of emotional stress by distancing themselves from the people with whom they work. Some professionals do it by avoiding interaction with the recipients of the services. College teachers who burn out shorten their office hours, come to them late, or find ways to avoid them altogether. We were told about a language professor who chose to spend his sabbatical leave on campus and who, in order to avoid being troubled by students, hung up a phony name tag on his door. Five years after his sabbatical, that name tag is still on the door.

In some mental hospitals, staff members never leave their glass cages to interact with patients; and in some counseling offices, the counselors take as much time as they can to get the clients' files. (As one counselor we interviewed said, "It gives me a little break in this crazy office.")

In some cases, this distancing occurs while the professional is in the process of interacting with the patient or client (e.g., "listening with only one ear"). In other cases, it functions as an anticipatory or retrospective device. For example, some professionals learn to turn off all thoughts and feelings about their patients or clients once these people have walked out the door. Within the medical professions, such objectivity and detachment are viewed as critical and essential to providing good health care for the individual. This philosophy of detached concern blends the notion of concern for the patient's well-being with the idea that some personal detachment from the stressful aspects of patient care is necessary in order to achieve that goal. However, in other professional situations, there is not even the recognition that such a psychological defense is operating. Insensitivity to the process of detached concern makes total burnout more likely.

DETACHMENT TECHNIQUES

Despite the differences in their functions, all the professional groups that we studied reported surprisingly similar changes in their perception of their clients or patients and in their feelings toward them. Furthermore, the specific verbal and nonverbal techniques used to achieve some degree of detachment were comparable. In different ways, each of these techniques helps the individual to see the other person as less human; to view the relationship with the other person in objective, analytic terms; and to reduce the intensity and scope of emotional arousal.

Semantics of Detachment

A change in the terms used to describe people is one way of making them appear more objectlike and less human. Some of these terms are derogatory (e.g., "they're all just animals"); others are more abstract, referring to large, undifferentiated units (e.g., "the poor"). Another form of objective language labels people in terms of the functional relationship that the professional has with them. For example, social-welfare workers often spoke of "my caseload" when referring to the people they deal with, and many a poverty lawyer talked about "my docket." Another way of divorcing one's feelings from a stressful event is to describe things as precisely, exactly, and scientifically as possible. This use of language is illustrated in several professions where the inclusion of jargon (e.g., "a positive GI series," "reaction formation") in patient interviews typically serves the purpose of distancing the person from a patient or client who is emotionally upsetting in some way. Furthermore, the patient who is only a "coronary" loses much of his or her complex humanness. In some mental hospitals, staff meetings function to distance the staff from the patients; the patient is not Joe Smith but a case of schizophrenia that can be described with objective, scientific terminology.

Intellectualization

A related technique is one in which the professional recasts the situation in more intellectual, less personal terms. By dealing with the abstract qualities of other people (rather than the more human ones), the professional can objectify the situation and react in a less emotional way. For example, in dealing with a mental patient who is being verbally abusive to her, a psychiatric nurse may stand back and look at the patient's problems more analytically ("he's exhibiting a particular delusional syndrome") to avoid becoming personally upset.

Situational Compartmentalization

In our interviews, professionals often made a sharp distinction between their job and their personal life. They did not discuss their family or personal affairs with their co-workers, and they often had explicit agreements with their spouses and friends not to "talk shop." Some prison personnel even refused to tell people what their job was; in response to questions, they would say only, "I'm a civil servant," or "I work for the state." By such devices, the emotional stress is confined to a smaller part of the professional's life. One social worker in child welfare stated that if he did not leave his work at the office, he could hardly stand to face his own children. Similarly, when he was at work, he could not think of his family because if he did, he would then repeatedly overidentify and overempathize with his clients and treat their misfortunes as his own, an emotional experience that he could not handle. Furthermore, some institutions have rules that promote compartmentalization by forbidding staff to socialize with their patients or clients outside of the job setting.

For many psychiatrists, one of the drawbacks of going into private practice is that the distinction between job and private life cannot be maintained because they are always on call. As one of our respondents put it, "Every time you hear your telephone ring at night, you think, 'Oh, no. I hope it's not a patient.' At times it seems like you can't ever get away from your patients' problems for some peace and quiet for yourself. When I worked at the hospital, there wasn't the same problem because when I went home for the day, another shift came on, and so I could relax in the evenings because I knew that if any of the patients needed help, there was someone else there to provide it."

Withdrawal

Another technique for reducing emotional arousal is to minimize one's physical involvement in the stressful interaction with other people. This is accomplished by professionals in a number of ways. One obvious approach that we observed was to distance oneself physically from the other person (by standing farther away, avoiding eye contact, or keeping one's hand on the doorknob). Withdrawal was also evidenced by professionals who communicated with patients or clients in more impersonal ways, such as superficial generalities and form letters. In some cases, the professionals simply spent less time with a patient or client, either by deliberately cutting down the length of the formal interview or therapy session or by spending more of their time talking and socializing with the other staff members. In more extreme forms of withdrawal, the professional did not interact at all with other people—either colleagues or clients. Taking longer lunch breaks, spending more time on paper work, leaving early on Friday, or simply being absent from work are all examples of such withdrawal.

Less obvious examples of withdrawal included poor performance (to assure that no one will refer problems to them); avoidance of tasks ("it's not my job"); and hiding behind rules. Rules protect professionals from direct *personal* interaction with the recipient of the services. For instance, a parole officer who was asked to be a co-signer of a loan for a parolee as an indication of her trust found, to her great relief, that there was a *rule* against it. That made it easier for her to say, "Look, it's nothing personal. It's the rule." We interviewed a first-year graduate student who was a teaching assistant in a class, a job that he started with great commitment, care, and enthusiasm. By the time the 313th student came to him with a plea that just one more point on the exam would make the grade higher, he had developed a cool and impersonal response: "Sorry, but I can't do it because those are the rules!"

Social Techniques

In attempting to deal with our own strong emotional feelings, we often turn to friends for help and emotional support. To the extent that such actions reduce psychological stress and discomfort, they can be used by professionals to develop detachment. One social technique used by the professionals in our samples was to solicit advice and comfort from other staff members after withdrawing from a difficult situation. Such social support not only helped to ease the stress and pain but also helped the individual to achieve intellectual distance from the situation. Getting together with fellow staff to "hash things out," "bitch a lot," "talk about new things to do," or "laugh about it" was the mainstay of the coping process for many of these professionals.

Social support also aided detachment because it promoted a perceived diffusion of responsibility. If several other staff people adopted a particular course of action, then an individual often had fewer qualms about doing the same thing. Another social technique was the use of humor. Being able to joke and laugh about a stressful event reduced the tension and anxiety that the professional felt. It also served to make the situation less serious, less frightening, and less overwhelming. The "sick" humor of the battlefield surgeons in *M*A*S*H* is a particularly apt example of this technique at work.

Many of these detachment techniques can be used by professionals either to reduce the amount of personal stress or to cope successfully with it while maintaining an appropriately effective level of concern and caring for the people they must work with. However, because some of these techniques preclude any continued caring, they can eventually lead to the total detachment and dehumanization that characterizes burnout. In these cases, the professionals' attempts at psychological self-protection come at the expense of the recipients.

REMEDIES FOR BURNOUT

When is burnout more likely to occur? Our research findings point to several factors in the professional's work situation that can have a major determining influence on whether he or she will burn out or will cope successfully with the personal stress of the job.

Ratio

The quality of the professional interaction is greatly affected by the number of people for whom the professional is providing care. As this number increases, the general result is a cognitive, sensory, and emotional overload for the professional. The importance of this ratio for understanding burnout is vividly demonstrated in the research on child-care workers that we recently conducted. We studied the staff members of eight different child-care centers that varied in their ratio of staff to children, ranging from 1:4 to 1:12. The staff from the high-ratio centers worked a greater number of hours on the floor in direct contact with the children and had fewer opportunities to take a break from work. They were more approving of supplementary techniques to make children quiet, such as compulsory naps and the use of tranquilizers for hyperactive children. They did not feel that they had much control over what they did on the job, and overall they liked their job much less than the staff from low-ratio centers did.

When the ratio is low, the individual staff member has fewer people to worry about and can give more attention to each of them. Furthermore, there is more time to focus on the positive, nonproblematic aspects of the person's life, rather than concentrating exclusively on his or her immediate problems or symptoms. For example, in psychiatric wards with low staff-patient ratios, the nurses were more likely to see their patients in both good times and bad. Even though there were occasions when their interactions were frustrating or upsetting, there were also times when the nurses could laugh and joke with the patients, play Ping-Pong or cards with them, talk with their families, and so on. In a sense, these nurses had a more complete, more *human* view of each patient.

Time-outs versus Escapes

Opportunities for withdrawing from a stressful situation are of critical importance for these professionals. However, the type of withdrawal that is available may spell the difference between burnout and successful coping. The most positive form of withdrawal that we observed is what we have called a *time-out*. Time-outs are not merely short breaks from work, such as rest periods or coffee breaks; rather, they are opportunities for the professional to choose to do some other, less stressful work while colleagues take over his or her responsibilities with clients or patients. For example, in one of the psychiatric wards that we studied, the nurses knew that if they were having a rough day, they could arrange to do paper work or dispense medications instead of working directly with the patients. The other nurses would cover for the one taking a time-out and would continue to provide adequate patient care. What makes this form of withdrawal positive is that good patient care can be maintained while the professional is getting a temporary emotional breather.

In contrast with sanctioned time-outs, most other types of withdrawals represented a negative form, an *escape*. In these cases, the professional's decision to take a break from work always came at the expense of clients or patients because there were no other staff people to take over the necessary duties. If the professional was not there to provide treatment or service, people in need simply had to wait, come back another day, or give up. These professionals were more likely to feel trapped by their total responsibility for their clients and could not temporarily withdraw without feeling some guilt. When guilt was heaped on the already heavy emotional burden they tenuously carried, the load often became too much to bear. Eventually, the guilt feelings would disappear for those professionals who began to lose both their sense of caring and concern. Thus, when institutional policies prevented the use of voluntary time-outs, we found lower staff morale, greater emotional stress, and the inevitable consequence of more dissatisfied citizens, frustrated at not getting the care they needed.

Amount of Direct Contact

The number of hours that a person works at a job is very likely to be related to that person's sense of fatigue, boredom, and stress. Consequently, one might suspect that longer working hours would result in a higher incidence of burnout. However, our data reveal a somewhat different pattern of behavior. Longer work hours are correlated with more stress and negative staff attitudes only when they involve continuous direct contact with patients or clients. Our study of child-care centers provides a good illustration of this point. Longer working hours were related to signs of burnout when those hours involved more work on the floor with children, but when the longer hours involved administrative, non-child-related work, burnout was less likely to occur. Basically, staff members who worked longer hours with children developed more negative attitudes toward those children. They were more approving of institutional restraints on the children's behavior, and when they were not at work, they wanted to get as far away as possible from children and child-related activities. In contrast with these people, the staff members who worked just as many hours but with a smaller proportion of time involving direct contact with children did not develop such negative attitudes toward the children; instead, they had positive feelings about the children and the child-care center in general. Perhaps the quality of caring, if not mercy, may have to be time-shared.

An additional variable is the severity or seriousness of the client's condition. It is generally believed that the most emotionally stressful wards in hospitals are those treating burned children and that the most difficult wards in mental hospitals are the closed psychiatric wards. Our recommendation, based on our study of many different samples, is for job rotations, lateral job changes, sharing of the difficult cases, and even the establishment of part-time positions.

Social-Professional Support System

The availability of formal or informal programs in which professionals can get together to discuss problems and get advice and support is another way of helping them to cope with job stress more successfully. Such a support system provides opportunities for analysis of the problems they face and their personal feelings about them, for humor, for comfort, and for social comparison. Burnout rates seem to be lower for those professionals who have access to such systems, especially if they are well developed and supported by the larger institution. Some of the psychiatrists reported being part of a social-professional support group when they were doing their residencies. After they entered private practice, they found that the lack of such a group was a serious, unanticipated loss to them, and they often made efforts (which were not always successful) to become part of such a support system again.

Analysis of Personal Feelings

Since the arousal of strong emotional reactions is a common feature of health and social-service occupations, efforts must be made to deal with them constructively and prevent them from being entirely extinguished, as they are in burnout. We were surprised to find that many of our subjects did not know that other people were experiencing the same changes in attitudes and emotions. Each thought that the personal reaction he or she was experiencing was unique (an illusion maintained by a tendency not to share feelings with fellow workers). They were unaware of the fact that the experience is a fairly common one, not an aberration. However, even though many of these professionals keep their feelings to themselves, it was painfully clear that they have a strong need to talk to someone about them.

Our findings show that burnout rates are lower for those professionals who actively express, analyze, and share their personal feelings with their colleagues. They not only consciously "get things off my chest" but also have an opportunity to get constructive feedback and to develop new perspectives and understanding of their relationships with their patients or clients. The process is greatly enhanced if an appropriate mechanism for it has been established by the relevant institution, such as an agency or hospital. This could include social-professional support groups, special staff meetings, or workshops. In general, we found that those professionals who are trained to treat psychological problems were better able to recognize and deal with their own feelings. For example, one clinical psychologist reported that she could not work well with passive, overly dependent female patients. By analyzing her personal reactions to this type of woman (which were related to childhood experiences and her own professional training), she was able to understand why she worked so poorly with this type of patient and could take appropriate steps to remedy the situation. In contrast, prison guards who experienced great fear were constrained from expressing or even acknowledging it by an institutional *macho* code, one consequence of which was the destructive channeling of this emotion into psychosomatic illnesses such as ulcers, muscle spasms, and migraines.

It is very important for the individual staff member to be aware of objective work stresses, recognize danger signs that indicate impending burnout, acknowledge vulnerability, put reasonable limits on the amount of work, and set up realistic, achievable goals. It is also important for the staff member, in spite of his or her idealistic, self-sacrificing education, to be able to set aside some time and resources for him- or herself.

Training in Interpersonal Skills

It seems clear from the research findings to date that health and social-service professionals need to have special training and preparation for working closely with other people. Although they are well trained in certain healing and technical service skills, they are often not well equipped to handle repeated intense emotional interaction with people. As one poverty lawyer put it, "I was trained in law but not in how to work with people who would be my clients. And it was that difficulty in dealing with people and their personal problems, hour after hour, that became the problem for me, not the legal matters per se."

From the point of view of the person seeking help, these professionals may need extra "people learning" to go along with their "book learning." Although many of our subjects stated that they wished they had had prior preparation in interpersonal skills, some reported that there was no time for it in their already packed curriculum. Others felt that such preparation was just "icing on the cake," that it was not an essential part of professional training. The view of several physicians was that the competent practice of medicine was all that they needed to know to be successful and that any psychological training simply amounted to knowing how to make "small talk" with their patients. Such a skill was viewed as pleasant but basically unimportant. In our opinion, such a viewpoint is sadly in error because it trivializes an essential aspect of the doctor-patient relationship and fails to recognize that both the doctor and the patient are human beings whose personal attitudes and emotions can affect not only the delivery of health care but also how—and even whether—it is accepted.

CONCLUSION

Is burnout inevitable? Some professionals seem to think so and assume that it is only a matter of time before they will burn out and have to change jobs. The period of time most often cited in one psychiatric ward was one and a half years; some poverty lawyers spoke of a reduction of what was commonly a four-year stint down to a quick and dirty two years, at most. We think that burnout is *not* inevitable and that steps can be taken to reduce and modify its occurrence. It is our belief that many of the causes of burnout are located not in permanent, fixed traits of the people involved, but in specifiable social and situational factors that can be influenced in ways suggested by our research.

However, regardless of the actual causes of burnout, its effects are dramatically clear in terms of social and personal costs. To the extent that people feel compelled to escape from their jobs or even to leave their professions entirely, it represents a tremendous waste of their training and talent. More importantly, burnout has detrimental psychological effects for both the professionals and their patients or clients. The professionals' perceptions of, and feelings about, people in general often show a cynical, negative shift. They begin to think of their patients or clients in more derogatory terms and to believe that they somehow deserve their problems. In telling us about their ideal jobs, professionals often described work situations in which they fantasized few (if any) people. For example, one social worker said that he loved art and would like most of all to work by himself in a museum, cataloging paintings in the back storage room.

A final detrimental consequence of burnout is the effect it can have on the professionals' relationships with family and friends. If stress cannot be resolved on the job, it is often unknowingly resurrected at home, which can lead to increased personal and family conflict.

Clearly, health and social-service professionals pay a high price for working in their chosen careers. But what about the costs to *us*, their patients and clients? It is equally clear that we, too, suffer from their burnout. We wait longer to receive less attention and less concern. The quality of the care we receive becomes poorer, and the experience of obtaining it becomes dehumanizing.

As this analysis has attempted to point out, burnout is not a function of bad people who are unfeeling and brutal. Rather, it is a function of bad situations in which once idealistic people must operate. It is our hope that implementation of some of the ideas proposed here can be a start toward changing these health and welfare situations so that they promote, rather than destroy, human values.

ON BEING SANE IN INSANE PLACES

DAVID L. ROSENHAN

Mental illness is commonly thought to be a characteristic that originates within the individual. That is, people considered crazy or mad are believed to have character flaws or personality problems. According to popular opinion, such people distinguish themselves by their aberrant, inappropriate, or dysfunctional behavior; whereas people who are sane and well adjusted behave in normal ways that would never be judged otherwise.

These are precisely the notions that Rosenhan challenges in his provocative article on mental hospitals, "On Being Sane in Insane Places." He argues that labeling someone "mentally ill" is often a response to the environmental setting, not to the person's behavior per se. Rosenhan believes that a sane person put in an insane place is likely to be viewed by others as being mentally disturbed.

Rosenhan's study generated tremendous controversy, some of which is reflected in the "Letters" column of the scientific journal in which the article appeared. These critiques of the research, along with Rosenhan's response to them, will give you an inside look at the process of scientific argument and debate.

If sanity and insanity exist, how shall we know them?

The question is neither capricious nor itself insane. However much we may be personally convinced that we can tell the normal from the abnormal, the evidence is simply not compelling. It is commonplace, for example, to read about murder trials wherein eminent psychiatrists for the defense are contradicted by equally eminent psychiatrists for the prosecution on the matter of the defendant's sanity. More generally, there are a great deal of conflicting data on the reliability, utility, and meaning of such terms as "sanity," "insanity," "mental illness," and "schizophrenia." Finally, as early as 1934, Benedict suggested that normality and abnormality are not universal (1). What is viewed as normal in one culture may be seen as quite aberrant in another. Thus, notions of normality and abnormality may not be quite as accurate as people believe they are.

To raise questions regarding normality and abnormality is in no way to question the fact that some behaviors are deviant or odd. Murder is deviant. So, too, are hallucinations. Nor does raising such questions deny the existence of the personal anguish that is often associated with "mental illness." Anxiety and depression exist. Psychological suffering exists. But normality and abnormality, sanity and insanity, and the diagnoses that flow from them may be less substantive than many believe them to be.

At its heart, the question of whether the sane can be distinguished from the insane (and whether degrees of insanity can be distinguished from each other) is a simple matter: do the salient characteristics that lead to diagnoses reside in the patients themselves or in the environments and contexts in which observers find them? From Bleuler, through Kretchmer, through the formulators of the recently revised *Diagnostic and Statistical Manual* of the American Psychiatric Association, the belief has been strong that patients present symptoms, that those symptoms can be categorized, and, implicitly, that the sane are distinguishable from the insane. More recently, however, this belief has been questioned. Based in part on theoretical and anthropological considerations, but also on philosophical, legal, and therapeutic ones, the view has grown that psychological categorization of mental illness is useless at best and downright harmful, misleading, and pejorative at worst. Psychiatric diagnoses, in this view, are in the minds of the observers and are not valid summaries of characteristics displayed by the observed.

Gains can be made in deciding which of these is more nearly accurate by getting normal people (that is, people who do not have, and have never suffered, symptoms of serious psychiatric disorders) admitted to psychiatric hospitals and then determining whether they were discovered to be sane and, if so, how. If the sanity of such pseudopatients were always detected, there would be prima facie evidence that a sane individual can be distinguished from the insane context in which he is found. Normality (and presumably abnormality) is distinct enough that it can be recognized wherever it occurs, for it is carried within the person. If, on the other hand, the sanity of the pseudopatients were never discovered, serious difficulties would arise for those who support traditional modes of psychiatric diagnosis. Given that the hospital staff was not incompetent, that the pseudopatient had been behaving as sanely as he had been outside of the hospital, and that it had never been previously suggested that he belonged in a psychiatric hospital, such an unlikely outcome would support the view that psychiatric diagnosis betrays little about the patient but much about the environment in which an observer finds him.

This article describes such an experiment. Eight sane people gained secret admission to 12 different hospitals. Their diagnostic experiences constitute the data of the first part of this article; the remainder is devoted to a description of their experiences in psychiatric institutions. Too few psychiatrists and psychologists, even those who have worked in such hospitals, know what the experience is like. They rarely talk about it with former patients, perhaps because they distrust information coming from the previously insane. Those who have worked in psychiatric hospitals are likely to have adapted so thoroughly to the settings that they are insensitive to the impact of that experience. And while there have been occasional reports of researchers who submitted themselves to psychiatric hospitalization, these researchers have commonly remained in the hospitals for short periods of time, often with the knowledge of the hospital staff. It is difficult to know the extent to which they were treated like patients or like research colleagues. Nevertheless, their reports about the inside of the psychiatric hospital have been valuable. This article extends those efforts.

From *Science*, Vol. 179, pp. 250–258 (January 19, 1973). Copyright © 1973 by the American Association for the Advancement of Science. Reprinted by permission.

PSEUDOPATIENTS AND THEIR SETTINGS

The eight pseudopatients were a varied group. One was a psychology graduate student in his 20's. The remaining seven were older and "established." Among them were three psychologists, a pediatrician, a psychiatrist, a painter, and a housewife. Three pseudopatients were women, five were men. All of them employed pseudonyms, lest their alleged diagnoses embarrass them later. Those who were in mental health professions alleged another occupation in order to avoid the special attentions that might be accorded by staff, as a matter of courtesy or caution, to ailing colleagues (4). With the exception of myself (I was the first pseudopatient and my presence was known to the hospital administrator and chief psychologist and, so far as I can tell, to them alone), the presence of pseudopatients and the nature of the research program were not known to the hospital staffs (5).

The settings were similarly varied. In order to generalize the findings, admission into a variety of hospitals was sought. The 12 hospitals in the sample were located in five different states on the East and West coasts. Some were old and shabby, some were quite new. Some were research-oriented, others not. Some had good staff-patient ratios, others were quite understaffed. Only one was a strictly private hospital. All of the others were supported by state or federal funds, or in one instance, by university funds.

After calling the hospital for an appointment, the pseudopatient arrived at the admissions office complaining that he had been hearing voices. Asked what the voices said, he replied that they were often unclear, but as far as he could tell they said "empty," "hollow," and "thud." The voices were unfamiliar and were of the same sex as the pseudopatient. The choice of these symptoms was occasioned by their apparent similarity to existential symptoms. Such symptoms are alleged to arise from painful concerns about the perceived meaninglessness of one's life. It is as if the hallucinating person were saying, "My life is empty and hollow." The choice of these symptoms was also determined by the *absence* of a single report of existential psychoses in the literature.

Beyond alleging the symptoms and falsifying name, vocation, and employment, no further alterations of person, history, or circumstances were made. The significant events of the pseudopatient's life history were presented as they had actually occurred. Relationships with parents and siblings, with spouse and children, with people at work and in school, consistent with the aforementioned exceptions, were described as they were or had been. Frustrations and upsets were described along with joys and satisfactions. These facts are important to remember. If anything, they strongly biased the subsequent results in favor of detecting sanity, since none of their histories or current behaviors were seriously pathological in any way.

Immediately upon admission to the psychiatric ward, the pseudopatient ceased simulating *any* symptoms of abnormality. In some cases, there was a brief period of mild nervousness and anxiety, since none of the pseudopatients really believed that they would be admitted so easily. Indeed, their shared fear was that they would be immediately exposed as frauds and greatly embarrassed. Moreover, many of them had never visited a psychiatric ward; even those who had, nevertheless had some genuine fears about what might happen to them. Their nervousness, then, was quite appropriate to the novelty of the hospital setting, and it abated rapidly.

Apart from that short-lived nervousness, the pseudopatient behaved on the ward as he "normally" behaved. The pseudopatient spoke to patients and staff as he might ordinarily. Because there is uncommonly little to do on a psychiatric ward, he attempted to engage others in conversation. When asked by staff how he was feeling, he indicated that he was fine, that he no longer experienced symptoms. He responded to instructions from attendants, to calls for medication (which was not swallowed), and to dining-hall instructions. Beyond such activities as were available to him on the admissions ward, he spent his time writing down his observations about the ward, its patients, and the staff. Initially these notes were written "secretly," but as it soon became clear that no one much cared, they were subsequently written on standard tablets of paper in such public places as the dayroom. No secret was made of these activities.

The pseudopatient, very much as a true psychiatric patient, entered a hospital with no foreknowledge of when he would be discharged. Each was told that he would have to get out by his own devices, essentially by convincing the staff that he was sane. The psychological stresses associated with hospitalization were considerable, and all but one of the pseudopatients desired to be discharged almost immediately after being admitted. They were, therefore, motivated not only to behave sanely, but to be paragons of cooperation. That their behavior was in no way disruptive is confirmed by nursing reports, which have been obtained on most of the patients. These reports uniformly indicate that the patients were "friendly," "cooperative," and "exhibited no abnormal indications."

THE NORMAL ARE NOT DETECTABLY SANE

Despite their public "show" of sanity, the pseudopatients were never detected. Admitted, except in one case, with a diagnosis of schizophrenia, each was discharged with a diagnosis of schizophrenia "in remission." The label "in remission" should in no way be dismissed as a formality, for at no time during any hospitalization had any question been raised about any pseudopatient's simulation. Nor are there any indications in the hospital records that the pseudopatient's status was suspect. Rather, the evidence is strong that, once labeled schizophrenic, the pseudopatient was stuck with that label. If the pseudopatient was to be discharged, he must naturally be "in remission"; but he was not sane, nor, in the institution's view, had he ever been sane.

The uniform failure to recognize sanity cannot be attributed to the quality of the hospitals, for, although there were considerable variations among them, several are considered excellent. Nor can it be alleged that there was simply not enough time to observe the pseudopatients. Length of hospitalization ranged from 7 to 52 days, with an average of 19 days. The pseudopatients were not, in fact, carefully observed, but this failure clearly speaks more to traditions within psychiatric hospitals than to lack of opportunity.

Finally, it cannot be said that the failure to recognize the pseudopatients' sanity was due to the fact that they were not behaving sanely. While there was clearly some tension present in all of them, their daily visitors could detect no serious behavioral consequences—nor, indeed, could other patients. It was quite common for the patients to "detect" the pseudopatients' sanity. During the first three hospitalizations, when accurate counts were kept, 35 of a total of 118 patients on the admissions ward voiced their suspicions, some vigorously. "You're not crazy. You're a journalist, or a professor [referring to the continual note-taking]. You're checking up on the hospital." While most of the patients were reassured by the pseudopatient's insistence that he had been sick before he came in but was fine now, some continued to believe that the pseudopatient was sane throughout his hospitalization (6). The fact that the patients often recognized normality when staff did not raises important questions.

Failure to detect sanity during the course of hospitalization may be due to the fact that physicians operate with a strong bias toward what statisticians call the type 2 error. This is to say that physicians are more inclined to call a healthy person sick (a false positive, type 2) than a sick person healthy (a false negative, type 1). The reasons for this are not hard to find: it is clearly more dangerous to misdiagnose illness than health. Better to err on the side of caution, to suspect illness even among the healthy.

But what holds for medicine does not hold equally well for psychiatry. Medical illnesses, while unfortunate, are not commonly pejorative. Psychiatric diagnoses, on the contrary, carry with them personal, legal, and social stigmas. It was therefore important to see whether the tendency toward diagnosing the sane insane could be reversed. The following experiment was arranged at a research and teaching hospital whose staff had heard these findings but doubted that such an error could occur in their hospital. The staff was informed that at some time during the following 3 months, one or more pseudopatients would attempt to be admitted into the psychiatric hospital. Each staff member was asked to rate each patient who presented himself at admissions or on the ward according to the likelihood that the patient was a pseudopatient. A 10-point scale was used, with a 1 and 2 reflecting high confidence that the patient was a pseudopatient.

Judgments were obtained on 193 patients who were admitted for psychiatric treatment. All staff who had had sustained contact with or primary responsibility for the patient—attendants, nurses, psychiatrists, physicians, and psychologists—were asked to make judgments. Forty-one patients were alleged, with high confidence, to be pseudopatients by at least one member of the staff. Twenty-three were considered suspect by at least one psychiatrist. Nineteen were suspected by one psychiatrist *and* one other staff member. Actually, no genuine pseudopatient (at least from my group) presented himself during this period.

The experiment is instructive. It indicates that the tendency to designate sane people as insane can be reversed when the stakes (in this case, prestige and diagnostic acumen) are high. But what can be said of the 19 people who were suspected of being "sane" by one psychiatrist and another staff member? Were these people truly "sane," or was it rather the case that in the course of avoiding the type 2 error the staff tended to make more errors of the first sort—calling the crazy "sane"? There is no way of knowing. But one thing is certain: any diagnostic process that lends itself so readily to massive errors of this sort cannot be a very reliable one.

THE STICKINESS OF PSYCHODIAGNOSTIC LABELS

Beyond the tendency to call the healthy sick—a tendency that accounts better for diagnostic behavior on admission than it does for such behavior after a lengthy period of exposure—the data speak to the massive role of labeling in psychiatric assessment. Having once been labeled schizophrenic, there is nothing the pseudopatient can do to overcome the tag. The tag profoundly colors others' perceptions of him and his behavior.

From one viewpoint, these data are hardly surprising, for it has long been known that elements are given meaning by the context in which they occur. Gestalt psychology made this point vigorously, and Asch (7) demonstrated that there are "central" personality traits (such as "warm" versus "cold") which are so powerful that they markedly color the meaning of other information in forming an impression of a given personality. "Insane," "schizophrenic," "manic-depressive," and "crazy" are probably among the most powerful of such central traits. Once a person is designated abnormal, all of his other behaviors and characteristics are colored by that label. Indeed, that label is so powerful that many of the pseudopatients' normal behaviors were overlooked entirely or profoundly misinterpreted. Some examples may clarify this issue.

Earlier I indicated that there were no changes in the pseudopatient's personal history and current status beyond those of name, employment, and, where necessary, vocation. Otherwise, a veridical description of personal history and circumstances was offered. Those circumstances were not psychotic. How were they made consonant with the diagnosis of psychosis? Or were those diagnoses modified in such a way as to bring them into accord with the circumstances of the pseudopatient's life, as described by him?

As far as I can determine, diagnoses were in no way affected by the relative health of the circumstances of a pseudopatient's life. Rather, the reverse occurred: the perception of his circumstances was shaped entirely by the diagnosis. A clear example of such translation is found in the case of a pseudopatient who had had a close relationship with his mother but was rather remote from his father during his early childhood. During adolescence and beyond, however, his father became a close friend, while his relationship with his mother cooled. His present relationship with his wife was characteristically close and warm. Apart from occasional angry exchanges, friction was minimal. The children had rarely been spanked. Surely there is nothing especially pathological about such a history. Indeed, many readers may see a similar pattern in their own experiences, with no markedly deleterious consequences. Observe, however, how such a history was translated in the psychopathological context, this from the case summary prepared after the patient was discharged.

> This white 39-year-old male . . . manifests a long history of considerable ambivalence in close relationships, which begins in early childhood. A warm relationship with his mother cools during his adolescence. A distant relationship to his father is described as becoming very intense. Affective stability is absent. His attempts to control emotionality with his wife and children are punctuated by angry outbursts and, in the case of the children, spankings. And while he says that he has several good friends, one senses considerable ambivalence embedded in those relationships also. . . .

The facts of the case were unintentionally distorted by the staff to achieve consistency with a popular theory of the dynamics of a schizophrenic reaction. Nothing of an ambivalent nature had been described in relations with parents, spouse, or friends. To the extent that ambivalence could be inferred, it was probably not greater than is found in all human relationships. It is true the pseudopatient's relationships with his parents changed over time, but in the ordinary context that would hardly be remarkable—indeed, it might very well be expected. Clearly, the meaning ascribed to his verbalizations (that is, ambivalence, affective instability) was determined by the diagnosis: schizophrenia. An entirely different meaning would have been ascribed if it were known that the man was "normal."

All pseudopatients took extensive notes publicly. Under ordinary circumstances, such behavior would have raised questions in the minds of observers, as, in fact, it did among patients. Indeed, it seemed so certain that the notes would elicit suspicion that elaborate precautions were taken to remove them from the ward each day. But the precautions proved needless. The closest any staff member came to questioning these notes occurred when one pseudopatient asked his physician what kind of medication he was receiving and began to write down the response. "You needn't write it," he was told gently. "If you have trouble remembering, just ask me again."

If no questions were asked of the pseudopatients, how was their writing interpreted? Nursing records for three patients indicate that the writing was seen as an aspect of their pathological behavior. "Patient engages in writing behavior" was the daily nursing comment on one of the pseudopatients who was never questioned about his writing. Given that the patient is in the hospital, he must be psychologically disturbed. And given that he is disturbed, continuous writing must be a behavioral manifestation of that disturbance, perhaps a subset of the compulsive behaviors that are sometimes correlated with schizophrenia.

One tacit characteristic of psychiatric diagnosis is that it locates the sources of aberration within the individual and only rarely within the complex of stimuli that surrounds him. Consequently, behaviors that are stimulated by the environment are commonly misattributed to the patient's disorder. For example, one kindly nurse found a pseudopatient pacing the long hospital corridors. "Nervous, Mr. X?" she asked. "No, bored," he said.

The notes kept by pseudopatients are full of patient behaviors that were misinterpreted by well-intentioned staff. Often enough, a patient would go "berserk" because he had, wittingly or unwittingly, been mistreated by, say, an attendant. A nurse coming upon the scene would rarely inquire even cursorily into the environmental stimuli of the patient's behavior. Rather, she assumed that his upset derived from his pathology, not from his present interactions with other staff members. Occasionally, the staff might assume that the patient's family (especially when they had recently visited) or other patients had stimulated the outburst. But never were the staff found to assume that one of themselves or the structure of the hospital had anything to do with a patient's behavior. One psychiatrist pointed to a group of patients who were sitting outside the cafeteria entrance half an hour before lunchtime. To a group of young residents he indicated that such behavior was characteristic of the oral-acquisitive nature of the syndrome. It seemed not to occur to him that there were very few things to anticipate in a psychiatric hospital besides eating.

A psychiatric label has a life and an influence of its own. Once the impression has been formed that the patient is schizophrenic, the expectation is that he will continue to be schizophrenic. When a sufficient amount of time has passed, during which the patient has done nothing bizarre, he is considered to be in remission and available for discharge. But the label endures beyond discharge, with the unconfirmed expectation that he will behave as a schizophrenic again. Such labels, conferred by mental health professionals, are as influential on the patient as they are on his relatives and friends, and it should not surprise anyone that the diagnosis acts on all of them as a self-fulfilling prophecy. Eventually, the patient himself accepts the diagnosis, with all of its surplus meanings and expectations, and behaves accordingly (3).

The inferences to be made from these matters are quite simple. Much as Zigler and Phillips have demonstrated that there is enormous overlap in the symptoms presented by patients who have been variously diagnosed (8), so there is enormous overlap in the behaviors of the sane and the insane. The sane are not "sane" all of the time. We lose our tempers "for no good reason." We are occasionally depressed or anxious, again for no good reason. And we may find it difficult to get along with one or another person—again for no reason that we can specify. Similarly, the insane are not always insane. Indeed, it was the impression of the pseudopatients while living with them that they were sane for long periods of time—that the bizarre behaviors upon which their diagnoses were allegedly predicated constituted only a small fraction of their total behavior. If it makes no sense to label ourselves permanently depressed on the basis of an occasional depression, then it takes better evidence than is presently available to label all patients insane or schizophrenic on the basis of bizarre behaviors or cognitions. It seems more useful, as Mischel (9) has pointed out, to limit our discussions to *behaviors*, the stimuli that provoke them, and their correlates.

It is not known why powerful impressions of personality traits, such as "crazy" or "insane," arise. Conceivably, when the origins of and stimuli that give rise to a behavior are remote or unknown, or when the behavior strikes us as immutable, trait labels regarding the *behaver* arise. When, on the other hand, the origins and stimuli are known and available, discourse is limited to the behavior itself. Thus, I may hallucinate because I am sleeping, or I may hallucinate because I have ingested a peculiar drug. These are termed sleep-induced hallucinations, or dreams, and drug-induced hallucinations, respectively. But when the stimuli to my hallucinations are unknown, that is called craziness, or schizophrenia—as if that inference were somehow as illuminating as the others.

THE EXPERIENCE OF PSYCHIATRIC HOSPITALIZATION

The term "mental illness" is of recent origin. It was coined by people who were humane in their inclinations and who wanted very much to raise the station of (and the public's sympathies toward) the psychologically disturbed from that of witches and "crazies" to one that was akin to the physically ill. And they were at least partially successful, for the treatment of the mentally ill *has* improved considerably over the years. But while treatment has improved, it is doubtful that people really regard the mentally ill in the same way that they view the physically ill. A broken leg is something one recovers from, but mental illness allegedly endures forever (*10*). A broken leg does not threaten the observer, but a crazy schizophrenic? There is by now a host of evidence that attitudes toward the mentally ill are characterized by fear, hostility, aloofness, suspicion, and dread. The mentally ill are society's lepers.

That such attitudes infect the general population is perhaps not surprising, only upsetting. But that they affect the professionals—attendants, nurses, physicians, psychologists, and social workers—who treat and deal with the mentally ill is more disconcerting, both because such attitudes are self-evidently pernicious and because they are unwitting. Most mental health professionals would insist that they are sympathetic toward the mentally ill, that they are neither avoidant nor hostile. But it is more likely that an exquisite ambivalence characterizes their relations with psychiatric patients, such that their avowed impulses are only part of their entire attitude. Negative attitudes are there too and can easily be detected. Such attitudes should not surprise us. They are the natural offspring of the labels patients wear and the places in which they are found.

Consider the structure of the typical psychiatric hospital. Staff and patients are strictly segregated. Staff have their own living space, including their dining facilities, bathrooms, and assembly places. The glassed quarters that contain the professional staff, which the pseudopatients came to call "the cage," sit out on every dayroom. The staff emerge primarily for caretaking purposes—to give medication, to conduct a therapy or group meeting, to instruct or reprimand a patient. Otherwise, staff keep to themselves, almost as if the disorder that afflicts their charges is somehow catching.

So much is patient-staff segregation the rule that, for four public hospitals in which an attempt was made to measure the degree to which staff and patients mingle, it was necessary to use "time out of the staff cage" as the operational measure. While it was not the case that all time spent out of the cage was spent mingling with patients (attendants, for example, would occasionally emerge to watch television in the dayroom), it was the only way in which one could gather reliable data on time for measuring.

The average amount of time spent by attendants outside of the cage was 11.3 percent (range, 3 to 52 percent). This figure does not represent only time spent mingling with patients, but also includes time spent on such chores as folding laundry, supervising patients while they shave, directing ward clean-up, and sending patients to off-ward activities. It was the relatively rare attendant who spent time talking with patients or playing games with them. It proved impossible to obtain a "percent mingling time" for nurses, since the amount of time they spent out of the cage was too brief. Rather, we counted instances of emergence from the cage. On the average, daytime nurses emerged from the cage 11.5 times per shift, including instances when they left the ward entirely (range, 4 to 39 times). Late afternoon and night nurses were even less available, emerging on the average 9.4 times per shift (range, 4 to 41 times). Data on early morning nurses, who arrived usually after midnight and departed at 8 A.M., are not available because patients were asleep during most of this period.

Physicians, especially psychiatrists, were even less available. They were rarely seen on the wards. Quite commonly, they would be seen only when they arrived and departed, with the remaining time being spent in their offices or in the cage. On the average, physicians emerged on the ward 6.7 times per day (range, 1 to 17 times). It proved difficult to make an accurate estimate in this regard, since physicians often maintained hours that allowed them to come and go at different times.

The hierarchical organization of the psychiatric hospital has been commented on before, . . . but the latent meaning of that kind of organization is worth noting again. Those with the most power have least to do with patients, and those with the least power are most involved with them. Recall, however, that the acquisition of role-appropriate behaviors occurs mainly through the observation of others, with the most powerful having the most influence. Consequently, it is understandable that attendants not only spend more time with patients than do any other members of the staff—that is required by their station in the hierarchy—but also, insofar as they learn from their superiors' behavior, spend as little time with patients as they can. Attendants are seen mainly in the cage, which is where the models, the action, and the power are.

I turn now to a different set of studies, these dealing with staff response to patient-initiated contact. It has long been known that the amount of time a person spends with you can be an index of your significance to him. If he initiates and maintains eye contact, there is reason to believe that he is considering your requests and needs. If he pauses to chat or actually stops and talks, there is added reason to infer that he is individuating you. In four hospitals, the pseudopatient approached the staff member with a request which took the following form: "Pardon me, Mr. [or Dr. or Mrs.] X, could you tell me when I will be eligible for grounds privileges?" (or ". . . when I will be presented at the staff meeting?" or ". . . when I am likely to be discharged?"). While the content of the question varied according to the appropriateness of the target and the pseudopatient's (apparent) current needs, the form was always a courteous and relevant request for information. Care was taken never to approach a particular member of the staff more than once a day, lest the staff member become suspicious or irritated. In examining these data, remember that the behavior of the pseudopatients was neither bizarre nor disruptive. One could indeed engage in good conversation with them.

. . . Minor differences between these four institutions were overwhelmed by the degree to which staff avoided continuing contacts that patients had initiated. By far, their most common response consisted of either a brief response to the question, offered while they were "on the move" and with head averted, or no response at all.

The encounter frequently took the following bizarre form: (pseudopatient) "Pardon me, Dr. X. Could you tell me when I am eligible for grounds privileges?" (physician) "Good morning, Dave. How are you today?" (Moves off without waiting for a response.)

. . .

POWERLESSNESS AND DEPERSONALIZATION

Eye contact and verbal contact reflect concern and individuation; their absence, avoidance and depersonalization. The data I have presented do not do justice to the rich daily encounters that grew up around matters of depersonalization and avoidance. I have records of patients who were beaten by staff for the sin of having initiated verbal contact. During my own experience, for example, one patient was beaten in the presence of other patients for having approached an attendant and told him, "I like you." Occasionally, punishment meted out to patients for misdemeanors seemed so excessive that it could not be justified by the most radical interpretations of psychiatric canon. Nevertheless, they appeared to go unquestioned. Tempers were often short. A patient who had not heard a call for medication would be roundly excoriated, and the morning attendants would often wake patients with, "Come on, you m—— f——s, out of bed!"

Neither anecdotal nor "hard" data can convey the overwhelming sense of powerlessness which invades the individual as he is continually exposed to the depersonalization of the psychiatric hospital. It hardly matters *which* psychiatric hospital—the excellent public ones and the very plush private hospital were better than the rural and shabby ones in this regard, but, again, the features that psychiatric hospitals had in common overwhelmed by far their apparent differences.

Powerlessness was evident everywhere. The patient is deprived of many of his legal rights by dint of his psychiatric commitment. He is shorn of credibility by virtue of his psychiatric label. His freedom of movement is restricted. He cannot initiate contact with the staff, but may only respond to such overtures as they make. Personal privacy is minimal. Patient quarters and possessions can be entered and examined by any staff member, for whatever reason. His personal history and anguish is available to any staff member (often including the "grey lady" and "candy striper" volunteer) who chooses to read his folder, regardless of their therapeutic relationship to him. His personal hygiene and waste evacuation are often monitored. The water closets may have no doors.

At times, depersonalization reached such proportions that pseudopatients had the sense that they were invisible, or at least unworthy of account. Upon being admitted, I and other pseudopatients took the initial physical examinations in a semipublic room, where staff members went about their own business as if we were not there.

. . .

THE SOURCES OF DEPERSONALIZATION

What are the origins of depersonalization? I have already mentioned two. First are attitudes held by all of us toward the mentally ill—including those who treat them—attitudes characterized by fear, distrust, and horrible expectations on the one hand, and benevolent intentions on the other. Our ambivalence leads, in this instance as in others, to avoidance.

Second, and not entirely separate, the hierarchical structure of the psychiatric hospital facilitates depersonalization. Those who are at the top have least to do with patients, and their behavior inspires the rest of the staff. Average daily contact with psychiatrists, psychologists, residents, and physicians combined ranged from 3.9 to 25.1 minutes, with an overall mean of 6.8 (six pseudopatients over a total of 129 days of hospitalization). Included in this average are time spent in the admissions interview, ward meetings in the presence of a senior staff member, group and individual psychotherapy contacts, case presentation conferences, and discharge meetings. Clearly, patients do not spend much time in interpersonal contact with doctoral staff. And doctoral staff serve as models for nurses and attendants.

There are probably other sources. Psychiatric installations are presently in serious financial straits. Staff shortages are pervasive, staff time at a premium. Something has to give, and that something is patient contact. Yet, while financial stresses are realities, too much can be made of them. I have the impression that the psychological forces that result in depersonalization are much stronger than the fiscal ones and that the addition of more staff would not correspondingly improve patient care in this regard. The incidence of staff meetings and the enormous amount of record-keeping on patients, for example, have not been as substantially reduced as has patient contact. Priorities exist, even during hard times. Patient contact is not a significant priority in the traditional psychiatric hospital, and fiscal pressures do not account for this. Avoidance and depersonalization may.

Heavy reliance upon psychotropic medication tacitly contributes to depersonalization by convincing staff that treatment is indeed being conducted and that further patient contact may not be necessary. Even here, however, caution needs to be exercised in understanding the role of psychotropic drugs. If patients were powerful rather than powerless, if they were viewed as interesting individuals rather than diagnostic entities, if they were socially significant rather than social lepers, if their anguish truly and wholly compelled our sympathies and concerns, would we not *seek* contact with them, despite the availability of medications? Perhaps for the pleasure of it all?

THE CONSEQUENCES OF LABELING AND DEPERSONALIZATION

Whenever the ratio of what is known to what needs to be known approaches zero, we tend to invent "knowledge" and assume that we understand more than we actually do. We seem unable to acknowledge that we simply don't know. The needs for diagnosis and remediation of behavioral and emotional problems are enormous. But rather than acknowledge that we are just embarking on understanding, we continue to label patients "schizophrenic," "manic-depressive," and "insane," as if in those words we had captured the essence of understanding. The facts of the matter are that we have known for a long time that diagnoses are often not useful or reliable, but we have nevertheless continued to use them. We now know that we cannot distinguish insanity from sanity. It is depressing to consider how that information will be used.

Not merely depressing, but frightening. How many people, one wonders, are sane but not recognized as such in our psychiatric institutions? How many have been needlessly stripped of their privileges of citizenship, from the right to vote and drive to that of handling their own accounts? How many have feigned insanity in order to avoid the criminal consequences of their behavior, and, conversely, how many would rather stand trial than live interminably in a psychiatric hospital—but are wrongly thought to be mentally ill? How many have been stigmatized by well-intentioned, but nevertheless erroneous, diagnoses? On the last point, recall again that a "type 2 error" in psychiatric diagnosis does not have the same consequences it does in medical diagnosis. A diagnosis of cancer that has been found to be in error is cause for celebration. But psychiatric diagnoses are rarely found to be in error. The label sticks, a mark of inadequacy forever.

Finally, how many patients might be "sane" outside the psychiatric hospital but seem insane in it—not because craziness resides in them, as it were, but because they are responding to a bizarre setting, one that may be unique to institutions which harbor nether people? Goffman (2) calls the process of socialization to such institutions "mortification"—an apt metaphor that includes the processes of depersonalization that have been described here. And while it is impossible to know whether the pseudopatients' responses to these processes are characteristic of all inmates—they were, after all, not real patients—it is difficult to believe that these processes of socialization to a psychiatric hospital provide useful attitudes or habits of response for living in the "real world."

SUMMARY AND CONCLUSIONS

It is clear that we cannot distinguish the sane from the insane in psychiatric hospitals. The hospital itself imposes a special environment in which the meanings of behavior can easily be misunderstood. The consequences to patients hospitalized in such an environment—the powerlessness, depersonalization, segregation, mortification, and self-labeling—seem undoubtedly countertherapeutic.

I do not, even now, understand this problem well enough to perceive solutions. But two matters seem to have some promise. The first concerns the proliferation of community mental health facilities, of crisis intervention centers, of the human potential movement, and of behavior therapies that, for all of their own problems, tend to avoid psychiatric labels, to focus on specific problems and behaviors, and to retain the individual in a relatively nonpejorative environment. Clearly, to the extent that we refrain from sending the distressed to insane places, our impressions of them are less likely to be distorted. (The risk of distorted perceptions, it seems to me, is always present, since we are much more sensitive to an individual's behaviors and verbalizations than we are to the subtle contextual stimuli that often promote them. At issue here is a matter of magnitude. And, as I have shown, the magnitude of distortion is exceedingly high in the extreme context that is a psychiatric hospital.)

The second matter that might prove promising speaks to the need to increase the sensitivity of mental health workers and researchers to the *Catch 22* position of psychiatric patients. Simply reading materials in this area will be of help to some such workers and researchers. For others, directly experiencing the impact of psychiatric hospitalization will be of enormous use. Clearly, further research into the social psychology of such total institutions will both facilitate treatment and deepen understanding.

I and the other pseudopatients in the psychiatric setting had distinctly negative reactions. We do not pretend to describe the subjective experiences of true patients. Theirs may be different from ours, particularly with the passage of time and the necessary process of adaptation to one's environment. But we can and do speak to the relatively more objective indices of treatment within the hospital. It could be a mistake, and a very unfortunate one, to consider that what happened to us derived from malice or stupidity on the part of the staff. Quite the contrary, our overwhelming impression of them was of people who really cared, who were committed and who were uncommonly intelligent. Where they failed, as they sometimes did painfully, it would be more accurate to attribute those failures to the environment in which they, too, found themselves than to personal callousness. Their perceptions and behavior were controlled by the situation, rather than being motivated by a malicious disposition. In a more benign environment, one that was less attached to global diagnosis, their behaviors and judgments might have been more benign and effective.

REFERENCES AND NOTES

1. R. Benedict, *J. Gen. Psychol.* **10**, 59 (1934).

2. E. Goffman, *Asylums* (Doubleday, Garden City, N.Y., 1961).

3. T. J. Scheff, *Being Mentally Ill: A Sociological Theory* (Aldine, Chicago, 1966).

4. Beyond the personal difficulties that the pseudopatient is likely to experience in the hospital, there are legal and social ones that, combined, require considerable attention before entry. For example, once admitted to a psychiatric institution, it is difficult, if not impossible, to be discharged on short notice, state law to the contrary notwithstanding. I was not sensitive to these difficulties at the outset of the project, nor to the personal and situational emergencies that can arise, but later a writ of habeas corpus was prepared for each of the entering pseudopatients and an attorney was kept "on call" during every hospitalization. I am grateful to John Kaplan and Robert Bartels for legal advice and assistance in these matters.

5. However distasteful such concealment is, it was a necessary first step to examining these questions. Without concealment, there would have been no way to know how valid these experiences were; nor was there any way of knowing whether whatever detections occurred were a tribute to the diagnostic acumen of the staff or to the hospital's rumor network. Obviously, since my concerns are general ones that cut across individual hospitals and staffs, I have respected their

anonymity and have eliminated clues that might lead to their identification.

6. It is possible, of course, that patients have quite broad latitudes in diagnosis and therefore are inclined to call many people sane, even those whose behavior is patently aberrant. However, although we have no hard data on this matter, it was our distinct impression that this was not the case. In many instances, patients not only singled us out for attention, but came to imitate our behaviors and styles.

7. S. E. Asch, *J. Abnorm. Soc. Psychol.* **41** 258 (1946); *Social Psychology* (Prentice-Hall, New York, 1952).

8. E. Zigler and L. Phillips, *J. Abnorm. Soc. Psychol.* **63,** 69 (1961).

9. W. Mischel, *Personality and Assessment* (Wiley, New York, 1968).

10. The most recent and unfortunate instance of this tenet is that of Senator Thomas Eagleton.

CRITICAL RESPONSE TO ROSENHAN'S RESEARCH

PSYCHIATRIC DIAGNOSIS

D. L. Rosenhan's article "On being sane in insane places," while full of important observations, is seriously flawed by methodological inadequacies and by conclusions that are inconsistent with—indeed, that directly contradict—the data he presents. . . . When Rosenhan's pseudopatients faked a history and were subsequently "misdiagnosed" by physicians at the psychiatric hospitals where they presented themselves, they established nothing about the accuracy of diagnosis per se, but merely reaffirmed the critical role of history-taking in medicine. Most physicians do not assume that patients who seek help are liars; they can therefore, of course, be misled. The so-called "Munchausen syndrome," of people who fake medical illness and may be admitted to hospitals repeatedly and receive years of extended treatment, is documented in the literature, as is, of course, simple effective malingering. It would be quite possible to conduct a study in which patients trained to simulate histories of myocardial infarction would receive treatment on the basis of history alone (since a negative electrocardiogram is not diagnostic), but it would be preposterous to conclude from such a study that physical illness does not exist, that medical diagnoses are fallacious labels, and that "illness" and "health" reside only in doctors' heads.

More misleading than Rosenhan's false conception of how diagnoses are reached, and his inaccurate conclusion therefrom that psychiatric diagnoses are empty labels, is his apparent total ignorance of the definitions of "insanity," "psychosis," "schizophrenia," and "schizophrenia in remission." Insanity is a legal term. It is not a psychiatric diagnosis. Though its exact definition varies among the states, it usually entails "the inability to decide right from wrong." This is a legal definition applied by *courts*. No psychiatrist ever "diagnoses" a patient as sane or insane. People legally insane at one point in time may be in general nonpsychotic (seizure disorder), and many, in fact most, people who are psychotic are never declared insane.

Most shocking, however, is Rosenhan's conclusion that "the normal are not detectably sane," by which he evidently means "not detectably nonpsychotic." In fact, all the pseudopatients were discharged with the diagnosis of "schizophrenia *in remission*," which means that they were clearly seen by the doctors to be nonpsychotic in the hospitals where they were observed but had been psychotic during the period described by their "history." Thus, Rosenhan's study demonstrates that despite false historical data and the set of the hospital environment, 12 nonpsychotics were observed by their psychiatrists to be nonpsychotic—a record of 100 percent accuracy.

In the rest of this article, Rosenhan poignantly describes neglect and abuses in psychiatric hospitals. He rightly reopens the door to this storehouse of bad practice and demands that the psychiatric professions enter, take responsibility, and change. But faulty application of concepts does not invalidate those concepts. The concept "psychosis"

From *Science*, Vol. 180, pp. 356–365 (April 27, 1973). Copyright © 1973 by the American Association for the Advancement of Science. Reprinted by permission.

(Rosenhan refers mostly to "insanity") is eminently justifiable not only by such symptoms as hallucinations, or by such responses to medication as one sees with lithium, but by the entire thrust of modern biology; how surprising it would be if the central nervous system of man—alone among all living tissue—were immune to biochemical or physiological pathology. . . .

Rosenhan might have summarized his important observations as follows: that given our current ignorance of biochemical and physiological parameters, psychiatric diagnoses may be inaccurate; that the psychiatric professions persist in overinterpretation and thereby increase the risk of type-2 errors; that given the ease with which histories of symptoms can be faked, coupled with the absence of positive chemical-biological diagnostic tests, the relationship between psychiatric diagnoses and the law needs reexamination and revision; and that the practice of psychiatry deviates disgracefully from accurate application of its concepts and ideals.

Unfortunately, through the publicity attracted by his methods, conclusions, and rhetoric, Rosenhan may have provided society with one more excuse for pursuing the current trend of vilifying psychiatric treatment and neglecting its potential beneficiaries.

PAUL R. FLEISCHMAN

Department of Psychiatry,
Yale University

. . .

. . . The 12 hospitals used in the study are intended, at least by implication, to be a representative sample of psychiatric institutions. We are given no meaningful data about any of these institutions—location, size, size of staff, kinds of staff, patient-staff ratio, training of staff, ward organization, therapeutic facilities, theoretical framework, admission and discharge procedures, patient involvement in ward management, off-ward activities and privileges, visiting arrangements, group and individual therapy provisions, and so on. Any one of these may have major impact on outcome of treatment or hospital experience. Without such data, we can make no comparisons of these hospitals with each other or with other hospitals. . . .

"Many" of the pseudopatients (how many is "many" out of eight?) "had never visited a psychiatric hospital," yet they immediately became experts in making complex interactional observations of patient and staff behavior which would

have taxed the skills of an experienced researcher. It appears that the pseudopatients gathered pseudodata for a pseudoresearch study. . . .

The article claims omniscience about what staff assumed or found—"*never* were staff found to assume that one of themselves or the structure of the hospital had anything to do with a patient's behavior." How was this "never" established? The author is a professor of law. Would he label this kind of evidence as anything but useless? I have sat in too many lengthy staff meetings and patient-staff meetings (were there none of those in the "excellent" hospital that was part of the study?) where hours were spent agonizing over the part played by staff and *their* behavior in patients' distress to give any kind of credence to the "never." . . .

OTTO F. THALER

Department of Psychiatry,
School of Medicine,
University of Rochester

. . . Rosenhan apparently lacks clinical knowledge and knowledge of the clinical mind; thus he fails to distinguish between what may have been a poor quality of practice and the reliability of current diagnostic criteria when properly applied.

Any expert clinical psychiatrist faced with the sudden onset of auditory hallucinations in a previously well person would think first of organic psychoses such as are associated with the use of drugs (hallucinogens), drug or alcohol withdrawal, endogenous or exogenous endocrine toxicity, intentional poisoning, cerebrovascular disease, and brain tumor. After the initial mental-status examination, which is a highly formal procedure, expert clinicians would be likely to order urine assays for hallucinogens, a neurological consultation, skull x-rays, and electroencephalograms in these cases. Careful interviews with the families and friends would have been conducted, since drug and alcohol abusers are notorious deniers.

One feature of the mental-status examination, namely, the hallucination of voices saying "thud," would have indicated intense case study. In 20 years of experience with hospitalized mental patients I have never encountered this hallucinatory content, nor read of it; experienced colleagues concur. How this unusual finding escaped interest is, as Rosenhan points out, puzzling.

If the organic work-up produced no conclusive positive findings, the clinician who failed to consider malingering in these cases would be considering schizophrenia. However, any psychiatrist trained in psychodynamics would be searching both for current precipitating interpersonal factors and severe early life traumas; the failure to find these would have created an urgent need for clinical psychological testing and, once again, interviews with family and friends.

No indication that any of the foregoing procedures were carried out is given in Rosenhan's article. . . .

HOWARD D. ZUCKER

Mount Sinai School of Medicine,
City University of New York

. . .

. . . Simulation is a challenge to the diagnostician in every area of medicine in which diagnosis rests primarily upon reports of subjective experiences, as it does, for example, in the case of angina pectoris, chronic neuralgia, or headache. Where there is something obvious to be gained by the simulation, such as compensation for injury or disability insurance payments, the examining physician is wary, though seldom able to make the distinction between the real and the simulated definitively. Since the psychiatrist deals with disease manifest primarily in subjective sensation and secondarily in overt behavior which he seldom has the opportunity to witness directly, mental illness can easily be simulated. That an illness can be successfully simulated does not make it any less "real" than one which cannot. . . .

Rosenhan claims that the only abnormal finding presented by his experimental subjects was the complaint of having heard voices. Review of his procedure discloses the presentation of at least two other phenomena which are ordinarily signs of illness. The first is the fact that the simulators sought admission to psychiatric hospitals. It is so rarely that this is done by anyone who is not indeed mentally ill that that alone must be taken seriously by a conscientious admitting psychiatrist as suggestive of illness.

Second, the voluminous note-taking which Rosenhan describes is a common occurrence among patients in mental hospitals. He expresses surprise that the hospital staff was not made suspicious by it. If anything, this note-taking would make the simulators seem more like compulsive paranoid patients than otherwise. . . .

I suspect that had these simulators applied for private care, most psychiatrists would have observed them without hospitalizing them. . . . However, the admitting room psychiatrist is not in private practice, and an admitting examiner who refuses hospitalization to an individual seeking it and presenting at least suspicious symptoms may face legal difficulties should the patient then commit suicide or homicide. Legal complications aside, there is considerably less harm done by admitting a patient who does not require hospitalization than by turning away one who does. . . .

A mental illness is not a diagnostic label; it is a pathologic process with its own natural history. . . . There is an important difference between sleep-induced or drug-induced hallucinations on the one hand and hallucinations of schizophrenia on the other. The difference is that when the period of sleep or of drug intoxication is over, the hallucinations and the behavior alteration associated with them will disappear. Once the diagnosis of schizophrenia has been correctly made, we may anticipate that during the rest of that patient's life he will be in danger of recurrent attack. . . . That the specific details of the subsequent course cannot be predicted is less important than the fact that the odds of recurrent or continuing difficulty in a schizophrenic individual are orders of magnitude greater than they are in the general population. Rosenhan may claim that it is the process of labeling which exerts such a deleterious effect upon the individual's life. The practicing psychiatrist, on the other hand, will at once be able to call to mind many patients whom he has seen in second or third attacks of schizophrenic illness whose first attacks were not recognized or diagnosed. . . .

MORTIMER OSTOW

Riverdale, New York

. . . What Rosenhan must wish to conclude is that the criteria for distinguishing sane from insane are not clear or unambiguous. This of course is a well-known fact. The question is, just how vague are the criteria? That in none of 12 cases was the phony patient spotted by the authorities gives the erroneous impression that these criteria are very, very vague. However, this is not necessarily borne out by the "data."

While it is true that psychosis is thought to "reside in" the patient (that is, the adjective "psychotic" is applied to a person), it is generally understood that the psychosis manifests itself only under certain conditions. The psychotic is not expected to be bizarre in everything he says or does. . . . The conditions on the ward are designed (rightly or wrongly) to make the patients manageable (hence to appear sane). Those whose psychosis is not suppressed are transferred from the admitting ward. Accordingly, a much more impressive demonstration of his point could be made by Rosenhan if he were to take obviously insane persons and, by giving them a new name and releasing them to a community where they were not known, successfully pass them off as sane. . . .

LEWIS R. LIEBERMAN

Columbus College,
Columbus, Georgia

. . .

The assertion that the diagnosis of schizophrenia written in a hospital record is a lifelong stigma has been repeated so often that one seldom hears scientific skepticism expressed about it. There has certainly been much question within psychiatry about the manner in which the term schizophrenia is to be defined. Those who apply the term widely do not understand what the fuss is all about, for many of their patients do quite well and appear to recover. Those who apply the diagnosis narrowly find that most of their patients do poorly, as did individuals with similar symptoms years before the label was invented, for it is the underlying illness, not the label, that accounts for the difficulties. The fact that the boundaries between normal and abnormal vary from culture to culture is cited in the article as an element of the proof that diagnosis of mental illness cannot be valid. But mental illness is diagnosed on the basis of definite criteria, not merely an impression of abnormality. Psychiatrists who have not mastered the criteria will of course make errors. . . .

It is interesting that the author adopted a misconception shared by most hospital patients. This is the narcissistic belief that what the nurses record is the abnormalities of patient behavior. Well-trained staff report, without evaluation, what they observe; the only criticism to be made of the nurse's report "exhibits writing behavior" is that it uses three words where one would suffice.

If patients "were viewed as interesting individuals rather than diagnostic entities, . . . would we not *seek* contact with them . . . ?" asks Rosenhan. To suggest that the diagnostic category so occupied the attention of the hospital staff that they could not respond to the individuality of their patients is to ignore what is known about institutions, roles, and even efficiency. People accept the fact that they can be guided along highways by traffic policemen who do not know their ultimate destination or motives for traveling, that they can be given money by bank clerks who do not know how they will spend it; but they

hate to come up against the fact that in a modern psychiatric hospital they are likely to recover from a psychotic illness without ever telling a psychiatrist about their fears and hopes. The old-time doctor who sat by the patient's bed while he died was held in higher esteem than the physician of today who provides a prescription and then absents himself while his patient recovers. . . .

HENRY PINSKER

Department of Psychiatry,
Beth Israel Medical Center

. . . Rosenhan overlooks some obvious and important conclusions:

1) In this country it is increasingly easy to obtain psychiatric care, including hospitalization. Often one need only ask; the request is taken seriously, and bizarre or uncontrolled behavior is not required as further proof of need. Whatever the impact of this on scientific accuracy of diagnosis, the humanitarian aspects are obvious.

2) The psychiatric hospital is not a pleasant place for "normal" people. This is perhaps appropriate: normals seldom want to get in, and it is probably good that they should want to leave soon. Few of those who are ill enjoy their hospitalization either, but many prefer the hospital environment with all its failings to any alternative available to them. They enter and remain voluntarily. I do not think one can accept without reservation Rosenhan's allegation that the hospital environment is "undoubtedly countertherapeutic." His lone scientific point is that "normals" don't like to be in a psychiatric hospital—a point I think no one doubted before reading his article.

3) The "medical model" of mental illness is moribund, at least where patient and hospital meet. Where the model survives in hospital records and official reports, its sustenance may well come from administrators and funding agencies such as insurance companies who expect to receive the reports. Insurors are notoriously reluctant to pay bills if the patient wasn't "really sick."

Rosenhan is puzzled because his pseudopatients were retained in hospital even though they were symptom-free and exhibited no abnormal behavior. Had he looked about him (at the "real" patients) his question might have been resolved, for many psychiatric wards are not marked by a great deal of bizarre behavior; behavioral abnormalities often decrease immediately on hospitalization or soon after. Subjective symptoms also are often relieved by hospitalization. Absence of symptoms while in a special environment does not necessarily mean absence of illness; a patient admitted for bleeding peptic ulcer may "feel fine" and not be bleeding 24 hours later—he has his ulcer still. . . .

S. M. BLAIR

Department of Physiology-Anatomy,
University of California,
Berkeley

. . .

The fact that any nomenclature which categorizes or applies to mental functioning eventually becomes a derogatory term or label is well-known—"idiot," "moron," and "imbecile" were coined as scientific terms but eventually became a form of invective and had to be replaced by "mentally retarded." Yet no scientific approach to physical or mental illness is possible without a nomenclature, unless one is willing to give up a scientific approach to illnesses altogether. Psychiatric nomenclature is not uniform and includes etiologic, psychodynamic, and even sociological aspects of mental and behavioral disorders. Yet the attack on psychiatric nomenclature as some kind of pernicious "labeling" comes very close to a denial that any mental disorders characterized by objectively ascertainable symptoms, behaviors, and tests altogether exist. In the not so distant past, "tuberculosis" and "syphilis" were words shunned by polite society. Fortunately this did not deter physicians and researchers from diagnosing and treating these conditions. If, as Rosenhan advocates, we avoided psychiatric diagnoses, labeled by him as labels, and replaced them by focusing "on specific problems and behaviors," then the verbal designations of these problems and behaviors would become labels, too. . . .

GEORGE H. WIEDEMAN

Columbia University,
School of Social Work

. . .

These letters deserve to be read with care. The issues they raise are important ones, and the feelings they convey need to be appreciated if one is to get a sense of where the crossroads in psychiatry are today. However much I wish it were otherwise, the authors and I simply do not agree on the major counts.

"On being sane in insane places" described two largely separate issues: diagnostic practices in psychiatric hospitals, and the experience of patienthood. Most of the comments are addressed to the first issue, and it is well that we review briefly the part of the study that is germane to that issue:

Eight people gained admission to 12 psychiatric facilities by simulating a single symptom, hallucinations. The contents of these hallucinations were of a kind that had never been reported in the literature. Beyond that simulation and some concomitant nervousness "no further alterations of person, history, or circumstances were made. The significant events of the pseudopatients' life histories were presented as they had actually occurred. Relationships with parents and siblings, with spouse and children, with people at work and in school, . . . were described as they were or had been." Eleven of the pseudopatients were diagnosed schizophrenic. All were discharged "in remission." None was found sane.

The theoretical predicates for the research derive from the large literature on the effects of contexts on perception (*1*). Perception is clearly an active process. While we tend personally to believe that we can always disembed a figure from its ground, the fact of the matter is that the meaning and value that are attributed to a figure are in some part contributed by the ground. A book found on your desk is perceived to be more valuable than one in your wastebasket. A hand in the air has different meaning according to whether you are sitting in a classroom, making a right turn in your car, or marching in a German parade during the 1940's.

While we may think that in examining a patient we have disembedded him from the context in which he is found, that assumption is open to reasonable question and is in fact the basis for our study. A recent experiment by Langer and Abelson (*2*) may make the effects of context more clearly germane to the present case. They videotaped an interview in which discussions were focused on a client's job histories and difficulties, then asked well-trained psychodynamic psychologists and psychiatrists to rate the degree of adjustment of the client, telling half the raters that they were observing a job interview and the other half that it was a psychiatric interview. Those who thought they were watching a job interview rated the patient as much better adjusted.

With respect to diagnosis, the issue that is implicated in the study has apparently been widely misunderstood. The issue is not that the pseudopatient lied. Of course he did. Nor is it that the psychiatrist believed him. Of course he must believe him. Neither is it whether the pseudopatient should have been admitted to the psychiatric hospital in the first place. If there was a bed, admitting the pseudopatient was the only humane thing to do.

The issue is the diagnostic leap that was made between the single presenting symptom, hallucinations, and the diagnosis, schizophrenia (or, in one case, manic-depressive psychosis). That is the heart of the matter. Had the pseudopatients been diagnosed "hallucinating," there would have been no further need to examine the diagnostic issue. The diagnosis of hallucinations implies only that: no more. The presence of hallucinations does not itself define the presence of "schizophrenia." And schizophrenia may or may not include hallucinations.

Lest the matter reduce to one scientist's word against another, let us look to the standard for diagnosis in psychiatry, the *Diagnostic and Statistical Manual* (DSM-II) of the American Psychiatric Association:

> 295. Schizophrenia. This large category includes a group of disorders manifested by characteristic disturbances of thinking, mood, and behavior. Disturbances in thinking are marked by alterations of concept formation which may lead to misinterpretation of reality and sometimes to delusions and hallucinations, which frequently appear psychologically self-protective. Corollary mood changes include ambivalence, constricted and inappropriate emotional responsiveness and loss of empathy with others. Behavior may be withdrawn, regressive, and bizarre.... .
>
> 295.3. Schizophrenia, paranoid type. . . . characterized primarily by the presence of persecutory or grandiose delusions, often associated with hallucinations. Excessive religiosity is sometimes seen. The patient's attitude is frequently hostile and aggressive, and his behavior tends to be consistent with his delusions. . . .

But, you will say, "hallucinations" is not a diagnosis at all but merely a description. Indeed that is so, and as we shall soon see, those descriptions are all that may be warranted by the current state of knowledge.

The matter of psychiatric diagnosis is qualitatively quite different from what it is in general medicine. Diagnostic reliability in medicine is not perfect, but it has much more going for it than psychiatric diagnosis. Consider Blair's example of bleeding ulcers. It is the case, as Blair points out, that the bleeding can abate but the peptic ulcers remain. The presence of that ulcer, however, is verifiable independently of the bleeding. It is precisely because we can check urine, perform blood tests, palpate, examine reflexes, look inside, and more, that we are on considerably better ground in medical diagnoses than we are in

psychiatry. To my knowledge, schizophrenia is not independently verifiable beyond what a patient says and does. Fleischman put it well: "Given our current ignorance of biochemical and physiological parameters, psychiatric diagnosis may be inaccurate"—regardless, I would add, of how intuitively convinced the diagnostician is of his own accuracy.

The impression given by the letters, as by textbooks in psychiatry and abnormal psychology, is that psychiatric diagnoses are sturdy and highly reliable. The fact is that the unreliability of psychiatric diagnoses as they are commonly made has been known for a long time, so long that it is remarkable that the impression of sturdiness could have been sustained in the face of such an overwhelmingly contrary literature.

As early as 1938, Boisen (3) pointed to the role of local convention in psychiatric diagnoses. He found that some 76 percent of patients were diagnosed hebephrenic schizophrenic in one Illinois hospital while only 11 percent were so diagnosed in another. Ash (4) found that three psychiatrists seeing the same male patients could agree on the diagnosis in only 20 percent of the cases. Agreement rose to 34 to 43 percent when two psychiatrists were diagnosing.

Examining the matter from a different angle, Zigler and Phillips (5) investigated the frequency of 35 common presenting symptoms among 793 hospitalized psychiatric patients. All 35 symptoms were found among both neurotics and schizophrenics, 34 were found among character disorders, and 30 in manic-depressives. With such overlap, how reliable or valid can diagnostic categories be? True, the investigators found many small relationships between specific symptoms and diagnostic categories, but the very triviality of those relationships itself underscores the magnitude of the problem of validity. The literature on the reliability of psychiatric diagnoses is large and spans more than three decades. Several extensive summaries are available (6).

It is tempting to disregard the data from our experiment and the earlier evidence and simply say that it is not diagnosis that has failed, only diagnosticians. We were ourselves tempted to that judgment during the early part of the study, before we had seen the spectrum of hospitals and diagnosticians that were included in the study. Let their characteristics speak for themselves. Eight of the 11 public hospitals conducted approved psychiatric residence programs, as did the private hospital. Three of the public hospitals were affiliated with university medical centers. The private hospital, while not directly affiliated, was closely associated. Moreover, it was not only the admitting officers who diagnosed. These diagnoses were confirmed by treating physicians and psychologists, in case presentation conferences and in discharge conferences.

Is it possible . . . that "more went on in the admitting offices than is reported" in the article? Of course it is. No one can do research in this area without being extraordinarily sensitive to the issues of experimenter bias . . . and demand characteristics that are continuously present in psychological research, and especially in efforts that involve participating and observing simultaneously. But some things can be said to establish the potential limits of these distortions. . . . Note. . . , that visitors' observations on the pseudopatients after they were admitted uniformly disclosed no departures from role in the direction of craziness. Moreover, the ease with which psychiatric diagnoses were questioned when a pseudopatient was expected (in the "challenge" experiment) raises some questions whether the "experimenter bias" was perhaps as much in the mind of the diagnostician as it might have been in the behavior of the pseudopatient.

On another matter, a writer questions whether the pseudopatients, several of whom had no previous experience in psychiatric hospitals, were capable of making the "complex" interactional observations reported in the article. In fact, those data were obtained in four hospitals by experienced researchers who had worked in similar settings. But that need not have been the case. Counting when and how often staff come and go from the "cage" hardly requires experimental know-how. Nor does asking standardized questions at fixed intervals and observing subsequent behaviors tax the skills of even a beginning researcher. These are quite simple matters, in fact.

As to the reality of psychological suffering, I made my views clear at the outset of the paper, in the third paragraph: ". . . Nor does raising such questions deny the existence of the personal anguish that is often associated with 'mental illness.' Anxiety and depression exist. Psychological suffering exists. But normality and abnormality, sanity and insanity, and the diagnoses that flow from them may be less substantive than many believe them to be." Let me be perfectly clear about this: To say that psychological suffering is a myth is to engage in massive denial. But to imply, as Wiedeman does, that psychological labeling does not itself create suffering is to similarly engage in denial.

Some assert that the appearance of this paper can only hurt psychiatry. The possibility that it might help psychiatry, that sensitization to issues in diagnoses and treatment might lead to beneficial change, seems not to arise. For the record, let me make clear that the theory that underlies this effort, and the report itself, do not support the vilification of psychiatric care. Psychiatry may be less knowledgeable than it believes itself to be but that is hardly surprising when one considers the magnitude of the problems which it must address. In the closing paragraph, I wrote, "It could be a mistake, and a very unfortunate one, to consider that what happened to us derived from malice or stupidity on the part of the staff. Quite the contrary, our overwhelming impression of them was of people who really cared, who were committed, and who were uncommonly intelligent. Where they failed, as they sometimes did painfully, it would be more accurate to attribute those failures to the environment in which they, too, found themselves. . . . Their perceptions and behavior were controlled by the situation. . . . In a more benign environment . . . their behaviors and judgment might have been more benign and effective."

D. L. Rosenhan

Department of Psychology and
*Stanford Law School,
Stanford University*

REFERENCES

1. See U. Neisser, *Cognitive Psychology* (Appleton-Century-Crofts, New York, 1967); R. Taguiri and L. Petrullo, Eds., *Person Perception and Interpersonal Behavior* (Stanford Univ. Press, Stanford. Calif., 1958); R. Brown. *Social Psychology* (Free Press, New York, 1967).

2. E. Langer and R. Abelson, "A patient by any other name . . .: Clinician group difference in labeling bias" (unpublished manuscript, Yale University).

3. A. T. Boisen, *Psychiatry* **2,** 233 (1938).

4. P. Ash, *J. Abnorm. Soc. Psychol.* **44,** 272 (1949).

5. E. Zigler and L. Phillips, *ibid.* **63,** 69 (1961).

6. P. London and D. Rosenhan, Eds., *Foundations of Abnormal Psychology* (Holt, Rinehart & Winston, New York, 1968); J. Zubin, *Annu. Rev. Psychol.* **18,** 373 (1967); L. Phillips and J. G. Draguns, *ibid.* **22,** 447 (1971).

PROJECTS

Name _____

Date _____

11.1: BEING DEVIANT FOR A DAY

In many instances, the kinds of behavior that people view as strange, bizarre, or even pathological are those that deviate from the normative standards in a particular situation. These standards are often unwritten and implicit, but their influence is quite strong, as we can see by people's reactions when someone violates them. The use of such situational norms to define what is deviant is an example of the social basis of human pathology.

This project is designed to help you gain an increased awareness of the power of normative standards through engaging in one of the norm-violating behaviors listed below:

a. Dress in a fashion that is very atypical of you (e.g., in a dress or suit if you usually wear jeans), and note your friends' reactions. Or dress in a fashion that is considered out of place or inappropriate for a particular situation (e.g., wear a sweat shirt and jeans to a formal dance).

b. Whenever someone asks you how you are or how you are feeling, respond with a detailed answer describing your feelings, recent activities, state of health, and so on.

c. When talking to someone, stand either too close to them (within one foot) or too far away (three feet). Try to maintain this distance even if the other person moves to change it.

1. How did people react to you when you violated a norm? List both their verbal and their nonverbal responses.

2. How did *you* feel while you were behaving in a deviant way?

Name _____

Date _____

11.2: ASPECTS OF DEPERSONALIZATION

Almost all of us have experienced being processed by some large institution, such as a hospital, a school, a service agency, or a military unit. During such an experience, we feel like numbers or objects rather than people. In short, we feel depersonalized. What factors contribute to this sense of depersonalization? Rosenhan alluded to such variables as powerlessness and lack of contact (both verbal and nonverbal) with other people. Think about one of your own depersonalizing institutional experiences, and try to identify, as concretely as possible, what caused you to feel that way.

1. How did *physical* aspects of the institution contribute to your depersonalization (e.g., identical equipment or uniforms for everyone, long corridors that make it difficult for people in their offices to see anyone else)?

2. How did *procedural* aspects of the institution contribute to your depersonalization (e.g., rules that restricted what you could say or do, long waits)?

3. How did *interpersonal* aspects of the institution contribute to your depersonalization (e.g., lack of eye contact, use of form letters)?

4. Keeping in mind the emotional stresses faced by institutional staff (as described by Maslach and Pines), what changes would you recommend to reduce the depersonalization experienced by an institution's clients or patients?

12
ETHICS

Imagine, for a moment, that you are required to do a research project in social psychology in order to graduate from college. You consider a number of possible topics and eventually decide to test a hypothesis derived from cognitive dissonance theory. You are especially intrigued with the theory that people come to love that which they have suffered for (the "severe initiation effect"), and you want to see if you can replicate the original findings in a new study. Because you are concerned about the contrived and artificial nature of many laboratory experiments, you decide to do a more "real-life" study which uses a naturally occurring situation. In thinking about the college setting, you soon realize that the hypothesis could be tested with students who study very hard for an exam but do not receive a good grade. Would they be more enamoured with their college after this experience, as dissonance theory would predict?

To do your study, you need a large group of subjects, so you look for an introductory course which has several hundred students enrolled in it. You arrange with the instructor to have all the students fill out a questionnaire in which they indicate their attitudes toward the college (a pre-experimental measure that will serve as a baseline). You then want to have some of the students who worked hard in the course to receive low grades while others receive high ones, and then to ask them again about their attitudes toward the college. You obviously cannot tamper with the students' actual grades, but you persuade the instructor to post a fictitious grade list at the end of the course on the condition that students will be told their true grade immediately after they complete the second attitude measure. Thus, many students who had actually earned high grades (and had presumably worked hard to get them) will find low scores next to their names on the posted grade list. The instructor then asks them to fill out a final course evaluation (in which they are again asked about their attitudes toward the college).

After collecting the questionnaires, the instructor tells the students that the grade list was fictitious, explains why this was done, and tells the students their actual grades. When you analyze the data, you discover that the results do indeed support the dissonance hypothesis—students who put in a lot of effort for a low grade came to like the college more.

As a budding researcher, how would you feel about your experimental achievement? Undoubtedly, you would feel very pleased and proud about your work, especially if it earned you special honors at graduation (as was the case for the student who actually conducted this study almost ten years ago). But what about the subjects in your study—how would *they* feel about it? If you now remove yourself from the researcher role and put yourself in the subject's position, your attitude toward the study might change. The fact is that you suffered some anguish and embarrassment over your unexpectedly poor mark. Also, you had been observed and studied without your knowledge or consent. All of this might cause you to feel extremely angry and upset about this study (as indeed the real subjects did).

The conflicting values involved in a research project of this kind—the importance of discovering new knowledge versus the subject's right to privacy—are the basis of the ethical dilemma that continually faces researchers in psychology, and social psychology in particular. How is such a dilemma resolved? Until recently, the resolution was left entirely up to the individual researcher. He or she might decide that the importance of the findings outweighed any possible discomforts of the subjects. Special safeguards might be added to the project to alleviate any negative reactions on the part of the subjects. Or the study might be redesigned so that no deception of the subject would be involved. At the present time, the researcher must submit to the review procedures of special committees established to protect the rights of human subjects. These committees evaluate all proposed studies and must give their approval before any research project can be carried out. Although the use of such review committees has helped ensure the ethical conduct of research, their decisions are often provisional and tentative. The last words have not been and may never be heard in the debate over the ethical issues raised by psychological research.

SOME THOUGHTS ON ETHICS OF RESEARCH: AFTER READING MILGRAM'S "BEHAVIORAL STUDY OF OBEDIENCE"

DIANA BAUMRIND

One of the classic and most controversial experiments in social psychology is Milgram's study of obedience. In a seemingly innocuous laboratory setting, subjects obeyed the experimenter's request and delivered what they thought were extremely painful electric shocks to another person. The results were dramatic because of both the number of subjects who obeyed and the extent to which they obeyed. Milgram's findings clearly violated people's expectations of how they (and everyone else) would respond in a comparable situation and aroused a great deal of interest and heated discussion. However, the ethical issues raised by the methods Milgram used to conduct his study aroused an even more intense debate.

The articles "Some Thoughts on Ethics of Research" and "Issues in the Study of Obedience" constitute a well-known and important exchange of views in which Baumrind and Milgram argue the ethical dilemmas underlying psychological research.

Certain problems in psychological research require the experimenter to balance his career and scientific interests against the interests of his prospective subjects. When such occasions arise the experimenter's stated objective frequently is to do the best possible job with the least possible harm to his subjects. The experimenter seldom perceives in more positive terms an indebtedness to the subject for his services, perhaps because the detachment which his functions require prevents appreciation of the subject as an individual.

From *American Psychologist*, 1964, *19*, 421–423. Copyright © 1964 by The American Psychological Association and reprinted with permission of author and The American Psychological Association.

Yet a debt does exist, even when the subject's reason for volunteering includes course credit or monetary gain. Often a subject participates unwillingly in order to satisfy a course requirement. These requirements are of questionable merit ethically, and do not alter the experimenter's responsibility to the subject.

Most experimental conditions do not cause the subjects pain or indignity, and are sufficiently interesting or challenging to present no problem of an ethical nature to the experimenter. But where the experimental conditions expose the subject to loss of dignity, or offer him nothing of value, then the experimenter is obliged to consider the reasons why the subject volunteered and to reward him accordingly.

The subject's public motives for volunteering include having an enjoyable or stimulating experience, acquiring knowledge, doing the experimenter a favor which may some day be reciprocated, and making a contribution to science. These motives can be taken into account rather easily by the experimenter who is willing to spend a few minutes with the subject afterwards to thank him for his participation, answer his questions, reassure him that he did well, and chat with him a bit. Most volunteers also have less manifest, but equally legitimate, motives. A subject may be seeking an opportunity to have contact with, be noticed by, and perhaps confide in a person with psychological training. The dependent attitude of most subjects toward the experimenter is an artifact of the experimental situation as well as an expression of some subjects' personal need systems at the time they volunteer.

The dependent, obedient attitude assumed by most subjects in the experimental setting is appropriate to that situation. The "game" is defined by the experimenter and he makes the rules. By volunteering, the subject agrees implicitly to assume a posture of trust and obedience. While the experimental conditions leave him exposed, the subject has the right to assume that his security and self-esteem will be protected.

There are other professional situations in which one member—the patient or client—expects help and protection from the other—the physician or psychologist. But the interpersonal relationship between experimenter and subject additionally has unique features which are likely to provoke initial anxiety in the subject. The laboratory is unfamiliar as a setting and the rules of behavior ambiguous compared to a clinician's office. Because of the anxiety and passivity generated by the setting, the subject is more prone to behave in an obedient, suggestible manner in the laboratory than elsewhere. Therefore, the laboratory is not the place to study degree of obedience or suggestibility, as a function of a particular experimental condition, since the base line for these phenomena as found in the laboratory is probably much higher than in most other settings. Thus experiments in which the relationship to the experimenter as an authority is used as an independent condition are imperfectly designed for the same reason that they are prone to injure the subjects involved. They disregard the special quality of trust and obedience with which the subject appropriately regards the experimenter.

Other phenomena which present ethical decisions, unlike those mentioned above, *can* be reproduced successfully in the laboratory. Failure

experience, conformity to peer judgment, and isolation are among such phenomena. In these cases we can expect the experimenter to take whatever measures are necessary to prevent the subject from leaving the laboratory more humiliated, insecure, alienated, or hostile than when he arrived. To guarantee that an especially sensitive subject leaves a stressful experimental experience in the proper state sometimes requires special clinical training. But usually an attitude of compassion, respect, gratitude, and common sense will suffice, and no amount of clinical training will substitute. The subject has the right to expect that the psychologist with whom he is interacting has some concern for his welfare, and the personal attributes and professional skill to express his goodwill effectively.

Unfortunately, the subject is not always treated with the respect he deserves. It has become more commonplace in sociopsychological laboratory studies to manipulate, embarrass, and discomfort subjects. At times the insult to the subject's sensibilities extends to the journal reader when the results are reported. Milgram's (1963) study is a case in point. The following is Milgram's abstract of his experiment:

This article describes a procedure for the study of destructive obedience in the laboratory. It consists of ordering a naïve S to administer increasingly more severe punishment to a victim in the context of a learning experiment. Punishment is administered by means of a shock generator with 30 graded switches ranging from Slight Shock to Danger: Severe Shock. The victim is a confederate of E. The primary dependent variable is the maximum shock the S is willing to administer before he refuses to continue further. 26 Ss obeyed the experimental commands fully, and administered the highest shock on the generator. 14 Ss broke off the experiment at some point after the victim protested and refused to provide further answers. The procedure created extreme levels of nervous tension in some Ss. Profuse sweating, trembling, and stuttering were typical expressions of this emotional disturbance. One unexpected sign of tension—yet to be explained—was the regular occurrence of nervous laughter, which in some Ss developed into uncontrollable seizures. The variety of interesting behavioral dynamics observed in the experiment, the reality of the situation for the S, and the possibility of parametric variation within the framework of the procedure, point to the fruitfulness of further study [p. 371].

The detached, objective manner in which Milgram reports the emotional disturbance suffered by his subjects contrasts sharply with his graphic account of that disturbance. Following are two other quotes describing the effects on his subjects of the experimental conditions:

> I observed a mature and initially poised business-man enter the laboratory smiling and confident. Within 20 minutes he was reduced to a twitching, stuttering wreck, who was rapidly approaching a point of nervous collapse. He constantly pulled on his earlobe, and twisted his hands. At one point he pushed his fist into his forehead and muttered "Oh God, let's stop it." And yet he continued to respond to every word of the experimenter, and obeyed to the end [p. 377].
>
> In a large number of cases the degree of tension reached extremes that are rarely seen in sociopsychological laboratory studies. Subjects were observed to sweat, tremble, stutter, bite their lips, groan, and dig their fingernails into their flesh. These were characteristic rather than exceptional responses to the experiment.
>
> One sign of tension was the regular occurrence of nervous laughing fits. Fourteen of the 40 subjects showed definite signs of nervous laughter and smiling. The laughter seemed entirely out of place, even bizarre. Full-blown, uncontrollable seizures were observed for 3 subjects. On one occasion we observed a seizure so violently convulsive that it was necessary to call a halt to the experiment . . . [p. 375].

Milgram does state that,

> After the interview, procedures were undertaken to assure that the subject would leave the laboratory in a state of well being. A friendly reconciliation was arranged between the subject and the victim, and an effort was made to reduce any tensions that arose as a result of the experiment [p. 374].

It would be interesting to know what sort of procedures could dissipate the type of emotional disturbance just described. In view of the effects on subjects, traumatic to a degree which Milgram himself considers nearly unprecedented in sociopsychological experiments, his casual assurance that these tensions were dissipated before the subject left the laboratory is unconvincing.

What could be the rational basis for such a posture of indifference? Perhaps Milgram supplies the answer himself when he partially explains the subject's destructive obedience as follows, "Thus they assume that the discomfort caused the victim is momentary, while the scientific gains resulting from the experiment are enduring" [p.

378]. Indeed such a rationale might suffice to justify the means used to achieve his end if that end were of inestimable value to humanity or were not itself transformed by the means by which it was attained.

The behavioral psychologist is not in as good a position to objectify his faith in the significance of his work as medical colleagues at points of breakthrough. His experimental situations are not sufficiently accurate models of real-life experience; his sampling techniques are seldom of a scope which would justify the meaning with which he would like to endow his results; and these results are hard to reproduce by colleagues with opposing theoretical views. Unlike the Sabin vaccine, for example, the concrete benefit to humanity of his particular piece of work, no matter how competently handled, cannot justify the risk that real harm will be done to the subject. I am not speaking of physical discomfort, inconvenience, or experimental deception per se, but of permanent harm, however slight. I do regard the emotional disturbance described by Milgram as potentially harmful because it could easily effect an alteration in the subject's self-image or ability to trust adult authorities in the future. It is potentially harmful to a subject to commit, in the course of an experiment, acts which he himself considers unworthy, particularly when he has been entrapped into committing such acts by an individual he has reason to trust. The subject's personal responsibility for his actions is not erased because the experimenter reveals to him the means which he used to stimulate these actions. The subject realizes that he would have hurt the victim if the current were on. The realization that he also made a fool of himself by accepting the experimental set results in additional loss of self-esteem. Moreover, the subject finds it difficult to express his anger outwardly after the experimenter in a self-acceptant but friendly manner reveals the hoax.

A fairly intense corrective interpersonal experience is indicated wherein the subject admits and accepts his responsibility for his own actions, and at the same time gives vent to his hurt and anger at being fooled. Perhaps an experience as distressing as the one described by Milgram can be integrated by the subject, provided that careful thought is given to the matter. The propriety of such experimentation is still in question even if such a reparational experience were forthcoming. Without it I would expect a naïve, sensitive subject to remain deeply hurt and anxious for some time, and a sophisticated, cynical subject to become even more alienated and distrustful.

In addition the experimental procedure used by Milgram does not appear suited to the objectives of the study because it does not take into account the special quality of the set which the subject has in the experimental situation. Milgram is concerned with a very important problem, namely, the social consequences of destructive obedience. He says,

Gas chambers were built, death camps were guarded, daily quotas of corpses were produced with the same efficiency as the manufacture of appliances. These inhumane policies may have originated in the mind of a single person, but they could only be carried out on a massive scale if a very large number of persons obeyed orders [p. 371].

But the parallel between authority-subordinate relationships in Hitler's Germany and in Milgram's laboratory is unclear. In the former situation the SS man or member of the German Officer Corps, when obeying orders to slaughter, had no reason to think of his superior officer as benignly disposed towards himself or their victims. The victims were perceived as subhuman and not worthy of consideration. The subordinate officer was an agent in a great cause. He did not need to feel guilt or conflict because within his frame of reference he was acting rightly.

It is obvious from Milgram's own descriptions that most of his subjects were concerned about their victims and did trust the experimenter, and that their distressful conflict was generated in part by the consequences of these two disparate but appropriate attitudes. Their distress may have resulted from shock at what the experimenter was doing to them as well as from what they thought they were doing to their victims. In any case, there is not a convincing parallel between the phenomena studied by Milgram and destructive obedience as that concept would apply to the subordinate-authority relationship demonstrated in Hitler's Germany. If the experiments were conducted "outside of New Haven and without

any visible ties to the university," I would still question their validity on similar although not identical grounds. In addition, I would question the representativeness of a sample of subjects who would voluntarily participate within a noninstitutional setting.

In summary, the experimental objectives of the psychologist are seldom incompatible with the subject's ongoing state of well-being, provided that the experimenter is willing to take the subject's motives and interests into consideration when planning his methods and correctives. Section 4b in *Ethical Standards of Psychologists* (APA, 1962) reads in part:

Only when a problem is significant and can be investigated in no other way, is the psychologist justified in exposing human subjects to emotional stress or other possible harm. In conducting such research, the psychologist must seriously consider the possibility of harmful aftereffects, and should be prepared to remove them as soon as permitted by the design of the experiment. Where the danger of serious aftereffects exists, research should be conducted only when the subjects or their responsible agents are fully informed of this possibility and volunteer nevertheless [p. 12].

From the subject's point of view, procedures which involve loss of dignity, self-esteem, and trust in rational authority are probably most harmful in the long run and require the most thoughtfully planned reparations, if engaged in at all. The public image of psychology as a profession is highly related to our own actions, and some of these actions are changeworthy. It is important that as research psychologists we protect our ethical sensibilities rather than adapt our personal standards to include as appropriate the kind of indignities to which Milgram's subjects were exposed. I would not like to see experiments such as Milgram's proceed unless the subjects were fully informed of the dangers of serious aftereffects and his correctives were clearly shown to be effective in restoring their state of well-being.

REFERENCES

American Psychological Association. *Ethical standards of psychologists: A summary of ethical principles.* Washington, D.C.: 1962.

Milgram, S. Behavioral study of obedience. *Journal of Abnormal and Social Psychology,* 1963, **67:** 371–378.

ISSUES IN THE STUDY OF OBEDIENCE: A REPLY TO BAUMRIND

STANLEY MILGRAM

Obedience serves numerous productive functions in society. It may be ennobling and educative and entail acts of charity and kindness. Yet the problem of destructive obedience, because it is the most disturbing expression of obedience in our time, and because it is the most perplexing, merits intensive study.

In its most general terms, the problem of destructive obedience may be defined thus: If X tells Y to hurt Z, under what conditions will Y carry out the command of X, and under what conditions will he refuse? In the concrete setting of a laboratory, the question may assume this form: If an experimenter tells a subject to act against another person, under what conditions will the subject go along with the instruction, and under what conditions will he refuse to obey?

A simple procedure was devised for studying obedience (Milgram, 1963). A person comes to the laboratory, and in the context of a learning experiment, he is told to give increasingly severe electric shocks to another person. (The other person is an actor, who does not really receive any shocks.) The experimenter tells the subject to continue stepping up the shock level, even to the point of reaching the level marked "Danger: Severe Shock." The purpose of the experiment is to see how far the naïve subject will proceed before he refuses to comply with the experimenter's instructions. Behavior prior to this rupture is considered "obedience" in that the subject does what the experimenter tells him to do. The point of rupture is the act of disobedience. Once the basic procedure is established, it becomes possible to vary conditions of the experiment, to learn under what circumstances obedience to authority is most probable, and under what conditions defiance is brought to the fore (Milgram, 1965).

The results of the experiment (Milgram, 1963) showed, first, that it is more difficult for many people to defy the experimenter's authority than was generally supposed. A substantial number of subjects go through to the end of the shock board. The second finding is that the situation often places a person in considerable conflict. In the course of the experiment, subjects fidget, sweat, and sometimes break out into nervous fits of laughter. On the one hand, subjects want to aid the experimenter; and on the other hand, they do not want to shock the learner. The conflict is expressed in nervous reactions.

In a recent issue of *American Psychologist*, Diana Baumrind (1964) raised a number of questions concerning the obedience report. Baumrind expressed concern for the welfare of subjects who served in the experiment, and wondered whether adequate measures were taken to protect the participants. She also questioned the adequacy of the experimental design.

Patently, "Behavioral Study of Obedience" did not contain all the information needed for an assessment of the experiment. But it is clearly indicated in the references and footnotes (pp. 373, 378) that this was only one of a series of reports on the experimental program, and Baumrind's article was deficient in information that could have been obtained easily. I thank the editor for allotting space in this journal to review this information, to amplify it, and to discuss some of the issues touched on by Baumrind.

At the outset, Baumrind confuses the unanticipated outcome of an experiment with its basic procedure. She writes, for example, as if the production of stress in our subjects was an intended and deliberate effect of the experimental manipulation. There are many laboratory procedures specifically designed to create stress (Lazarus, 1964), but the obedience paradigm was not one of them. The extreme tension induced in some subjects was unexpected. Before conducting the experiment, the procedures were discussed with many colleagues, and none anticipated the reactions that subsequently took place. Foreknowledge of results can never be the invariable accompaniment of an experimental probe. Understanding grows because we examine situations in which the end is unknown. An investigator unwilling to accept this degree of risk must give up the idea of scientific inquiry.

Moreover, there was every reason to expect, prior to actual experimentation, that subjects would refuse to follow the experimenter's instructions beyond the point where the victim protested; many colleagues and psychiatrists were questioned on this point, and they virtually all felt this would be the case. Indeed, to initiate an experiment in which the critical measure hangs on disobedience, one must start with a belief in certain spontaneous resources in men that enable them to overcome pressure from authority.

It is true that after a reasonable number of subjects had been exposed to the procedures, it became evident that some would go to the end of the shock board, and some would experience stress. That point, it seems to me, is the first legitimate juncture at which one could even start to wonder whether or not to abandon the study. But momentary excitement is not the same as harm. As the experiment progressed there was no indication of injurious effects in the subjects; and as the subjects themselves strongly endorsed the experiment, the judgment I made was to continue the investigation.

Is not Baumrind's criticism based as much on the unanticipated findings as on the method? The findings were that some subjects performed in what appeared to be a shockingly immoral way. If, instead, every one of the subjects had broken off at "slight shock," or at the first sign of the learner's discomfort, the results would have been pleasant, and reassuring, and who would protest?

PROCEDURES AND BENEFITS

A most important aspect of the procedure occurred at the end of the experimental session. A careful postexperimental treatment was administered to all subjects. The exact content of the dehoax varied from condition to condition and with increasing experience on our part. At the very least all subjects were told that the victim had not received dangerous electric shocks. Each subject had a friendly reconciliation with the unharmed victim, and an extended discussion with the experimenter. The experiment was explained to the defiant subjects in a way that supported their decision to disobey the experimenter. Obedient subjects were assured of the fact that their behavior

was entirely normal and that their feelings of conflict or tension were shared by other participants. Subjects were told that they would receive a comprehensive report at the conclusion of the experimental series. In some instances, additional detailed and lengthy discussions of the experiments were also carried out with individual subjects.

When the experimental series was complete, subjects received a written report which presented details of the experimental procedure and results. Again their own part in the experiments was treated in a dignified way and their behavior in the experiment respected. All subjects received a follow-up questionnaire regarding their participation in the research, which again allowed expression of thoughts and feelings about their behavior.

The replies to the questionnaire confirmed my impression that participants felt positively toward the experiment. In its quantitative aspect (see Table 1), 84 percent of the subjects stated they were glad to have been in the experiment; 15 percent indicated neutral feelings, and 1.3 percent indicated negative feelings. To be sure, such findings are to be interpreted cautiously, but they cannot be disregarded.

Further, four-fifths of the subjects felt that more experiments of this sort should be carried out, and 74 percent indicated that they had learned something of personal importance as a result of being in the study. The results of the interviews, questionnaire responses, and actual transcripts of the debriefing procedures will be presented more fully in a forthcoming monograph.

The debriefing and assessment procedures were carried out as a matter of course, and were not stimulated by any observation of special risk in the experimental procedure. In my judgment, at no point were subjects exposed to danger and at no point did they run the risk of injurious effects resulting from participation. If it had been otherwise, the experiment would have been terminated at once.

Baumrind states that, after he has performed in the experiment, the subject cannot justify his behavior and must bear the full brunt of his actions. By and large it does not work this way. The same mechanisms that allow the subject to perform the act, to obey rather than to defy the experimenter, transcend the moment of performance and continue to justify his behavior for him. The same viewpoint the subject takes while performing the actions is the viewpoint from which he later sees his behavior, that is, the perspective of "carrying out the task assigned by the person in authority."

TABLE 1. EXCERPT FROM QUESTIONNAIRE USED IN A FOLLOW-UP STUDY OF THE OBEDIENCE RESEARCH

NOW THAT I HAVE READ THE REPORT, AND ALL THINGS CONSIDERED . . .	DEFIANT	OBEDIENT	ALL
1. I am very glad to have been in the experiment	40.0%	47.8%	43.5%
2. I am glad to have been in the experiment	43.8%	35.7%	30.2%
3. I am neither sorry nor glad to have been in the experiment	15.3%	14.8%	15.1%
4. I am sorry to have been in the experiment	0.8%	0.7%	0.8%
5. I am very sorry to have been in the experiment	0.0%	1.0%	0.5%

Note: Ninety-two percent of the subjects returned the questionnaire. The characteristics of the nonrespondents were checked against the respondents. They differed from the respondents only with regard to age; younger people were overrepresented in the nonresponding group.

Because the idea of shocking the victim is repugnant, there is a tendency among those who hear of the design to say "people will not do it." When the results are made known, this attitude is expressed as "if they do it they will not be able to live with themselves afterward." These two forms of denying the experimental findings are equally inappropriate misreadings of the facts of human social behavior. Many subjects do, indeed, obey to the end, and there is no indication of injurious effects.

The absence of injury is a minimal condition of experimentation; there can be, however, an important positive side to participation. Baumrind suggests that subjects derived no benefit from being in the obedience study, but this is false. By their statements and actions, subjects indicated that they had learned a good deal, and many felt gratified to have taken part in scientific research they considered to be of significance. A year after his participation one subject wrote:

> This experiment has strengthened my belief that man should avoid harm to his fellow man even at the risk of violating authority.

Another stated:

> To me, the experiment pointed up . . . the extent to which each individual should have or discover firm ground on which to base his decisions, no matter how trivial they appear to be. I think people should think more deeply about themselves and their relation to their world and to other people. If this experiment serves to jar people out of complacency, it will have served its end.

These statements are illustrative of a broad array of appreciative and insightful comments by those who participated.

The five-page report sent to each subject on the completion of the experimental series was specifically designed to enhance the value of his experience. It set out the broad conception of the experimental program as well as the logic of its design. It described the results of a dozen of the experiments, discussed the causes of tension, and attempted to indicate the possible significance of the experiment. Subjects responded enthusiastically; many indicated a desire to be in further experimental research. This report was sent to all subjects several years ago. The care with which it was prepared does not support Baumrind's assertion that the experimenter was indifferent to the value subjects derived from their participation.

Baumrind's fear is that participants will be alienated from psychological experiments because of the intensity of experience associated with laboratory procedures. My own observation is that subjects more commonly respond with distaste to the "empty" laboratory hour, in which cardboard procedures are employed and the only possible feeling upon emerging from the laboratory is that one has wasted time in a patently trivial and useless exercise.

The subjects in the obedience experiment, on the whole, felt quite differently about their participation. They viewed the experience as an opportunity to learn something of importance about themselves, and more generally, about the conditions of human action.

A year after the experimental program was completed, I initiated an additional follow-up study. In this connection an impartial medical examiner, experienced in outpatient treatment, interviewed 40 experimental subjects. The examining psychiatrist focused on those subjects he felt would be most likely to have suffered consequences from participation. His aim was to identify possible injurious effects resulting from the experiment. He concluded that, although extreme stress had been experienced by several subjects,

> none was found by this interviewer to show signs of having been harmed by his experience. . . . Each subject seemed to handle his task [in the experiment]

in a manner consistent with well established patterns of behavior. No evidence was found of any traumatic reactions.

Such evidence ought to be weighed before judging the experiment.

OTHER ISSUES

Baumrind's discussion is not limited to the treatment of subjects, but diffuses to a generalized rejection of the work.

Baumrind feels that obedience cannot be meaningfully studied in a laboratory setting: The reason she offers is that "The dependent, obedient attitude assumed by most subjects in the experimental setting is appropriate to that situation" [p. 275 in this book]. Here, Baumrind has cited the very best reason for examining obedience in this setting, namely that it possesses "ecological validity." Here is one social context in which compliance occurs regularly. Military and job situations are also particularly meaningful settings for the study of obedience precisely because obedience is natural and appropriate to these contexts. I reject Baumrind's argument that the observed obedience does not count because it occurred where it is appropriate. That is precisely why it *does* count. A soldier's obedience is no less meaningful because it occurs in a pertinent military context. A subject's obedience is no less problematical because it occurs within a social institution called the psychological experiment.

Baumrind writes: "The 'game' is defined by the experimenter and he makes the rules" [p. 275]. It is true that for disobedience to occur the framework of the experiment must be shattered. That, indeed, is the point of the design. That is why obedience and disobedience are genuine issues for the subject. *He must really assert himself as a person against a legitimate authority.*

Further, Baumrind wants us to believe that outside the laboratory we could not find a comparably high expression of obedience. Yet, the fact that ordinary citizens are recruited to military service and, on command, perform far harsher acts against people is beyond dispute. Few of them know or are concerned with the complex policy issues underlying martial action; fewer still become conscientious objectors. Good soldiers do as they are told, and on both sides of the battle line. However, a debate on whether a higher level of obedience is represented by (*a*) killing men in the service of one's country, or (*b*) merely shocking them in the service of Yale science, is largely unprofitable. The real question is: What are the forces underlying obedient action?

Another question raised by Baumrind concerns the degree of parallel between obedience in the laboratory and in Nazi Germany. Obviously, there are enormous differences: Consider the disparity in time scale. The laboratory experiment takes an hour; the Nazi calamity unfolded in the space of a decade. There is a great deal that needs to be said on this issue, and only a few points can be touched on here.

1. In arguing this matter, Baumrind mistakes the background metaphor for the precise subject matter of investigation. The German event was cited to point up a serious problem in the human situation: the potentially destructive effect of obedience. But the best way to tackle the problem of obedience, from a scientific standpoint, is in no way restricted by "what happened exactly" in Germany. What happened exactly can *never* be duplicated in the laboratory or anywhere else. The real task is to learn more about the general problem of destructive obedience using a workable approach. Hopefully, such inquiry will stimulate insights and yield general propositions that can be applied to a wide variety of situations.

2. One may ask in a general way: How does a man behave when he is told by a legitimate authority to act against a third individual? In trying to find an answer to this question, the laboratory situation is one useful starting point—and for the very reason stated by Baumrind—namely, the experimenter does constitute a genuine authority for the subject. The fact that trust and dependence on the experimenter are maintained, despite the extraordinary harshness he displays toward the victim, is itself a remarkable phenomenon.

3. In the laboratory, through a set of rather simple manipulations, ordinary persons no longer perceived themselves as a responsible part of the causal chain leading to action against a person. The means through which responsibility is cast off, and individuals become thoughtless agents of action, is of general import. Other processes were revealed that indicate that the experiments will help us to understand why men obey. That understanding will come, of course, by examining the full account of experimental work and not merely the brief report in which the procedure and demonstrational results were exposed.

At root, Baumrind senses that it is not proper to test obedience in this situation, because she construes it as one in which there is no reasonable alternative to obedience. In adopting this view, she has lost sight of this fact: A substantial proportion of subjects do disobey. By their example, disobedience is shown to be a genuine possibility, one that is in no sense ruled out by the general structure of the experimental situation.

Baumrind is uncomfortable with the high level of obedience obtained in the first experiment. In the condition she focused on, 65 percent of the subjects obeyed to the end. However, her sentiment does not take into account that, within the general framework of the psychological experiment, obedience varied enormously from one condition to the next. In some variations, 90 percent of the subjects *dis*obeyed. It seems to be *not* only the fact of an experiment, but the particular structure of elements within the experimental situation that accounts for rates of obedience and disobedience. And these elements were varied systematically in the program of research.

A concern with human dignity is based on a respect for a man's potential to act morally. Baumrind feels that the experimenter *made* the subject shock the victim. This conception is alien to my view. The experimenter tells the subject to do something. But between the command and the outcome there is a paramount force, the acting person who may obey or disobey. I started with the belief that every person who came to the laboratory was free to accept or to reject the dictates of authority. This view sustains a conception of human dignity insofar as it sees in each man a capacity for *choosing* his own behavior. And as it turned out, many subjects did, indeed, choose to reject the experimenter's commands, providing a powerful affirmation of human ideals.

Baumrind also criticizes the experiment on the grounds that "it could easily effect an alteration in the subject's . . . ability to trust adult authorities in the future" [p. 276]. But I do not think she can have it both ways. On the one hand, she argues the experimental situation is so special that it has no generality; on the other hand, she states it has such generalizing potential that it will cause subjects to distrust all authority. But the experimenter is not just any authority: He is an authority who tells the subject to act harshly and inhumanely against another man. I would consider it of the highest value if participation in the experiment could, indeed, inculcate a skepticism of this kind of authority. Here, perhaps, a difference in philosophy emerges most clearly. Baumrind sees the subject as a passive creature, completely controlled by the experimenter. I started from a different viewpoint. A person who comes to the laboratory is an active, choosing adult, capable of accepting or rejecting the prescriptions for action addressed to him. Baumrind sees the effect of the experiment as undermining the subject's trust of authority. I see it as a potentially valuable experience insofar as it makes people aware of the problem of indiscriminate submission to authority.

CONCLUSION

My feeling is that viewed in the total context of values served by the experiment, approximately the right course was followed. In review, the facts are these: (*a*) At the outset, there was the problem of studying obedience by means of a simple experimental procedure. The results could not be foreseen before the experiment was carried out. (*b*) Although the experiment generated momentary stress in some subjects, this stress dissipated quickly and was not injurious. (*c*) Dehoax and follow-up procedures were carried out to insure the subjects' well-being. (*d*) These procedures were assessed through questionnaire and psychiatric studies and were found to be effective. (*e*) Additional steps were taken to enhance the value of the laboratory experience for participants, for example, submitting to each subject a careful report on the experimental program. (*f*) The subjects themselves strongly endorse the experiment and indicate satisfaction at having participated.

If there is a moral to be learned from the obedience study, it is that every man must be responsible for his own actions. This author accepts full responsibility for the design and execution of the study. Some people may feel it should not have been done. I disagree and accept the burden of their judgment.

Baumrind's judgment, someone has said, not only represents a personal conviction, but also reflects a cleavage in American psychology between those whose primary concern is with *helping* people and those who are interested mainly in *learning* about people. I see little value in perpetuating divisive forces in psychology when there is so much to learn from every side. A schism may exist, but it does not correspond to the true ideals of the discipline. The psychologist intent on healing knows that his power to help rests on knowledge; he is aware that a scientific grasp of all aspects of life is essential for his work and is in itself a worthy human aspiration. At the same time, the laboratory psychologist senses his work will lead to human betterment, not only because enlightenment is more dignified than ignorance, but because new knowledge is pregnant with humane consequences.

REFERENCES

Baumrind, D. Some thoughts on ethics of research: After reading Milgram's "Behavioral study of obedience." *American Psychologist*, 1964, **19**: 421–423.

Lazarus, R. A laboratory approach to the dynamics of psychological stress. *American Psychologist*, 1964, **19**: 400–411.

Milgram, S. Behavioral study of obedience. *Journal of Abnormal and Social Psychology*, 1963, **67**: 371–378.

Milgram, S. Some conditions of obedience and disobedience to authority. *Human Relations*, 1965, **18**: 55–76.

ETHICAL ISSUES IN FIELD EXPERIMENTS

Ethical problems of a rather obvious nature arise in the experiments in which deception has potentially harmful consequences for the subject. Take, for example, the brilliant experiment by Mulder and Stemerding on the effects of threat on attraction to the group and need for strong leadership.[1] In this study—one of the very rare examples of an experiment conducted in a natural setting—independent food merchants in a number of Dutch towns were brought together for group meetings, in the course of which they were informed that a large organization was planning to open up a series of supermarkets in the Netherlands. In the High Threat condition, subjects were told that there was a high probability that their town would be selected as a site for such markets, and that the advent of these markets would cause a considerable drop in their business. On the advice of the executives of the shopkeepers' organizations, who had helped to arrange the group meetings, the investigators did not reveal the experimental manipulations to their subjects. I have been worried about these Dutch merchants ever since I heard about this study for the first time. Did some of them go out of business in anticipation of the heavy competition? Do some of them have an anxiety reaction every time they see a bulldozer? Chances are that they soon forgot about this threat (unless, of course, supermarkets actually did move into town) and that it became just one of the many little moments of anxiety that must occur in every shopkeeper's life. Do we have a right, however, to add to life's little anxieties and to risk the possibility of more extensive anxiety purely for the purposes of our experiments, particularly since deception deprives the subject of the opportunity to choose whether or not he wishes to expose himself to the risks that might be entailed?

[1] M. Mulder and A. Stemerding, "Threat, Attraction to Group, and Need for Strong Leadership," *Human Relations*, 1963, *16*, 317–334.

LEGAL AND ETHICAL ASPECTS OF NONREACTIVE SOCIAL PSYCHOLOGICAL RESEARCH: AN EXCURSION INTO THE PUBLIC MIND

DAVID W. WILSON and EDWARD DONNERSTEIN

Many social psychologists have discussed the concept of the implicit contract that exists between an experimenter and a subject who participates in a study voluntarily. They maintain that because the subject has, in effect, contracted to be part of a research project, the use of some deception is less objectionable. Although this argument may be valid for laboratory experiments, in which the subject is aware of his or her experimental participation, it may not hold true for nonreactive field research, in which the subject is unaware that a study is taking place and that his or her behavior is being observed. Clearly, no contract, even an implicit one, exists between experimenter and subject in such a situation. That fact gives rise to a question: Is it ethical to collect data or to induce an experimental manipulation under such conditions? This is one of the issues explored in "Legal and Ethical Aspects of Nonreactive Social Psychological Research," by David Wilson and Edward Donnerstein. Rather than speculating about the general public's reaction to nonreactive research methods, they actually sampled public attitudes and feelings.

In recent years there has been a growing criticism of laboratory research in psychology, particularly in social psychology. It has been argued that such research is susceptible to many types of artifacts which decrease the validity of the findings. Such artifacts include demand characteristics . . . , evaluation apprehension . . . , experimenter expectancy . . . , early versus late-term participation . . . , and volunteer subjects. . . . Related to this last artifact is the problem of the generalizability of laboratory results. Volunteer subjects do differ from nonvolunteers on a number of important dimensions . . . , but even beyond this problem, psychologists tend to be biased in their selection of subjects . . . , with most subjects being college males. The generalizability of results from such a select population has been viewed as hazardous, if not wrong.

A further problem of laboratory research in social psychology is the use of deception. Although the use of deception has been for the purpose of reducing subject awareness of the experimenter's hypothesis, it has produced both methodological and ethical problems of its own. . . . Adair (1973) argues that the "deception-searching" attitude that develops with the widespread use of deception is an issue of great concern. For example, Silverman, Shulman, and Wiesenthal (1970) have shown that subjects who have participated in prior deception experiments tend to present themselves in a favorable manner in later experiments. On the ethical side, Kelman (1967) has argued that the use of deception has several negative aspects. First, he believes that many

deceptions may result in harmful consequences to subjects even though they are debriefed. A recent study by Holmes and Bennett (1974), however, does not support this conclusion. In their study, it was found that debriefing eliminated the arousal associated with the threat of shock. They concluded that debriefing effectively eliminates deceptions and the stress associated with them. Second, Kelman argues that the use of deception results in a demeaning of the relationship between experimenter and subject. In sum, Kelman's argument is that the use of deception should be reduced and that attempts should be made to find methods that do not require deception.

In response to many of these laboratory problems, there has been an increased interest in naturalistic experimentation in which subjects are unaware that their behavior is being studied. McGuire (1967, 1969) has outlined a number of "forces" making field research attractive. He believes that theory-oriented research in natural settings is "the best of both worlds for social psychology." While many advantages exist for doing naturalistic research, most writers are quick to point out the potential ethical problems of such research. Opinions as to the seriousness of such problems, however, are quite varied. Toward one end of the continuum are writers such as Johnson (1973), who feels that laboratory research is preferable to field research on ethical grounds. Johnson feels that ethical problems are multiplied in field research, because there is no informed consent and no attempt at debriefing. At the other end of the continuum are writers such as Campbell (1969) and Bickman and Henchy (1972), who argue that because most field experiments study behavior that falls within the "public domain," and because these experiments do not disrupt a subject's normal behavior, a subject's permission is not required. Toward the middle of the continuum are Crano and Brewer (1973), who question

From *American Psychologist*, 1976, *31*, 765–773. Copyright © 1976 by The American Psychological Association and reprinted with permission of authors and The American Psychological Association.

what "public" behaviors really are and feel that the issue of privacy is still at stake if individuals in field settings do not normally *expect* to be observed. Crano and Brewer further voice concern over the cumulative effects of field research possibly leading to a "candid camera" complex among the public. As a solution to such ethical problems, they suggest that field experimentation be limited to settings and activities in which the researchers would typically engage. For example, a researcher connected with a volunteer service could study persuasion techniques as part of a fund-raising campaign. A more liberal position, but yet still rather middle-of-the-road, is taken by Aronson and Carlsmith (1968), who feel that field experimentation is ethically more extreme than laboratory research and should be undertaken only with a "great deal of caution." Their argument is based on the grounds that in field experimentation, subjects do not enter a contractual relationship with the experimenter. Subjects' behaviors are affected by the experimenter without their consent or knowledge that they are participating in an experiment.

. . .

The present study assessed the general public's reactions to nonreactive methods in a context in which they could express their views without a feeling of obligation or pressure. Our goal was to collect data that would serve as an aid in resolving ethical anxieties about conducting nonreactive field research. We feel that such an approach is consistent with Gergen's (1973) proposal that we, in part, base ethical guidelines on empirical evidence indicating precisely what subjects feel about certain experimental procedures.

METHOD

Subjects

The subjects were 93 males and 81 females who were selected randomly (with the restriction that the subject be college age or above) at various field locations such as parking lots, shopping centers, and parks. Ages ranged from 17 to 85, with a median age of 27.83. Included in the sample were 139 nonstudents and 35 students. Sampling was done in midwestern locations, with the population generally being middle class. An attempt was made to sample in locations that were comparable to those that are typically used as research locations. Consequently, 30% of the subjects came from a small university town of approximately

45,000, and 43% of the subjects came from a large city with a population of approximately 300,000. This latter city, although more urbanized than the small university town, does contain several colleges and a university. Most of the remaining subjects came from small midwestern towns smaller in population than the university town described above.

Interviewers

The interviewers were 35 students from the authors' introductory psychology and social psychology classes. All interviewers were instructed in the techniques and problems of interviewing. The number of subjects interviewed by each student ranged from 3 to 7, with the mode being 5.

Nonreactive Methods

The 8 nonreactive methods that were described to subjects were taken from 10 methods that were used by Silverman (1975). These included the methods of Latané (1970)—asking for money; Freedman and Fraser (1966)—subjects are asked a small, then a large request by an experimenter misrepresenting himself; Piliavan and Piliavin (1972)—subjects witness a staged emergency on a subway; Milgram (1969)—letters are dropped in various locations; Milgram (1970)—asking to enter home and use telephone; Zimbardo (1969)—filming of subjects who have contact with abandoned automobiles; Schaps (1972)—experimenter's accomplice rejecting whatever the shoe salesman shows her during busy store hours; and Abelson and Miller (1967)—subjects are personally insulted. The summaries that appeared in Silverman (1975, p. 765) were used verbatim to describe the methods to the subjects. These summaries are reproduced in the following section.

Summaries of Nonreactive Methods—Taken from Silverman (1975)

1. Experimenters, walking singly or in pairs, ask politely for either 10¢ or 20¢ from passerby, sometimes offering an explanation for why they need the money (Latané, 1970).

2. The experimenter comes to a home, says that he has misplaced the address of a friend who lives nearby, and asks to use the phone. If the party admits him, he pretends to make the call (Milgram, 1970).

3. Automobiles, parked on streets, look as if they were abandoned. (License plates are removed and hoods are raised.) Experimenters hide in nearby buildings and film people who have any contact with the cars (Zimbardo, 1969).

4. A female and a confederate experimenter visit shoe stores at times when there are more customers than salesmen. One of them is wearing a shoe with a broken heel. She rejects whatever the salesman shows her. The confederate, posing as a friend of the customer, surreptitiously takes notes on the salesman's behavior (Schaps, 1972).

5. Housewives are phoned. The caller names a fictitious consumer's group that he claims to represent and interviews them about the soap products they use for a report in a "public service publication," which is also given a fictitious name. Several days later the experimenter calls again and asks if the housewives would allow five or six men into their homes to "enumerate and classify" all of their household products for another report in the same publication. If the party agrees, the caller says he is just collecting names of willing people at present and that she will be contacted if it is decided to use her in the survey. No one is contacted again (Freedman & Fraser, 1966).

6. People sitting alone on park benches are asked to be interviewed by an experimenter who gives the name of a fictitious survey research organization that he claims to represent. At the beginning of the interview, the experimenter asks a person sitting nearby, who is actually a confederate, if he would mind answering the questions at the same time. The confederate responds with opinions that are clearly opposite those of the subject and makes demeaning remarks about the subject's answers; for example, "that's ridiculous"; "that's just the sort of thing you'd expect to hear in this park" (Abelson & Miller, 1967).

7. A person walking with cane pretends to collapse in a subway car. "Stage blood" trickles from his mouth. If someone approaches the victim, he allows the party to help him to his feet. If no one approaches before the train slows to a stop, another experimenter, posing as a passenger, pretends to do so and both leave the train (Piliavin & Piliavin, 1972).

8. Letters, stamped and addressed to fictitious organizations at the same post office box number, are dropped in various locations, as if they were lost on the way to being mailed. Some are placed under automobile windshield wipers with a penciled note saying "found near car" (Milgram, 1969).

Four of the eight summaries were described to each subject. Half of the subjects heard descriptions of the first four experiments described above, and the other half heard the second four.

Procedure

Upon randomly choosing a subject, the interviewer approached the subject, introduced him/herself, and asked if the subject would be willing to take 10 minutes to answer some questions for a psychology class project. Subjects were told that the interview would be totally anonymous. If the subject agreed or at least tentatively agreed to be interviewed, the interviewer went on to explain by stating:

> What we would like to do is simply find out how people like yourself feel about certain procedures that are sometimes used in research in social psychology, particularly that research which is conducted in natural settings using people like yourself as subjects. As I describe these various procedures to you, try to put yourself in the position of a subject in one of these experiments and judge as best and honestly as you can how you would feel about being a subject in such an experiment. Keep in mind as you hear each description that the purpose in each of these experiments is simply to observe the reactions of the subject. For each question I ask you, answer "no," "not sure," or "yes."

The interviewer then read the descriptions of four nonreactive methods to the subject. After reading each description, the interviewer asked a series of questions regarding legal and ethical aspects of the method. These questions included: (1) If you discovered that you had been a subject in this experiment, would you feel that you had been harassed or annoyed? (2) If you discovered that you had been a subject in this experiment, would you feel that your privacy had been invaded? (3) Do you feel that such an experiment is unethical or immoral? (4) Would you mind being a subject in such an experiment? (5) Do you feel that psychologists should be doing such an experiment? (6) Is doing such an experiment justified by its contribution to our scientific knowledge of behavior? (7) Does such an experiment lower your trust in social scientists and their work? (8) Do you feel that the psychologist's actions in this experiment are against the law? (9) If you discovered that the psychologist's actions were illegal, would you attempt to see a lawyer and press charges? (10) If you discovered that you had been a subject in this experiment, would you feel that trespassing had been committed?

After all four descriptions had been read and responded to, five more general questions were asked. These were: (1) Should psychologists stop deceiving the public as they do in these experiments? (2) Should the public protest against the actions that were described in these examples? (3) Is it all right for social scientists to deceive the public? (4) Is it all right for politicians to deceive the public? (5) Is it all right for the military to deceive the public?

Following the completion of these questions, the subject was thanked for participating in the study and the interview was completed.

RESULTS

The results of the interviews are presented in Tables 1 and 2. No systematic sex, age, or locale differences were found, so, consequently, the data were collapsed over these variables for all other analyses. Table 1 shows the percentages of subjects responding "no," "not sure," or "yes" to each question for each nonreactive method. Table 2 shows the results of the subjects' responses to the five general questions. As can be seen in Table 1, the largest percentage of subjects who expressed feelings of harassment responded to the Schaps (1972) study (72%). Subjects felt least harassed by the Zimbardo (1969) study (24%). For four of the eight studies, a majority of the subjects expressed feelings of harassment. For the other four studies, the minority expressing such feelings was quite sizable, being as high as 44% in one case. With regard to feelings of invasion of privacy, none of the studies elicited such feelings from the majority of the subjects, with the largest percentage (47%) being in the case of Freedman and Fraser (1966), followed closely by 46% for the Milgram (1970) study. The lowest percentage (11%) was in the case of Milgram (1969). Clearly these are noteworthy minorities, however. Also, the majority of subjects did not see the studies as being unethical, although the percentages in several cases were considerable, with the highest being 47% for Piliavin and Piliavin (1972) followed by 43% for Latané (1970). The lowest such

percentage was 18% for Zimbardo (1969). When asked if they would mind being subjects in the experiments, a majority said they would mind in five of the experiments, the highest percentage being 65% for Schaps (1972), the lowest 28% for Zimbardo (1969).

When the subjects were asked if psychologists should be doing such an experiment, the responses were much more varied than on the questions thus far. For two of the studies, half or more of the subjects said that psychologists should not be doing the experiment. These two studies were Latané (1970) (54%) and Piliavin and Piliavin (1972) (50%). For the remaining studies, rather large minorities felt that the experiments should not be done. Responses were again quite varied with regard to whether the experiment was justified by its contribution to our scientific knowledge of behavior. For none of the studies did a majority of the subjects say it was *not* justified. However, neither did a majority in any case feel the experiment *was* justified. In general, rather substantial minorities saw the experiments as not being justified. A large majority of the subjects felt that the experiments did *not* lower their trust in social scientists and their work. Still, a respectable number of people in many cases felt the experiments *did* lower their trust, with the highest percentage being 37% for Piliavin and Piliavin (1972). When asked if the methods were against the law, very few subjects in general perceived them as such, with the highest percentage being 26% for Milgram (1970). Given that the methods were known to be illegal, a majority of the subjects in each case said they would not see a lawyer, with the largest percentage (73%) being in the case of Schaps (1972). Nevertheless, sizable minorities of subjects, as high as 32% for Piliavin and Piliavin (1972), said they *would* see a lawyer. For three of the methods, subjects were asked if they felt the experimenter committed trespassing. Rather large minorities of subjects felt this to be the case, with 40% indicating this for Milgram (1970), 33% for Freedman and Fraser (1966), and 14% for Schaps (1972).

It is also possible to get some indication of which particular methods were most or least acceptable overall. To do this, the methods were ranked from the most to the least objectionable for each interview question. Each method's mean ranking was then computed. The methods as listed in Table 1 are in precisely this order, from most to least objectionable. As can be seen, Latané's (1970) method was the least acceptable while

EXPERIENCING SOCIAL PSYCHOLOGY

TABLE 1. SUBJECTS' RESPONSES TO QUESTIONS ASKED ABOUT EACH NONREACTIVE METHOD

					QUESTION					
ANSWER	FEEL HARASSED?	PRIVACY INVADED?	UNETHICAL?	MIND BEING SUBJECT?	DO SUCH EXPERIMENT?	JUSTIFIED BY SCIENTIFIC CONTRIBUTION?	LOWER TRUST?	AGAINST LAW?	SEE LAWYER?	TRESPASSING COMMITTED?
Latané (1970)—Asking for Money										
No	40	56	46	38	54	48	62	57	64	—
Not sure	3	1	1	8	27	23	9	23	10	—
Yes	57	43	43	54	19	29	29	20	26	—
Piliavin & Piliavin (1972)—Blood Study										
No	55	81	43	42	50	38	59	60	58	—
Not sure	2	1	10	5	18	36	4	19	11	—
Yes	43	18	47	53	32	27	37	20	32	—
Milgram (1970)—Ask to Enter Home and Use Telephone										
No	51	46	48	46	46	41	64	55	60	48
Not sure	5	8	15	10	22	24	5	19	21	12
Yes	44	46	38	44	31	35	31	26	19	40
Freedman & Fraser (1966)—Foot-in-the-door Technique										
No	45	50	53	41	36	38	69	59	58	63
Not sure	1	3	12	6	30	30	10	24	13	4
Yes	54	47	35	53	34	32	22	17	29	33
Abelson & Miller (1967)—Personal Insult Study										
No	28	48	42	40	35	30	68	73	68	—
Not sure	9	7	16	9	28	27	7	12	19	—
Yes	63	44	42	52	37	43	25	15	14	—
Schaps (1972)—Shoe Store Study										
No	20	60	52	28	49	42	68	75	73	72
Not sure	8	14	16	8	20	16	11	18	16	14
Yes	72	26	31	65	31	41	21	8	10	14
Milgram (1969)—Lost Letter Technique										
No	70	87	68	54	34	37	70	75	69	—
Not sure	3	2	8	8	33	31	10	15	10	—
Yes	26	11	24	38	32	32	20	10	22	—
Zimbardo (1969)—Abandoned Automobiles Study										
No	72	74	65	65	22	18	78	75	72	—
Not sure	5	5	16	6	28	32	5	18	18	—
Yes	24	21	18	28	49	49	17	6	10	—

Note: All data are given as percentages. Number of subjects on which percentages are based range from 79 to 93. . . . .

TABLE 2. SUBJECTS' RESPONSES TO GENERAL QUESTIONS

RESPONSE	QUESTION				
	STOP DECEIVING PUBLIC?	PUBLIC PROTEST?	ALL RIGHT FOR SOCIAL SCIENTISTS TO DECEIVE PUBLIC?	ALL RIGHT FOR POLITICIANS TO DECEIVE PUBLIC?	ALL RIGHT FOR MILITARY TO DECEIVE PUBLIC?
No	41	45	61	91	81
Not sure	21	17	13	6	10
Yes	38	38	26	2	9

Note: All data are given as percentages. Percentages based on *N* = 172. . . .

Zimbardo's (1969) method was the most acceptable.

As can be seen in Table 2, responses to whether psychologists should stop deceiving the public were consistent with the responses presented thus far. Thirty-eight percent of the subjects felt that such deception should be stopped. A rather sizable minority (21%) were uncertain on the issue. As to whether the public should protest against the methods, again 38% felt that they should. A rather interesting comparison can be made for the final three questions. While 91% and 81% said it was not all right for politicians and the military, respectively, to deceive the public, 61% believed that it was not all right for social scientists to do so.

. . .

DISCUSSION

The results of the present study pose somewhat of a dilemma. That is, one can make several opposing conclusions from the data. We will point out these possible interpretations and let debate take its course.

It seems reasonable that one possible interpretation of the present data is that the public generally does not negatively view the use of nonreactive methods. Such an interpretation, of course, must be based on the premise that one's concern is with what the "majority" of the public feels. That is, this view dictates that if the majority of the public views a particular technique as acceptable, then we will consider that technique to be as such. The implicit assumption here is that no technique will be acceptable to all potential subjects and that we must therefore use a "majority rule" criterion for deciding the acceptability of a particular procedure.

The data do in fact indicate that in many cases the majority of subjects did not react negatively to the unobtrusive measures. Four of the eight studies were seen as harassing by a majority of the subjects, but in no case did a majority see the procedures as invading their privacy or as unethical. In only one case did a strong majority indicate that they would mind being a subject in the experiment, while in four other cases a little more than half of the subjects indicated that they would mind being a subject. In only two cases did half or more of the subjects say the experiment should not be done. In no case did a majority feel that an experiment was unjustified by its scientific contribution, and usually strong majorities indicated that the experiments did not lower their trust in social scientists. For experiments in which it is conceivable that trespassing may have been committed, less than a majority felt this to be the case. Interestingly, a majority of the subjects did not perceive any of the methods as illegal, and more interesting, they indicated that they would not see a lawyer even if such illegality existed.

Furthermore, less than a majority felt that deception in nonreactive research should be stopped or that a protest should be mounted against such research. Also, while most subjects felt that it was not all right for social scientists, politicians, and the military to deceive the public, more leeway was given to social scientists.

If one does indeed interpret the results in terms of "public acceptance" of nonreactive techniques, then these results are obviously contrary to what some believe to be the case. It is probably true that one reason for having ethical guidelines in the first place is that if we did not, subjects would react negatively. It is interesting, then, that the picture painted thus far is much different than that presented by Warwick (1975), who feels that nonreactive research is highly frowned upon by the public and is contributing to a growing feeling of mistrust in America. Apparently, there is still some feeling among the public that anything done for the sake of science is legitimate. Furthermore, the present findings could be viewed as being consistent with many findings cited earlier which show that subjects are not as concerned about ethical issues as we might think.

A totally different interpretation of the present results is perhaps more appealing to many readers. This interpretation puts less of an emphasis on the majority and instead emphasizes the substantial minorities in many cases who view the procedures negatively. Such an approach has as its basic premise the belief that if *any* number of subjects find a particular technique unacceptable, then such a technique will indeed be classified as such. The extreme case, of course, with such an interpretation is when only one individual objects to a given technique. This may in fact be rare, but nevertheless this approach assumes that only one negative response is enough to cause concern. It takes only one person to publicly protest the use of nonreactive methods or only one person to take us to court to convince us that a negative response can be devastating. With this attitude in mind, the data of the present study are indeed quite alarming. Obviously, many subjects were quite distressed with the techniques. More than one in three of our subjects felt that social scientists should stop deceiving the public and that a public protest should be mounted. It is interesting to speculate as to why such protests have not occurred. Presumably, public awareness of the extent of usage of nonreactive techniques is not great. As public awareness does increase, however, 38% of the potential subject population is more than enough to lay to rest any ambitions social scientists may once have had regarding the use of nonreactive methods. In general, one might take the following attitude. Can we justify using a nonreactive measure when we know that maybe one third or more of our subjects would be distressed if they were aware of what we were doing and probably would not want to be in the experiment? After all, we must remember that they have not entered a contractual relationship with us. Subjects may also view our laboratory procedures as unacceptable, but at least there they would be aware that they were being studied. If the researcher chooses to proceed with the knowledge that one third of the subjects would object, the risks involved are unlikely to be precisely known but can be potentially very costly, especially in terms of legal repercussions to the researcher.

The data of the present study were intentionally collected in such a way as to minimize feelings of obligation or pressure to respond in certain ways. There is always the possibility, however, that subjects would react differently toward these nonreactive methods if they were actually subjects in one of the described experiments. Such a possibility could be investigated by debriefing subjects in a nonreactive experiment and asking them their reactions to the experiment. It might be that in such a case, subjects would react even more positively than they did in the present study if they were told the rationale for the experiment. Or on the other hand, the immediacy of the situation and the knowledge that they had been deceived might result in more negative reactions. Data on this issue are clearly needed.

The implied theme of this article is that in the future, investigators using nonreactive methods should take into consideration the public's attitudes toward that method. . . . Presently, most researchers are likely to consider only their own views or those of their peers without considering the views of their potential subjects. By finding out from the subject pool the aspects of the method that are objectionable, the researcher can explore other viable alternatives, possibly even with the aid of members of the subject pool. Not only would such a procedure keep the researcher from using an objectionable technique but it also would allow him or her to use a particular method without feelings of guilt or the burden of having to justify the use of the method to others. The APA Committee on Ethical Standards in Psychological Research (1973) has noted that disguised field experimentation "can be considered only with misgivings, for which the help of ethical consultants will be needed to resolve" (p. 33). We simply feel that potential subjects should have the opportunity to participate in this consulting process.

The use of potential subjects as consultants raises several issues. One issue is how much weight should be given to the public view. For instance, it might be that the investigator and his or her peers feel that the use of a particular method is justified by the scientific contribution made by the study. Potential subjects, on the other hand, may object to the technique. What, then, does the experimenter do? We have suggested that the public view be taken into account, but how much weight it should be given is a matter for debate.

A second issue that has already been dealt with is the problem of what percentage of the public must object to a particular method before we conclude that the general public attitude toward that technique is "negative." That is, assuming that the public opinion is weighted heavily in the investigator's decision, what percentage of subjects expressing a negative attitude is enough to veto use of the method? Must it be a majority? 5%? Is *one* negative response enough? Again, this is not an issue with an easy solution and we do not pretend to have the answer.

· · ·

In summary, an experimenter, in deciding whether to use a particular nonreactive technique, has recourse to several bodies of ethical consul-

tants. We have suggested that the general public be considered as one such consultant by gauging the public attitude toward the method. The results of the present study can be used as a gauge for investigators wanting to use methods similar to those described to our subjects. If a method different from the ones described here is desired, the experimenter should conduct his or her own survey to determine its viability. Given that ethical guidelines are constructed to protect the rights of subjects, we feel that the most ethical study is one in which subjects themselves have had a voice in determining its methods.

REFERENCES

Abelson, R. P., & Miller, J. C. Negative persuasion via personal insult. *Journal of Experimental Social Psychology*, 1967, *3*, 321–333.

Adair, J. G. *The human subject: The social psychology of the psychological experiment.* Boston, Mass.: Little, Brown, 1973.

APA Committee on Ethical Standards in Psychological Research. *Ethical principles in the conduct of research with human participants.* Washington, D.C.: American Psychological Association, 1973.

Aronson, E., & Carlsmith, J. M. Experimentation in social psychology. In G. Lindzey & E. Aronson (Eds.), *The handbook of social psychology* (Vol. 2). Reading, Mass.: Addison-Wesley, 1968.

Bickman, L., & Henchy, T. (Eds.). *Beyond the laboratory: Field research in social psychology.* New York: McGraw-Hill, 1972.

Campbell, D. T. Prospective: Artifact and control. In R. Rosenthal & R. L. Rosnow (Eds.), *Artifact in behavioral research.* New York: Academic Press, 1969.

Crano, W. D., & Brewer, M. B. *Principles of research in social psychology.* New York: McGraw-Hill, 1973.

Freedman, J. L., & Fraser, S. C. Compliance without pressure: The foot-in-the-door technique. *Journal of Personality and Social Psychology*, 1966, *4*, 195–202.

Gergen, K. J. The codification of research ethics: Views of a doubting Thomas. *American Psychologist*, 1973, *28*, 907–912.

Holmes, D. S., & Bennett, D. H. Experiments to answer questions raised by the use of deception in psychological research: I. Role playing as an alternative to deception; II. Effectiveness of debriefing after a deception; III. Effect of informed consent on deception. *Journal of Personality and Social Psychology*, 1974, *29*, 358–367.

Johnson, D. W. (Ed.). *Contemporary social psychology.* Philadelphia, Pa.: Lippincott, 1973.

Kelman, H. C. Human use of human subjects: The problem of deception in social psychological experiments. *Psychological Bulletin*, 1967, *67*, 1–11.

Latané, B. Field studies of altruistic compliance. *Representative Research in Social Psychology*, 1970, *1*, 49–60.

McGuire, W. J. Some impending reorientations in social psychology. *Journal of Experimental Social Psychology*, 1967, *3*, 124–139.

McGuire, W. J. Theory-oriented research in natural settings: The best of both worlds for social psychology. In M. Sherif & C. W. Sherif (Eds.), *Interdisciplinary relationships in the social sciences.* Chicago, Ill.: Aldine, 1969.

Milgram, S. The lost-letter technique. *Psychology Today*, June 1969, pp. 30–33; 66; 68.

Milgram, S. The experience of living in cities. *Science*, 1970, *167*, 1461–1468.

Piliavin, J. A., & Piliavin, I. M. Effect of blood on reactions to a victim. *Journal of Personality and Social Psychology*, 1972, *23*, 353–361.

Schaps, E. Cost, dependency and helping. *Journal of Personality and Social Psychology*, 1972, *21*, 74–78.

Silverman, I. Nonreactive methods and the law. *American Psychologist*, 1975, *30*, 764–769.

Silverman, I., Shulman, A. D., & Wiesenthal, D. L. Effects of deceiving and debriefing psychological subjects on performance in later experiments. *Journal of Personality and Social Psychology*, 1970, *14*, 203–212.

Warwick, D. P. Social scientists ought to stop lying. *Psychology Today*, February 1975, pp. 38; 40; 105–106.

Zimbardo, P. The human choice: Individuation, reason and order versus deindividuation, impulse and chaos. In W. J. Arnold & D. Levine (Eds.), *Nebraska Symposium on Motivation* (Vol. 17). Lincoln: University of Nebraska Press, 1969.

PROJECTS

Name _____

Date _____

12.1: WHAT IS THE ETHICAL PROBLEM?

This exercise presents various ethical problems raised by research in social psychology. As you evaluate each of the studies summarized below, consider whether the potential findings were important enough (either theoretically or practically) to justify the procedure that was used. In a class discussion, compare your responses with those of your fellow students.

A. After the subjects had performed an experimental task, the investigator made it clear, through words and gestures, that the experiment was over and that he would now "like to explain what this has been all about so you'll have some idea of why you were doing this." The explanation was false and was designed to serve as a basis for the true experimental manipulation, which involved asking subjects to serve as the experimenter's accomplices. The task of the accomplice was to tell the next subject that the experiment in which he had just participated had been interesting and enjoyable. (It was, in fact, a rather boring experience.) He or she was also asked to be on call on unspecified future occasions when his or her services as accomplice might be needed because "the regular fellow couldn't make it, and we had a subject scheduled." These newly recruited accomplices were, of course, the true subjects, and the subjects were the experimenter's true accomplices. For their services as accomplices, the true subjects were paid in advance. Half of them received $1; the other half, $20. However, when they completed their tasks, the investigators asked them to return the money. (Festinger, L., and Carlsmith, J. M. Cognitive consequences of forced compliance. *Journal of Abnormal and Social Psychology*, 1959, **58**, 203–210.)

1. What are the ethical problems raised by the study?

2. Was the dignity or privacy of the subjects endangered? If so, how?

B. Bramel led male undergraduates to believe that they were homosexually aroused by photographs of men. Bergin gave subjects of both sexes discrepant information about their level of masculinity or femininity. In one experimental condition, that information was presumably based on an elaborate series of psychological tests in which the subjects had participated. In all three studies, the deception was explained to the subject at the end of the experiment. (Bramel, D. A Dissonance theory approach to defensive projection. *Journal of Abnormal and Social Psychology*, 1962, **64,** 121–129; Selection of a target for defensive projection. *Journal of Abnormal and Social Psychology*, 1963, **66,** 318–324. Bergin, A. E. The effect of dissonant persuasive communications on changes in a self-referring attitude. *Journal of Personality,* 1962, **30,** 423–438.)

1. What ethical problems do you see in these studies?

2. Was there a danger to the subjects' physical or psychological well-being? If so, what was it?

C. The subject was led to believe that he was participating in a learning study and was instructed to administer increasingly severe shocks to another person, who, after a while, began to protest vehemently. In fact, the victim was the experimenter's accomplice and did not receive any shocks. Depending on the conditions, sizable proportions of the subjects obeyed the experimenter's instructions and continued to shock the other person up to the maximum level, which they believed to be extremely painful. (Milgram, S. Behavioral study of obedience. *Journal of Abnormal and Social Psychology*, 1963, **67,** 371–378; Some conditions of obedience and disobedience to authority. *Human Relations*, 1965, **18,** 57–76.)

1. What are some of the ethical problems posed by this research?

2. How stressful do you think the experience was for the subject? How would you assess the level of stress?

D. In an experiment designed to study the establishment of a conditioned response in a situation that is traumatic but not painful, the experimenters used a drug to induce a temporary interruption of respiration in their subjects. "This has no permanently harmful physical consequences but is nonetheless a severe stress which is not in itself painful. . . ." The subjects' reports confirmed that this was a "horrific" experience for them. All the subjects . . . said that they thought they were dying." Of course, the subjects, "male alcoholic patients who volunteered for the experiment when they were told that it was connected with a possible therapy for alcoholism," were not warned in advance about the effect of the drug, because that information would have reduced the traumatic impact of the experience. (Campbell, D., Sanderson, R. E., & Laverty, S. Characteristics of a conditioned response in human subjects during extinction trials following a single traumatic conditioning trial. *Journal of Abnormal and Social Psychology*, 1964, **68**, 627–639.)

1. What ethical problems does this study raise?

2. What difficulties would be introduced if the experimenter first obtained the subjects' informed consent?

Name _____

Date _____

12.2: EVALUATING ETHICAL ISSUES

This project presents you with a complex task in order to help you understand the spirit in which social scientists approach their research. It involves a rather detailed description of a research program carried out in military settings by Berkum, Bialek, Kern, and Yagi ("Experimental Studies of Psychological Stress in Man," *Psychological Monographs,* 1962, **76,** 15). This program investigated cognitive stress in general and the effect of battle stress on performance in particular. The specific question addressed was: Is there a deterioration of performance during combat?

A. Sixty-six men who were passengers aboard an airplane served (without their prior knowledge) as subjects in the study. (All were in their first eight weeks of army basic training.) When the plane had reached an altitude of 5,000 feet, subjects saw that one propeller had stopped turning and heard about other malfunctions over the intercom; they were then informed directly that there was an emergency. A simulated pilot-to-tower conversation was provided to the subjects over their earphones to support the deception. As the aircraft passed within sight of the airfield, subjects could see firetrucks and ambulances on the airstrip in apparent expectation of a crash-landing. After several minutes, the pilot ordered the plane steward to prepare the passengers for ditching in the nearby ocean because the landing gear would not function properly. This was a signal for the steward to administer the questionnaires (which was the test of impaired performance). The subjects were asked to fill out two forms: one, an emergency form, involving deliberately complicated directions for twenty-three categories of items, that included a description of, and instructions for, disposition of the individual's personal possessions in case of death; the other, emergency instructions that had twelve multiple-choice items testing retention of airborne emergency instructions that all subjects had been required to read as a standard operating procedure before the flight. These papers were supposed to be put in a waterproof container and jettisoned before the aircraft came down on the ocean. After a specific time had elapsed, the aircraft made a safe landing at the airport. Blood and urine samples were then collected from all subjects. A postexperimental inquiry indicated that subjects suffered various degrees of anxiety about the possibility of death or injury. (See next page.)

What ethical problems does the study raise? That is, do you think that the study involved undue or unnecessary risks, invasion of privacy, disrespect for human dignity, and/or physical, physiological, or social harm? Was the requirement of informed consent fulfilled? Do you think that the beneficial outcomes of the research outweigh the risks to which the participants were subjected? Did the use of deception involve a particular ethical problem?

B. Subjects were new recruits not yet in basic training. They were transported by bus eighty-five miles from the army base to a large, desolate mountain area, undeveloped, dry, and rugged. Before they boarded the bus, an officer told the men that they were to be used to test new concepts of atomic-age warfare and that they would be called upon to perform individually rather than as a group. He also told them that a novel concept of extremely wide dispersal of troops was under study in a large-scale exercise simultaneously involving many units and that experimental communication equipment was to be used. Certain units, not currently in contact with the subjects, were said to be concerned with actual testing of nuclear weapons and conventional artillery. Subjects were also cautioned about the danger of forest fires.

Each subject was then taken in turn to an isolated outpost. A two-way radio purposely overburdened with dials, lights, and knobs (intended to camouflage the performance measures) served as his only contact with the command post. Once subjects reported that they were in position, the experimenter played a tape recording that the subjects heard on their earphones; it consisted of miscellaneous, extremely convincing radio transmissions dealing with the military exercise. After approximately twenty-five minutes, the studies were started. In all three experimental situations, the subjects were led to believe that they were in immediate danger of losing their lives or of being seriously injured. The situations differed only in the events contrived to cause the emergency: accidental nuclear radiation in the area (the radiation dosimeter needle began to fluctuate, and the subject received messages that his area was in danger), a sudden forest fire in the area (a smoke generator was started, and the subject heard messages regarding the existence of a forest fire in the area), misdirected incoming artillery shells (subjects experienced the first of the series of nearby explosions simulating incoming artillery shells and heard reinforcing messages confirming the unexpected hazard).

In all three situations, the subject was led to believe that immediate rescue was possible for him only if he could report his location over his radio transmitter, which had failed quite suddenly. The effect of stress on performance was measured by how fast the subject could repair the prearranged defect in the transmitter. After seventy-five minutes, the study was terminated, subjects were picked up at the outpost, and after they had given blood and urine samples, they were thoroughly debriefed. (See next page.)

What ethical problems do these three studies present? (Refer to the specific issues raised concerning the experiment described in question A.)

C.   In this study, there was no threat of injury to the subject himself. Rather, he was made to feel responsible for an injury to someone he knew or with whom he had been working. (This, by the way, proved to be the most stressful situation for the subjects.) Army trainees were brought individually to an isolated area on the edge of a military post. They were told that a crew was wiring some explosives in the canyon below but needed a remote control circuit to blow up a charge of TNT. The subjects were then told how to build the circuit and to throw the switch. Each was also told that his radio was the only communication he and the crew in the canyon had with the army base. After the subject threw the switch and set off a five-pound charge of TNT, he heard over the intercom that someone was hurt by the explosion and that it was his responsibility to get help. But when he tried to transmit his call for help, he discovered that his radio did not work. Again, impaired performance was measured by how long it took subjects to repair the radio. Blood and urine samples were collected from the subjects after the termination of the experimental situation. (See next page.)

What ethical problems do you see with the study?

Name _____

Date _____

D. Put yourself in the place of the scientist who wants to find out whether stress really impairs performance. This is a very important issue. For example, it is vital to understand and thus be able to anticipate the responses of people who work in highly stressful jobs (e.g., police, hospital emergency room staff, firemen). How would you study the general issue of the effect of stress on performance and yet avoid the ethical issues you have raised in your answers in the previous questions?

ABOUT THE AUTHORS

AYALA PINES is a Lecturer and Research Associate in the Psychology Department at the University of California, Berkeley. She received her B.A. in Psychology and Sociology from the Hebrew University at Jerusalem in 1967, and her Ph.D. from Boston University in 1973. Her research interests in applied social psychology (especially job burnout, life tedium, and the social-psychological double-bind of professional women) have resulted in numerous scientific publications.

CHRISTINA MASLACH is Associate Professor of Psychology at the University of California, Berkeley. She received her B.A. in Social Relations from Radcliffe College in 1967, and her Ph.D. from Stanford University in 1971. She is the coauthor of *Influencing Attitudes and Changing Behavior* and the coeditor of *Psychology For Our Times*. She has contributed numerous articles to a variety of journals and edited collections. At present, she is conducting research on emotion and the emotional exhaustion syndrome known as burnout, as well as on the processes of individuation.